ABOUT THE AUTHORS

Martin Parker is Professor of Organization and Culture in the Management Centre at the University of Leicester.

Valérie Fournier is Senior Lecturer in Organization Studies in the Management Centre at the University of Leicester.

Patrick Reedy lectures at the Business School of the University of Newcastle upon Tyne.

D0994527

The
Dictionary *of*
Alternatives

Utopianism and Organization

MARTIN PARKER, VALÉRIE FOURNIER, PATRICK REEDY

Zed Books
LONDON & NEW YORK

The Dictionary of Alternatives was first published in 2007 by
Zed Books Ltd, 7 Cynthia Street, London N1 9JF, UK and
Room 400, 175 Fifth Avenue, New York, NY 10010, USA.

www.zedbooks.co.uk

Cover designed by Andrew Corbett
Set in 10½/13 pt Bembo by Long House, Cumbria, UK
Printed and bound in Malta by Gutenberg Press Ltd

Distributed in the USA exclusively by Palgrave Macmillan, a division of
St Martin's Press, LLC, 175 Fifth Avenue, New York, NY 10010.

A catalogue record for this book
is available from the British Library

US Cataloging-in-Publication Data
is available from the Library of Congress

ISBN: 978 1 84277 332 1 hb
ISBN: 978 1 84277 333 8 pb

Contents

CONTENTS

Introduction

'[T]he cause of the vices and unhappiness of mankind is to be found in the *bad organization* of society' Etienne Cabet (in Berneri, 1971: 220)

Etienne Cabet wrote a fictional utopia titled *Voyage to Icaria* which was published in France in 1839. After travelling to London to consult with Robert Owen, who had established an alternative community and form of factory organization in New Lanark in Scotland, Cabet eventually established an 'Icarian' commune at Nauvoo, near St Louis in the USA. Though Cabet died in 1856, several other Icarian colonies were also established, the last existing until 1898. Cabet's utopia was based on order, on bureaucracy. He put forward a vision of a democratic and well-organized society in which all were equal, and there was no waste or conflict. In addition, he was keen on elastic, because it would allow for one-size-fits-all clothing, especially hats. This odd little story could be classified as an interesting mixture of history, fiction and idealist politics, but what relevance might it have for contemporary debates about the politics of organizing and economy?

One of the most common pieces of common sense nowadays is that there is no real alternative to market managerialism, to the sort of free market liberalism that currently dominates certain parts of the planet. We disagree, and think that this dictionary should convince you to disagree too. In fact, what we think this book proves (and we do think 'proof' is the right word here), is that there are many alternatives to the way that many of us currently organize ourselves.

The words 'organize' or 'organization' are important here. For us 'organization' refers not to a fixed entity – a corporation, a university, a hospital – but rather to the processes through which human beings pattern or institutionalize their activities in order to achieve a fairly stable state of affairs. Thus we understand organization as a verb, the act of structuring, ordering, dividing things and people to produce order, rather than a noun – the state of being organized. This conceptualization of organization means that it is not a term restricted to the economic sphere, but is relevant to all human activities and social relations: everything has to be organized, from the family, to the city, the community, the state.... And more fundamentally for the purpose of this dictionary, organization is an eminently political activity. Defining organization as a verb rather than a noun brings to the fore the many decisions and choices that have to be made in structuring and ordering human activities. Organization is contingent upon choices relating to questions of means and ends. What is organization for? What should its size be? How should activities be coordinated and controlled, and by whom? How should ownership be distributed? How should work be divided, rewarded? And so on.

All too often, ordinary people across the world are being told that the problem of organization is already solved, or that it is being solved somewhere else, or that it need not concern them because they have no alternatives. We think this is wrong in two ways. Wrong, because the evidence we have gathered here is that (both geographically and historically) organizing is a highly varied, continually contested and negotiated matter; not a matter which is easily reduced to certain inexorable economic laws. Wrong also because, in an ethical and political sense, it is an attempt to persuade people that they cannot organize themselves, and that they need to wait for experts to tell them how they should live.

Defining organization as open to decisions and choices means that it can always be otherwise; it is open to change; it contains utopian possibilities. The word 'utopian' also needs clarification here. Traditionally utopia has been taken to refer to a literary genre of fiction that describes the perfect society. More's *Utopia*, Cabet's *Voyage to Icaria*, Gilman's *Herland*, Morris' *News from Nowhere*, Skinner's *Walden II*, Piercy's *Woman on the Edge of Time* – to take a few examples – all offer blueprints of ideal societies. Utopias in this sense have been denounced, especially from the mid-twentieth century, as static blueprints, impossible and undesirable dreams. Perhaps they are dangerous and oppressive places where the quest for the 'best order' imposes closure on what can be imagined and demanded, because the 'perfect society' is not to be contested or changed.

In this dictionary, we depart from this understanding of utopia as fictional representations of perfect societies; instead we see utopia as the expression of what Ernst Bloch (1986) called the 'principle of hope'. In this respect, we follow many other contemporary utopians who see utopia in terms of its critical, transgressive and transformative functions rather than in terms of its particular form or content (Bammer, 1991; Goodwin, 2004; Harvey,

2000; Jameson, 2005; Levitas, 1990; Moylan, 1986; Sargisson, 1996). From this perspective, utopia is not so much the naturalistic representation of the good society, as what inspires and drives people to imagine and work for a better world; thus 'what is important about utopia is less what is imagined than the act of imagination itself, a process which disrupts the closure of the present' (Levitas, 2004: 39).

In short, for us utopia is the expression of the possibility of alternative organization, organization understood in the broad sense signalled above. These alternatives could be expressed as fictions, as utopian novels and stories which attempt to put forward a different way for human beings to live together (Davis, 1984). These fictional depictions, by imagining a world built on 'better principles', call into question the current order and can be seen as thought experiments in alternative ways of organizing society. Alternatives could also be discovered historically, in terms of the rich history of dissent and heterodox thinking that is all too often hidden by the stories of kings and empires. Or, they could be described in terms of the contemporary politics of anti-corporate protest, environmentalism, feminism, localism and so on. But, perhaps most importantly, they form a rich picture in which fiction, history and today's politics provide an alternative way of thinking about how we organize ourselves at the beginning of the twenty-first century.

In this dictionary we have gathered what may seem like an eclectic collection of entries that include fictional utopias; political theories, theorists and ideas (Marxism, Anarchism, Feminism, Fourier, St Simon, democracy…); social movements (environmentalism, anti-capitalism…); and concrete alternatives (American utopian experiments such as Brook Farm or Oneida, cooperatives, ecovillages, Local Exchange Trading Schemes…). The common thread that runs through these diverse entries is that they embody and have inspired hope in the possibility of alternative organization. Together, these entries stand as testimony to the wide range of possibilities for organizing ourselves; they demonstrate that throughout history people have had the courage and imagination to believe that a better world was possible.

This dictionary is therefore perhaps best described as a source book, pattern book or almanac of possibilities. We have organized it as a 'dictionary', so it is alphabetical, with UPPER-CASE CROSS-REFERENCES to the whole maze of entries, the references in this introduction and the suggestions for further reading collected together at the end. There is no particular consistency to the cross referencing, as you might find in a comprehensive reference work. Most of the entries were written by the three of us. Martin wrote mainly about fiction, Valérie about contemporary politics, and Patrick about history, but these certainly are not exclusive categories, and we have all edited everything, and so take collective responsibility for it. Some of the entries were written by specialists in those fields. We have edited these, too, but first authorship is indicated by the initials at the end of the entry, and a list of who these people are follows this introduction. We thank them all, as well as all those who have suggested entries, and been so supportive about the project. Particularly we thank Warren Smith, whose enthusiasm for the book was infectious, and who wrote quite a few entries at short notice.

We are well aware that this dictionary is not comprehensive. In many ways it is far too white, too English, too Western and too focused on theory rather than practices. We could have included so much more, but the fact that we had to cut 5,000 words from the original, combined with our ignorance, has left some huge gaps and silences. We are sure that many readers will be irritated by this, but it is worth thinking about these omissions in a more positive way, too. Part of our project for some years now has been to put market managerialism 'in its place' as only one form of organizing amongst many. The partiality of our selection reflects the fact that dissent and alternatives arise from a particular historical tradition, even as we struggle to emerge from the culture that we find ourselves within. In that sense the wildest forms of utopianism are grounded in the experience of their creators and draw on their social context. There are, of course, many more traditions of dissent and alternative ways of living than we can adequately write about ourselves. So, the more forms of organizing that you, as a reader, can think of that we have missed out, the better our argument becomes. Please contact us with your suggestions, so that future versions of this book can be improved and extended.

That being said, we have also had to draw our own boundaries, and we think they fall into four categories. First, we have excluded many fictional utopias because we did not feel that they added that much in terms of ideas about organization or economy. This was particularly the case where the good society was simply brought about by fantastic technological solutions, like the miraculous fluid Vril, found in Edward Bulwer Lytton's *The Coming Race* (1871). This is utopia by magic, rather than by human efforts. Nonetheless, if you want to know more about utopias, see for example Claeys and Sargent (1999), Fortunati and Trousson (2000), Kumar (1991), Manguel and Guadalupi (1999), Manuel and Manuel (1979), Schaer, Claeys and Sargent (2000) or Trahair (1999) for more comprehensive surveys. Second, we offer no more than a geographically representative sample of communes and co-ops, and hence ignore many large and well-established examples. If you want to know more about these, see for example Bunker *et al.* (2006), Coates (2001), Fellowship for Intentional Communities (2005), Sutton (2005), Trainer (1995) or Volker and Stengel (2005). Third, on the whole we ignore religion and spirituality, except in so far as it is an animating principle for particular entries. For some people, such matters are the stuff from which their politics is made, but for us they seem rather too much like a version of Vril. Finally, we are only including more orthodox terms from management and politics in order to stress their radical potential. This means that quite a lot of new age managerialism and third way politics doesn't make it into the dictionary, but both currents of thought seem to have plenty of other ways of making themselves heard, so we doubt that their enthusiasts will be too distressed.

Of course, one person's alternative is another person's orthodoxy, and we have included quite a few terms that (at first glance) might be thought to sit uneasily in this collection. But this isn't simply a collection of things that we think are 'good'. It is a wider attempt to show the massive diversity of ways in which human organization can be imagined. Inevitably, our book visits worlds that its authors and readers would probably rather not live in, and examines practices that they would rather not engage in. Our whole point is that this dizzying network of ideas presents alternatives, and not the straight line that leads to the one best way. Open the book at random, and then follow your nose. We hope you find it as interesting to read as we did to write.

LIST OF CONTRIBUTORS

AC   Abby Cathcart (Queensland University of Technology)
CW   Colin Williams (University of Sheffield)
DH   David Harvie (University of Leicester)
DL   Davina Landsman (Member of Kibbutz Givat Brenner 1988–1994)
HM/IU   Hakeem I Mobolaji and Ibrahim Umar (University of Leicester)
GL   Geoff Lightfoot (University of Leicester)
GP   Geoffrey Parker (University of Birmingham)
JB   Jo Brewis (University of Leicester)

JC   Jude Courtney (North Staffordshire Combined Healthcare)
KD   Karen Dale (University of Leicester)
MC   Martin Corbett (University of Warwick)
PD   Peter Davis (University of Leicester)
SB   Simon Bainbridge (University of Lancaster)
SS   Stevphen Shukaitis (Queen Mary, University of London)
WIRC   Tom Keenoy, Len Arthur, Molly Scott-Cato and Russell Smith
        (Wales Institute for Research into Cooperatives)
WS   Warren Smith (University of Leicester)

ABBEY OF THELEME The last chapters of book one of *Histories of Gargantua and Pantagruel*, a bawdy satire written by François Rabelais between and 1532 and 1553, describe an Abbey that reverses the assumptions about religious orders that pertained in sixteenth-century France. It has no walls, both men and women are admitted, and members can marry, become rich and come and go as they please. There are no clocks, because 'the greatest nonsense in the world was to regulate one's life by the sound of a bell, instead of by the promptings of reason and good sense'. There is considerable architectural detail about the six-storey hexagonal tower which contained 9,332 apartments (each with chamber, closet, wardrobe and chapel), all opening onto a central hall. Inside were also libraries of Greek, Latin, Hebrew, French, Italian and Spanish books, galleries painted with histories and views, a riding ring, a theatre, swimming baths, falconry facilities, stables, orchards, perfumeries, barbershops and so on. Above the great gate was an inscription noting the various characters who were not welcome (hypocrites, swindlers, lawyers, usurers, the poor, old and sick) as well as those who were (witty and wealthy gentlemen, vigorous preachers and upright modest ladies). They could all, men and women, read, write, sing and play musical instruments. Both women and men dressed exceptionally well, no doubt assisted by the 'smart and well-arranged' block of houses nearby, which contained 'goldsmiths, jewellers, embroiderers' and so on working at their trade. Most importantly, 'in their rules there was only one clause: DO WHAT YOU WILL, because people who are free, well-born, well-bred and easy in honest company have a natural spur and instinct that drives them to virtuous deeds and deflects them from vice'.

It seems clear that parts of this utopia are a satire on the asceticism and submission required by the MONASTIC life, but Rabelais also seems to be suggesting that human beings are perfectible creatures, if they have free will and the right circumstances. It is the same assumption about human beings that underlies ANARCHISM, COMMUNISM and SOCIALISM. Given its place in the text, after pages and pages of food, drink, shit and sex, the effect of the story of the Abbey is curiously touching and inspiring. Rabelais founds a utopia that is certainly materialistic, but is also founded on liberty and a certain sort of equality, both sentiments too radical to be openly voiced in France until a few centuries later.

AGORA The centre of public life in the Ancient and Classical Greek city (see CITY STATE; POLIS). It was a physical space that enabled a wide range of interconnected economic, social, legal, political and religious activities; each influencing the other. The agora in essence was nothing more than a MARKETPLACE where people came together to meet and to buy and sell, exchanging all the social and material necessities of life. The most important feature of the agora was thus accessibility for all. It also needed to be an *open* space which contrasted with the narrow and constricted spaces characteristic of many other parts of the city. Although the most prestigious temple in a city would be set apart, perhaps on a fortified acropolis, the temples used every day would tend to be in the agora, again because of its accessibility. And so the agora became more than a simple marketplace.

As monarchical power gave way to a variety of more participative forms of government, and particularly to the DEMOCRACY of Athens, the agora presented itself as a space for new institutions. Thus Athenians might visit the agora 'to get information, meet their friends (or enemies), gamble, torture a slave, hire or get hired as wage labourers, accost a prostitute, seek asylum (if a slave), have a haircut, go begging, fetch water, watch cock-fighting, and find out the time from a public water clock'. One might also take part in a trial, a religious procession, a philosophical debate (Socrates spent much of his time in the agora discussing ethical questions with any willing Athenian) or attend the *ekklesia,* the popular assembly that voted on community decisions. More conservative figures, including Plato and Socrates, were concerned at this mix of day-to-day activities with more 'elevated' ones such as law, philosophy and politics. They worried at the ability of the poor to mingle with the rich, fearing that the status quo might be inverted as a result. There was also concern that the areas of the city most concerned with trade would be 'too' democratic and, by their nature, would have a high concentration of foreigners present. Solutions to this perceived problem were suggested, including having a separate agora for trade or not allowing citizens to engage in trade.

An idealized agora provides a possible model for forms of participative democracy. Its accessibility and openness to all, the integration of everyday exchange with COMMUNITY and political functions, and its development through a continuing dialogue between all those who come to use it, contrast strongly with current forms of organizational and political governance. It is not surprising that the word crops up across a range of organizations and institutions wishing to claim democracy, openness and accessibility as governing principles, from the Treaty of Rome to open systems software developers. One application of these principles is AGORA, a UK community organization, largely sponsored by the churches, whose aims include identifying and creating new places of meeting for public conversation; ensuring that these spaces are inclusive and accessible; and building on people's life experience while resisting domination by experts.

ALBIGENSIANS, see CATHARS

ALTERNATIVE GEOPOLITICS A term first used by the French geographer Yves Lacoste after the 1968 student demonstrations in Paris. Lacoste used it as part of his advocacy of the use of geography for purposes other than the support of the authority of the state and the making of war. This, he claimed, had been its principal use in the past. Lacoste revived the term 'geopolitics' which had become highly suspect as a result of its use to justify the territorial expansionism of the Third Reich. He and other French geographers turned to an examination of the work of early twentieth century ANARCHISTS such as Peter KROPOTKIN and Elisée Reclus, who had seen the subject as having the potential to liberate the peoples of the world from their oppressors. This alternative geopolitics centred on the use of the world's resources for the benefit of its peoples rather than the wealth and power of the few. It entailed putting in place alternative structures of government to those that had been associated with power and domination.

The new schools of geopolitics in the Anglo-Saxon countries which rose in the later twentieth century were more concerned with peace than with war. However, even when concerned with the prevention of conflict such thinking did not fundamentally challenge the existing state system. All the evidence suggests that, left to themselves, the existing territorial states are unlikely to change their behaviour to any really significant extent. During the last half-century they have shown that they remain wedded to the use of force in pursuit of their own interests and that their policies reflect an underlying nationalism and xenophobia. The alternative geopolitics seeks to bring radical change to this situation by replacing the existing system

3

of territorial states with a new one. This entails the replacement of the present components of the world system by alternatives that are likely to prove more amenable to the establishment of genuinely COOPERATIVE structures. Such possible alternative components of the world system include CITY STATES, SMALL STATES and regions.

Because of their small size, limited power and natural interdependence, such alternative states are more likely to see it as in their interest to become willing participants of an inter-state order. An example of an alternative process with a successful outcome was the Hanseatic League, which came into being in the transition period between the decline of the medieval empires and the rise of the modern state powers. Its component city states were highly successful in facilitating trade over large areas and establishing both economic and political internal order. In a similar way, following the First World War, the small nations of Eastern Europe gained a brief independence before they were once more incorporated into a new quasi-imperial structure. After the Second World War, the German *länder* were resurrected and proved to be highly successful forms of autonomous administration within a state. Subsequently, the desire to recreate the pre-national world of the Renaissance city states has produced political parties devoted to greater autonomy for regions such as the Basque country or Lombardy.

The European Union is the principal heir to earlier ideas of inter-state cooperation. Fundamental to the ideas of its founder Jean Monnet was the transfer of power away from the existing territorial states and the underlying philosophy of the EU is thus basically UTOPIAN. The idea of subsidiarity contained in the Maastricht Treaty is in accord with the FEDERALISM implicit in alternative geopolitics. However, by the beginning of the twenty-first century it had become evident that some of the more powerful member states, which had formerly been great powers, had increasing reservations about the continuation of integration and showed signs of wishing to revert to the assertion of their own political and economic power. The extent to which the alternative geopolitics will continue to make progress is now open to question. The great powers have demonstrated their propensity to act unilaterally and the latest crop of small nations, which emerged following the collapse of the SOVIET UNION, have yet to make much impact. Despite this, there is evidence of the continued existence of the alternative geopolitical process in the form of small states, non-state nations, city states and regions. There are also continued devolutionary tendencies within the existing states that give some indication of the steady erosion of their power from within. This all demonstrates the continued existence of the alternative geopolitics and the possibilities that it holds. (GP)

ALTERNATIVE TECHNOLOGY, see APPROPRIATE TECHNOLOGY

AMANA COLONIES, see AMISH, ANABAPTISTS

AMAZONS A tribe of brave female warriors whose existence is first described in print by Sir John Mandeville in 1357, and later by Sir Walter Raleigh in 1596 (see also EL DORADO). The Amazons treat men with contempt, using them for reproduction once a year, and then emasculating them and using them as slaves. Boy children are expelled. They are said to cut one of their breasts off in order to draw their bows more easily. The legend of Amazonia now often functions as a FEMINIST myth, perhaps of a matriarchal GOLDEN AGE, and has certainly been influential in the construction of (usually ARCADIAN) separatist FEMINIST UTOPIAS (see, for example, HERLAND).

AMERICA In this context 'America' means what is now the 'United States of America', and not primarily Canada, and certainly not Central or South America. As an idea, the 'American Dream', it has been both the inspiration and tragedy of much alternative and UTOPIAN thinking. As a place, it has been the site for many alternatives, and the most successful MARKET economy ever created. From the seventeenth century onwards, many NON-CONFORMIST and DISSENTING migrant groups left Europe for the 'New World', in an attempt to escape poverty or persecution (see ANABAPTISTS; AMISH). The MASSACHUSETTS BAY COLONY was established by Puritans fleeing from England, and begins a story of colonization in which previous inhabitants are notable by their absence. Like the protagonists of so many utopian romances, the Puritans set sail for lands over the sea, hoping to begin again. In 1776, the United States was established with ringing declarations of 'liberty and justice for all', the separation of church and state, an independent judiciary and so on. Compared to the cramped and divided societies they left behind, the wide-open spaces of North America offered seemingly boundless opportunity and natural resources. This idea of America as ARCADIA made a great deal of sense to authors such as Thoreau (see WALDEN), for whom the journey Westwards (towards the sunset) expressed a deep human need for exploration.

The many alternative communities that were established in the nineteenth century were often inspired by European ideas – Robert OWEN's 'New Harmony', ONEIDA, the SHAKERS, the Zoarites, Rappites, Moravians, Fruitlanders, Ephratans, Nashobans and so on – but increasingly required separation from the emerging capitalist economy in order to survive. It is the version of America with capitalism retained at its core that has become both utopia and DYSTOPIA. A land of social and geographical mobility, of unlimited resources and gigantic plates of food (see COCKAIGNE), of towering cities, free speech and democratic institutions. While all these aspects of America clearly organize a global imaginary, so does a mirror image which is echoed in many twentieth-century dystopian fictions. This is the America founded on the genocide of the first people and currently policing a *Pax Americana* in which resistance is met by overwhelming military force. An America in which the homeless sleep on the doorsteps of the wealthiest people on the planet, the MAFIA really run things, and forms of religious fundamentalism divide the deserving from the undeserving, both within America and the rest of the world. American exceptionalism has been the dominant theme in the way it has been imagined by European com-mentators for centuries. Hegel, in his 1837 *Philosophy of History*, suggested that America 'is the land of the future.... It is a land of desire for all those who are weary of the historical lumber-room of old Europe.' Alexis de Tocqueville, in his *Democracy in America* (1840) acknowledged that the Puritan influence was central to the busy-ness of America, but worried about the paradoxical extremes of individualism and centralization that resulted from democratic liberalism. Friedrich Engels felt that the collapse of capitalism was most likely on the 'more favoured soil of America, where no mediaeval ruins bar the way' (from the US edition of *The Condition of the Working Class in England*, 1887). More recently Jean Baudrillard has commented that America 'is an utopia which has behaved from the very beginning as though it were already achieved'. It is 'built on the idea that is the realization of everything that others have dreamt of – justice, plenty, rule of law, wealth, freedom: it knows this, it believes in it, and in the end, the others have come to believe in it too'.

When compared with the other major actually existing utopia of the twentieth century, COMMUNISM, it is difficult not to accept that American market managerialism was the winner, both ideologically and practically. However, if we narrow down the choice of alternatives to two, then it is

6

hardly any choice at all. As this dictionary suggests, there are many different ways to imagine alternative organization and utopia. To assume that the end of history is represented by McTopia, or Disney's town of Celebration, might be to sell the very idea of America too cheaply.

AMISH An enduring group of Christian NON-CONFORMIST communities mostly concentrated in the US states of Pennsylvania and Ohio, well known for their 'plain' lifestyle and suspicion of modern technology. Derived from the Mennonite section of the ANABAPTISTS, the Swiss followers of Jacob Amman distinguished themselves in the seventeenth century by their strict adherence to shunning deviant members ('Meidung') and washing the feet of others to demonstrate humility. Many emigrated to the US in the eighteenth century, along with many other similar religious sects such as the Amana Communities. All were particularly attracted by the tolerance implied in the separation of church and state, but the Amish were among the most successful and they currently number about 150,000 people. Depending on the conservatism of the particular Amish community, new technologies are assessed for their potential use or complication, and may be permitted in a limited form. Most groups would avoid the use of motor vehicles and modern fabrics, but there might be one communal telephone, or limited voltage electricity might be used if it is produced by Amish-owned generators. More traditional groups refuse to use buttons or belts, but all would share a fundamentalist view of the Bible and the avoidance of an evangelical mission to convert outsiders.

Like all Anabaptists, the Amish insist that baptism is only meaningful if it is entered into by an adult. The emphasis on the individual choosing God and community reasonably is one element of a highly ordered community of equals, though age and gender cut across this in fairly predictable ways. The character of the virtuous Amish comprises quietness, modesty, obedience and community service. Children come of age at sixteen, and are then permitted to try out the 'English' lifestyle during a period of 'Rumspringa' (jumping around). Most then return to the German-speaking communities, where they are expected to follow the 'Ordnung' or Amish Charter, unwritten laws which rule almost every aspect of life, including the growth of beards or length of skirt. The division of labour follows gender lines, family size is large, and children are expected to work. Insurance is avoided because of the considerable emphasis on collective support. They recognize the authority of the state, and pay most taxes, but are clear about the limitations of state power. Recent US court cases have contested their views of Amish private schooling, the non-payment of welfare taxes, the refusal to serve in the armed forces and child labour. Despite some discrimination, the Amish (like many similar groups) are now generally seen as a tourist and commercial asset for the areas that they live in. Their continuation as a community for almost three centuries is remarkable, and has presumably been sustained by a generalized shunning of the outside world combined with an intense stress on community responsibility.

ANABAPTISTS One of the largest and most influential groups from the radical wing of the Protestant Reformation in the sixteenth century. The name comes from the Greek for 're-baptizers' because of their insistence that only adult consenting baptism was valid. The Anabaptists were strong in Southern Germany, the Netherlands and Eastern Europe, and rejected many of the traditional rites and doctrines of both Catholic and new Protestant churches. It is difficult to generalize about Anabaptist groups because of their diversity of both belief and practice but they can be seen as part of the tradition of religious dissent reaching back to the various MILLENARIAN sects. Ultimately such groups looked even further back to the early Apostolic Church and accompanying ideas of holding property in common and forming self-sufficient COMMUNITIES. For example, in Moravia, Anabaptists washed each other's feet, had goods in common, worked at crafts, and educated their children separately from their parents in communal schools.

In the late medieval period religious reform was synonymous with social reform. It also frequently required COMMUNITARIAN separatism as religious freedom was considered automatically to challenge both secular and religious authority. Two attempts at revolutionary theocracy by Anabaptist groups provoked the authorities into widespread repression. In 1521, under the leadership of Thomas Müntzer, the 'Peasants' War' took place in Southern Germany. Until its failure, these revolutionary Anabaptists fought against feudal oppression and opposed all constituted authorities. They attempted to establish an ideal Christian COMMONWEALTH, with equality and the community of goods. A second attempt to establish such a theocracy took place in Münster, Germany, in 1532–5.

The main result of these attempts was the persecution of Anabaptists by both Catholic and Protestant churches. Thousand of Anabaptists were martyred. This persecution also had the effect of scattering Anabaptists and their beliefs throughout Europe and eventually to the promise of freedom in North AMERICA. This dispersion enabled Anabaptist ideas to take root in many different places and to have a significant effect on the development of all subsequent NON-CONFORMIST sects as well as on the later emergence of ANARCHISM and SOCIALISM. Their legacy lives on directly in the surviving communities of the Amana, AMISH, Hutterites, and Mennonites. Some have also argued that they were a significant influence on both the QUAKERS and the Mormons. Their history is also a powerful illustration of the extraordinary historical continuity of ideals central to almost all UTOPIAN experiments and the ambivalent power of religious belief in motivating groups of people to stand against the weight of institutional and state authority in pursuing these experiments.

ANARCHISM The word comes from the Greek for 'without rulers' which encapsulates the consensus amongst anarchists that all forms of authority, and particularly state authority, are oppressive as well as socially dysfunctional. Rather, the principles of individual autonomy and voluntary cooperation, undistorted by authority, will lead to a society of free human beings. Anarchism may be viewed as both a social philosophy and a political movement but, given its insistence on autonomy and diversity, there are many different anarchisms. Anarchists have often stressed the historical continuity of anarchist ideas and practice. For example, Colin Ward argues that anarchism is always a feature of human COMMUNITY and organization and lies just under the surface of all societies as a network of reciprocal relationships and MUTUAL arrangements. Thus primitive communities are often taken as precursors or exemplars of anarchism in practice. KROPOTKIN used the model of the *obshchina*, or Russian village community as one possible model of anarchist community.

Some anarchists look back to Greek philosophers such as Zeno and the stoics as providing the start of an anti-statist tradition in political theory. Later heretical religious and radical social movements such as the CATHARS, ANABAPTISTS and DIGGERS are also often seen as forerunners of anarchism. However, anarchism as a coherent set of ideas and practices is usually dated back to William GODWIN's 'An Enquiry Concerning Political Justice' (1793). The term first begins to be used as a positive self-description following Pierre-Joseph PROUDHON's 'What is Property?' (1840). Anarchism as a political movement was at its zenith during the revolutionary decades of

9

the nineteenth and early twentieth centuries. It developed alongside Marxism and shares much of MARX's critique of the capitalist system. Anarchists were also a significant part of the First International Working-men's Association until the dispute between their leader, Mikhail BAKUNIN, and Marx over political strategy led to their expulsion from the First INTERNATIONAL in 1872. The ensuing hostility between many Marxists and Anarchists continues to the present time. Anarcho-syndicalism, the anarchist wing of the labour movement, also developed in the latter decades of the nineteenth century.

In the twentieth century, anarchists played an important role in the Russian REVOLUTION, Italian revolutionary politics, and the Spanish Civil War. It dispersed to both the US and Latin America, where it continued to have an influence on the development of WORKER SELF-MANAGEMENT in the US and revolutionary movements in Latin America. This influence is still evident in the beliefs and organizational principles of the ZAPATISTAS. By the 1960s a resurgence in anarchist ideas was evident in the student protest movements, the counter-culture and the activities of autonomous groups such as the SITUATIONISTS and the Angry Brigade. The founding of INTENTIONAL COMMUNITIES in order to escape mainstream society also drew on an insistence on individual autonomy combined with a desire for more communal, SELF-SUFFICIENT forms of life. The 1960s also saw the emergence of green anarchism and anarcho-feminism. In the 1970s Punk Rock adopted the symbolism and some of the rhetoric of anarchism, if not its political and social objectives.

Since the 1980s anarchism, it could be argued, has been the dominant theoretical and tactical model for the resistance movements against global capitalism. The various ways in which DIRECT ACTION has been utilized by groups such as Reclaim the Streets or the BLACK BLOC is firmly in the anarchist tradition, as is the organizational model for large scale ANTI-CAPITALIST protests such as the BATTLE FOR SEATTLE. The WORLD SOCIAL FORUM and its various regional and local counterparts are also heavily influenced by anarchist thinking and organizational principles. Because of the diversity of anarchist thought it is easiest to outline some key ideas under different strands. It should be borne in mind that different strands frequently combine to produce variations that cannot be captured in a brief overview. Key anarchist thinkers are also identified through the ideas for which they are best known but again may be associated with more than one strand.

Individualist Anarchism has its origins in the work of Max STIRNER, who argued that the only principled form of political action was the pursuit of individual self-interest and self-realization. All institutions, authorities and belief systems are repudiated as empty and oppressive because they limit individual autonomy (see also BLAKE). Even within more COMMUNITARIAN forms of anarchism the belief that individuals should not be compelled to abide by collective decisions is widespread. Individualist anarchism is particularly associated with American writers such as Josiah Warren and Benjamin Tucker. Henry Thoreau advocated similar ideas in WALDEN. The individualist tradition has been developed in a particular way by Libertarian and Right anarchists.

Libertarian and Right Anarchism is primarily a US development and not accepted as a part of the anarchist tradition at all by many. Writers such as Robert NOZICK, Murray Rothbard and Lew Rockwell combine anti-statist liberalism (or 'minarchism') and the individualist tradition. They reject COLLECTIVIST approaches to social organization in favour of private property held by autonomous individuals who are free to exchange their property and labour through free markets. They argue that all aspects of society can be organized through individual contracting. Unlike other forms of anarchism there is no commitment to equality or workers' control of their labour and products. As such it can be seen as a UTOPIAN variant of neoliberalism.

Anarcho-communism is the most widespread form of anarchism, having its roots in the work of Mikhail BAKUNIN, Peter KROPOTKIN and Emma GOLDMAN. It strives for the abolition of private property and of monetary exchange. Instead, work should be under the direct control of producers. Goods and services are directly exchanged or given according to desire and need. Production and society in general are organized through self-directed communities and organization is based on the principles of free association and individual affinity. More complex social structures are built from networks based on voluntary federation by smaller units. Modern forms of production and information technology are sometimes claimed to have made such federal social structures a viable way to organize society at large. The ultimate aim of communo-anarchism is essentially the same as that of COMMUNISM as envisaged by LENIN amongst others, although the tactics to achieve this aim are generally a matter of dispute.

Anarcho-syndicalism denotes the anarchist labour movement, whose aim is primarily large-scale political change rather than local disputes. SYNDICALISM may not be specifically anarchist in nature and forms a part of the broader SOCIALIST tradition. The use of industrial action, particularly the GENERAL STRIKE, is seen as a means of defending the universal interests of workers and of overthrowing capitalism. In addition labour organizations develop, as part of their struggle, the self-governing structures that will form the basis of eventual direct workers' control of production.

Anarcho-feminism (or anarcha-feminism) is a branch of radical FEMINISM that has its primary origins in the work of Emma Goldman. Patriarchy is argued to be the original form of oppressive authority from which all others develop. Feminists should thus struggle against all forms of hierarchy. Anarcho-primitivism and Green Anarchism advocate a return to a pre-industrial (sometimes even a pre-agricultural) existence, notably argued for by John Zerzan. This is based on a belief that technology, urbanization, the division of labour and other aspects of human civilization are inherently alienating and destructive. Only small scale non-hierarchical communities will enable human beings to live freely and ethically. SOCIAL ECOLOGY has been a major influence on the development of Green Anarchism, whilst DEEP ECOLOGISTS advocate primitivism as the only possible way to live in harmony with the natural world. Green activist organizations such as Earth First also utilize anarchist forms of political practice and organization.

Religious Anarchists are inspired by forms of political and social radicalism, not least because heresy has often led to the expulsion of believers from mainstream society. TOLSTOY'S Christian Anarchism was partly inspired by the COMMUNISM of the Apostolic Church and the rejection of all forms of authority other than that of the divine. GANDHI was strongly influenced by Tolstoy's ideas, particularly the opposition to secular authorities through non-violent mass protest. Post-structuralist Anarchism is a largely theoretical development which seeks to take classical anarchist theory beyond what are argued to be its humanistic assumptions, such as a belief in the 'natural' goodness of humanity and in an unfettered autonomous rationality. Thinkers such as Michel Foucault, Gilles Deleuze and Félix Guattari have called for a multiplicity of beliefs and practices and regard any overarching political discourse as potentially oppressive and representing yet another form of authority. One implication of this is a move away from traditional forms of left-wing mass action to more local and individualistic micro-politics aimed at personal emancipation (see AUTONOMIA).

ANARCHO-SYNDICALISM, see ANARCHISM; SYNDICALISM

ANTI-CAPITALISM In some ways as old as capitalism itself, for the latter has met with some forms of resistance ever since its emergence. But contemporary understandings of the term tend to see the BATTLE OF SEATTLE as a significant turning point in that it challenged the idea that the promotion of free trade and financial liberalization would bring economic growth which would eventually benefit the poorest. Mass protests in Seattle, and later in Prague, Genoa, and so on, suggested that this 'consensus' was not shared, and that many saw global capitalism and neoliberalism as the cause of, not the solution to, increasing global injustice, poverty and environmental destruction.

Thus 'anti-capitalism' is defined by its critique of contemporary capitalism, and in particular of its global, corporate and neoliberal nature (indeed the 'anti-capitalist' movement is also sometimes referred to as the anti-globalization or anti-corporate movement). This critique takes the following form: the liberalization of trade and capital movement has meant that businesses have been able to travel the globe in search of cheap labour and low environmental regulation, encouraging a 'race to the bottom' among developing countries to attract capital investment from multinational companies. The globalization of capitalism has been accompanied by its increasing concentration around large multinational corporations that have acquired not only growing profits, but also increasing power over the lives of workers, consumers and citizens through the pressures they have been able to exercise over international institutions such as the International Monetary Fund, the World Bank and the World Trade Organization, as well as over national governments. In short, global corporate capitalism, driven by the search for ever-greater profits, is plundering the earth, destroying the lives of entire communities, particularly in the South, and hijacking democracy.

Anti-capitalism builds upon the 1968 legacy that saw the explosion of the Left into multiple movements, and the substitution of official oppositional politics by a proliferation of 'unofficial' movements and groups operating mainly outside the mainstream political process of parties, elections and parliaments. Instead it privileges DIRECT ACTIONS such as mass protests, sit-ins, disruptions, the creation of alternative media and various forms of GRASSROOTS action. Another factor that defines anti-capitalism is its mode of (dis)organization, and in particular its capacity to coordinate the voices and activities of a myriad of different groups into a global dialogue. The anti-capitalist movement, mainly thanks to the internet, has

13

made many small marginal groups visible, and helped them develop links that have given particular and local forms of oppression and struggle a global dimension. For example, the ZAPATISTAS' demands for Mayan rights to access common land has resonated with the struggles of many other oppressed groups throughout the world.

But anti-capitalism is defined as much by the differences as the similarities within itself; it is a 'movement of movements' (Tormey, 2004) more clearly defined by a 'common enemy' (Starr, 2000) than a common agenda. Thus anti-capitalism is not a singular organization but a loose and decentralized network of groups, movements and organizations. In particular, it contains many different views about what political tactics should be used to challenge global capitalism, and what should replace it. Not all within the movement are against capitalism as such. The 'reformists' challenge capitalism as it currently operates; they are anti-global capitalism, or anti-corporate capitalism, but they can see a way in which capitalism can be regulated to operate in the interest of society generally rather than merely of big business. This would involve re-invigorating social DEMOCRATIC traditions to harness the productive energies of capitalism whilst ensuring that its benefits are more equally distributed. Here we find various proposals for designing legal and political frameworks that would regulate capitalism and make it more caring, more responsible. For example some would like to transform existing global institutions into forms of governance that would guarantee minimum rights, standards of living and environmental protection, or introduce fiscal policies that would ensure the redistribution of wealth from rich to poor countries (see ATTAC), or promote the development of FAIR TRADE.

On the other side of the spectrum are more radical views that would do away with capitalism altogether. These radical views are informed by various ideological currents – ANARCHISM, AUTONOMISM, ENVIRON-MENTALISM, FEMINISM, MARXISM and SOCIALISM. Moreover, many of the radical grassroots groups that form the anti-capitalist movement do not claim affiliation to any particular ideology but rather develop their own response to local contexts. For example the ZAPATISTAS, whilst often associated with the autonomist movement or with anarchism, stress the empowerment of local COMMUNITIES in designing their own alternative to global capitalism. Another line of division within the anti-capitalist movement concerns tactics. Some argue that the anti-capitalist movement should present a more united front if it is to challenge global capitalism successfully. Others see its disparate nature as a strength: first, it makes the movement more difficult for anyone to control, contain or attack; and second, it creates the conditions in which people can decide for themselves what alternative world they want to construct. Despite these differences, the anti-capitalist movement has been united in challenging the idea that there is a consensus around neoliberal policy, and in calling for a democratization and politicization of the economy, as well as the empowerment of people in making the decisions that affect their lives.

ANTI-UTOPIA, see DYSTOPIA

APPROPRIATE TECHNOLOGY The development and use of technologies that are designed to enable people with few resources to work their way out of poverty (sometimes also called Intermediate Technology). It is inspired by SCHUMACHER'S idea that 'Small is Beautiful' and aims to develop small-scale (see SMALLNESS) projects to help people satisfy their basic needs whilst making the most of their time, capabilities, environment and resources. Technology here refers to more than 'hardware' and includes related knowledge and skills, as well as the capability to organize and manage technology.

Important features of Appropriate Technology include its sensitivity to local contexts and resources – for example, the knowledge, skills, natural resources and capital available, as well as the prevailing environmental conditions. The majority of technological innovations occur in industrialized countries and are driven by capital-intensive production. But these technologies are often not affordable for people in developing countries. For example, the development of high-yielding varieties of rice is dependent on the availability of a wide range of supporting services and technologies (irrigation systems, pesticides and fertilizers, machinery) which limits its application among poor farmers in the South. Appropriate Technology aims to build technological solutions that are commensurate with local contexts. This emphasis on context leads to a participative approach to the development of technology. Involving users in the development of technology is a step towards ensuring that it will respond to their needs, constraints and requirements. Appropriate Technology clearly targets the problem of poverty by providing sustainable livelihoods for people with few resources. Its deployment should help people meet their basic needs, either by generating an income (by starting businesses, for example, or selling farm products) or by providing them with the means

15

of self-subsistence (such as simple irrigation systems that enable them to grow food, ways to produce clean water, or solar cookers). Finally, Appropriate Technology aims to increase SELF-SUFFICIENCY in developing countries. The idea is not to tackle poverty through 'aid' or technology transfer from industrialized countries, but rather to equip people with the skills to help themselves. There is an emphasis on developing technologies that local people can design, manage and control, as well as on decreasing dependency on industrialized countries (see also GRAMEEN BANK).

ARCADIA A region of contemporary Greece, made famous by its use as a rural utopian setting for Virgil's (70–19 BCE) *Eclogues*, in which happy shepherds sing about love and poetry. Virgil appropriated the 'bucolic' poetic form from the much earlier Sicilian poet Theocritus (third century BCE) but located his poems in this savage rustic area whose native god was the half-animal Pan. This pastoral imagery became popularized and domesticated in the European Renaissance, and the idea of an idyllic setting of forests and hills, populated by naïve but healthy Arcadians became popular in the sixteenth and seventeenth centuries. It influenced garden design, and helped to construct the common picturesque image of man and nature in perfect harmony, with animals peacefully grazing in pastures beyond. In Christian myth this would be assumed to be the original state of human beings in the Garden of EDEN before the fall. A famous 1647 painting by Nicholas Poussin shows a group of shepherds examining a tomb upon which is written 'Et In Arcadia Ego' ('I am also/even in Arcadia'). This could mean that Death comes to Arcadia, too, or that the dead person now lives in Arcadia. More contemporary uses of the word express a nostalgic sense of a naturally ordered utopia or wilderness, uncontaminated by modern forms of organization and civilization and populated by temperate people with simple appetites (see Henry David Thoreau's WALDEN). Many contemporary ECOVILLAGES and aspects of ENVIRON-MENTALISM are partly inspired by ideas of harmony and tranquillity such as these (see also ECOFEMINISM). Compare this to the rather more excessive COCKAIGNE or to the many ordered CITY STATE utopias.

ARTS AND CRAFTS An English reformist movement primarily inspired by the ideas of John RUSKIN and William Morris (see NEWS FROM NOWHERE). At its peak between 1880 and 1910, the aesthetic principles of Arts and Crafts influenced architecture, textiles, garden design, interior decoration, pottery, printing, and many other areas. Its inspiration comes from a resistance to machine production, both in terms of the anonymity of its mass-produced items and in terms of the degradation it causes to workers. Hence, rather than speed, profit or efficiency, the criteria for design was the beauty inherent in careful and skilful craft production. The often rather sentimental SOCIALISM that followed on from this required a certain ROMANTICIZATION of the medieval GUILD relationships that were supposed to have existed before the advent of urban capitalism (see GOLDEN AGE). In practice, this meant a certain neo-gothic style that echoed Victorian understandings of the mediaval, combined with asymmetric, rustic and cottage garden influences. The slightly more modernist and later variants of Arts and Crafts are often classified as Art Nouveau or Art Deco, particularly in the US.

The radical elements of Arts and Crafts are tempered by the attitudes of its (often wealthy) adherents. It is at its heart an anti-modern movement, though this does necessarily involve a substantial political criticism of the alienated worker, of the division of labour, and of consumerism. It shares with FOURIER and early MARXISM a conviction that work is a central part of what makes us human, and that such work has been made meaningless for many within industrial societies. A few English craft cooperatives were established upon these general principles, the best known probably being Charles Robert Ashbee's 'Guild of Handicraft' established in East London in 1888. The guild produced a variety of artefacts for architects and designers, supported a lively social life, and purchased country cottages for worker holidays. Craft Guilds and Schools of Handicraft later became common across the UK, often with substantial involvement and leadership from women, and similar guilds were established in the USA (The Roycroft Community in 1895, The United Craftsmen in 1898). Ashbee's guild eventually moved out to the rural setting of Chipping Campden in 1901 but (under pressure from machine-made Arts and Crafts objects) eventually went bankrupt in 1907. The influence of Arts and Crafts on both the aesthetic and politics of GARDEN CITIES is clear, and there are links to many later ANARCHIST and COOPERATIVE ideas. It is sad that the central insight, that work can be collective and meaningful, was often buried beneath a middle class anti-urbanism.

ASSOCIATIONS, see MUTUALISM, SOCIAL CAPITAL

ATLANTIS A legendary island originally referred to by Plato in his dialogues *Timaeus* and *Critias* around 360 BCE. The land was populated by a wise and powerful people and was founded by Poseidon, the god of the sea. According to him, the Atlanteans used circular canals to irrigate the ten districts of their island and engaged in trade and commerce. They also had hot and cold running springs, underground harbours, wild elephants, and a metal called 'orichalc' which can no longer be found. Eventually corrupted by greed and power, the entire population perished as the island was sunk under the sea as a punishment from Zeus. For Plato, this account may have been a parable concerning an ideal government, such as that described in The REPUBLIC. The name was resurrected in Francis Bacon's scientific utopia The NEW ATLANTIS, but more recent treatments tend to focus on proving the existence or location of this highly developed ancient civilization, with discussions of the various ancient authorities who also mention legends of similar islands. Apart from its many fictional incarnations, the name now functions as a missing utopian CITY STATE, a GOLDEN AGE that had glories that we might one day recapture. Esoteric speculations about Atlantis are also common, and they are often related to the supposedly related lost island of Lemuria, or Mu, in what is now the Indian Ocean. The late-nineteenth-century psychic Madame Blavatsky claimed that Lemuria was inhabited by a peace-loving, egg-laying race with a psychic third eye who lived on an island in what is now the Indian Ocean 150 million years ago. Their downfall came when they discovered sex. A slightly different version of the legend, to be found in Breton mythology, concerned the beautiful drowned city of Ys, built in Douarnenez Bay by the King of Cornouaille. It was flooded by the devil as punishment for the decadence of its inhabitants. A similar fate overcame the Cornish island of Lyonnesse, which will rise again when King Arthur returns. HyBrasil, off the south-west coast of Ireland, had psalm-singing birds and fountains that spouted wine. It only became visible every seven years, and was last seen on maps in 1865. See also COCKAIGNE; EDEN; EL DORADO; SHANGRI-LA.

ATTAC The Association for a Taxation of financial Transactions and for the Aid of Citizens originated in France in the summer of 1998 and was launched as an international movement in December 1998. At the beginning of 2005, it counted over 80,000 members worldwide, and was represented in nearly 40 countries. ATTAC was born out of a critique of financial globalization, and its undermining of state sovereignty and citizens' power to determine their own destiny. It is argued that the speculative logic of financial markets fosters economic insecurity and social inequality, whilst serving the particular interests of multinational corporations. In order to disarm global capital and recapture the spaces of democracy lost to financial power, ATTAC promotes measures such as the taxation of international financial transactions (named the Tobin Tax, after the American economist who proposed it in 1972), the introduction of sanctions on tax havens, and the abolition of pension funds and their replacement by state pensions. For example, in its 1998 Platform, ATTAC suggests that even a relatively low Tobin Tax of 0.1 per cent would bring in close to £100 billion every year, mostly from industrialized countries; it goes on to suggest that this money could be redistributed towards poor countries to fight against poverty and inequality, and to promote food security and sustainable development. This critique of global capital extends to neoliberal policies that promote the opening of MARKETS to 'free trade'. ATTAC does not believe that government will change things of their own volition, and instead encourages citizens to take DIRECT ACTION, 'to take back, together, the future of our world'. ATTAC is not affiliated to any political party and is keen to stress its pluralism; it is a loose, non-hierarchical network that brings together people who identify with the 'Platform statement'. It has been actively involved in the ANTI-CAPITALIST MOVEMENT and the WORLD SOCIAL FORUM.

AUROVILLE An utopian city-in-the-making whose purpose is to 'realize human unity' and promote SUSTAINABILITY. Founded in 1968 in the South of India, it counted approximately 1,800 residents from 35 countries in 2005. Auroville is based on the vision of Indian political leader, scholar, teacher, poet and spiritual visionary Sri Aurobindo and his disciple Mirra Alfassa (also known as 'the Mother'). They wish to create a town where men and women of all countries can live in peace and harmony, above all creeds, all politics and all nationalities. Auroville is meant as a place of spiritual realization that is not bound to any religious dogma but envisaged in terms of a gradual awakening to our true selves. It aims to be a place where all 'fighting instincts' are used to conquer the causes of suffering, weakness and ignorance; where the needs of the spirit get precedence over desires or material enjoyments; where work becomes a means of expressing oneself because the COMMUNITY provides for every resident's subsistence;

19

and where human relations are based on cooperation and solidarity rather than competition.

Auroville is designed to have 50,000 citizens, a number that would enable the participation of all in the life of the community, as well as the production of goods and services to meet all needs (see GARDEN CITIES). Its architectural design is based on different zones for different activities: a green belt designed for agricultural and leisure activities, an industrial zone including small arts, crafts and manufacturing businesses meant to cover the needs of the city; a residential zone; a cultural zone providing arts and science education and research in APPROPRIATE TECHNOLOGY and a democratic school (see SUMMERHILL). It will also have an international zone with houses for each nation acting as embassies of different cultures, and finally the Matrimandir: a 100-foot-high elliptical sphere with surrounding gardens and walkways representing the physical and spiritual centre of Auroville.

AUTO-DIDACTICISM A term meaning 'self-education' or 'self-directed learning'. The great age of auto-didacticism in England was during the formation of radical working-class organizations and movements at the end of the eighteenth and in the first half of the nineteenth century. According to E. P. Thompson, 'The articulate consciousness of the self-taught was above all a political consciousness.... The towns, and even the villages, hummed with the energy of the autodidact.' The hunger for access to radical books and the plethora of polemical pamphlets in circulation led to a rapid increase in literacy. This had largely to be self-taught as formal education was limited and the few day and Sunday schools often provided only the most basic reading skills. Skilled artisans, for whom literacy became increasingly useful in the practice of their crafts, were often highly skilled readers and writers, well able to mount scholarly rebuttals of the repressive policies of the government. Auto-didacts operated either individually or sometimes in groups based in working-class self-help and MUTUAL organizations such as the MECHANICS INSTITUTES and FRIENDLY SOCIETIES.

Many radical movements place education at the centre of attempts to further their aims. Educational theories such as the deschooling ideas of Ivan ILLICH or the critical pedagogy of Paulo FREIRE are also (to some extent) practised in radical and democratic schools such as SUMMERHILL in Suffolk, where lessons are voluntary and the pupils run the affairs of the school on a democratic basis.

AUTONOMIA Developed in Italy in the 1970s, the movement was to inspire a new current of left-wing politics: 'Autonomist Marxism'. The Autonomist movement was born out of a critique of the reformist politics and hierarchical nature of the Italian Communist Party and trade unions; it found its first expression in *operaismo* ('workerism') in 1960s Italy. 'Potere Operaio' was created in the late 1960s to capture factory workers' mounting frustration with TRADE UNION policies of compromise. *Operaismo* did not aim to ameliorate the work situation, but to abolish it. "Refusal of work" became the main strategy for asserting workers' independence from the domination of capital.

Undermined by unions and the decline of the industrial sector, Potere Operaio dissolved in 1973. But many of its members went on to form a more diffuse movement – Autonomia Operaia ('Workers' Autonomy') – that sought to harness the momentum of protest to new groups such as students, the unemployed and women. This shift of politics away from the factory to a broader terrain led to various, often illegal, practices: from collective 'free shopping' to the self-reduction of charges for bus fares or rent, or the SQUATTING of 'social centres' (see CENTRI SOCIALI). The refusal of work extended into a generalized rejection of organized society, and the search for alternative spaces operating autonomously from the state and the capitalist political economy. For some this meant taking politics into the cultural domain, and part of the movement centred on creative or cultural interventions, such as free radio stations, artists' collectives, or small independent publishers. Whilst the use of illegal practices was considered a legitimate rejection of capitalist law and order, the use of violence was more ambivalent. Symbolic violence was used in demonstrations, but the Autonomist movement generally condemned TERRORIST organizations for what they considered élitist and counter-productive use of violence. However in the late 1970s, Autonomia was caught between an Italian state that became increasingly repressive following the kidnapping and murder of Aldo Moro (leader of the Christian Democratic Party) by the Red Brigades, and armed groups (including the MAFIA) that kept 'raising the stakes'. In 1979 Antoni Negri, one of Autonomia's most famous proponents, and hundreds of others were arrested on trumped-up charges of involvement with the Red Brigades; many were jailed whilst others escaped abroad. Due to the political persecution of many of its exponents, Autonomia was marginalized in the 1980s, but enjoyed a resurgence in the 1990s following the publication of *Empire* by Negri and Hardt (see

MULTITUDE). It has since become an influential voice within the ANTI-CAPITALIST movement (see DISOBBEDIENTI).

Autonomia not only broke away from the Left of official parties and trade unions, but also from state MARXISM. In particular, autonomists insist on workers' autonomy from capital. Rather than seeing capitalist development as being governed by the logic of capital accumulation, autonomism emphasizes the role of working-class struggles in shaping capitalist development. Thus the working class is not seen as having to wait for capitalism to follow its logic towards its own eventual downfall, but as a potential agent of change which can overturn capitalism through its own actions, such as the refusal of work. A second way in which Autonomia challenges orthodox Marxism is in its understanding of the composition of the 'working class'. According to Negri, the rise of post-Fordism since the 1970s and its increasing reliance on 'immaterial labour' (for example, emotional or intellectual labour) has been accompanied by the broadening of the working class from the 'mass worker' typical of Fordist production to the 'social worker', or the 'MULTITUDE', to employ the most recent term used by Hardt and Negri. The multitude is a broad category that includes all those whose labour is directly or indirectly exploited by and subjected to capitalist norms of production and reproduction. Indeed, in its latest stage, capitalism, referred to as 'empire', 'lives off the vitality of the multitude'. However, this all-encompassing force of late capitalism is also its weakness because it also exposes its dependent, parasitic nature. The more capitalism encroaches upon the lives and subjectivities of the multitude, the more dependent it becomes on the multitude, and the more possibility for resistance it opens up.

B

BAKUNIN, MIKHAIL One of the founding figures (1814–76) of both ANARCHIST theory and tactics. Born into the Russian aristocracy to a politically liberal father, he undertook military training at the Artillery University in St Petersburg. He took up a commission with the Russian Imperial Guard and served in Lithuania, resigning three years later in disgust at the repression of the local people. He then threw himself into reading and translating Hegel's writings, which took him to Germany in 1842 where he came into contact with the German SOCIALIST movement. He went on to live in Paris, meeting and being heavily influenced by PROUDHON. Settling in Switzerland, he became active in the socialist movement there. After taking part in an attempted REVOLUTION in Dresden in 1849, he was captured and condemned to death. Instead of executing him, however, the authorities handed him back to the Russian government. He was sentenced to life imprisonment in the notorious Peter and Paul fortress. Eight years later, after petitions by his family, his sentence was commuted and he was sent to Eastern Siberia. Eventually he escaped to AMERICA, becoming an influence on the American anarchist tradition via the thought of Benjamin Tucker. He arrived in England in 1861, and lived the rest of his life in various Western European countries.

Bakunin led the COMMUNIST anarchists in the First INTERNATIONAL but came into conflict with MARX. Bakunin accepted Marx's analysis of capitalism and the need for its overthrow by revolution but strongly disagreed with Marx's insistence on the need for a transitional worker's state, believing that it would simply lead to new forms of repression and authoritarianism. Bakunin believed that workers should organize their own institutions from the ground up, achieving more complex forms by voluntary FEDERALISM. It was not only this political difference that was to blame for the rupture with Marx, as Bakunin also frequently displayed the casual anti-semitism common at the time. Eventually Bakunin and his followers were expelled from the International in 1872.

Bakunin's ideas developed from LIBERTARIAN socialism to full-blooded anarchism over his lifetime. He rejected all forms of government and external authority, believing that human nature was essentially benign. It was the distorting effects of external restraint, inequality and privilege that were responsible for the ills of society. He fell briefly under the influence of the nihilist revolutionary Nachaev, who considered that revolutionaries needed to be completely ruthless, pursuing their ends by whatever means without taking any account of personal or moral feelings. This link earned Bakunin an unfair reputation as a proponent of TERRORISM and assassination.

Although Bakunin is sometimes held to be more of an activist and charismatic leader than theoretician, his contribution to anarchist and libertarian thinking is significant if not always systematic. This is not to say that his achievements as an activist were insignificant. He helped develop historically important anarchist movements in France, Switzerland, Belgium, Italy, Spain and Latin America. His political philosophy combines Proudhonian politics and Marxist economics. His lack of coherence was partly a result of his suspicion of what he saw as Marx's over-abstract systems of thought, divorced from the realities of workers' struggles on the ground. Despite this suspicion, he developed anarchism from utopian aspiration to a theory of political action, paving the way for anarcho-SYNDICALISM. He was also the first to argue for the need for an international social revolution, anticipating the thinking of Trotsky. Unlike Marx, with his disdain for the peasantry and 'lumpen-proletariat', Bakunin saw their revolutionary potential, a belief entirely vindicated by the history of the twentieth century. Most would also see his predictions concerning the authoritarian tendencies of state socialism as prophetic. More recently, the resurgence in anarchist thinking and politics that began in the 1960s has led to his becoming an influential thinker within contemporary COMMUNITARIAN movements.

BALL, JOHN An English Lollard priest who became one of the leaders of the PEASANT'S REVOLT in 1381. He fled London after the defeat of the revolt by the authorities, but was captured and subsequently hung, drawn and quartered before Richard II. He forms part of the long tradition of dissident monks and priests who identified themselves with the cause of the poor and sometimes built up considerable followings amongst them. Their teaching generally called for the establishment of the KINGDOM OF HEAVEN ON EARTH in the here and now, a feature of which was social equality and the dissolution of hierarchies. Such teaching was highly threatening to both church and secular authorities. Little is known about John Ball before his prominent role in the Revolt. He followed and preached the doctrines of John Wycliffe, a priest who opposed church hierarchy and translated the bible into English. Ball particularly stressed Wycliffe's anti-authoritarianism and preached social equality and the need for simplicity of life for the priesthood and MONASTIC orders.

His teaching struck a chord with the peasantry, whose position had been deteriorating due to the pressure of an increasing population and attempts to strengthen the obligations and ties of feudalism by manorial landowners. John Ball thus became a spokesman for the poor, which brought him into serious conflict with the Church. The Archbishop of Canterbury had him imprisoned three times for his teaching, but he continued to speak out. The rebelling peasants released him from Maidstone Gaol and he accompanied them on their way to London to confront the King. His most famous sermon was preached to the rebels at Blackheath, just outside London. One account has him saying:

'When Adam delved and Eve span, who was then the gentleman? From the beginning all men by nature were created alike, and our bondage or servitude came in by the unjust oppression of naughty men. For if God would have had any bondmen from the beginning, he would have appointed who should be bond, and who free. And therefore I exhort you to consider that now the time is come, appointed to us by God, in which ye may (if ye will) cast off the yoke of bondage, and recover liberty.'

John Ball is noteworthy because he has become part of the iconography of SOCIALISM and ANARCHISM. William Morris's 'A Dream of John Ball' typifies the way in which figures such as Ball come to be seen as part of a long historical tradition of opposition to the prevailing order.

BARTERING Trading goods or services for other goods or services, without the exchange of money. The simplest forms of bartering depended on the mutual coincidence of needs; thus a wheat grower needing shoes had to find not just a cobbler but a cobbler who needed wheat. To overcome this problem, especially as transactions became more complex, common media of exchange were developed. These were commodities that could be easily stored, were portable, durable and widely desirable – precious metals, grain, beads, shells, cattle and, eventually, metallic coins developed in Ancient Greece and China.

Barter is often regarded as an old-fashioned and inefficient means of exchange, and in virtually all civilizations it was superseded by money. But while money has been the dominant mode of modern commercial exchange, bartering has persisted. For example, during times of economic depression and currency instability, people have reverted to bartering, as they did in Germany after the two World Wars. Barter has also played an important role in international trade with countries whose currencies are not readily convertible. In 1972, PepsiCo did a deal with the government of the USSR that allowed it to sell Pepsi not for roubles but for vodka to be sold in the USA. Barter remains influential and the internet can be seen as one of the factors that has helped revitalize it. In addition, other forms of barter that rely on local networks of cashless exchange, such as LETS and TIME BANKS, have developed rapidly since the 1990s and have been promoted as ways of rebuilding COMMUNITY economies. Barter also remains a significant instrument of business trading, not only among cash-poor small businesses, but also as a medium of international trade. International bartering between businesses is enjoying a regeneration, thanks to a 'new generation' of intermediaries: companies that act as brokers of exchange between businesses wishing to swap their products or services against other products or services.

BATTLE OF SEATTLE In December 1999, up to 70,000 people converged on Seattle to protest against the neoliberalism of the World Trade Organization (WTO). This was the largest popular uprising in the USA since protests against the Vietnam war. The 'Battle of Seattle' opposed 'people power' to 'corporate power', and became a defining moment in the making of the ANTI-CAPITALIST MOVEMENT. This was a decentred protest that brought together groups as diverse as environmentalists, Third World debt campaigners, trade unionists, human rights activists, AIDS activists, church groups, peasants and small farmers. Although all these groups came with different agendas and demands (from saving turtles to abolishing capitalism), the police beatings and arrests they met in the streets reinforced the resolve and unity of the protesters. With Seattle, protest became a more open and inclusive activity; it was no longer the preserve of a few marginal, hard-core activists, but involved anyone who shared the belief that the logic of neoliberalism was wrong, whether their concern was primarily with war, sweatshops, deforestation, genetic engineering, increased poverty, growing global inequalities, cuts in social services, or global warming. Another factor in explaining the significance of Seattle was the development of new media

26

forms and activities to capture public attention. In particular, INDYMEDIA was established by independent and alternative media organizations and activists to provide grassroots coverage of the Seattle protest. Its website has since served as a major alternative source of information on various direct action campaigns and protests.

As a result of the Seattle protest, the WTO aborted its round of talks, and this constituted a symbolic victory for the movement. The note of triumph in the aftermath of Seattle has fuelled further actions by the anti-capitalist movement, and defined a new politics of protest that was manifested, for example, in the demonstrations aga5ints the IMF/World Bank in Washington DC in April 2000, the gathering of protesters in Millau, France, in June 2000 to oppose the trial of José Bové and local farmers for dismantling the town's McDonald's, the protest against the IMF/World Bank in Prague in September 2000, the gathering of anti-capitalist protesters during an EU summit in Nice in December 2000, the Genoa protest against the G8 in July 2001, and so on. All these protests have sullied the global perception of the WTO, and neoliberal economics more generally, by denouncing its anti-democratic nature, its privileging of corporate power and profits, and its neglect of social justice, the poor and the environment.

BLAC(K) BLOC An ephemeral group of activists, often with ANARCHIST affiliations, who organize together for a particular protest action. Black Bloc is not an organization that one can join, even less 'lead', but a tactic used during demonstrations to provide safety and solidarity in the face of repressive police action. Black blocs as a tactic reflect anarchists' preference for spontaneity and individual autonomy over the hierarchy, authority and structure of an 'organization'. Black blocs are named after the black (the colour of anarchism) clothing and masks they wear at demonstrations to provide anonymity for individuals, yet visibility as a group. The masks also symbolize egalitarianism and the anarchist refusal to recognize a leader. Typical actions of a Black Bloc include distracting police, misleading police about protesters' movements, 'unarresting' people who have already been arrested by the police, building barricades, attacking and disarming police, as well as the destruction of property deemed to have symbolic significance, such as banks, institutional buildings, or the outlets of multinational corporations.

Black bloc tactics originated in the AUTONOMIA movement in Germany in the 1980s and were first seen in AMERICA during the protests against the

27

first Gulf War. They have been present in all ANTI-CAPITALIST protests since the BATTLE OF SEATTLE, where their use of violence has been highly controversial both within and outside the movement. Against accusations of 'vandalism', Black blocs have defended their actions on the grounds that the police often attack protesters without prior provocation, or that they only target the property of the 'rich'. In addition, they have suggested that the police and neo-Nazi groups have infiltrated Black blocs at various anti-capitalist protests and have engaged in acts of vandalism and violence in order to discredit the movement. Black bloc activists were given heavy sentences for alleged 'TERRORIST activities' after GENOA.

BLAKE, WILLIAM An English artist and poet born into a lower-middle-class family in 1757. His father was a hosier and the family lived in relative poverty. Blake received little education as a child but obtained an apprenticeship with the engraver James Basire in 1771. A short, unsuccessful time as a student at the Royal Academy was followed by equally unproductive periods working for a bookseller and running his own engraving business. Until his death, Blake scraped a living as an independent craftsman surviving on commissions from wealthy patrons. Only two of his own works were printed,, neither was published. His prolific output was therefore almost entirely self-produced. His work was exhibited only once in his lifetime (in 1809) and that was a financial and critical disaster. In fact, the only review of the exhibition described Blake as 'an unfortunate lunatic, whose personal inoffensiveness secures him from confinement'. He rarely travelled, and for two years he did not leave his house save for short trips to the shops. In 1803, however, he did manage to get himself charged for sedition at the Chichester assizes after swearing at a soldier he caught urinating in his garden. He was acquitted.

But Blake in time came to be seen as an important forerunner of both ROMANTICISM and British ANARCHISM. He moved for a while in the circle of William GODWIN, Mary Wollstonecraft and Thomas Paine whilst working for their publisher, Joseph Johnson. Blake produced *Natural Religion*, the first of his illuminated works, in 1788, developing a unique method of production in which the text and illustrations were drawn in reverse on copper plates. After the prints were taken they were coloured by hand. Between 1789 and 1800 he was extraordinarily prolific, producing *Songs of Innocence* (1789), *The Marriage of Heaven and Hell* (1790), *The French Revo- lution* (1791), *America: A Prophecy* (1793), *Visions of the Daughters of Albion*

(1793), *Songs of Experience* (1794) and *Europe: A Prophecy* (1795). He was stimulated by the political upheavals in Europe and AMERICA at the time. His writings opposed the consequences of industrialism, those 'dark satanic mills', slavery and sexual inequality, but his anti-authoritarian spirit and belief in individual freedom was so strong that he would always be frustrated by earthly movements. Driven by rebellion itself, and rejecting all forms of imposed authority, he sought nothing less than transcendence, once affirming 'I must create my own system or be enslaved by another man's.' Blake saw society as inevitably restricting the freedoms derived from intuition and spontaneity. For him the State and the Church served only to oppress; his project therefore was to break free of these impositions and create a society in which an unorganized, unmediated state of being was possible. This England, his 'Jerusalem', could therefore only be envisioned through poetry, art and the power of the imagination. He died in 1827, leaving no debts.

BOOKCHIN, MURRAY Born in 1921 in New York, the son of poor Russian immigrants, he spent his early years as an industrial worker. Initially a MARXIST, he became disillusioned with what he saw as the authoritarianism of Marxist thinking and began to develop his own ideas combining ANARCHIST and ecological theory. Throughout he has stressed the need for, and interconnection between, social transformation and individual autonomy. He was a member of the anarchist American Libertarian League in the 1960s and went on to found the Institute for Social Ecology in the 1970s. His thinking has been highly influential in a number of areas, particularly the Green Movement, the ANTI-CAPITALIST Movement and recent anarchist theory and practice.

His first important book was *Post-Scarcity Anarchism* (1971), a collection of essays. In it he argues that modern technology, for the first time in history, makes abundance for all a real possibility and provides the preconditions for a free society of autonomous but interdependent individuals. In the vitriolic essay *Listen, Marxist* he argues that MARX's thinking was based on a scarcity capitalism that was now outmoded. Bookchin was also developing his ideas on ENVIRONMENTALISM, beginning with his earlier work on the problems of chemicals in food and environmental pollution in the 1950s and 1960s. He published a series of critical studies of urbanism including *Crisis in our Cities* (1965), *The Limits of the City* (1973), and *The Rise of Urbanization and the Decline of Citizenship* (1987). Bookchin's response to the problems of modern urban living is to argue that CITY STATES on a human

29

scale should be a central goal of anarchist politics. Local municipalities should be run by local citizens' assemblies, which would foster autonomy as well as providing an ideal form of participatory **DEMOCRACY**.

The two strands of Bookchin's thought, his environmentalism and his **COMMUNISM**, have been integrated into his development of a cultural politics within an ecological context. His anarchism draws heavily on the thinking of **PROUDHON, BAKUNIN,** and **KROPOTKIN,** as well as his Marxist background. Bookchin is a firm advocate of **UTOPIANISM**. He argues that utopian thinking is essential because it provides a way of harnessing the power of imagination in order to question the assumptions of the current order. It also enables the consideration of alternative social arrangements and the proposal of concrete proposals for change. He follows **FOURIER** and Morris in believing that work must both provide sensuous satisfaction and be an outlet for the creativity of human beings. Whilst retaining a Marxist commitment to **REVOLUTIONARY** change, he argues that it is not enough simply to dissolve the State. Rather, new institutions need to be developed that enable the transformation of daily lives. The process of revolutionary change should thus not merely be seen as a means to an end, but as a way for individuals to become aware of their autonomy and the possibilities for the actualization of their hopes.

Bookchin links this to his perspective on ecology. Within nature he sees an essential harmony between living and non-living things. Human consciousness is the highest expression of what he sees as nature's tendency towards self-awareness. This ecological model provides Bookchin with ideal principles on which to base human society, the most important of which might be termed 'harmony in diversity'. Bookchin has written 'From an ecological viewpoint, balance and harmony in nature, in society and, by inference, in behaviour, are achieved not by mechanical standardization but by its opposite, organic differentiation.' In other words, individuals and communities should strive to enable multiple forms of life but in ways that recognize their **NETWORKED** interdependence. Thus we need to move from a hierarchical technocratic rationality to the 're-enchantment of humanity by a fluid, organismic and dialectical rationality.' These views place him at odds with radical ecocentric environmentalists because of his insistence on the primacy of human life.

His own utopian vision is that of **ECOTOPIA**, comprising relatively small-scale communities using advanced technologies in carefully applied ways so as to sustainably use and indeed enhance the supporting eco-systems (see

WOMAN ON THE EDGE OF TIME). Human relationships and material exchange would be based on the principle of *usufruct*. All would receive the basic minimum to live and give freely without consideration of return. Care, responsibility and obligation would replace interest, cost and profitability. Bookchin's thought can be criticized as overly dependent on the belief that history is inevitably leading towards social progress, with modern technology enabling the achievement of an ideal society. There are plenty of arguments that can be made about the regressive direction in which modern technological developments are taking us. The assumption that the planet can provide abundantly for all is also open to question. However, the combination of environmentalism and radical cultural and social politics make Bookchin a highly original thinker and one of the most important anarchist theorists of the twentieth century (see also ILLICH).

BOURNVILLE This model community was established by George and Richard Cadbury in 1878. The Cadbury business had been started by their father John Cadbury in 1824. Originally a retailer selling tea, coffee and drinking chocolate, Cadbury soon moved into manufacture and set up his first factory in Birmingham. The Cadbury family were members of the Society of Friends, or QUAKERS. Such NON-CONFORMIST groups were known for their commitment to social reform. Barred from entering the universities, Quakers were restricted from joining the established professions and therefore turned to business, which was also seen as a means of furthering their progressive ideals. In the late 1870s the Cadbury brothers decided to move from the centre of Birmingham to a new site. They therefore purchased land about four miles south of the city. The site was predominately meadow, with a trout stream called 'the Bourn'. Plans for the Bournville 'factory in a garden' were drawn up and production commenced in 1879.

There were also strong commercial advantages to the move as many of Cadbury's competitors were transferring production to purpose-built, single-site factories. And although it is said that the brothers searched for a site where they could pursue their social welfare commitments, by 1892 only 16 semi-detached residences had been built. As the Cadbury's factory grew in size, land values increased. To prevent the surrounding land from falling into the hands of developers, the brothers purchased more land and began to develop the housing stock. They were aware of the valuable favourable publicity that often accompanied such developments. The

31

French firm Menier (Cadbury had adopted the name Bournville to associate with the positive image of French chocolate) had started building houses for its workers in 1870 and became known as a 'model employer' as a result. Ideas were also drawn from the developing GARDEN CITY movement, of which George Cadbury became an instrumental member. Cottages were grouped and set back from tree-lined roads. All had their own front garden with a vegetable patch, and fruit trees were planted at the rear. Cottages were well built (costing a minimum of £150) with good sanitation, and further building was controlled on sites to prevent overcrowding. The first houses were sold on leases of 999 years and mortgages were available for purchasers.

By 1900 the estate comprised 330 acres of land with 313 cottages. Whilst Cadburys invested significantly in welfare, recreation and social provision for its workers, there existed a degree of detachment between these initiatives and the Bournville project. By following the 'Garden City' model, Bournville was developed differently from the earlier-nineteenth-century philanthropic tradition (see PORT SUNLIGHT; SALTAIRE). For example, George Cadbury chose to establish the charitable Bournville Village Trust. Its deed of foundation provided land for both residential and community purposes and gave particular importance to parks and other open spaces in its planning schemes. The trust remained entirely separate from the Cadbury business and all revenue was devoted to the extension of the estate and the promotion of housing reform. According to some, George Cadbury thereby resisted the temptation to become a kind of feudal lord. The trust continues today. Presently the Bournville estate covers 1,000 acres and contains 7,600 dwellings. It also manages properties in nearby towns and participates in architectural and environmentally related projects aimed at improving planning and housing conditions. Residents in properties covered by an original trust covenant continue to have to abide by a strict code of conduct relating to the preservation of their property. (WS)

BRAY, JOHN FRANCIS Born in 1809 in the United States of an immigrant English family from Leeds, he undertook his intellectual development in England. He wrote two books: *Labour's Wrongs and Labour's Remedy* (1839), which contains all his key ideas; and *A Voyage around Utopia*, a satire never published in his lifetime. After his return to AMERICA, his literary output was channelled into labour movement papers such as the

Labor Leaf, and he died in 1897. His ideas stand at the meeting place between the COMMUNITARIAN self-sufficiency of Robert OWEN and CHARTIST ideas for change through political reform.

In *The Poverty of Philosophy* MARX categorized Bray as UTOPIAN, whilst later historians labelled him a Ricardian SOCIALIST. Yet his central idea of the incremental accumulation of workers' savings was a direct contradiction of Ricardo. Bray felt that there were sufficient funds in the hands of various MUTUAL societies and TRADE UNIONS to establish common-stock institutions, and that a subscription of one penny per week would eventually be enough to buy out the capitalists. He criticized OWEN's notion of self-sufficiency (see SUBSISTENCE WORK) as impractical given the advantages of technology and economy of scale, and called for fixed capital to be transferred from capitalists to workers. Even Marx, forty years later, whilst questioning the ability of worker COOPERATIVES to overtake capitalism, did acknowledge that a national level strategy might be successful.

Bray's ideas were radical but based on gradualism and consent, not expropriation by the state. He held to a belief in cooperative association as the building block for the emancipation of labour – but insisted that technological conditions must determine an appropriate scale of economic activity. His ideas took the COMMUNITY of labour beyond self-sufficiency and towards recognition of the importance of specialization. For Bray the MARKET, not a centralized planning system, would ensure that COLLECTIVISM provided benefits whilst avoiding the exploitation of capitalism (see also MUTUALISM). Bray argued for intermediate organizational forms to develop DEMOCRATIC attitudes within what he perceived to be a brutalized proletariat. He expected a gradual cultural transition through learning and development driven by practical experience. In Bray the community of labour was not something that emerged automatically but was rather an ideal to evolve towards. The market remained the ultimate reality for the economic viability of the community of labour and (unlike Marx) he never doubted that workers' businesses would outstrip capitalism.

The challenges of combining size, collectivism and hierarchy towards the realization of distributive justice and economic democracy remain, but the economic and institutional platform for a sector-by-sector strategy that Bray envisaged exists. The global cooperative movement is as much Bray's legacy as any labour strategist of his period. CREDIT UNIONS, ESOPS, MONDRAGÒN and so on all bear witness to the practicality and contemporary relevance of his ideas. (PD)

BRETHREN OF THE FREE SPIRIT Followers of the MILLENARIAN Heresy of the Free Spirit emerged at the close of the twelfth century. They are thought to have been inspired by the Sufis, a group of Islamic mystics based in Seville in Spain. Although less well known than the CATHARS or ANABAPTISTS, the Brethren of the Free Spirit have probably had greater influence on the social history of Europe. The RANTERS of seventeenth-century England were their spiritual descendants and the radical English Civil War 'Left' of LEVELLERS and DIGGERS owed much to their influence. The mysticism of BLAKE has striking affinities with Free Spirit thinking as does the LIBERTARIAN eroticism of 1960s counter-culture. The Brethren can thus be seen as medieval individualist ANARCHISTS.

The Heresy of the Free Spirit included the belief that God is in all created things, which are thus divine. Followers did not believe in a heaven or hell as rewards or punishment in an afterlife; rather they are states of the soul of human beings in this world. Most significantly, the Brethren believed that once they had achieved a sufficient knowledge of God they were perfected and could not sin. They were therefore above all the restraints of laws, doctrines and earthly authorities and were licensed to follow any desire without the fear of committing sin. Indeed this belief developed so that the pursuit of any desires without feeling remorse was a sign that a follower had become an adept, achieving a divinity that placed them on the same level as God himself. The adepts thus advocated complete amorality and this sometimes included self-assertion at the expense of others. There were frequent incidents where members of the sect exploited and oppressed non-members. Brethren rejected private property and the marriage tie, extending the same freedom of sexual promiscuity to male and female alike.

Those who followed the heresy became 'holy beggars', travelling throughout Europe and spreading their ideas. Though they were intent on achieving their own individual enlightenment, they became a sort of travelling intelligentsia, encouraging the rebellion of the poor and dispossessed. The notion that one might reject the crushing weight of secular and spiritual authority and do as one pleased without fear of hell or the pangs of conscience was a REVOLUTIONARY one often cited as a justification in PEASANT REVOLTS during the medieval period. The idea that one might attain a state of innocence where all was permitted and sin did not exist was often interpreted as an attempt to recreate EDEN, where all were equal. Social distinctions, inequality and moral restraint could thus be seen as a result of original sin, and therefore as intrinsically evil.

BROOK FARM

'Democracy was not enough, it should be raised up into life and made social.' Charles Dana

An INTENTIONAL COMMUNITY in West Roxbury, Massachusetts that lasted from 1841 to 1847 (see also MASSACHUSETTS BAY COLONY). Despite its short existence, 'The Brook Farm Institute for Agriculture and Education' became well known because of its famous members and visitors – Nathaniel Hawthorne, Charles Dana, Ralph Waldo Emerson and others. It was also gently satirized in Hawthorne's *The Blithdale Romance* (1852), in which a group of middle-class intellectuals discover that they don't really like manual labour after all (see also RUSKIN). It was founded by George Ripley, an ex-Unitarian minister, who raised the capital as a joint stock company with 24 shares at $500 per share. Initially it was largely based on the philosophy of 'American transcendentalism', a form of European ROMANTICISM that stressed nature, intuition and the rejection of contemporary civilization (see WALDEN for further details). In practice this meant a combination of an experiment in Christian living, self-sustaining COOPERATIVE economics, and an attempt to avoid a hierarchy of labour or intellect. In order to achieve a union between spirit and flesh, all members had to spend a few hours a day engaged in physical effort, but there were also endless educations and amusements open to all. Due to perceived problems in sharing work, it was agreed that 300 days were the equivalent of one year's labour (ten hours in the summer, eight in the winter), and eventually that labour hours should be formally recorded (see TIME BANK).

Brook Farm's school was highly successful (boarding pupils either paying, or working to pay for their tuition) but attempts at agriculture were not helped by sandy soil and inexperienced farmers. From 1844 onwards Brook Farm became more influenced by the ideas of Charles FOURIER (see HAYDEN). *The Harbinger*, a Fourierist newspaper, was initially edited and printed at Brook Farm. A large communal building called the 'Phalanstery' was begun, but in 1846 it burned down before completion and the COMMUNITY never really recovered.

BULLOCK REPORT, see INDUSTRIAL DEMOCRACY

BUREAUCRACY

To call someone a 'bureaucrat' is to suggest that they have substituted means for ends, to say that they are strangling themselves and others with red tape, and that (as Eichmann famously argued at his trial) they are only following orders. *Bureaucratie*, rule from the desk, was coined by Vincent de Gourney, one of the French 'physiocrats' who stressed MARKET liberalism against centralized state protectionism. The subsequent history of the word often marks it as a pathological condition, as an impediment to the exercise of commercial freedoms and as opposed to the small-scale autonomy of COMMUNITIES. These views are echoed in the present concern of the World Trade Organization to 'liberate' trade from regulation, and the endless claims by politicians to want to get rid of bureaucrats and give power to ordinary citizens.

The most influential author for contemporary understandings of bureaucracy was Max Weber at the beginning of the twentieth century. Weber saw the advance of bureaucratization as inevitable but tied it to a larger sociological thesis about the development of forms of legitimacy. He argued that, in every sphere of social life, from music to war, charismatic and traditional forms of authority were increasingly routinized into legal-rational, or bureaucratic, authority. In this regard, he appears rather like Comte, but Weber's ambivalence about the advance of bureaucracy is clear. He praises its technical advantages but is also painfully aware of its dehumanizing consequences.

Weber's diagnosis echoes through the twentieth century. Much of US sociology and psychology after the Second World War was concerned with various ways in which the FASCIST version of bureaucracy could be better understood and avoided. Descriptions of authoritarian and bureaucratic personality types, experiments on the willingness of subjects to obey people in white coats, and accounts of the inefficiencies and dysfunctions of bureaucracy set the tone for a pervasive suspicion of bureaucrats. William Whyte's *Organization Man* (1961) is a dull conformist and more lately both MacIntyre and Bauman have characterized both management and bureaucracy as being amoral, in the latter case even complicit with the holocaust. Yet despite such sustained criticism for nearly 250 years, the concept seems to be remarkably resilient. Many UTOPIAS have relied on some conception of bureaucracy (LOOKING BACKWARD, VOYAGE TO ICARIA, WELLS) and many theorists have defended the impartiality and due process necessary for the functioning of state bureaucracies. In any case, it can be argued that Weber's 'ideal type' of bureaucracy is actually a description of the problems that any formal organization needs to solve – hierarchy, decision making, communication and so on. The problem hinges on whether all organizations should be regarded as bureaucratic. To some degree, this is a useful starting point, since any form of organization (alternative, UTOPIAN or not) must have a set of rules (formal or informal) that constitutes the organization as organized. However, not all organizations need to be hierarchical, separate public from private, have written policies and organization charts, and so on. Perhaps bureaucratization is better seen as a continuum, with extremely formalized organizations at one end, and extremely informalized ones at the other, but bearing in mind that no organizations can be entirely constituted by formal rules, and that no organizations can have no rules (see ANARCHISM).

C

CADBURY, see BOURNVILLE

CAPTAIN SWING The mythical leader of a series of uprisings by British farm labourers which took place around 1830. The absence of a rural peasantry meant that the majority of the British rural population in the eighteenth and nineteenth centuries were farm labourers. By the early 1800s in south and east England, due to rapid population growth, mechanization, and the demobilization of soldiers from the Napoleonic wars, there was a surplus of agricultural labour. Workers were employed on a casual basis for short periods for harvesting, hedging, ditching, threshing and so on. Wages fell and poor relief could not meet the growing demand.

The run of bad harvests in the 1820s meant that many of the poor could not cover their basic expenses and grew short of food. However the harvest of 1830 promised better and the labourers saw this as an opportunity to press for better conditions. By June riots had taken place in Kent and then spread to Surrey and Sussex. Before the end of the year Hampshire and Wiltshire had been affected. Farm buildings were set alight and threshing machines were broken. On 25 November there was fighting between labourers and the military in Wiltshire. The government appointed a special commission of three judges to try those arrested in the affected counties. Some men were deported; others were jailed or fined.

These 'Swing' riots were the first collective demonstrations by agricultural labourers and they influenced the passing of the 1834 Poor Law Amendment Act. However, wages and conditions generally did not improve and agricultural labourers continued to have the worst conditions of all labouring communities. The name 'Captain Swing' derived from the supposed author of a number of letters written by the protesters and sent to farmers and others, and followed in the tradition of mythical leaders set by the LUDDITES. It is generally believed that few were actually produced by the labourers themselves. According to *The Times* of 29 November 1830, one letter was produced by the schoolboys of Eton. The uprising gradually ebbed away and most of the wage increases secured were reversed. However, the use of threshing machinery did decline for a while. (WS)

CARNIVAL The origin of the term is open to dispute but one common interpretation is that is comes from the Latin *carne* (meat) and *levare* (to remove). Carnival is mostly a Roman Catholic tradition and marks a period of unbridled celebration and excess to use up all remaining meat and animal products before the Lent period of fasting and sacrifice.

Carnivals also draw upon pagan festivals, the earliest of which was Saturn's festival, Saturnalia, celebrated in Ancient Rome. This was a period of temporary subversion of civil order in which rules and roles were turned upside down; slaves became masters and masters became slaves. Like the Roman Saturnalias, carnivals are an expression of freedom and renewal, they conjure up a GOLDEN AGE of plenty that has often captured the imagination, for example through the powerful imagery of COCKAIGNE, or in the Rabelaisian world of giants Gargantua and Pantagruel (see ABBEY OF THELEME). Carnival is thus part of a strand of UTOPIAN tradition that contrasts with the emphasis on self-restraint and simplicity that characterizes many other visions of the utopian CITY STATE. Carnival is a rite of renewal that celebrates life by symbolically evoking abundance (excess and waste of food and drink) and fecundity (manifested in ubiquitous obscenity). As opposed to the official feast, carnival celebrates temporary liberation from the prevailing truth and the established order. It marks the suspension of hierarchical ranks, privileges, norms and prohibitions. For a period of time, the hardship, order and routine of ordinary life give way to abundance and freedom. Masks and laughter are used to blur and transgress boundaries. The costumes used in carnivals enable participants to become someone else, whilst laughter, ridicule, the grotesque and satire give licence to critique those in power.

But the carnival is also a deeply ambivalent practice for it places the transgression of social order within a clear temporal and spatial frame. It is not meant to last but serves as a channel for the expression of discontent and tension, so that social order may remain unchallenged during the rest of the year. The carnival is therefore a paradoxical practice since it simultaneously destabilizes and reinforces order. It marks an interruption, rather than a transformation.

CASTRO, FIDEL, see CUBA

CATHARS A heretical CULT similar to the MILLENARIAN tradition. It first appeared in the middle of the tenth century and lasted, despite the crusades and the inquisition sent against it by the Pope, into the first decades of the fourteenth. Even after its disappearance, Catharism influenced the development of radical Protestant groups such as the ANABAPTISTS and Hussites that emerged during the Reformation, as well as later groups such as the LEVELLERS. It also contributed to the direction in which some NON-CONFORMIST denominations developed. Although they existed elsewhere, Cathars were mainly associated with what is now the Languedoc in France, Lombardy in Italy and Catalonia in Spain. In medieval times this was a region known as Occitania, a land with its own language and distinctive culture that was politically independent of France. The Cathars were also known as the Albigensians from the end of the twelfth century, after the town of Albi in southern France.

Their beliefs were derived from Gnosticism, a reinterpretation of Christianity that sees Satan and God as two sides of the same coin. The material world, including the flesh, was created by the Devil and was essentially evil; the soul was good and belonged to God. They believed in reincarnation as a curse, as it meant assuming another material form. The objective of the devout Cathar was to escape reincarnation and return the soul to God. The leaders were known as the 'Perfects' or 'Good Men'. They pursued a strict and frugal way of life, claimed to be able to forgive sins and were responsible for administering the 'Consolation' on the deathbed of believers, who were then guaranteed a place in heaven. Believers did not eat after the Consolation in order not to pollute them-selves with worldly matter. This sometimes led its adherents to starve themselves to death rather than risk losing a place in heaven. Cathars also tried to avoid reproducing and so condemning another generation to material existence.

Although the Good Men generally led lives of voluntary poverty and piety, their followers were effectively freed from any moral prohibition by Cathar teaching. They were guaranteed salvation by the Consolation no matter what they had done. Having said this, in practice there is only evidence of a modest level of sexual permissiveness. Accusations by the Church regarding the lasciviousness of Cathars were a response to heresies of all kinds and were in turn reciprocated by heretics in their criticisms of the clergy. Although women were generally subordinate there were some female Perfects. In addition, the tendency of Cathar beliefs was to reject both social and gender inequalities as one's bodily form was considered irrelevant. Moral codes in Cathar-dominated COMMUNITIES tended to be based upon neighbourliness and MUTUALITY. Private property was respected but not wealth. Voluntary poverty was widely valued, particularly as it was believed that the current social order would be reversed after death. Hard work was not valued particularly highly, although the Good Men were compared favourably to Catholic priests because they worked to support themselves.

Their teaching appealed to the poor because it valorized poverty and criticized the accumulation of wealth. It also freed the poor from many irksome aspects of Catholicism, not least their subordination to priests. Unusually, the Cathars also received support and protection from a large proportion of the local nobility, including the Dukes of Aquitaine. The nobility were also determined to demonstrate their independence from France and from the Papacy. In 1204 the Pope sent legates to the Occitan bishops ordering the suppression of the Cathars. The bishops refused to recognize the authority of the legates and were then suspended by the Pope. The local nobility were excommunicated but continued to protect the Cathars. Eventually the Pope sponsored the Albigensian Crusade in 1209 and guaranteed to the northern French nobility that they could seize the land of heretic southern nobles. Even by medieval standards the crusade was brutal. In one famous atrocity the entire population of Béziers was slaughtered after the invading forces asked the Abbot of Citeaux how they might tell the difference between good Catholics and heretic Cathars: 'Kill them all, God will know his own,' he replied. The breaking of the power of the southern nobles severely weakened Catharism but it carried on as a SECRET SOCIETY in the isolated mountain VILLAGES of Occitania until the last Cathar leaders were burnt at the stake in 1329.

Catharism was unique amongst dissident religious movements in its gentleness and its promise of universal, as opposed to exclusive, redemption. The Cathars opposed all forms of killing, human and animal alike. Their egalitarian beliefs inspired peasants and many of the nobility to give up their lives fighting the authority of the powers of the day. It survived against this onslaught for around 300 years and mounted a serious challenge to orthodox belief. Many of its ideas survived and eventually influenced the emergence of politically radical and UTOPIAN movements in our own time.

CENTRI SOCIALI Regarded as laboratories of cultural innovation and political subversion, centri sociali ('social centres') have spread across Italian towns and cities since the 1990s, but have their roots in the country's underground scene of the 1970s, and the SQUATTING of public spaces and abandoned buildings that developed out of the AUTONOMIA movement. These centres attracted many young people who fled from employment and the family to live collectively. They survived on precarious jobs, the 'expropriation' of food in supermarkets and restaurants, and the self-reduction of bus fares, concert or cinema tickets. One of the oldest and largest centri sociali – Leoncavallo in Milan (see DISOBBEDIENTI) has been shut down by the police and re-opened many times and is a self-contained community that includes several restaurants, gardens, a bookstore, a cinema, a bar, a club and a radio station.

Today it is difficult to identify one ideological line that would apply to all centri sociali. Whilst they have often been associated with ANARCHISM or autonomism, many have tended to reject any particular label, and the campaigns they organize or participate in tend to span a wide range of issues (such as the anti-war movement, anti-racism, reform of the criminal justice system, the granting of asylum to refugees, ANTI-CAPITALISM). They are also centres of urban counter-culture and have a long-standing association with the alternative music scene in Italy (many are equipped with recording studios). The cultural production of centri sociali includes radio broadcasting, the publication of magazines, fiction and poetry, art exhibitions, and theatre workshops. Some centri sociali also provide community services such as Italian language courses for asylum seekers, day care, AIDS prevention, or drug counselling. Altogether, centri sociali define a 'new Italian underground', that involves political action, the production and consumption of alternative culture and the voluntary provision or MUTUAL exchange of services. They provide a self-managed space, autonomous from the state or the MARKET, for cultural, political and economic experimentation.

CHIPKO MOVEMENT 'Tree-hugging' was developed mainly by women peasants in Uttar Pradesh, India, in the 1970s to oppose the commercial logging of forests. These forests are a critical resource for the subsistence of indigenous people both because of their direct provision of food, fuel and fodder and because of their role in stabilizing soil and water resources. As these forests have been felled for commerce and industry, villagers have sought to protect their livelihoods through mainly GANDHIan methods of non-violent DIRECT ACTION. Whilst tree logging had been going on in the area since British colonial rule and had already disrupted subsistence agriculture, the situation was exacerbated in the early 1970s when a series of landslides devastated the Uttar Pradesh region.

The first Chipko action took place spontaneously in April 1973 when a group of 27 women hugged trees to save them from the contractors' axes and stop further deforestation. Over the next five years similar actions spread to many Himalayan districts in Uttar Pradesh, and the movement has since developed in other regions of India. The Chipko movement has been successful in forcing a fifteen-year ban on felling in the hills of Uttar Pradesh, and in generating pressure for a national forest policy which is more sensitive to people's needs and to the ecological development of the country. The movement is the result of hundreds of decentralized and locally AUTONOMOUS initiatives, with diverse experiences and motivations. Its leaders and activists are primarily village women, acting to save their means of subsistence and their COMMUNITIES. But although it is mainly a GRASS-ROOTS movement, Vandana Shiva, an ecofeminist writer and activist involved in the movement, has been an influential spokesperson. The Chipko movement has inspired ENVIRONMENTALISM both nationally and globally, and contributed substantially to the emerging philosophies of ECOFEMINISM and DEEP ECOLOGY.

CHRISTIANIA This self-governing part of the Christianshavn district of the Danish capital Copenhagen was established by a mass SQUAT in 1971. The site of an old military barracks, it covers an area of 85 acres and (in 2004) about 1,000 people lived there. Since 1972, the residents of the freetown have being paying utility bills and state taxes, but have been under continual threat of eviction as various city administrations attempt to deal with perceived problems, and renegotiate the taxes and benefits that apply within the area. Whilst the selling of cannabis on street stands has been prohibited by the freetown residents since 2004, over the years it has often resulted in sustained police operations and multiple arrests. The Christianians' response has involved cultural and political organization with large scale SITUATIONIST protests and theatre events, and (since 1978) the freetown has had an elected representative on the city council.

Christiania is governed by a series of meetings, the 'common' meeting being the key one. There are fifteen smaller area meetings and functional

43

meetings for economy, business, buildings and so on. All residents may attend all meetings. Residence depends on a room being advertised in the local newspaper and applicants interviewed by an area meeting. A common purse is funded by rents from individuals and businesses which pays for some state taxes and internal institutions, whilst electricity is metered. The key public issues for self-government have been dealing with rocker violence, banning cars, restricting cannabis dealing to particular areas, prohibiting heroin use and (in 1997) introducing the local currency, the Løn. The gradual normalization of relationships between the freetown and the state is re flected in the growing number of tourists, small businesses and entertainment venues. It is also increasingly branded as a model of sustainable urban living, both in terms of recycling and impact, but also for its preservation of substantial green spaces within the city. Christiania has been a successful and lengthy social experiment which has sustained a hippy lifestyle whilst taking issues of structure and democracy seriously (see also CENTRI SOCIALI). Whether it can avoid being incorporated as a merely bohemian quarter of a liberal city is probably the important issue for the next part of its history.

CHRISTIANOPOLIS Johann Valentin Andreae, a German scholar and humanist (1586–1654), published this Christian reformist UTOPIA in 1619, and it reflects a Renaissance interest in education and social improvement. His association with a SECRET SOCIETY seemingly intended for religious reform has meant that he is also included in histories of Rosicrucian mysticism. Though Andreae is clear that human beings can never be as perfect as God, he thinks that they be can improved through their circumstances. In this sense, Andreae was a practical utopian who founded an early mutual protection association at Calw to support the working people from the cloth factories and dye works.

In one hundred short chapters, the *Reipublicae christianopolitanae descriptio* provides considerable detail on utopian organization. After sailing across the Academic Sea on the good ship Phantasy, the adventurer arrives at the triangular island of Capharsalama through being shipwrecked (Andreae was the first to use this device) and there finds the city of Christianopolis. He is allowed entrance after a three-stage examination and enters the square, symmetrical, stone-built and fortified city within which about four hundred people live. The city is divided according to function, with different parts for different industries, and these parts again divided by levels of skill. Governance is carried out by a triumvirate of well-respected men, and beneath them by officials and councillors representing different parts of the city. There is no private property but a system of central planning that ensures, amongst other things, that work duties are rotated so that all take their turns at the more unpleasant manual duties. By this method, the citizens are not coarsened by certain forms of labour, and working hours are kept to a minimum. Families are small. Plainly dressed according to season, age or gender, they eat their meals privately in simple accommodation (with food provided from the public storehouse). Education (which is described in considerable detail, and almost certainly influenced Bacon's NEW ATLANTIS) is the same for girls and boys, and consists of classes on logic, rhetoric, languages, music, astronomy, history, ethics and theology, taught by active and generous instructors (see NEW JERUSALEM). Despite this equality in education, women have no public voice, and (even within marriage) sex is only permissible for the purposes of reproduction.

The influence of Luther, ideas of the CITY STATE as enshrined in Calvin's Geneva, and traditions of brotherly craft GUILDS a re clear in Andreae's work. So too is the endless struggle between a metaphysics of human corruption and a severely practical Protestant ethic. For example, Andreae discourses on the virtues of street lighting, which can both make the streets safer for the night watch and prevent useless wandering around, as well as metaphorically causing the darkness and fog of the Antichrist to shrink in the citizens' hearts. Or, in terms of discipline, petty thefts will incur sensible penalties ('for anyone can destroy a man, but only the best one can reform'), whilst blasphemy and adultery will result in the severest forms of punishment. These tensions between a tyrannical Christian moralism and a tempered anti-authoritarian reformism are similar to those found in the CITY OF THE SUN, but not, for example, in the rather more sumptous setting Rabelais designed for the ABBEY OF THELEME.

CINCINNATI TIME STORE, see MUTUALISM, TIME BANKS

CITY OF THE SUN The visionary UTOPIA of Thomasso Campanella (1568–1639) was written in prison and at least four different versions exist (in Italian and Latin), composed in between 1602 and 1631. Most were written in prison, where Campanella spent much time as a result of falling foul of the Roman Inquisition during the counter- re fo mation. He believed that the Catholic Church should be at the heart of a new Holy Universal

Republic, and hence (at various times) backed the aspirations of his native Calabria, Spain and France because he thought they would be able to reform the Church of Rome. *City of the Sun* was written despite episodes of madness, trials and tortures, and reflects (in a disguised and fantastic manner) his own political aspirations. The fact that the early versions were written in Italian (the language of the people) indicates that he wished for his 'poetical dialogue' to be read widely, and the dialogue form allows Campanella to voice comments about contemporary issues through his characters.

The text takes the form of a dialogue between a grandmaster of the Knights Hospitallers and a Genoese sea captain who has journeyed across the entire world. Coming ashore at Taprobane, a large plain just underneath the equator, the captain is taken to the City of the Sun by a large crowd of people. A hill rises in the middle of the plain, around which are built seven fortified concentric walls (named after the planets) with four gates that look to the corners of the earth. In the centre of the walls is a circular temple with a globe over the altar. Founded by Sol, the city is governed by O (or Hoh) which means 'metaphysic', and he is helped by Pon (who governs miltary power), Sin (who governs knowledge) and Mor (who governs love and reproduction). O is a learned man who is generally chosen by astrologers and can rule from the age of 35 until a wiser man has been found. Sin has caused all the walls of the city to be painted with maps, alphabets, herbs, animals, inventions and so on. All children are taught by looking at the paintings, and watching people at work until they find the trade to which they are best suited. Members work for about four hours a day, and spend the rest of the time in exercising the mind and body (though this does not include any game that can be played whilst sitting down, such as dice or chess).

In the City of the Sun, all property is held in common, and crimes are punished by being deprived of the common table and of commerce with women. All the 'Solarians' wear white clothing (which is washed once a month) and a system of plumbing allows them to have good access to washing water. Because of their accommodation and medicinal diet, they live up to 100 years, and sometimes up to 200. Sexual relations are allowed and wives are held in common, though homosexuality is punishable by death. Reproduction is organized by the magistrates on eugenic grounds, and the women are tall and beautiful from exercise (the wearing of make-up or high heels also being punishable by death). The Captain claims that women are given the same jobs as men, including military ones, though their tasks are usually physically lighter. Nonetheless, jobs are generally allocated on the basis of gender and age. There is considerable detail about military organization, but the only wars fought are those to preserve the liberty of others from tyrants.

Hardly surprisingly, in view of Campanella's biography, they have no prisons or torture but a rapid judgement of the merits of a particular case. Though death sentences are rare, the executions are carried out by those who have been wronged. Every so often, sacrifices are made to God, which involves suspending a willing participant under the central dome whilst they are fed a little by priests. After twenty or thirty days, they are released and themselves become priests. Campanella's utopia (like CHRISTIANOPOLIS) is a strange mixture of social engineering, Calvinism and the craft traditions of the CITY STATE. The uniqueness of *City of the Sun* rests on its frequent mention of astrology and mediaeval metaphysics, together with some remarkable inventions, and a curiously detailed description of eugenic sexual practices.

CITY STATE Both an ideal to which many thinkers have subscribed over the centuries and a reality that has been in existence for over three thousand years (see POLIS). From Aristotle's *Politics* to Thomas More's UTOPIA the city state has framed ideas about a better society. It can be viewed as an alternative to the territorial state that has dominated the world scene for most of that period (see ALTERNATIVE GEOPOLITICS). Whilst history has been dominated by territorial states, for most of the time city states have existed alongside them. The territorial state has usually been concerned with the imposition and assertion of political and military control and the maintenance and increase of its power. However, the city state has normally had little to do with the assertion of territoriality and more to do with economic, political and cultural aspirations. The POLIS was the progenitor and model of later European city states. Historically, the impact of the city state outside Europe and the Mediterranean has been very slight. The periods when the city state has flourished in Europe have usually coincided with those during which the territorial state, in the form of empires or great powers, has been too weak to maintain its position of dominance.

Since the city state represented an alternative to the territorial state, the latter inevitably saw it as representing a danger. Basic to this animosity were the inherent characteristics of the city state. These included its assertion of freedom from control by the territorial powers and its aspiration to greater internal freedom. Within the Holy Roman Empire this was defined in the concept of the *freistadt* that secured rights from the emperor. The existence of the city state was thus a major challenge to the absolute authority of princes. In addition to this, the participation in city government which evolved over the centuries was a further challenge to the absolutism of princely rule in a way that was rare in any territorial state before the French REVOLUTION. Economic development, innovation and wealth creation also took place to a far greater extent in the city state than was usual in the territorial state.

To its principal protagonists, such as Plato (see REPUBLIC) and Aristotle, the *polis* constituted an ideal, and the ancient philosophers considered it to be in all ways a superior form of organization to the empire. Its small size was the characteristic that encouraged popular participation in all aspects of its life and this in turn protected that freedom which was its most important asset and without which its other positive characteristics would not be possible. For Aristotle, this freedom was based on *eunomia,* the balance within the state ensuring that no individual or group was able to gain and retain control in its own narrow interests. The vital importance of freedom is encapsulated in the German assertion that *die stadtluft macht frei* (city air makes for freedom). This distinguished the *freistädte* from the o p p ressive authority of the empire and implied freedom from its own former internal oppressors as well as from the external princes.

Since early times a major problem of the city state system has been that of the regulation of relationships among them and this has posed a considerable problem. Conflict among city states characterized both ancient times and the Renaissance period. However, the *Hanse* of northern Europe and – briefly – the *Comunidades* of Spain established COOPERATIVE organizations that put the interests of the whole above those of individual cities and enabled them to work together. Thomas More's *Utopia* was actually a FEDERATION of cities which, while retaining their own freedoms, delegated authority over specified matters to a central administration.

The city state has always been viewed as a model of good government by those for whom the SMALL STATE is a more satisfactory form of organization than the large one. It has been viewed by its protagonists as representing the form of government which is most in accord with human scale. Thus participation, tolerance and freedom constitute a totality that has commended the city state though the ages to those who sought 'the good life' in the Aristotelian sense. This is encapsulated in the Renaissance concept of the *città ideale* which envisages the city state as a harmonious architectural, artistic, intellectual and political whole. Those times when the concept of the *città ideale* has approached realization have remained through the ages in the collective memory and have encapsulated hopes for a better society. (GP)

CIVIL DISOBEDIENCE, see DIRECT ACTION; GANDHI; NON-VIOLENT RESISTANCE; WALDEN

COCKAIGNE (or Cockaygne) In various European cultures there is a fictional country of plenty, the sort of place where there is no work and lots of sex; where wine flows in the rivers and pigs walk around with carving knives in their backs for the convenience of their consumers. The name is derived from 'land of cakes', but there are equivalent versions of this land of milk and honey in other languages too. In Dutch 'Luilekkerland', in German 'Schlarraffenland', in Spanish 'Jauja' (an abundant region of Peru). In a 1567 painting 'The Land of Cockaigne', Bruegel the elder depicts drunken peasants and food in the trees and the rooftops. This working class UTOPIA directly confronts poverty with material excess and can be contrasted to the calm pastoralism of ARCADIAN utopias, or the urban order of the CITY STATE. In some sense, Cockaigne is not an organized utopia at all, just a CARNIVALesque dream where the troubles and hardships of the ordinary world have been turned upside-down. However, like many imaginary lands, such as ATLANTIS, EDEN and SHANGRI-LA, it can form an image of a GOLDEN AGE or a world to come that can have a powerful mobilizing effect.

CO-HOUSING, see COOPERATIVE

COLLECTIVISM Denotes an emphasis on the group as opposed to the individual. The word is usually used to imply that the group ought to form the basic unit of social, economic and political organization rather than the individual. Some libertarians use the term in a derogatory sense as posing a threat to individual liberty. Collectivism has a long tradition as a form of social organization, with the idea of the COMMONS and COMMONWEALTH being extremely ancient. The DIGGERS and LEVELLERS used the concept for reclaiming private land for common ownership. As the relatively self-sufficient COMMUNITY has formed the basic unit of society for most of humanity for most of history, some degree of collectivization and MUTUALITY has been essential for survival. Many on the Left have seen an idealized form of the collective VILLAGE as the model for improved forms of society in the future. KROPOTKIN based his ideal collective on the Russian obschina, or collective peasant village. The SOVIETS that were a feature of the first stage of the RUSSIAN REVOLUTION had similar antecedents.

In practice there is no simple opposition between collectivism and individualism because COMMUNITARIANS, SOCIALISTS and COMMUNISTS (as well as some ANARCHISTS) argue that individuals can only achieve their full autonomy within a group. In other words, individual freedom implies moral action within the collective rather than a simple absence of restraint. Much collectivist thinking would also see many different levels of human groups. This viewpoint, characteristic of ENVIRONMENTAL politics, ultimately sees humanity itself as a collective that must cooperate if a sustainable future for all individuals is to be achieved. COMMUNISM proposes a complete end to private property and the collective ownership both of the means of production and of the products of human labour. Communism also envisages an end to wage labour and markets as, to paraphrase MARX's well-known phrase, each would contribute according to their ability and receive according to their need. The collectivization of agriculture that took place in the era of Stalin perhaps explains why the term has negative connotations for so many today. LENIN saw collectivization of the backward peasant agriculture of the SOVIET UNION as a way of improving production and increasing equality. The wealthier peasants or kulaks resisted the initially voluntary collectivization of farming. Under Stalin collectivism was brutally imposed and, by 1936, 90 per cent of farms had been collectivized. In the meantime millions had died either due to forced resettlement or because of the famine exacerbated by Stalin's attempt to hide the failure of his policy.

ANARCHISTS have had a more ambivalent view of collectivization because of the strong individualist LIBERTARIAN strand in their tradition. They have often worried that obligatory collectivization, where individuals are forced to accept the will of the majority, is essentially repressive. PROUDHON, despite his famous maxim that 'property is theft' suggested that, though society should be organized into self-managed collectives, property could still be privately owned. BAKUNIN called for all property to be held in common, although workers would still be rewarded according to their contribution. KROPOTKIN argued for full communal collectivism in a similar way to Marx. The anarchist solution to the tension between collectivism and liberty has usually been to suggest that society might consist of a diversity of different collective models linked into more complex FEDERAL structures by DEMOCRATIC delegatory councils.

Marshall (1993) points to the organization of the Catalan economy during the short-lived Spanish Revolution of the 1930s as an example of such a desirable diversity. The land was pooled and a system of common storehouses set up. Farming collectives were voluntarily organized based on solidarity and mutual aid for all who wished to join, whether they were producers or not. In many areas money was abolished and surplus produce directly traded with neighbouring collectives and towns. Farmers who did not wish to join continued in individual production and were able to trade with the collectives. Factories were also collectivized and WORKER SELF-MANAGED. However, they often retained wages and even kept on the old pre-revolutionary managers to help run the plants. The Spanish revolutionary experience demonstrates that collectivization can accommodate a significant degree of individual autonomy, retain a diversity of forms and yet be an effective way to provide for the material needs of society.

COMMONS Land over which members of the community could exercise customary rights, such as the right of grazing or collecting fodder. In England, the rights of commons were eroded by the enclosures that began in the twelfth century. Despite various acts of resistance and attempts to reclaim the commons (see the DIGGERS), in Europe at least, enclosure was largely completed by the end of the nineteenth century. In modern usage, the commons has acquired a broader meaning to include not only land but also other natural resources (water, biodiversity) and cultural resources (traditional knowledge, information and creative works) traditionally openly available to all. Drawing on a long history of protest, there have been many attempts to protect the commons from modern forms of enclosure, in particular corporate encroachment through privatization and marketization. Reclaiming the commons has become one of the rallying calls of the ANTI-CAPITALIST movement.

Examples include protest movements against biopiracy, the patenting of life forms such as plants, and the exploitation of traditional knowledge about their qualities (see Shiva, 1997). The OPEN SOURCE SOFTWARE movement is also an attempt to keep software within the public domain through copyleft licensing that ensures that anyone can use or modify a programme, but no one can appropriate it through copyright or patent laws. This movement has inspired similar initiatives to place creative work (literature, photography, music) or information in the public domain (see WIKIPEDIA). In addition, there have been campaigns to reclaim privatized water as a common resource; to defend the right of small farmers to use common land against the threat of eviction and privatization; or to reclaim public spaces for public use by taking DIRECT ACTION against the invasion of cars, shopping malls and business parks (see, for example, the website of Reclaim the Streets).

COMMONWEALTH A term that now suggests a FEDERATED alliance (for example, The British Commonwealth of Nations, and many other states and organizations, for example the SCOTT BADER COMMONWEALTH), but originally (fifteenth century) was, like commonweal, a term for the common good. In the mid-sixteenth century it acquired republican and egalitarian connotations by being applied during the English REVOLUTION by the Rump parliament after they had abolished the House of Lords and the monarchy. The Commonwealth and Free State lasted from 1649 to 1660, and Oliver Cromwell was termed the 'Lord Protector of the Common-wealth' in 1653 (see also OCEANA). On independence, four US states adopted the term in order to distance themselves from the monarchy. The term 'ideal commonwealth' now usually means UTOPIA. William Morris's (see NEWS FROM NOWHERE) COMMUNIST magazine was titled 'The Commonweal'.

COMMUNE A term used to refer to historically specific, relatively large-scale political experiments (as in for example the PARIS COMMUNE, the People's Communes of the Republic of China), or more broadly to smaller-scale INTENTIONAL COMMUNITIES based on some degree of common ownership and shared responsibility. Beyond this definition, communes can take many different forms: they can vary in size, structure, goals, and what aspects of life are shared. A commune could be a household of a handful of people, a VILLAGE of hundreds or a town of thousands (AUROVILLE, CRYSTAL WATERS, FINDHORN). It could be based on sharing living accommodation (as in housing COOPERATIVES), or more radically on sharing economic activity, incomes, or childcare. Andrew Rigby identifies six different types of communes on the basis of their underlying purposes. Self-actualizing communes aim to provide an environment in which individual members can feel free to explore and develop themselves and their creative potential. Communes for mutual support provide members with a sense of togetherness and a supportive environment they have not been able to find in the world 'outside'. Activist communes are oriented towards political critique and transformation, aiming to provide a base from which members can engage in activism and experiment with different forms of social organization. Practical communes are defined primarily in terms of the economic and practical advantages of sharing resources. THERAPEUTIC communes are oriented towards creating a social, physical, or spiritual environment in which people considered to be in need of care and attention can be looked after. Finally, religious communes are based primarily on shared religious and spiritual beliefs and have MONASTICISM as their archetype.

In reality it is difficult to maintain a clear distinction between these different purposes as they tend to overlap within the same commune. Most members join communes at least partly because of the felt need for mutual support; most communes are, at least in part, born out of a rejection of some aspects of conventional society (the nuclear family, capitalism, consumerism, individualism) and the desire to create alternatives, and as such are to some degree oppositional and transformative. Religious communes may have therapeutic goals, such as the care of children or adults with special needs; and in some communes spiritual and political vision may be closely intertwined.

Whilst the commune movement is often associated with hippy experiments in the 1960s and 1970s, its history reaches far back and can be traced, in fictional or concrete form, from the DIGGERS in the seventeenth century, to various religious groups inspired by the QUAKERS or SHAKERS, to nineteenth-century utopian SOCIALIST experiments inspired by Cabet, OWEN or FOURIER (like BROOK FARM, ONEIDA, New Harmony), to the anarchist Spanish collectives in the first half of the twentieth century or the KIBBUTZ movement in Israel. Today, communes are central to the political articulation of (at least parts of) movements such as ANARCHISM, ENVIRONMENTALISM, ANTI-CAPITALISM and AUTONOMIA, where they are seen to address concerns for social justice and environmental SUSTAINABILITY. For these reasons, communes have been the privileged forms of organising adopted by, for example, ECOVILLAGES, or CENTRI SOCIALI. Throughout history, communes have been a strong motif of UTOPIAN imagination and experiments by providing an alternative to the predominant social order.

53

COMMUNISM A society in which property and the means of production are owned communally. It is one instance of a COLLECTIVIST rather than an individualist vision of the good life. Within a communist society, states and social classes would disappear. The COMMUNE, as a DEMOCRATIC, self-governing entity, would form the basic unit of society. Such an ideal does not necessarily imply the absorption of individuality within the mass. Many communists, often claiming inspiration from MARX, have seen it as the only way of achieving autonomy and individual fulfilment. It is probably true to say that some form of communism is the ideal to which much UTOPIANISM aspires, although what form such a society should take and how it should be arrived at are matters for disagreement.

Writing about communism immediately requires one to make a distinction between two common usages of the term. Much of the history of the twentieth century was determined by political parties and state systems described as 'communist'. In many cases states such as the SOVIET UNION preferred to describe themselves as 'state SOCIALIST' to indicate that they had not completed the transition to full communism, despite being governed by a 'communist' party. Left-wing critics of such states used the term 'state capitalism' to indicate that they saw them as very distinct from anything that could meaningfully be described as communism. Rather they were simply BUREAUCRATIC centrally-planned versions of the MARKET capitalism that dominated Western states.

The link between these two usages is to be found in the work of Marx. He was dedicated to forging what he saw as 'scientific SOCIALISM', founded on his combination of philosophy, historical studies and political economy. His work as a political activist ensured that this theoretical contribution dominated left-wing politics for the next hundred years and has led to the association of the term communism with Marxism. However, many societies have practised some form of communism. Marx and Engels regarded the first stage of human history as having been characterized by 'primitive' communism. For most of history the communal VILLAGE has been the fundamental social and productive unit. The origin of communism as an ideal form of society in Western thought may be traced to the Apostolic Church, where all property was pooled and 'held in common'. The combination of the desire to return to this form of Christianity, where all property was shared, together with a strong sense of what were believed to be the ancient rights of 'COMMONWEALTH' led to a long tradition of communism as a key part of religious dissent. Such groups included the various MILLENARIAN SECTS, the CATHARS and later, the ANABAPTISTS. It is also evident in the sermons attributed to John BALL and some radical Protestant groups such as the DIGGERS. It was from this tradition that the ideal came down to the SOCIALIST and ANARCHIST movements in the nineteenth century, via such thinkers as ROUSSEAU. Marx, in turn, took communist thinking largely from French socialists and anarchists such as PROUDHON.

Marx saw communism as the final stage of human society. He argued that history was proceeding through identifiable stages, characterised by different ways of organizing production, with conflict between the privileged and the dispossessed providing the 'engine' of historical development. Past stages included primitive communism, the slave empires of antiquity, and feudalism, arriving at the capitalism of Marx's own day. Capitalism in turn would be overthrown by the industrial working class or proletariat. Following this REVOLUTION a transitory stage of SOCIALISM would occur. It would be necessary to take over the existing institutions in order that society could remain stable whilst the 'withering away of the state' was in process.

Marx was very reluctant to define what a future communist society would be like, and was critical of UTOPIAN writers such as FOURIER and SAINT-SIMON. He argued that, as social conditions changed on the road to communism, then so should the vision of the good life. It is clear, however, that his thinking is utopian in many ways. In *The German Ideology* Marx gives us a rare clue to his desired future world: 'In communist society, where nobody has one exclusive sphere of activity but each can become accomplished in any branch he wishes, society regulates the general production and thus makes it possible for me to do one thing today and another tomorrow, to hunt in the morning, fish in the afternoon, rear cattle in the evening, criticise after dinner. Just as I have a mind, without ever becoming hunter, fisherman, herdsman or critic.'

The first political organization describing itself as 'communist', at the instigation of Marx and Engels, was the Communist League in 1847. They wrote the 'Communist Manifesto' for the League which was wound up in 1852. The League was a factor in the uprising of the PARIS COMMUNE. The International Workingmen's Association, otherwise known as the First INTERNATIONAL, was founded in 1864 and led by Marx. It was broadly committed to the establishment of communism and was made up of a variety of elements from the labour movement, including British TRADE

UNIONISTS, anarchists, French utopian socialists and Italian republicans. After a bitter dispute between BAKUNIN and Marx over revolutionary tactics, the anarchists were expelled. Bakunin was highly critical of the notion of retaining state institutions even as a transitional arrangement, believing that the state was likely to perpetuate itself and prevent any move towards full communism. The First International was disbanded in 1876.

The Second International was founded in 1889 in order to continue the work of the First in promoting international socialism. It continued to do this until the lack of consensus over the First World War led to its demise. In 1917, the Bolshevik wing of the Russian Social Democratic Party took power after the October Revolution. In 1918 the party changed its name to the Communist Party. Many other socialist parties renamed themselves communist and affiliated to the Third International under the leadership of the Communist Party of the SOVIET UNION. In 1949 MAO's Chinese Communist Party came to power. Further revolutions took place in the Third World, sponsored by the Soviet Communist Party. By the 1980s, one third of the world's population lived in states described as communist.

Stalinism caused a widespread disillusionment with the Soviet model of communism within a state. Trotsky founded the Fourth International in 1938 to propound what he saw as a return to the idea of revolution without national boundaries that would continue until full communism was achieved – 'permanent revolution'. Despite being a major influence on the development of Marxist thinking and revolutionary groups in the 1960s and 1970s, no successful revolution or governing communist party was ever avowedly Trotskyist. The term Euro-communism was coined to describe parties which were not affiliated to the Soviet party and which often took a reformist approach to social change rather than being committed to revolution. With the break-up of the Soviet Union in 1991 and the acceleration of China away from anything that resembled Marxist communism, it could be argued that Communism as a political movement is dead, despite the survival of a few states such as CUBA.

The popularity of this term within the Left has declined markedly. The descent of the Russian Revolution into totalitarianism is seen by the right and individualist libertarians as indicating a flaw in collectivist UTOPIANISM. Others, including many anarchists, would argue that the danger of new forms of state authoritarianism were inherent in the idea of a vanguard political party, despite its effectiveness as a revolutionary force. Still others might argue that, though a tragic failure and missed opportunity, the

Revolution, particularly in its early stages, demonstrated the possibility of radical social change in the interests of the common people, and the emancipatory potential of a communist society. Perhaps communism remains an idea that has never been implemented; perhaps its time will and should still come. A free, equal and unexploitative society, in which individuals share the products of voluntarily given labour, remains a central aim of alternative visions. Communism, the spectre that once haunted Europe, remains both a dream that lingers in the utopian imagination and a nightmare reminder of the fragility of human endeavours to realize that dream.

COMMUNITARIANISM One version expresses a romanticized cultural conservativism, in which COMMUNITY becomes the oppressive solution to society's moral problems. Another is an inspiration for many contemporary organizations and movements which oppose the individualism and LIBERALISM of market MANAGERIAL societies. The term originated in the US in the late twentieth century, primarily as a philosophical and ideological response to the Thatcher/Reagan consensus of the 1980s (Mulhall and Swift 1992). The organizational sociologist Amitai Etzioni, partly inspired by his early experiences on a KIBBUTZ, has been one of the key writers in this area (see, for example, Etzioni 1993).

The usual starting point for communitarian arguments is the idea that humans are necessarily produced by society and the POLIS, and hence the free individual of liberalism is a theoretical impossibility (see NOZICK). This also then leads into policy and organization debates, with an emphasis on COLLECTIVE responsibilities being deployed to counter-balance liberalism's emphasis on individual rights. The power of majorities to make decisions that affect minorities and constrain their freedoms is a contentious area, and one that distinguishes DEMOCRATIC communitarians from most ANARCHISTS or extreme libertarians. Like the word community itself, communitarianism is a vague term that appears to signify a certain left-of-centre position on social issues, but on closer examination can embrace many different claims. However, since there are no globally agreed definitions of the central purposes and values of communities, this is not a surprising state of affairs.

COMMUNITY The power of this word partly resides in its multiplicity and vagueness but what unifies most of its meanings is the idea that it is a good thing, and a form of social organization that is preferable to many

57

others. In general, it seems to stand for a NETWORK of close relationships between a limited number of people, usually based on face-to-face inter-action within a particular geographical area. It is also often suggested that it is something that is under attack from social changes but was stronger in the past, and that one community can be distinguished from another on the basis of their shared understandings. There is also often an implication that communities are somehow more 'natural' than other forms of social organization. Beyond this, it is very difficult to define what this hopeful word actually means at all.

Perhaps what is more instructive is to consider the various binaries that the concept is organized around. Probably the most enduring is the distinction between rural pre-industrial societies, and urban industrial ones. Here, community suggests a greater density of social ties and agreement on norms (see ARCADIA), compared to the confusions and contradictions of complex societies. A second distinction is between community and MARKET, with the implication being that, in the former, exchange is based on some sort of long-term collective reciprocity, whilst the latter reduces all transactions to impersonal numbers which take no account of local or personal circumstance. A further dualism exists between community and society, state or government. Whilst the former suggests decision making at a local level, informed by immediate perceptions of need (see COMMUNE), the latter implies distanced planning, probably with all the attendant defects and insensitivity that critics identify in BUREAUCRACY. Finally, community is often taken to be based on informal rules and norms, unlike formal organizations that make their rules explicit in their policies and structure.

Many UTOPIAS and forms of alternative organization have been partly inspired by the idea of community in order to distance themselves from a marketized urban bureaucratic state (see COOPERATIVES, GRAMEEN BANK, ISLAMIC FINANCE, MUTUALITY). However, the varied use of the word rapidly begins to overwhelm any attempt at an inclusive definition. Communities can exist in cities (see CHRISTIANIA, GARDEN CITIES), or be partially marketized (see LETS), or be sponsored by a state or planner attempting delegation of power and responsibility, or engineered (together with traditions) for many other purposes (nationalism, for example). Further, the concept can be used (as in the 'gay community') without implying some form of co-residence or even any physical interaction at all (communities can be virtual: see WIKIPEDIA). Neither should it be assumed that communities do not need rules. As the many examples in this dictionary illustrate, the point is that the rules are different, not that there are no rules at all (see, for example, AMISH). For many classical MARXISTS, the withering away of the state that would happen as part of the advent of a COMMUNIST society seems to suggest a future of self-governing communities without hierarchy. Yet all forms of organization have rules, otherwise they would have no division of labour, no boundaries, and no conception of belonging. What the word community often implies is that rules have not been made into formal artefacts, such as organization charts or strategic plans.

While it is undoubtedly a powerful concept, it is also one that can encourage some rather imprecise thinking (such as the idea of a European Community), as well as being used as a warm word in contexts that might otherwise be less comfortable. The idea that communities are caring places can just as easily be set against the freedoms and independence generally experienced in large cities, and the claustrophobia of living somewhere where everybody feels they have a right to interfere. The extent to which community needs to be balanced against personal freedoms is the key element in a lengthy debate between COMMUNITARIANS and liberals, as well as being an element in debates about the coercive effects of organizational or corporate culture. In a sense then, it is more helpful as a term that highlights opposing elements of contemporary society than as an actual description of a particular form of social organization.

COMMUNITY CREDIT, see CREDIT UNIONS

COMMUNITY CURRENCY, see BARTERING; LETS; TIME BANKS

COMMUNITY GARDENS Developed as a reaction against the concentration of land, community gardens draw on the traditions of the COMMONS to reclaim the use of land for COMMUNITY ends, either through lease agreements or SQUATTING. They are usually set on waste lands in cities, and are converted into productive spaces by and for local people. Beside growing food, community gardens serve a range of social objectives that may involve giving children the opportunity to experience gardening and nature, providing training or employment opportunities to the unemployed or disadvantaged, and developing community cohesion by bringing together people of different cultures, ages and abilities. In short, community gardens act as a catalyst for community development by placing local people in charge of a common project, by encouraging self-reliance, and by creating opportunities for recreation, education and work.

COMMUNITY-SUPPORTED AGRICULTURE   A group of consumers commit to pay a farmer in advance for a fixed period in exchange for a share of products, usually distributed weekly. This mutual commitment between farmers and consumers allows for a sharing of the risks and rewards of agriculture. CSA differs from box schemes, farm shops or markets in that, although these methods of distribution may be employed, the consumer members make an advance financial contribution. In addition, the partnership between consumers and farmers usually involves more than the exchange of cash for produce; it may include activities designed to bring farmers and consumers closer together through the publication of newsletters, visits, or help with farm work. CSA may involve one or more farmers, and a group of consumers that may range from just a few families to hundreds.

The idea behind CSA originated in Japan with *teiki* groups – 'tie-up' or partnerships requiring the consumer to pay a weekly fee in return for a box of fresh produce. Since the 1990s, similar schemes have developed in many other countries where, together with other direct exchange schemes between producers and consumers, they have enjoyed rapid growth. For example, in 2003 there were around 40 CSAs operating in the UK, and a further 60 farms establishing a scheme, whilst in the USA thousands of schemes were operating in 2002. By setting up alternative systems of exchange which short-circuit the MARKET and bring producers and consumers into direct contact, CSA enables small farmers to practise organic agriculture. Whilst CSA does not require organic certification, it usually proscribes the use of chemical pesticides and fertilizers. It also allows farmers to escape the downward pressure on price exercised by the retail sector, and to retain their independence. Through the advance payment, farmers can raise capital and receive a secure income; and by cutting out intermediaries, they can obtain a higher and fairer return (see FAIR TRADE). By making farms directly accountable to their consumers, CSA also encourages farmers to provide high-quality food at affordable prices. More broadly, CSA has been seen to encourage more environmentally sustainable and socially responsible farming by reducing food miles, encouraging local biodiversity, and securing local circulation of money in the community (see ENVIRONMENTALISM, LOCALIZATION, SUSTAINABILITY).

COOPERATIVES O rganizations where ownership and control rest with members rather than outside owners. According to the International Cooperative Alliance (ICA) 'a cooperative is an autonomous association of persons united voluntarily to meet their common economic, social, and cultural needs and aspirations through a jointly owned and democratically controlled enterprise'. Drawing on the traditions started by the ROCHDALE PIONEERS, cooperatives are based on the values of self-help, DEMOCRACY, equality and solidarity, and are guided by principles (discussed below) laid down by the ICA.

Cooperatives are voluntary organizations, open to all persons who wish to use their services and are willing to accept the responsibilities of membership, without gender, social, racial, political or religious discrimination. Members actively participate in setting policies and making decisions. Cooperative members contribute to and control the capital of their cooperative. They usually receive limited compensation, if any, on the capital they subscribe; and decisions regarding the distribution of surplus (whether towards the development of the cooperative, for compensation of members, or supporting COMMUNITY activities) are taken democratically. Cooperatives are AUTONOMOUS, self-help organizations controlled by members. If they raise funds from external sources, they do so on terms that ensure democratic control by members and maintain the cooperative's autonomy. Cooperatives are committed to the education and training of their members, but also to raise awareness about the nature and benefits of cooperation among the general public. Cooperatives work together through local and international networks to strengthen the cooperative movement. Cooperatives work for the sustainable development of their communities through policies and programmes funded and approved by their members.

The idea of cooperation has a long history. For example, Thomas More's UTOPIA is built around a cooperative system; during the English Civil War, the LEVELLERS and DIGGERS used the establishment of the COMMONWEALTH to propose the COMMON ownership of land; in the 1760s many cooperative mills were set up in response to the rise in the price of corn and the establishment of monopoly. But it was not until the nineteenth century that cooperation as a social movement spread. OWEN in England and FOURIER in France, both considered as the founding fathers of the cooperative movement, promoted cooperative principles as a more humane alternative to the greed and competition fostered by capitalism (see also BRAY). To combat poverty and exploitation, Owen proposed the development of 'villages of cooperation', in which members (about a thousand people) would pool resources to acquire land and capital that would enable them to live SELF-SUFFICIENTLY, exchanging only among themselves on the basis of 'fair deals'.

Consumers' co-ops developed mainly from the nineteenth century, largely in response to the 'truck' system that forced workers to accept goods – often adulterated and extortionately priced – from company stores in lieu of wages. In 1844 the Rochdale Pioneers set up a shop selling wholesome, unadulterated food at fair prices. This idea of consumers getting together to buy quality food in large quantities and sell to each other at low prices was to become the founding principle of consumers' cooperatives. The Rochdale Pioneers also developed cooperative production, insurance, wholesaling and education. These various cooperatives came together to form the Cooperative Wholesale Society in 1863, and this has grown into a large supermarket and banking chain.

Workers' co-ops developed in response to industrial capitalism and its disempowering effects on workers. Skilled workers created co-op workshops by drawing on their savings and MUTUAL credits in order to maintain their independence of factory owners (see AUTONOMIA). These are businesses owned and controlled democratically by those who work in them, with membership restricted to employees. WORKER SELF-MANAGEMENT has been heralded as providing a way in which people can control their own labour, and enjoy a flexible friendly working environment. Workers' co-ops have also been seen as an instrument of social change: through the egalitarian and democratic principles they promote, they potentially offer an alternative to neoliberal capitalism (see MONDRAGÒN, SUMA, TOWER COLLIERY).

Housing co-ops are usually set up to provide affordable housing by applying cooperative principles to the domestic economy. The idea of housing co-ops is that the property is bought or leased and rented out to tenant members. Through their rents, tenants eventually build up a share account that corresponds to the value of their house. Several schemes emerged in the late nineteenth century to provide communal housing for women or particular communities, for example. Some of these schemes tended to resonate with the architectural idea of the GARDEN CITY: sets of houses surrounded by countryside and encircled by a railway, with sites for a library, schools, recreation, and a communal kitchen (see COOPERA-TIVE CITY; HAYDEN). There are many housing cooperatives, and some of these also provide a focal point or home for community projects, campaigns, resource centres or social centres (see CENTRI SOCIALI).

Cooperatives have also been embraced by radical FEMINISTS as challenging 'patriarchal' practices based on competition, hierarchy or the division of labour, and reflecting 'women's values' such as participative decision making, empowerment and equality. Thus for many radical feminist organizations, such as women's health centres, bookshops and shelters for battered women, co-op structures and principles are not only means to an end, but have become ends in themselves, a central expression of a feminist politics (see also ECOFEMINISM; FEMINIST UTOPIAS).

In its diverse forms, the cooperative sector represents an alternative to the MARKET economy: in 2004, the ICA estimated that there were 800 million cooperators worldwide, with a further 100 million persons employed by cooperatives. But the economic significance of the cooperative sector is not limited to members and employees. The number of people whose livelihoods rely to a significant extent on cooperative ventures approaches three billion, half of the world's population.

COOPERATIVE CITY Bradford Peck, in his *The World, a Department Store. A Story of Life under the Cooperative System* (1900), presents a COOPERATIVE version of UTOPIA. An imaginary Christian and temperate city, 'Cooperative City' is built in the first quarter of the twentieth century, in the state of Maine, AMERICA and has a population of 100,000. The city makes regular payments into the accounts of its citizens that reflect their contributions, and must be spent within the city (see CITY STATE). This minimum payment is raised according to age, academic attainment and labour. There is no unemployment, or charity, and labour is allocated where it is needed by an Executive Board. Money has disappeared altogether and been replaced by 'coupon cheques' so that there is no lending, no speculation and no payment of interest. No member is permitted to transact any business outside the city. Because competition, middle-men and bankers no longer exist, production is now much more efficient and people work for only six hours a day.

The city is built on a grid plan, with harmonious and symmetrical a p a rtment blocks, public dining rooms (with no alcohol) and meeting places, electric trains for transport and large areas of green space (see GARDEN CITIES). Education and health are organized according to efficient and humane principles, and religion is closely connected with the work of the

Department of Education. There is a central publishing house which produces all the reading matter, including a newspaper (*The Daily American*) which contains no advertising or sensationalism. Peck's utopia is similar to Cabet's VOYAGE TO ICARIA and Bellamy's LOOKING BACKWARD in its rather authoritarian faith in planning, but has a more sophisticated financial structure which in some ways anticipates LETS. As with many of the organized utopias from Plato's REPUBLIC onwards, whether Peck's vision is utopia or repressive DYSTOPIA is an arguable point.

COPYLEFT, CREATIVE COMMONS, see COMMONS; OPEN SOURCE SOFTWARE; WIKIPEDIA

CREDIT UNIONS Financial institutions owned and controlled by their members, and sharing the values and principles of COOPERATIVES such as open membership, DEMOCRATIC control, and an emphasis on members' financial education. Their aim is to provide access to saving and affordable loans to disadvantaged communities and individuals excluded from the conventional financial system or charged exorbitant rates for borrowing. The bill-payment facility offered by many credit unions enables individuals without bank accounts to benefit from purchasing in a more cost-effective manner. To counter the trend of predatory lending, credit unions encourage savings among low-income households and use these resources to provide affordable credits to the least well-off. Members' savings form a common pool of money from which loans are made to other members. The income generated by interest paid on loans serves to pay dividends to savers, and any remaining profit is shared among the members – there are no shareholders to pay. The loans granted can be personal, or to help set up micro-enterprises and community projects. Each credit union has a 'common bond' that determines who can join. The common bond may be based on a neighbourhood, a workplace or an association (such as a TRADE UNION or a church-based group).

Various other microcredit arrangements also attempt to address similar problems, such as the informal *hawala* or *hundi* systems of trusted financial intermediaries used in parts of Africa and Asia, or the internet-based 'Ripple Project' (see GRAMEEN BANK). The idea emerged out of the cooperative movement in the nineteenth century (see FRIENDLY SOCIETIES); the first credit union opened in Germany and was quickly followed by similar experiments in Canada and AMERICA, where it became particularly popular during the Great Depression. In the UK, the first Credit Union was set up in 1964 by members of the West Indian community in Wimbledon and grew out of informal relationships between extended family groups clubbing together to save and give each other loans. The World Council of Credit Unions estimated that there were 123 million credit union members worldwide in 2004 and that membership was growing fast in Eastern Europe, South America, Africa and the Far East.

CRYSTAL WATERS An ECOVILLAGE created in 1987 to demonstrate and practise SUSTAINABLE living. It is set on impoverished land in an economically depressed rural area north of Brisbane in Australia. By applying PERMACULTURE principles it aims to revitalize the bio-region, improve land quality, and create opportunities for sustainable living to attract new residents to the area. At the end of 2005, Crystal Waters counted about 200 residents and included various small businesses that provided incomes and jobs for people in the COMMUNITY.

Residential and commercial lots occupy 20 per cent of the land, whilst the rest (the best land) is held in COMMON and licensed for agricultural, forestry or recreational projects. Crystal Waters was financed by people who wanted to live there in order to avoid property speculation; and the profit made on the sales of the residential and commercial areas was reinvested in community facilities. Residents are encouraged to build and live in sustainable ways through a set of by-laws and the 'Crystal Waters Owner's Manual' explains the concepts behind living lightly on earth. Crystal Waters has provided fertile experimental grounds for green technologies in house construction from the use of natural materials, to composting toilet systems, passive solar energy, or the recycling of wastewater.

Crystal Waters does not aim to become totally SELF-SUFFICIENT as it wants to encourage interaction with the surrounding area; however, it produces a large amount of its food and timber. It relies on its several businesses to bring in incomes, the most important of which centres around educational tourism and training courses, notably in permaculture.

CUBA Cuba has been a focus for the utopian imagination since the 1959 REVOLUTION. This proved to be one of the seminal political events heralding the great cultural shift of the 1960s. Both Fidel Castro and, to an even greater extent, Guevara, became ROMANTIC icons of the counter-culture and the New Left. The Cuban revolution has survived both the SOVIET

65

UNION and intense and sustained opposition and interference from its near neighbour, AMERICA. It is one of the few SOCIALIST revolutions to have remained reasonably true to its initial principles. There have unarguably been curbs on individual liberty, a lack of DEMOCRACY, and an uncomfortably frequent resort to state violence, sometimes in the form of executions. It may be that these authoritarian tendencies were inevitable for a SMALL STATE trying to maintain its independence in a condition of almost permanent crisis caused by the hostility of its powerful neighbour. Despite this, the government has remained reasonably popular with its people and delivered nearly 50 years of peace and relative prosperity. This popularity is perhaps not surprising given the experience of the Cuban people of decades of corrupt and repressive government up until the Revolution.

From the second half of the nineteenth century internal insurrection was mostly aimed at independence from Spain, an objective increasingly supported by the US. These struggles met with little success until 1895, when the radical intellectual José Martí landed with his men. He was killed in battle a month later but became an iconic figure in Cuba's struggle for independence. Castro claimed to be his heir in the 1959 Revolution. Despite Martí's death, his struggle was successful as the rebellion spread and received US support. The Spanish granted Cuba independence in 1902, but the US then took responsibility for ensuring Cuban stability. The US often interpreted 'stability' as the protection of its own political and economic interests, which were extensive. The US maintained a constant military presence and continues to lease the military base of Guantánamo to this day.

From the Second World War, Fulgencio Batista dominated Cuban politics. Despite early reforms and LIBERALISM, his rule became increasingly repressive and corrupt. He instituted a dictatorship from 1952. Opposition from GUERRILLA groups and other, mostly left-wing, activists, grew. In 1953, Fidel Castro's militia attacked the Moncada Barracks. The attack failed and Fidel Castro was exiled to Mexico, where he met Che Guevara. With his brother Raúl and Guevara, Castro trained a small army and planned an invasion. In 1956, he landed in the south of Cuba and formed a number of alliances with other revolutionary groups. Batista fled Cuba in 1959, leaving Castro to organize the government. Despite initially leaning towards the US, Castro's government moved into the orbit of the SOVIET UNION following US hostility to Cuba's relatively modest programmes of land reform and nationalization. After the abortive US-backed Bay of Pigs invasion in 1961, Castro declared himself a COMMUNIST and moved towards a one-party state on the Soviet model, though this was never as repressive as its Eastern European counterparts. Castro made free healthcare and education for all Cubans his central domestic policies. Although pre-revolutionary Cuba had some of the best health provision in Latin America its benefits were very unevenly available. Cuba has built a free, universal healthcare system of the highest quality and can now earn foreign exchange by selling surplus capacity to 'health tourists'. It also sent 10,000 doctors to Venezuela in support of ally Hugo Chávez, to improve medical provision in the shanty towns. In 1961, the government sent 100,000 student teachers into the countryside, who taught one million people to read and write in a year, eradicating widespread illiteracy. This was the first stage in the creation of an education system still without parallel in Latin America.

The Soviet Union kept Cuba economically afloat with subsidized sugar purchases and supplied it with cheap oil. The Soviet system's collapse in 1991, combined with the punitive US trade embargo, have led to tough times for Cuba. The support of Venezuela has been essential for Cuba's ailing economy. Tourism is now the most important source of revenue for Cuba, overtaking sugar in 1995. Castro has largely retired from actively steering the country but a new generation is apparently determined to preserve his legacy. For the first time in its history Cuba has enjoyed an extended period of peace, stability and prosperity, whose effects have been widely distributed amongst the population. Cuba continues to stand up to the economic and military might of a hostile US and has now produced several generations of well-fed, healthy, well-educated citizens with a widespread affection for their country and their government. Almost uniquely amongst the revolutions of the twentieth century, Cuba's did not descend into struggle and has continued to provide an actually existing example of the potential for revolutionary change: a deeply flawed UTOPIA, but one that gives cause for hope rather than despair.

CULT For our purposes, we will treat cults and sects as the same, though sociologists have made distinctions between the two. Any definition of a cult (or sect) generally involves three elements – charismatic leadership, a distinctive set of beliefs and practices, and some sort of control system. What distinguishes a cult from a business corporation, religion, COOPERATIVE or COMMUNITY is ultimately a matter of wider social acceptability. In some senses, this is an alarming conclusion, because it blurs distinctions that are normally rather secure, but it does also point to the similarity of induction and socialization processes, as well as group affiliations, within many formal organizations. The standard criticism of cults, a word that has its origins in ideas of care and nurturing (as in culture and cultivation), has been (since the 1960s) that they make excessive demands on their followers, including the routines of worship or meditation, rejection of property, non-standard sexual or child-rearing practices and so on. However, alterations to these practices are also constitutive of most UTOPIAN organization. Some cult beliefs are indeed bizarre, their organization is often totalising, and some practices (such as mass suicide) are difficult to comprehend or condone. Nonetheless, it is highly unlikely that any watertight definition could be constructed that would clearly distinguish the AMISH (for example) from a group who thought Jesus would be arriving in a spaceship next Tuesday.

Within the sociology of religion, it is common (following the work of Max Weber) to make a distinction between cults, sects, denominations, churches and ecclesia (with supranational membership) usually ordered along a continuum of increasing formalization, and decreasing divergence from the social order. The idea that early members must be converted, and may hence have intense beliefs, whilst later ones are born into the beliefs, has also been used to explain the decline of strength of evangelical commitment over time. The implication would also be that a long-lasting cult might become a sect, which eventually might become a denomination and so on. This model captures an element of the BUREAUCRATIZATION that Weber assumed would follow the routinization of charismatic leadership, but it also underscores the way in which there seems to be a convergence between beliefs inside and outside the organization. It is unclear whether this is because the organization becomes less extreme, or because its ideas begin to permeate more widely, but, either way, it does open the possibility that alternative organization could become mainstream over time. The sociologist Bryan Wilson famously distinguished between sects on the basis of their view of salvation. Within that typology he notes the existence of 'conversionist', 'revolutionist', 'introversionist', 'reformist' and 'utopian' sects. Ideas about a possible future GOLDEN AGE are common to both sects and alternative organizations, though clearly the methods for achieving it differ widely. Nonetheless, many forms of alternative organization have been dismissed as insane or extreme by those with power and/or status within the status quo.

D

DECROISSANCE / DEGROWTH A term coined by French radical economists to refer to and call for economic downscaling, or 'degrowth', as it has been translated in English. Whilst the term was first used by Romanian-born economist Nicholas Georgescu-Roegen, it has been popularized by Serge Latouche and has since been at the centre stage of radical political debates about alternative economic systems in France, for example in a monthly magazine entitled *La Decroissance* and in the *Institut d'Etudes Economiques et Sociales pour la Decroissance Soutenable*. The idea of degrowth was put forward to free economic thinking from the 'tyranny of growth' and provoke thought about alternatives. Proponents of degrowth denounce economic thinking and systems that see growth as holding the promise of a better world and solving its environmental and social problems. In much the same way as radical ENVIRONMENTALISTS, they point out that growth and consumption are unsustainable. Measures of growth such as the Gross National Product only take into account the production and sale of commodified goods and services, ignoring the damaging effects this has on other 'goods': justice, equality, DEMOCRACY, the health of humans and ecosystems, and social relations. They insist that economic growth and the increase in material wealth can only be pursued at the expense of these other more qualitative sources of wealth.

Proponents of degrowth are not only opposed to neoliberal policies privileging growth, but also to the increasingly popular notion of 'sustainable development'. This rests on the idea that it is possible to reconcile growth with the earth's natural capacities by switching to more ecologically efficient technologies (recycling, renewables). Advocates of degrowth argue that the reduction in ecological damage achieved by these 'green technologies' is more than offset by the increase in production they generate. Thus the solution is not to make growth greener or more socially equitable but rather to challenge the very principle of growth: to produce and consume less, especially in the North. Supporters of degrowth do not have a blueprint but rather insist that degrowth should be a process that emerges out of GRASSROOTS initiatives. They embrace notions of LOCALIZATION, 69

SMALLNESS and simplicity. They point to ECOVILLAGES, LETS, and COMMUNITY-SUPPORTED AGRICULTURE as examples of initiatives from below that produce economic and social relations outside the MARKET economy. Finally, they argue that promoting degrowth is not merely an economic question but must entail challenging and reconstructing society. Introducing degrowth in a society constructed around growth could have dire consequences (such as unemployment and the withdrawal of social or cultural services). Proponents want to encourage political debates on the COLLECTIVE choices facing societies, and on alternative models of social and economic organization; for example by questioning our relationship to work and calling for much reduced working hours. The notion of degrowth and the debates it has generated are clearly inscribed within a broader critical tradition that includes ILLICH and SCHUMACHER. Moreover, the notion of degrowth has clear resonance with many of the concerns raised by the ANTI-CAPITALIST movement.

DEEP ECOLOGY A movement within ENVIRONMENTALISM that defines itself against anthropocentric approaches and instead puts forward an ecocentric or biocentric ethic. The term was coined by Arne Naess in an essay written in 1973, 'The Shallow and the Deep: Long Range Ecological Movement'. Naess argued that the technological fixes and reformist measures the environmental movement put forward (recycling, renewable energies) did not go far enough in addressing ecological problems. Instead what was required was a radical overhaul in individual values, lifestyles and consciousness that stressed respect for, and cooperation with, nature. Deep Ecology describes itself as 'deep' because it questions the place and role of human life on Earth. It stresses the inherent and equal value of all living beings, irrespective of their usefulness for human purposes; indeed human beings are not seen as having more value than any other beings. According to Deep Ecology, no species has any more right to live and flourish than any others. This decentring of human life has an important spiritual dimension that is expressed in terms of holism. Deep Ecology draws upon various forms of Eastern and aboriginal spiritualism to challenge the dualism between human being and nature and invokes the close connections between all forms of life. This emphasis on holism calls for new forms of individual consciousness that move away from the ego-centred and individualistic self towards an expanded self that is realized through identification with all forms of life on the planet.

This leads to a strong critique of Western industrial societies and their tendency to treat the earth and non-human beings as resources to be exploited and manipulated. It contrasts strongly with the SOCIALIST and ANARCHIST traditions that generally see nature as a resource to be exploited for the satisfaction of human needs. In practice, Deep Ecology promotes a shift away from industrialism towards the creation of decentralized eco-regions that foster a sense of 'place' and respect the diversity of cultures and natural environments. More controversially, Deep Ecology also advocates the reduction of human population as a necessary measure for all forms of life to flourish. Deep Ecology has been subject to many criticisms, not least from its main rival SOCIAL ECOLOGY. Deep Ecology has been accused of misanthropy, and of verging on totalitarianism or eco-FASCISM for the measures it promotes to save the planet. In their defence, Deep Ecologists have argued that they value human life as much as other forms of life, not more but not less. BOOKCHIN argues that Deep Ecology fails to link environmental problems to power relationships within society. By concentrating on changes in individual consciousness, it fails to confront the power structures (capitalism, social hierarchy) that may be responsible for environmental devastation. In a similar vein, ECOFEMINISTS have argued that the roots of environmental problems are not anthropocentrism but androcentrism and men's domination of women.

DEMOCRACY From the Greek meaning 'rule by the people', the idea has its roots in the democracy of fifth-century BCE Athens, where all citizens could speak and vote in the CITY-STATE assembly, initially located in the AGORA. Citizenship was very restricted, including only about one quarter of the male population and excluding all women. Who should be able to vote and under what circumstances remains one of the problematic aspects of democracy to this day. In current political discourse, the term is commonly used in three ways: first, as a description of Western-style representative democracy. Second, it may be used more generally as a descriptor of COLLECTIVE decision-making practices. Third, it may be a UTOPIAN ideal in the sense of something that has not yet come to pass, such as a society based on participation. All often have the connotation of an ethically superior way of organizing society and institutions.

The concept central to all usages is the idea of collective, usually majoritarian, decision making by a defined group. The way in which this principle is applied varies greatly. The most widespread use of the term

71

refers to the representative democratic nation state often associated with LIBERALISM. Representative democracy refers to the system of government whereby the *demos*, usually the adult citizens, elect representatives to an assembly that is empowered to make decisions on behalf of the electorate for a fixed term. Such assemblies may govern a local region, nation state, or international federations of states. The ability of elected representatives to make decisions that are oppressive to minority groups, or that undermine the democratic system itself, is usually limited by a constitution, overseen by a judiciary at least theoretically independent of the executive. The other element of representative democracies usually considered essential within liberalism is the existence of alternative political parties and candidates. As participation by the citizen is largely limited to a periodic vote, there must be a choice of parties and candidates, often differentiated on ideological lines, for the system to count as democratic. Thus the elections that have taken place in one-party states (such as those in the SOVIET UNION) are not generally accepted as democratic.

Neoliberals have made a strong association between representative democracy and MARKET capitalism on the basis of a general argument about 'freedom'. The universality and desirability of this notion of democracy is hotly disputed by those on the Left who argue that the forcible spread of market liberal democracies, whether by military intervention or by the economic muscle of large corporations, is profoundly undemocratic. Opponents of free MARKET models of representative democracy may still support the link between markets and democracies but object to the US neoliberal model because it erodes the constitutional checks and balances notionally guaranteed by the state. More effective regulation of the operation of corporations by a system of international law is the usual remedy advocated by these proponents of liberal democracy.

Opposition may also come from those advocating social democracy. Social democracy is usually associated with centre-left positions and advocates a greater role for state intervention in markets and a larger welfare sector. Social democrats are concerned that there should be a strong civil society, so that citizens are more involved in the political process, often through local political institutions. As a result social democrats tend to favour the participation of COMMUNITY organizations, including organized labour in the form of TRADE UNIONS, themselves usually governed by various forms of representative democracy.

Libertarians, SOCIALISTS and ANARCHISTS tend to object to representative democracy on more fundamental grounds, arguing that it amounts to the tyranny of the majority over the minority and the individual. Many would argue that, once in power, governments tend not to pay much attention to the wishes of the electorate. Also, despite ostensible differences between political parties that supposedly guarantee choice to the electorate, political parties in power increasingly come to resemble each other. The effective use of the mass media is considered essential for electoral success and this requires massive financial resources, making the rich the paymasters. This sense of the lack of 'real' democracy is encapsulated in the anarchist slogan 'no matter who you vote for, the government always gets in'.

Participative democracy requires that all those affected by decisions directly participate in them. It is often argued that this is only feasible if decisions are made at a local level whenever possible (see LOCALIZATION; PORTO ALEGRE; SMALL STATES). Larger units could be achieved through delegatory assemblies, where local assemblies elect delegates who cannot act independently of their electors. Alternatively, the decisions of delegatory assemblies would not necessarily be binding on those represented. Power would thus always reside at the lowest possible local level. Likewise, individuals would not necessarily be bound by any collective decision, although continued membership might be dependent upon some acceptance of the collective will. The democratic principle might also be assumed to apply to all areas of social life in a wholesale rejection of hierarchy and authority, extending to the family and work organization. The idea that free human beings should reach collective decisions by consensus and be full participants underwrites many modern visions of the good life, both for individuals and communities.

DEMOCRATIC SCHOOL, see SUMMERHILL

DE SADE, see SADE

DIDEROT, see SUPPLEMENT TO BOUGAINVILLE'S VOYAGE

DIGGERS A DISSENTING group (also known as the True LEVELLERS) that emerged from the English Civil War. The term 'Leveller' was applied to disparate groups whose common bond was a desire for a more egalitarian society without the strictly enforced social hierarchy of the seventeenth century. Such groups included the Fifth Monarchists, Muggletonians and

73

early QUAKERS. They mainly appealed to the poor and dispossessed, as well as to radicalized soldiers of the NEW MODEL ARMY, themselves often drawn from the bottom rungs of society. The Diggers were significant because of the leadership provided by Gerrard Winstanley, an outstanding thinker who developed a version of ANARCHIST and COMMUNIST thought. His ideas provided a link between the MILLENARIAN and other religious dissenters of medieval times such as the CATHARS, contemporaneous religious dissenters such as the ANABAPTISTS of Germany, and the nineteenth-century work of PROUDHON, MARX, BAKUNIN and KROPOTKIN. Leveller groups were eventually suppressed by Cromwell and his aides in the new COMMON-WEALTH, ensuring that the English Revolution paved the way for the rise of the middle classes and a capitalist industrial REVOLUTION.

The years 1620 to 1650 were exceptionally hard for the English poor. As well as the disruption of the Civil War, there were rising levels of taxation and a series of disastrous harvests. The more radical supporters of the Revolution, including the Leveller elements of the New Model Army, felt betrayed by Cromwell, not least because the electoral franchise was to be severely restricted by property qualifications. Many regiments mutinied and bands of beggars, Clubmen, recommenced their food 'reappropriation' activities until forcibly dispersed. Against this background there were increasing calls for a much more fundamental reorganization of society and the rise of groups desperate enough to take matters into their own hands and to begin the process of transformation at the local level. In 1649, around twenty people occupied St George's Hill, at Walton-on-Thames. Inspired by Winstanley, they claimed the land for themselves, intending to farm it COLLECTIVELY. They sent out messages inviting all to come and join them, promising the poor 'meat, drink and clothes'. The colony soon attracted about two hundred inhabitants and its proximity to London gave it particular prominence. A second Digger colony was established at Wellingborough in Northamptonshire at about the same time. The owners of the land organized armed raids to harass the colonists and attempted to evict them through the courts. After several months the St George's colony moved to Cobham Heath, a few miles away, hoping to escape persecution, but it was forcibly dispersed in 1650.

Like many other Leveller groups, the Diggers advocated a form of communism derived from a nostalgia for what they thought of as pre-Norman Conquest liberties, and from the organization of the Apostolic Church. This was the continuation of the English radicalism that is apparent in the PEASANT'S REVOLT and the preaching of JOHN BALL. They demanded a redistribution of wealth and land as well as direct democracy at the local level, rejecting both spiritual and temporal authority as at odds with the equality of God's original creation. Winstanley argued that around one third of all land was barren waste. Enclosure prevented its cultivation by the poor. He believed that communal cultivation would enable the investment required to improve the land and obtain better yields from it. This would ensure the end of starvation, begging and crime. Winstanley did not restrict his attention to food production. He also argued for an end to buying and selling with money. Industrial and craft enterprises would be WORKER SELF-MANAGED. In order to bring about his new society, Winstanley believed that the extension of free education to all classes was essential and, unusually, this included both sexes. He was also an internationalist, believing that the poor of other nations would follow England's example. His communism was rooted in religious belief but this was far from orthodox. He followed a pantheism closer to BLAKE's thinking than to the Puritanism of his own day. The divine was to be found in creation and so the pursuit of knowledge was to be encouraged as a way of discovering the mind of God. It was thus also God's will that society be organized on rational and humane principles.

It may seem surprising that the Diggers still loom so large in radical UTOPIAN thought, given the small numbers involved, their swift suppression and the obscurity of Winstanley after 1660. Christopher Hill argues that the St George's Hill uprising was simply the best documented instance of a much more widespread popular social movement, one that very nearly propelled the English Revolution in a communistic, egalitarian and democratic direction. Their memory is preserved in folk song and in the martyrology of the utopian Left.

DIRECT ACTION Refers to protests designed to change 'objection-able' conditions directly, rather than through parliamentary politics, although it may also seek or attract indirect support from the media or political institutions. GANDHI's teaching of Satyagraha (truth force) and civil disobedience have inspired many practitioners of NON-VIOLENT Direct Action (NVDA), a tactic seen as the tool of the powerless against the power-ful. Direct Action follows several logics; for some it is a way of exerting pressure on the powers that be (the state, or a multinational corporation) by willingly undergoing discomfort or self-sacrifice. For example, environmental activists have created situations of personal vulnerability (chaining themselves to trees, inhabiting tunnels dug under planned roads) that give them the moral advantage and compels their opponents to resort to force. Another motive for direct action is to 'bear witness' and dramatize one's opposition by disrupting, delaying and escalating the cost of a project one opposes. Direct action is also an expression of people taking power over their lives, and as such is a central principle of ANARCHIST theory and practice. Direct action embodies anarchists' objectives of creating a free society where people can govern themselves DEMOCRATICALLY without domination or hierarchy.

Direct Action has played a key part in many social struggles. For example, the labour and TRADE UNION movements have developed out of various forms of worker action, from strikes to sabotage (see LUDDITES). Direct action was also central to the British Suffragettes, who chained themselves to the railings of the House of Commons to demand the vote. It was an important tactic of the civil rights movement in AMERICA, and contributed to the end of apartheid in South Africa. It has been used by the anti-nuclear movement, which has occupied air bases or set up peace camps outside them. Animal rights groups have broken into laboratories and 'liberated' animals subjected to experimentation, and more recently environmental activism (see ENVIRONMENTALISM) and the ANTI-CAPITALIST movement have direct methods. Throughout these campaigns, activists have favoured demonstrated a variety of tactics: blockades, boycotts, pickets, sabotage, SQUATTING, tree spiking, lockouts, occupations, slowdowns, attacks on property, blocking roads by staging street parties, the destruction of GM crops, and concrete lock-ons.

Whilst direct action is primarily a method of protest and resistance, it often has constructive elements, for through direct action alternative forms of organization emerge. For example, groups of people squatting in empty homes, or workers taking over factories, are not only engaging in protest action but also creating embryonic alternative organizations based on COMMUNAL or COOPERATIVE principles.

DISOBBEDIENTI An extra-parliamentary radical NETWORK that emerged from the Tute Bianche in the aftermath of the demonstrations in Genoa in July 2001. The Tute Bianche (white overalls) were named after the mayor of Milan ordered the eviction of the Leoncavallo social centre (see CENTRI SOCIALI), saying that from that point SQUATTERS would be no more than 'ghosts wandering about the city'. As a response activists put on white overalls (padded to provide protection against the police) and took to the streets to defend the squat. After saving Leoncavallo, they became involved in protests against precarious working conditions and immigrants' rights. They were also part of various anti-capitalist demonstrations, notably against the WTO in Seattle in 1999, and sent delegates to Chiapas to support the ZAPATISTAS. At Genoa the Tute Bianche decided to take off their trademark white overalls and join the MULTITUDE of 300,000 demonstrators. The transition from the Tute Bianche to the Disobbedienti also marked a development from 'civil disobedience' to 'social disobedience'. The repressive actions by the police force in Genoa brought the practice of social disobedience to more diverse social realms. One of the Disobbedienti spokespersons, Luca Casarini, describes the Tute Bianche as a small army, and the Disobbedienti as a multitude and a movement.

However, the Disobbedienti have maintained the political project of the Tute Bianche and their roots in AUTONOMIA. They have engaged in various forms of social disobedience, including the occupation and creation of self-managed centri sociali, 'free shopping' and the distribution of stolen goods to passers-by, and campaigns for asylum rights for refugees and migrant labourers. They also continue to carry out spectacular DIRECT ACTIONS, for example dismantling a detention camp for clandestine immigrants in Bologna in 2002. By the middle of the decade internal tensions between the Autonomists, those affiliated with the Rifondazione Comunista (an offshoot of the old COMMUNIST Party), and the Green Party were emerging. Discontent has also been expressed with the 'strong leadership' that is deemed to threaten the autonomy of the various political groups with whom the Disobbedienti are affiliated.

DISPOSSESSED, THE A 1974 SCIENCE FICTION novel by Ursula Le Guin which contains both UTOPIAN and DYSTOPIAN elements. It describes the relationship between twin planets – Anarres, an ANARCHIST culture, and Urras, a DYSTOPIAN hierarchical capitalist state. Anarres is a harsh planet, originally colonized by one million radicals from Urras who had been inspired by the writer Odo, a philosopher radical who stressed freedom and interdependence. These Odonian beliefs are personified in Shevek, a brilliant theoretical physicist who is the first Anarresti to visit Urras in 150 years. Through Shevek's eyes we see the luxuries and horrors of 'propertarian' and profiteering society, as compared to the hardships and dangers of anarchism on Anarres.

77

On Anarres, the language does not use hierarchical terms as synonyms for power or superiority, and neither does the language of property get used for relationships or even body parts. So, to praise someone, you might suggest that they are 'more central' and not 'higher', whilst children would refer to 'the father', or even 'the leg', rather than using the word 'my'. There is no government, but the Production and Distribution Coordination administers the syndicates, federatives and individuals engaged in productive labour. The Anarresti assume that a combination of work postings (which can always be refused), combined with the individual's natural enthusiasm and energy for labour, will result in the minimal coordination that is needed to allow members to benefit from collective production. Apart from this, almost everything is decentralized (apart from the allocation of names, to ensure that everyone living has a different name from everyone else). There are no examinations, because students are only taught if they want to learn. There are no laws, because laws do not stop people from wanting to do things. There are no police, because exclusion or violence are possible responses to behaviour that a community doesn't like, and 'freedom is never very safe'. There are no families, though there can be voluntary partnerships for sex, or to bring up children. Gender differences are irrelevant, since everyone is expected to find their own places, regardless of who they are.

The Arresti have no property, no walls, no doors. The only gift they have to give is their freedom, and their decision to engage in MUTUAL aid because their lives will be better together than apart. No one is rich, but no one is poor. Shevek tries to explain to a rich Urrasti why he prefers his world.

> You have, we do not have. Everything is beautiful, here. Only not the faces. On Anarres nothing is beautiful, nothing but the faces.... Here you see the jewels, there you see the eyes. And in the eyes you see the splendour, the splendour of the human spirit. Because our men and women are free, possessing nothing they are free. And you the possessors are possessed.

Le Guin's utopia is barely that. Anarres is a hard world that bears almost no resemblance to the utopias of previous centuries. It is a world that struggles against the encrustations of power, uses Odonion phrases in clichéd and thoughtless ways, and falls too easily into easy condemnations of 'others'. Yet, in its honesty and self-criticism, Le Guin manages to make a certain kind of anarchism live in the imagination in a way that almost no other author has achieved.

DISSENTERS A broad term for English NON-CONFORMIST religious groups who questioned the authority of the state-sanctioned church to interfere in religious matters. Despite differences in doctrine, they tended to stress forms of equality, DEMOCRACY and the ability of individuals and COMMUNITIES to worship in ways unmediated by the BUREAUCRACY of the official church. They were often central to the establishment of non-conformist communities in AMERICA from the sixteenth century onwards. There were many different groups, but the better-known ones were the ANABAPTISTS (see also AMISH), the DIGGERS, the LEVELLERS, the Puritans (see MASSACHUSETTS BAY COLONY), QUAKERS and RANTERS. In their more pronounced forms, their beliefs could be understood as forms of ANARCHISM and COMMUNISM, in which spirituality and politics merged, but they can more generally be understood as part of an English radical tradition (see also DISSENTING ACADEMIES).

DISSENTING ACADEMIES Independent educational institutes set up in opposition to the official system of schools and universities in England in the seventeenth century. They initially existed to prepare DISSENTERS or NON-CONFORMISTS for the ministry, but their curriculum broadened in time to include a fuller range of subjects than were available in the universities. They flourished between 1660 and the later decades of the eighteenth century. Eventually they were to surpass Oxford and Cambridge and many of the gentry preferred to send their sons to dissenting academies even when they were Anglicans. It should be borne in mind that, radical in many ways though they were, the academies did not educate women. At their zenith the academies were both considered better value for money than the universities and providers of the best education available. Many of the gentry and even the nobility pursued their studies in them. They also enabled many of modest means, who would not have been admitted to the universities, to pursue advanced studies, notably including Daniel Defoe (see ROBINSON CRUSOE), educated at the Newington Green Academy in London.

After the restoration of the monarchy in 1660, the Clarendon Code largely outlawed the practice of religious non-conformity. Charles II was well aware of the links between political radicalism and Puritanism, and of the dangers this might pose to his throne and indeed to his life, given his father's fate. The Conformity Legislation of 1662 forced all who taught to swear an oath that they would conform to the official liturgy. Such teachers also had to be licensed by their bishop. A great many non-conformist university lecturers, ministers and teachers were ejected as a result of this policy. The dissenting academies flourished because non-conformist ministers and laymen would not allow their sons to be educated within the official system. Also many of the ejected clergy and teachers were considered the most effective within their profession. The academies required no oath of religious conformity and so Anglicans were also able to attend them. They were persecuted by the authorities in the early years. Tutors were liable to heavy fines and premises often had to be changed to avoid official harassment. Academies were often run on relatively DEMOCRATIC lines and their founders and teachers were generally motivated by their religious and political convictions.

The traditional universities went into a steep decline while the dissenting academies flourished. Universities were rooted in a restricted classical education, bastions of a narrow orthodoxy. The academies embraced 'modern' philosophies such as utilitarianism and paid more attention to science, modern languages and 'practical' subjects. Their curricula were a major influence on the educational reformers of the nineteenth century. The academies also provide a striking example of highly successful and long-lived voluntaristic organizations, set up in opposition to the prevailing order. Along with the MECHANICS' INSTITUTES, they form part of the tradition of radical AUTO-DIDACTICISM. Present-day alternative schools such as SUMMERHILL owe a good deal to their example.

DYSTOPIA Literally an anti-UTOPIA (or cacotopia/kakotopia), the dystopian form presents something of a paradox. Some commentators distinguish between dystopias and anti-utopias on the basis that the former leave the possibility of progressive change open, whilst the latter offer no way out. Whichever classification we adopt, the earliest are probably comic dystopias, such as those written by Aristophanes, and such works are almost satires that parody the good intentions of some reform of society or people (see EREWHON). By the ROMANTIC period, the dystopia was becoming European society itself, with works such as Hall's *Mundus Alter et Idem*, Swift's GULLIVER'S TRAVELS, Diderot's SUPPLEMENT TO BOUGAINVILLE'S VOYAGE and de Foigny's NEW DISCOVERY OF TERRA INCOGNITA AUSTRALIS criticizing religion, law and social organization from the safety of 'virgin' islands. These sort of echoes of the 'noble savage' can be seen in elements of Romantic and MARXist utopianism right the way up to the end of the nineteenth century. But it is in the twentieth century that dystopia really comes of age, partly because the rise of a BUREAUCRATIC society and the idea of social planning (see LOOKING BACKWARD, GARDEN CITIES, LE CORBUSIER) underwriting ideas of progress in both North AMERICA, Western Europe and the Soviet Union.

An early, and often neglected example is Richter's *Pictures of a Socialistic Future* (1891), a satire on the dangers of totalitarian socialism where everyone eats the same sized portions of food at the same time. Another is Gregory's *Meccania the Super State* (1918), where failure to follow and understand the intricate rules means that you have to be confined to a lunatic asylum. Better known works in this genre are WELLS's *When the Sleeper Wakes* (1899), Forster's *When the Machine Stops* (1909), Zamyatin's *We* (1924), Kafka's *The Trial* (1925) and *The Castle* (1926), Huxley's *Brave New World* (1932) and Orwell's *Nineteen Eighty-four* (1949), or films such as *Metropolis* (1926) and *Modern Times* (1936). Most of these works are forms of SCIENCE FICTION which presented 'realist' nightmares in order to criticize Stalinism, technocracy, bureaucracy and the dehumanization of the world. The paradox is that it is at about this time that the novelistic utopia begins to decline in frequency and importance, but that forms of space cowboy science fiction legitimate a different way of writing imaginative fantasy. The dystopia, it could be argued, then becomes a kind of cynical utopia, written for an audience who no longer believe in fairy stories or central planning. Central to its logic is the idea that this is the sort of world that neither the writer nor reader wishes to inhabit, and its presentation is hence in the nature of a cautionary tale.

In most dystopias, the problems of human freedom are played out against the backdrop of a strong state, technological matrix, or military industrial complex, though there is also a sub-genre of post-apocalypse dystopias which are usually premised on the dangers of nuclear war, environmental collapse or overpopulation. Since the 1980s, the cyberpunk genre of science fiction, together with associated films, computer games and so on, has particularly emphasized the dangers of corporate domination and brutal versions of market managerialism. For examples, see Gibson's *Neuromancer* (1986), Stephenson's *Snow Crash* (1992), Barry's *Jennifer Government* (2003) or Morgan's *Market Forces* (2004). In this way, contemporary dystopianism engages with the dominance of certain organizational forms (as well as consumerism and commodification).

Just as utopias reflect the contexts from which they were written, so too do dystopias. But this also opens the possibility that utopias could become dystopias, and vice versa. Reading More's original *Utopia* (1516), there is a stern moralism that makes it difficult to imagine this as a good place to live. Many of the other utopias in this book contain extreme punishments, prohibitions on sexuality and gender, assumptions about the uniformity of character, hierarchical regimes and so on. Correspondingly, More might have read Huxley and understood *Brave New World* to be a well-run regime which guaranteed the happiness, safety and stability of all obedient citizens, which was precisely what Skinner later did with his WALDEN TWO (1949). (Though Huxley later responded with ISLAND, a utopia which reversed the perspective once more.) Contemporary dystopias also often have strong messages about human agency and individuality, and the characters that populate the plots are involved in active forms of struggle, unlike the settled arrangements and contentment that characterizes most utopias. Even utopias such as Le Guin's THE DISPOSSESSED (1974) and Piercy's WOMAN ON THE EDGE OF TIME (1976) contain clear dystopian contrasts which give the novels their narrative drive. Perhaps the rise of dystopianism is in itself a caution against the possibility of any final utopia coming to realization, the triumph of a principled realism over facile optimism.

ECOFEMINISM Emerged during the 1980s from the ENVIRONMENTALIST and FEMINIST movements, and draws connections between the exploitation of nature and the exploitation of women. It interrogates the dualism between humanity and nature, and the association between women and nature, that have been used to justify sexual hierarchy. For ecofeminists, the feminization of nature as well as the 'naturalization' of women in patriarchal societies suggest that feminist and environmentalist agendas are closely aligned and that environmental degradation and womens' subordination are mutually implicated. Both require challenging the patriarchal 'logic of domination' (Warren, 1997). Ecofeminism is also the product of a rebellion against the 'patriarchal' thinking of radical environmentalist movements. It addresses a wide range of issues from deforestation to toxic waste, militarism and nuclear weapons, reproductive rights and technologies, animal rights, and agricultural development. It is divided not only by its multiple concerns but also by different conceptualizations of the special connections between women and nature (Sturgeon, 1997).

For some, it is women's biology and their reproductive bodies that bring them close to nature's seasonal and cyclical rhythms, and give them a better understanding of the environment. Others draw a spiritual connection between women and nature and find their inspiration in forms of spirituality that contains strong images of female power (for example witchcraft or goddess worship). A third position sees the close relationship between women and nature as the product of material conditions and, in particular, the sexual division of labour: women's role in traditional agriculture and household management (cooking, food production, childcare, healthcare). As will be apparent, these different interpretations rest upon incompatible assumptions. In particular, whilst the first two see the connections between women and nature as 'natural', the product of some universal and fixed 'feminine' traits grounded in biology or spirituality, the third position sees the connection as socially constructed. Ecofeminism has attracted much criticism, not least within feminism, for its essentialist account of women, that is, for proposing definitions of women grounded in biology. However, as the discussion above should make clear, this criticism reduces ecofeminism to its 'biological' or maybe spiritual versions, and ignores other forms of ecofeminism.

ECOTOPIA The subject of two UTOPIAN novels by Ernest Callenbach – *Ecotopia* (1975) and *Ecotopia Emerging* (1981). Using a SCIENCE FICTION genre Callenbach describes a territory west of the Rocky Mountains which broke away from the USA in 1980. In 1999, a reporter called William Weston becomes one of the first people to visit. Ecotopia covers most of the US states of Oregon and Washington, as well as Northern California. Its capital city is San Francisco, and its economy is based on ENVIRONMENTAL technologies and SUSTAINABILITY. For example, the use of any wood to build a timber structure has to be repaid with sufficient work in the 'forest service' to replace the biomass that has been used. Sexual freedom and equality are now dominant, though, due to LIBERAL education and birth control, the population fell after independence. The governing party are the female-dominated 'Survivalists'. Air and car travel has disappeared, and been replaced with railways and bicycles. The media contain no consumerist advertising and are largely concerned with public information, and there are no competitive sports. Economically, Ecotopia is not an ECOVILLAGE, but a SMALL STATE which practises an environmentally aware form of capitalism (compare with WOMAN ON THE EDGE OF TIME).

Importantly, *Ecotopia* is largely based on a realistic assessment of the environmental technologies which were known when Callenbach was writing. It is a fiction that is intended to change the future, not merely a fantastic account of an imaginary world, or a wishful romance (see NEWS FROM NOWHERE). Its influence has been substantial, and it is difficult for anyone who encounters Ecotopia not to want, like William Weston, to become an Ecotopian themselves. Many other fictions are now termed 'ecotopias' too, such as Kim Stanley Robinson's *Mars Trilogy* or Ursula Le Guin's (1986) *Always Coming Home* (see also The DISPOSSESSED), and the term has also been applied to the work of the ANARCHIST philosopher Murray BOOKCHIN.

ECOVILLAGES In a definition that has become widely cited, Gilman described ecovillages as 'human-scale, full-featured settlements in which human activities are harmlessly integrated into the natural world in a way that is supportive of healthy human development and can be successfully continued into the indefinite future'. Since then, many definitions have been suggested, but all make reference to three central dimensions. 'Ecovillages are COMMUNITIES in which people feel supported by and responsible to those around them'; to this end they should be small enough to enable members to know each other and to participate fully in community decisions (see SMALLNESS). An ecological dimension involves lifestyles that have a low impact on the environment. In practice this often points towards a combination of community SELF-SUFFICIENCY in food and energy, and LOCAL exchange. A spiritual and cultural dimension: whilst not all ecovillages have an explicit spiritual dimension, they are supportive of diversity, and they encourage cultural enrichment and artistic expression.

Ecovillages are based on ANTI-CAPITALISM, reject the pursuit of growth (see DECROISSANCE) and provide living examples of attempts to develop SUSTAINABLE alternatives. Indeed, in 1998, ecovillages were named among the United Nations' list of 100 best practices for sustainable living. Despite some fictions that prefigure many of their ideas (see NEWS FROM NOWHERE; WOMAN ON THE EDGE OF TIME) the ecovillage movement is still in its early stage and only began to organize in 1991, when various sustainable communities met to create the Global Ecovillage Network (GEN). This includes a wide variety of settlements, from well-established communities such as FINDHORN, CRYSTAL WATERS, AUROVILLE and CHRISTIANIA to many smaller groups. Ecovillages vary enormously in terms of size, location, composition, and activities. Most have between 50 and 500 members and are experimenting with a variety of social and ecological practices such as consensus decision making, inter-generational care, alternative economic models, ecological building techniques, PERMACULTURE, renewable energy systems, and alternative modes of education and social welfare. They are seen by some as providing an alternative to social welfare systems. For example, the senior citizens' co-housing trend in Denmark offers one solution to the problems of isolation and low income of pensioners. To communities in the global South, the idea has offered an alternative path of development. The Senegalese government has embraced the idea. Whilst the word may suggest a rural setting, ecovillages have also developed in cities, where they have focused for example on ecological 'retrofitting' of buildings, energy saving, the creation of social networks, or the establishment of COMMUNITY-SUPPORTED AGRICULTURE projects with local farmers.

EDEN In Christian mythology, an abundant and self-sufficient ARCADIAN UTOPIA from which human beings were forever expelled as a result of disobeying God and eating the forbidden fruit. This transgression was instigated by Satan in the form of a serpent, who encouraged the woman (Eve) to tempt the man (Adam) with an apple from the Tree of Knowledge of Good and Evil. The name now functions to indicate a primitive state of innocence, a PARADISE which has been lost. See also ATLANTIS; COCKAIGNE; EL DORADO; KINGDOM OF HEAVEN ON EARTH; SHANGRI-LA, and, for its development into Romantic Utopias see SUPPLEMENT TO BOUGAIN-VILLE'S VOYAGE; NEW DISCOVERY OF TERRA INCOGNITA AUSTRALIS.

EL DORADO Spanish for 'The Gilded One', a mythical city or land of gold somewhere in the South American jungle, probably based on stories about gold and treasures in the fabulous city of Manoa told to the Spanish conquistadores in the sixteenth century and recounted in English by Sir Walter Raleigh in 1596 (see also AMAZONS). Gold and jewels lay on the floor, and, once a year, the King is oiled and covered in gold dust. The name now functions as a utopian CITY STATE, a dream of wealth which is always beyond reach, and usually results in the destruction of those who seek it. A similar story was told by Chief Donnacona, an Iroquois taken prisoner by the French in the 1530s. He told stories of the 'Kingdom of the Saguenay', a land of vast riches in Quebec. See also ATLANTIS; COCKAIGNE; SHANGRI-LA.

EMPLOYEE OWNERSHIP see COOPERATIVES; MONDRAGÒN; WORKER SELF-MANAGEMENT

EMPLOYEE SHARE OWNERSHIP PLANS, see ESOP

EMPOWERMENT The term has its origins in the turn within radical politics away from COLLECTIVISM and towards issues of individual consciousness and emancipation. It could be argued that empowerment, as an oppositional practice rather than a term, has always been a feature of radical UTOPIAN movements. No such movement or group would ever have existed without people believing that taking their lives into their own hands and acting individually or collectively, often at the risk of torture and death, could lead to the realization of a better life for themselves and a transformed society. By the 1930s MARXIST thinkers were beginning to grapple with the problem of the failure of the proletariat to achieve the class-consciousness required for mass revolutionary action, despite the example of the Russian REVOLUTION and the existence of the SOVIET UNION. Indeed, all over Europe, sizeable sections of the working class were embracing fascism. Thinkers such as Antonio Gramsci argued for the need for individuals to free themselves from dominating systems of thought that naturalized an oppressive order. The idea reached its apogee in the social movements of the 1960s counter-culture. Empowerment was the objective of groups such as the SITUATIONISTS and many self-help groups of the time. It has always been a strong strand in the ANARCHIST tradition, particularly in the thinking of individualist anarchists such as STIRNER. The process of developing alternative lifestyles was partly an attempt to free the mind from the shackles of convention. Radical FEMINISM encouraged women to escape from the unconscious values of patriarchy which caused women to be complicit in their own oppression.

The most common use of the term 'empowerment' currently is within MANAGEMENT discourse (KALMAR; QUALITY OF WORKING LIFE). It retains its appeal through the connotation of individual autonomy and emancipation, whilst simultaneously emptying practices of these very features. The managerialist deployment of the term is designed to extend managerial control by persuading employees that embracing the interests of the organization and their managers constitutes an act of individual emancipation. Typically this empowerment is implemented through giving employees more responsibility and a small degree of AUTONOMY in how these responsibilities are to be carried out. For example, a work team may be given a set of overall objectives but allowed to organize themselves as to how these should be achieved. In practice such empowerment is usually very limited and frequently the rhetoric is greeted with cynicism by workers already weary of a rapid succession of management fads.

The irony is that the power of 'empowerment', even in its debased managerialist form, derives from its UTOPIAN promise of freedom and the possible escape from alienated forms of work. The ability to reappropriate concepts such as empowerment becomes part of the struggle over meaning that is part of the assertion of one's self against prevailing orthodoxies and social institutions. Critics of the LIBERAL implications of the term might argue that only within COLLECTIVES and COMMUNITIES may one escape through the actual creation of alternatives. Either way, empowerment has to be engaged in, and cannot be given ready-made.

87

ENVIRONMENTALISM Emerged out of concerns over pollution, global warming, soil erosion, deforestation, waste disposal, and resource depletion. To the extent that many of these environmental problems have been created by industrial production, economic growth and Western-style consumption, environmentalists often offer a critique of the model of economic growth on which they are based. Although environmentalism has a long historical lineage that can be traced back to ROMANTICISM and critiques of the impacts of industrial development on the environment during the Industrial REVOLUTION (NEWS FROM NOWHERE; WALDEN), as a modern social movement, it emerged in the 1960s. A significant milestone was the publication of Rachel Carson's (1962) *Silent Spring*, which denounced the impact of agricultural chemicals on wildlife. The early 1970s saw the emergence of two major groups: Friends of the Earth and Greenpeace, as well as the first Earth Summit. Another defining moment was the publication of a report by the Club of Rome in the early 1970s entitled *Limits to Growth* (Meadows *et al.*, 1972). The report put forward the notion of 'natural limits': because the earth has finite resources and a limited ability to support growth and absorb pollution, continued economic growth is unsustainable.

The notion of natural limits has since become central to the environmental movement, as has SUSTAINABILITY. However, environmentalists are divided over the proposals they put forward. One line of division within the environmental movement concerns ethics, and in particular the question of why we should care for the environment. Those holding biocentric views, such as DEEP ECOLOGISTS, argue that nature has value in itself and should be preserved for its own sake. They call for changes that promote closer harmony between all forms of life on the planet such as voluntary simplicity and the replacement of materialistic values with spiritual ones. Other environmentalists place humans at the centre and suggest that we should care about environmental problems because they are deeply connected with human and social issues such as justice or health. For example, for SOCIAL ECOLOGY environmental problems are rooted in an economic system that is deeply exploitative not only of nature but also of humans; overcoming the environmental crisis involves a radical overhaul of economic and social organization, and in particular the overthrowing of capitalism. The Environmental Justice Movement that emerged in AMERICA in the 1980s also links environmental and social problems by denouncing environmental racism: the dumping of toxic waste or polluting industries in locations or neighbourhoods inhabited by non-whites.

Another line of division within the environmental movement opposes reformists and radicals. Reformists argue that the switch to environmentally friendly technologies (renewable energies, recycling, non-polluting technologies), the use of green taxes, and increasing pressures from consumers for 'green products' will ensure the greening of capitalism and economic growth. Those on the radical side, on the other hand, do not think that these measures would go far enough in addressing environmental problems and propose drastic measures that include reduced levels of consumption and economic growth (see DECROISSANCE). They also often call for the breakdown of the global economy into SMALL communities relying on SELF-SUFFICIENCY and LOCAL exchange in order to lower the environmental cost of transportation and sensitize people to the environmental impact of their actions.

Environmentalism does not constitute a united movement but has many currents associated with different political orientations. It interacts with various other social movements such as the peace movement, the anti-nuclear movement, the animal rights movement, the human rights movement, or FEMINISM (see ECOFEMINISM). It consists of a variety of groups ranging from well-funded large international organizations, to Green political parties, to small GRASSROOTS groups that may campaign on single issues (CHIPKO) or organize to create more sustainable ways of living (ECOVILLAGES). In addition, its critique of industrial development, economic growth and Western patterns of consumption has made it, in particular its more radical currents, a central part of the ANTI-CAPITALIST movement.

EREWHON A satirical UTOPIA (and so probably a DYSTOPIA too) written by Samuel Butler and first published in 1872. Much of Butler's writing was pro-evolutionary, though *Erewhon* also satirizes a determinist Darwinian universe, in which machines could evolve and people are not responsible for their characters. Our hero treks to 'Erewhon' (an anagram of 'nowhere') over a mountain range and discovers a society which he takes to be the lost tribes of Israel. Like Swift's GULLIVER'S TRAVELS, much of the irony is produced by the narrator's rather pompous Christian assumptions about the perversity of the Erewhonian's beliefs. For example, rather than punishing criminals, they pity them and send them to 'straighteners', on the assumption that they can't help what they do. However, physical illness is taken to be a sign of moral weakness, and is hence punished most severely.

As a result, citizens hide the most trivial disease, but talk openly about the various crimes that they have been tempted to commit. Further examples of the reversal of common Victorian beliefs are their fear of technology (on the grounds that it will eventually enslave humans) and arguments in favour of treating animals and vegetables as if they were like humans. Butler also parodies Victorian institutions such as the church ('musical banks' which issue what everybody knows is useless coinage, but no one says so), and universities ('colleges of unreason', with complex justifications for why they never teach anything useful).

There is little in the way of practical advice for utopians in Butler's book, though Morris admired the book greatly, and may have borrowed the anagram for his NEWS FROM NOWHERE. Butler uses the fantastic journey genre with ironic precision in order to show the poor reasoning that justified so many Victorian institutions (and still does), and hence to open alternative ways of thinking about social issues. If we accept that people's actions are determined by their circumstances, why blame them for their immorality but not for their illness? If we accept that animals feel pain, then how can we claim to be good and still eat them? Butler is the sort of modern sceptic who doubts any received authority, whether parent, professor or judge. His skill at rooting out hypocrisy and diagnosing the various maladies of well-intentioned reformers (whether on the basis of logic or prejudice) is exemplary. 'I can see no hope for the Erewhonians till they have got to understand that reason uncorrected by instinct is as bad as instinct uncorrected by reason.' The novel ends with the protagonist escaping in a balloon with his Erewhonian love, but making plans to return and convert these heathens (see *Erewhon Revisited* 1901).

ESOP Employee Share Ownership Plans (called Employee Stock Ownership Programmes in the USA) are a system of allocating shares to workers based on certain criteria usually related to length of employment. There is some evidence that ESOP firms are more profitable since there is less incentive for the short-term profit taking which can be characteristic of the drive to increase shareholder value. It can be combined with a system of DEMOCRATIC governance that echoes ideas of INDUSTRIAL DEMOCRACY, or (as in the case of US 401 (K) plans) merely be a tax-efficient way of investing for retirement. For examples of the former see JOHN LEWIS PARTNERSHIP; SCOTT BADER COMMONWEALTH.

F

FAIR TRADE Seeks to establish equity in trade relations, particularly between developing and developed countries, by promoting international labour, environment and social standards. The aim is to support social justice and relieve poverty by ensuring that SMALL producers and workers get a 'fair deal' on the products exported to developed countries. Fair Trade can be traced back to the late 1950s in various European countries as well as AMERICA. For example, the UK-based Oxfam played a leading role and opened its first 'World Shop' in 1959. Whilst these early initiatives were mainly concerned with handicrafts and clothing, fair trade has since extended to agricultural products (coffee, chocolate, tea, bananas).

The notion of fair trade implies that 'free trade' is unfair, and there are at least two reasons why it is said to be so. First, whilst rich traders insist on developing countries removing 'barriers to trade' (in the form, for example, of employment or environmental regulation), they themselves use PROTECTIONISM against poor nations by submitting products imported from these countries to tariffs that vastly inflate their price. Critics of 'free trade' also condemn the 'dumping' of subsidized products from rich countries on poor countries, a practice that drives out local producers in developing countries by depressing prices. The second line of argument is that the fluctuation in commodity prices, combined with the downward pressures on prices exerted by powerful companies on commodity markets, results in starvation wages and does not generate the means for sustainable development in developing countries, forcing them into debt and poverty.

Whilst some propose to counter this situation with PROTECTIONISM or re-LOCALIZATION, fair trade supporters agree with free trade advocates that international trade could provide a way out of poverty for developing countries; however it needs to be made 'fair' by ensuring that more of the returns go to producers, workers, and programmes of social and environmental protection in developing nations. To this end, the Fair Trade movement promotes the implementation of international standards that set fair prices for farmers and decent working and living conditions for workers, promote workers' COOPERATIVES, and encourage sustainable development (for example by restricting the use of agrochemicals). The certification and labelling of products that meet fair trade standards enables consumers to choose to consume these products. Thus the fair trade movement effectively uses the MARKET principles of fair competition and consumer choice to achieve social justice.

FARMERS' MARKETS A long-standing feature of town and village life throughout the world, and the traditional way of exchanging food products. However, in the face of the escalating corporate takeover of the food market, farmers' markets have recently enjoyed increased popularity in Western countries. They are seen as a way of responding to health concerns about the quality of food, and ENVIRONMENTAL concerns about the negative ecological impact of the globalization of food. Like COMMUNITY-SUPPORTED AGRICULTURE, farmers' markets aim to bypass corporate retail chains and to establish closer relationships between local producers and consumers. As such they can form part of LOCALIZATION strategies. Farmers' markets can also contribute to the development of SUSTAINABLE agriculture by supporting producers who cannot withstand the pressures on prices imposed by retail chains, and by reducing food miles.

FASCISM Michel Foucault suggested that it is 'fascism that causes us to love power, to desire the very thing that dominates and exploits us' (in the preface to Deleuze and Guattari's *Anti-Oedipus*). Whilst this is a generous definition, it captures something of the worship of submission which is common to fascist regimes. As an organizational form, fascism is totalizing and totalitarian. It represents a form of UTOPIA which has, as Mussolini put it, 'Everything in the State, nothing outside the State, nothing against the State.' This is a comforting and complete vision, one in which many troubles can be MANAGED away though a strong (and non-negotiable) form of administered COMMUNITY. Many utopian fictions (see, for example, Plato's REPUBLIC, More's UTOPIA, Andreae's CHRISTIANOPOLIS, Cabet's VOYAGE TO ICARIA, Bellamy's LOOKING BACKWARD and Skinner's WALDEN TWO) and alternative regimes (see, for example, AMISH; SOVIET COMMUNISM) have been more concerned with constructing a coherent system of behavioural compliance than with encouraging or guaranteeing personal freedoms. In that sense, fascism is not extraordinary, simply an example of a tendency taken to its extreme.

However, if the word 'fascism' is not going to be applied to any authoritarian order that the commentator does not approve of, then it needs to be more precisely defined. The word has its origins in the 'fascio' which were small groups of peasant revolutionaries, usually SOCIALIST, which developed in southern Italy in the 1890s. Each 'fasci' developed in a slightly different direction, but Mussolini's version developed a set of ideas reliant on SYNDICALISM and corporatism in order to create an anti-MARXist and anti-MAFIA populism. That is to say, they proposed solving the conflicts between workers and capital through strong government, and not attacking the state or private property (see LE CORBUSIER). Key elements of Italian fascism were a nostalgic form of nationalism, a leadership CULT, and repressive tactics (including violence and propaganda). German fascism added to this a racial version of nationalism, but in both cases the upper and working classes were the key constituencies. The diagnosis of threat from free MARKETS (combined with the idea of a Jewish conspiracy), or the threat from supposedly class-obsessed revolutionary COMMUNISTS, legitimized the need for strong protection. This in turn underwrote a form of GUILD system in which capitalists in particular sectors, in combination with the state, cooperated on behalf of all citizens. This meant that, in principle, private profit had become a matter of public good, whilst in practice industrial dynasties were effectively untouched.

Few would now advocate fascism as a serious utopian or alternative form of organization. However, it is important to recognize the lessons that an authoritarian love of power teaches, because Nazi fascists were not simply evil monsters, but craft medievalists (see NEWS FROM NOWHERE), vegetarians, supporters of local organic agriculture and constructors of nature reserves. So the question is perhaps how much order we are prepared to embrace, or tolerate. Debates concerning COMMUNITARIANISM, LIBERALISM and BUREAUCRACY are clearly inflected by different degrees of toleration of diffe rence, and the corresponding rights of a group to impose their defin i-tions of utopia on others. It is often difficult to distinguish supposedly communist regimes (such as those headed by Stalin and M AOTSE-TUNG) from fascist ones. The certainty that the strong must rule and the weak must be ruled is an easy one to slip into. It is a shadow that haunts any utopian.

FEDERALISM A means of achieving voluntary large-scale organizational forms made up of SMALLER units, whilst trying to avoid hierarchy. The most common use of the idea in modern political discourse is as a state comprised a number of self-governing regions, sometimes themselves referred to as states, as in the United States of AMERICA. A number of modern nation states describe themselves as federations but the degree of autonomy the individual members of a federation have varies considerably. Often federations have their origin in an original agreement between previously entirely independent SMALL STATES. The main advantage of a federal state, it is argued, is that power cannot be centralized in large BUREAUCRATIC administrations with little accountability to the citizens they are meant to serve. In theory the component states reserve powers that may not be wielded by the federal government. However, important aspects of national sovereignty are usually ceded, such as foreign policy and defence. In the liberal DEMOCRATIC federal state, the rights and limits of the member states and federal government are enshrined in a constitution that cannot be altered at will by either tier. It is argued that federal states are more democratic than unitary states because of the balance of power held between the two tiers, the LOCALIZATION of many decisions and the subsequent expansion of opportunities for direct democracy.

The European Union possesses some characteristics of a federal state, albeit one with a very weak central government. It has its origins in the idea, dating from ANARCHIST federalists in the nineteenth century, that the European powers could be prevented from going to war with each other if they became a federal state. There are considerable arguments between member states about how far along the path of becoming a full federal state they wish the Union to go. The original constitution of the SOVIET UNION provided for a voluntary federation of soviet SOCIALIST republics. Each was to be governed by its own supreme council and had a formal right to secede. In practice, individual republics were governed centrally from Moscow and attempts to follow a more independent line were sometimes suppressed with military force.

For the nineteenth-century UTOPIAN socialists and anarchists, federalism was a key part of their vision of society as a vast federation coordinated by councils at the local, regional and, in some cases, global level. Members of councils would be delegates rather than representatives. They would not be able to make independent decisions on behalf of their COMMUNES and would be subject to recall. Councils would not have any authority in themselves; they would merely be coordinating bodies. PROUDHON, in *The Federal Principle* (1863), advocated federalism as a way of preventing the centralization of power in nation states which, he argued, should be broken up into a federation of autonomous regions. A 'political contract' or agreement would be drawn up between regions and would be amended by mutual consent. The fundamental unit of society would be the commune, a MUTUAL associations of property-owning and independent workers who would exchange the products of their labour with other communes and federations via bilateral contracts based on equal exchange. The largest units in a federation would be assigned the fewest powers: the higher levels would thus be subordinated to the lower ones.

BAKUNIN had a similar view, but rejected Proudhon's advocacy of a binding form of political contract. For Bakunin, the principle of local sovereignty required that 'each individual, each association, commune or province, each region and nation, has the absolute right to determine its own fate, to associate with others or not, to ally itself with whomever it will, or break any alliance, without regard to so-called historical claims or the convenience of its neighbour'. KROPOTKIN described a federal society as 'an interwoven network, composed of an infinite variety of groups and federations of all sizes and degrees, local, regional, national and international – temporary or more or less permanent – for all possible purposes'. He looked forward to the time when one might be a member of a variety of COLLECTIVES through a diversity of interrelated federal structures. The commune would eventually cease to be geographically bounded but become

> a generic name, a synonym for the grouping of equals, knowing neither frontiers nor walls.... Each group of the commune will necessarily be drawn towards other similar groups in other communes; it will be grouped and federated with them by links as solid as those which attach it to its fellow citizens, and will constitute a commune of interests whose members are scattered in a thousand towns and villages.

Federations are proposed as one solution to the problem of combining the autonomy of individuals with larger-scale institutions. Federalism has also been used as a coordinating mechanism by left-wing political movements, particularly in the First and Second INTERNATIONALS, and by TRADE UNIONS. In the full blown communistic vision of anarchism, federalism would be the fundamental social principle whereby local collectives form part of a society whilst retaining diverse and AUTONOMOUS forms of life.

FEMINISM To the extent that it has been concerned with providing a critique of gender inequity, and with envisaging ways in which gender relations could be freed of oppression, feminism is clearly inscribed within

UTOPIAN thinking. Broadly speaking, feminism refers to a diverse body of theories, movements and practices that have challenged sexual hierarchy and re-centred women or the experience of womanhood. However, beyond this broad orientation it is difficult to find common ground. Feminism is a highly divided field and its terms of reference – such as gender, sex, womanhood, equality or difference – have been much disputed.

Although the history of feminist ideas and activism is older, feminism as an organized movement emerged in the late eighteenth century, and the term itself was first used in the 1890s in France. Mary Wollstonecraft's (1792) *A Vindication of the Rights of Woman* is often considered the first 'feminist' manifesto and was concerned to establish women's rights to education and work. More generally, feminists in the nineteenth and early twentieth centuries were mainly concerned with women's rights to vote, to work, to hold property, and to be educated. The Suffragette movement was of particular significance during this period; sometimes employing extremely militant tactics, it earned women the vote in most Western countries in the first part of the twentieth century. This agenda of equal rights marked what subsequently became known as 'first-wave feminism'.

However, the provision of equal rights through legislation did little to overcome women's subordination; sexism seemed deeply rooted in cultural and institutional practices. From the 1960s and 1970s, 'second-wave feminists' called attention to a broad range of issues: the cultural association of women with nature and emotion (and men with culture and rationality); their confinement to the private sphere of domestic care; their financial dependence on men; their unequal pay at work. One important aspect of this fight for women's independence and equality was sexual liberation and birth control. Simone de Beauvoir insisted that women's control of reproduction was essential to their freedom from the 'burden of mother-hood' and their access to economic independence; only then could women become equal to men. Three theoretical perspectives are often said to form the 'canon' of second-wave feminism – LIBERAL, MARXIST or SOCIALIST, and radical feminism.

Liberal feminism does not call for radical social change but simply for reforms that would entitle women to the same rights as men. It draws upon the liberal emphasis on individual freedom and thus the main issue is to obtain equal opportunities through legal and institutional frameworks that enable women to participate freely and equally in the public sphere. Underlying the claim for equal rights and opportunities is a presumption of sameness. The liberal tradition has been the most influential, but it has been criticized for not going far enough in its challenge to sexual hierarchy. For example, Marxist feminists argue that sexual hierarchy, or patriarchy, is intertwined with capitalism, and can only be defeated by a strategy that embraces ANTI-CAPITALISM. The central focus of analysis here is the sexual division of labour in capitalism, in particular women's unpaid domestic labour, and their position at the periphery of the labour MARKET. The argument is that the sexual division of labour in capitalist economies both draws upon and reinforces patriarchy by locking women into financial dependence on men. The liberation of women rests upon a redrawing of the sexual division of labour (the redistribution of household work and childcare equally between men and women, and the abolition of sex segregation in the workplace), and the eradication of women's dependence on men through equal participation in paid work. These changes, it is argued, cannot be achieved under capitalism.

In contrast to both liberal and Marxist feminism, radical feminism does not seek to gain women 'equal' access to the public sphere, at least as defined by men, but rather to revalue the experiences of women in the private sphere. For radical feminists the roots of female oppression lie in male control over female bodies and sexuality. Radical feminists do not seek to distance themselves from their childbearing bodies, or to redistribute more equally their 'mothering' role with men; rather, they embrace female biology as the source of women's special life-giving power, their ability to act as reproducers, carers and nurturers. Radical feminists do not seek to establish their 'sameness' with men, but rather to embrace their difference. It is to protect and revalue this difference that they emphasize the creation of 'womanspaces' where women can develop their identities and activities beyond the gaze of men. From this perspective, women's liberation from patriarchy tends to be associated with a separatist agenda that seeks to free women from male science (and especially the male medical gaze, by developing alternative knowledge and centres of women's health) and institutions (for example by setting up women's COOPERATIVES deemed to be more in tune with 'female sensibilities').

Each of these three theoretical perspectives has attracted its own share of criticisms (partly from the other two). However, the three traditions have all been condemned more recently for their neglect of differences between women. Mirroring the cultural shift and growing interest in identity politics, (some) feminists since the 1980s and 1990s have been increasingly concerned

97

to highlight the diversity, fluidity and instability of gender identity. One body of theory that has emerged at the juncture of feminism and black activism (sometimes referred to as 'black feminism') suggests that dominant representations of 'woman' within feminist theory are in fact drawn from the experiences of white middle-class women who universalize their own experience and silence the experiences of women from different ethnic and cultural backgrounds. Another body of theories that has sought to explode the category of 'woman' has emerged out of the encounter between feminism and poststructuralism. From this perspective, the main task of feminism is to deconstruct understandings of the category of 'woman' (or 'man') through attention to historical and cultural specificities of race, class, sexuality, religion and nationality. Here gender differences do not provide the starting point of feminist critique but the very focus of inquiry as an 'effect' that requires explanation. The promise of emancipation comes not from freeing 'women' from the domination of 'men', as if these two categories provided a fixed line of identification, but rather in loosening the hold that gender identities have over us, in denaturalizing gender identity by looking at how it is made.

Feminism has been constituted in various ways by different theoretical perspectives, and in different historical and cultural contexts; and there are many different ways of mapping it out. Here some of the most influential and commonly discussed positions have been outlined, but this is by no mean an exhaustive 'list', and in addition feminism has combined with other movements, for example within ENVIRONMENTALISM, to give birth to new perspectives (see, for example, ECOFEMINISM).

FEMINIST UTOPIAS Many UTOPIAS have described women as fuller participants in their imaginary societies, whether in terms of politics, education, reproduction, sexuality or whatever (see, for example, FOURIER; NEWS FROM NOWHERE; WALDEN TWO). However, until the twentieth century it would gave been difficult to describe these as FEMINIST in terms of their paying systematic attention to issues of gender, sex, and sexuality. While there is no inclusive or exclusive definition of what a feminist utopia might be, generally it can be taken to refer to utopias that are structured with particular reference to gender equity, female separatism, or imaginary alternative arrangements for gender, sex or sexuality. As far as we are aware, it is always women who write them, though this probably should not be regarded as a necessary part of any definition. Most of these utopias would also be in some way influenced by feminist or ECOFEMINIST theory or practice, with particular reference to INTENTIONAL COMMUNITIES that have attempted to rethink actually existing gender relationships (see HAYDEN).

The obvious example of a gender equity utopia would be Marge Piercy's WOMAN ON THE EDGE OF TIME, a presentation of a society with fluid roles for gender, sex and sexuality. However, it is the separatist utopias that are more common, and perhaps more challenging for many readers as they echo the ancient myth of the powerful and proud AMAZONS. An early example of a separatist solution is Mary Bradley Lane's *Mizora: A World of Women* (1890), which portrays a world of white, blonde, beautiful women in the centre of the earth who live without animals (food is synthetically produced) and engage in eugenics to weed out undesirable types. Charlotte Perkins Gilman's HERLAND (1915) presents a tribe of women who have no need to measure themselves against men. Monique Wittig's *Les Guérillères* (1971) tells of a lesbian band of GUERRILLAS who wage war on men, and on male representations of their names, symbols and histories. Even the language and narrative is fractured, as if everything has to begin again in order for the ghosts of patriarchy to be laid to rest. Sally Miller Gearhart provides a more conventional piece of storytelling in *The Wanderground: Stories of the Hill Women* (1979). This is an ecofeminist parable in which men become impotent when they leave their cities, whilst wise women live in an ARCADIAN relationship with nature.

The possibilities of SCIENCE FICTION have also been used as thought experiments. Freed from the constraints of the 'real', writers have explored and challenged the normative structures of patriarchy, as well as its connections to imperialism and violence. For example, in Ursula Le Guin's *The Left Hand of Darkness* (1969), a society with only one sex is described. Reproduction is achieved when one person goes into the monthly cycle of Kemmer as either male or female, and stimulates another to take the opposite sex. For the rest of the time, everyone is a-sexual, and Le Guin explores what this might mean in terms of psychology and social institutions. Joanna Russ's *The Female Man* (1975) describes an all-female society that comes back into contact with the sex wars on Earth after 600 years of isolation, and Lois McMaster Bujold in *Ethan of Athos* (1986) describes an all-male society which has to send a representative to get new artificial wombs. Elizabeth Moon's *Serrano Legacy* series (1994–) is fairly orthodox space opera, but with a strong female lead character, whilst the work of Octavia Butler (particularly the *Xenogenesis* trilogy, 1987–9) engages with issues of gender, race and genetic engineering.

Paradoxically, a further sub-type of the feminist utopia is probably the feminist DYSTOPIA. The classic example is Margret Atwood's *The Handmaid's Tale* (1985), which describes a repressive patriarchy, but speaks from a powerfully feminist position. This in itself is an important clue to the power of feminist utopianism. Feminism, indeed any radical form of theory, is concerned with opening possibilities in the present that might encourage or anticipate a different future. This necessarily positions the present as dystopian and articulates utopianism as a radical act of imagination by those who are currently outside the structures of power. Forms of story-telling which inspire women (and perhaps men) to think and act differently can then easily be understood as political acts, and hence as a potential contribution to alternative forms of organization. As Joanna Russ puts it, 'they supply in fiction what their authors believe society … and/or women, lack in the here and now' (in Lefanu 1988: 70).

FINDHORN With approximately 400 members in 2005, one of the largest INTENTIONAL COMMUNITIES in Britain. From the outset, this COMMUNE set in rural Scotland experimented with SUSTAINABLE living and worked to develop connections between spiritual, social and economic life whilst working with the natural environment. The COMMUNITY was started in a caravan park in 1962 by Peter Caddy, Eileen Caddy and Dorothy MacLean, all three recently made unemployed. They brought their many years of spiritual practices to the development of a garden to grow their own food, and Findhorn became famous for the development of its productive gardens in adverse conditions. Although Findhorn has no formal religious creed or doctrine, it has a strong spiritual dimension that is expressed in values of planetary service, co-creation with nature and attunement to the divinity within all beings. In 1972 it created the Findhorn Foundation, an educational centre running programmes related to spiritual guidance, communal living and ECOVILLAGE design. In addition to running training courses, Findhorn includes about 40 other community businesses such as the Findhorn Press, a complementary medicine centre, and an organic food box scheme. Members have also worked to develop ecological buildings made of natural materials and using renewable energy systems. Drawing on its experience of sustainable communal living, Findhorn became a founder member of the Global ECOVILLAGE Network, and through its programmes continues to promote the development of sustainable settlements.

FOCOLARE The Italian word for hearth is a symbol of family, love, security and warmth. From the 1940s the Focolare Movement aimed to 'do unto others what you would like them to do unto you'. Its intention is to promote greater unity within the family by transforming interpersonal relationships. To achieve this, in 1991 the Movement established the Economy of Communion (EOC) in Sao Paulo, Brazil, as an attempt to address inequalities in wealth, first of all within the Focolare Movement, initially within Brazil and subsequently on a global scale. Small commercial businesses were set up or transformed so that their profits could be redistributed to the poor. By 2002, 778 businesses in 45 countries were participating in the project, redistributing a proportion of their profits to promote welfare and to spread a 'culture of giving'.

The distinctive vision was at first applied on a LOCAL scale. In the early days the circulation of personal possessions among members of the COMMUNITY was based on the common bond of shared spirituality, such as people giving away once a year all that they no longer required. In some ways, this was the first stage in the widening out of the hearth by extending it to the family and then the local community. Over time, it began to be supposed that larger spaces could also become hearths of sharing where the culture of giving might be lived out. This is what the EOC seeks to do through the extension of the Focolare into the realm of business. The EOC was a recognition that the 'communion of goods' was insufficient as a strategy to overcome inequalities on a global scale. What was new was that it would involve the participation of enterprises, not just individuals, to share their profits: one-third to be given to the poor (see ZAKÂT), one-third kept for reinvestment and one-third for the creation of educational structures to further promote the culture of giving. The EOC was thus reviving the tradition of 'tithing' within modern businesses but also insisting that it should become one of the chief motivations behind new businesses.

The practice begins with each individual making a self-assessment of what they need once a year. Once the needs of each community are totalled, every attempt is made to cover these needs through making use of local resources. This is in many cases, especially in Western nations, sufficient to cover needs and to generate surpluses which can be shared with other communities. If the local needs cannot be met through this local communion of goods, these needs are put forward to the regional Focolare and the same process occurs. If the regional Focolare is still unable to cover

101

these needs, the International EOC commission is contacted. Decisions on how much people need are not based on some predetermined criteria but on personal knowledge and understanding. If the total requests equal the fund available, everyone receives what they requested. In 1997, the amount of EOC funds was 80 per cent of the total requests, so each zone received 80 per cent of what they requested. The Focolare Movement's EOC thus demonstrates that it is also wholly possible to enact and imagine how capitalist practices themselves might be coopted by alternative economic logics in order to promote just and equitable ends.

FOURIER, CHARLES It might be suggested that many UTOPIANS are obsessive fantasists, and more than a little detached from the world that they live in. Charles Fourier (1772–1837) is almost the archetypal figure in this regard, a grey clerk who hated his job but built one of the most imaginative and lunatic utopias in this dictionary. In it he uses the tools of (a sort of) natural science of human interaction ('passionate attraction') and comes out with a social order that combines sexual liberation with a COOPERATIVE organization. He condemns bourgeois moralizing, and instead suggests that the arrangements of society and economy should work with our god-given passions, and not against them. The influences of English thinkers (utilitarianism and the economics of SMITH and Ricardo) can also be seen in his thought – though this self-appointed 'Newton' of human behaviour denied them strenuously. Fourier wants us to begin with a scientific approach that describes how human beings behave, and then to build a society accordingly. Though his writings are lengthy and repetitious, his most representative book is probably *Le Nouveau Monde Industriel et Sociétaire* (1829).

Fourier's imaginary world was called 'Harmonia' or 'Harmony', an organization of communities ('Phalanxes', named after the tightly knit ancient Greek fighting unit) which could communicate with each other through a system of signal towers. Each Phalanstery consisted of apartments for 1,620 people, each with its own palatial meeting rooms, private rooms with toilets, and grounds (see CITY STATE; GARDEN CITIES). This exact number had been arrived at by a calculation of the 810 different personality types which could be constructed from different combinations of the twelve basic passions. The point of this calculation was that it ensured that each person would be attracted to someone else who could satisfy their erotic and emotional needs, and the whole would form a 'passionate series'. Basic minimums of food, childcare, clothing and access to cultural events are met for all members of the phalanx, and people are free to choose to work at what interests them, in rivalry with others, or with people to whom they are attracted. For the 'Harmonians' work can become play, and jobs can be done for as long as they are interesting. A complicated daily exchange operates for each phalanx to ensure that people choose to go where they are needed, and neighbouring phalanxes can also bid for extra labour, organize meetings, and so on. Work, like sex, is only worth doing if it reflects a person's passions. So savage people will work as butchers; small children (with a fascination with dirt) will form a 'little horde' that rides a round on small ponies dressed as hussars emptying toilets and killing snakes; and so on. Large-scale tasks will be performed by 'industrial armies' manned by 'industrial athletes', serviced by female 'sexual athletes'.

On gender, Fourier was again highly radical, suggesting that the best measure of civilization was the extent to which women were liberated from patriarchy and bondage to the family. Fourier's interest in ensuring sexual gratification echoes other writers at the same time (see Diderot's SUPPLEMENT TO BOUGAINVILLE'S VOYAGE and SADE), but his arrangements are more organized than most. There are no sexual deviations, or expectations of monogamy, merely the problem of matching like with like and allowing desire to find its most productive purpose. Hence the passions of the young are scientifically and sympathetically assessed by more experienced match-makers at various complicated ceremonies, inspections and orgies, and the old will then also be more likely to find someone who suits their needs too. Whilst it is easy enough to classify Fourier as a ROMANTIC in terms of his view of what civilized repression does to the passions (he despised the 'MONASTIC-industrial discipline' of SAINT-SIMON) his utopia is nonetheless a highly organized one, involving a complex (if temporary) division of labour and a form of order in which 'science' and planning play key roles. He even describes how the shelling and sorting of peas can be done by two-year-olds, if they are organized correctly. The phalanx is unequal because people's natural talents will determine their position in society, and 'regents, proctors and special officers' are entrusted with co-ordinating responsibility. Further, there would be dividends paid on the initial capital invested in setting up each phalanx, because it would be necessary that one-eighth of the initial members be capitalists, scholars and artists.

Fourier, like Saint-Simon and OWEN, was criticized by MARX for wanting to build 'pocket editions of the New Jerusalem' and by Engels in *Socialism,*

Utopian and Scientific (1892) for being a bourgeois fantasist who wanted to solve everyone's problems at one stroke. Whether valid for the other two, this seems fair for Fourier, since even other utopians have found some of his ideas rather unlikely. His fascination with numbers and fondness for grand prophecies led him to suggest that the era of perfect harmony would last 8,000 years, the world would contain 37 million scientists equal to Newton, and the seas would turn to lemonade. However, his influence has been considerable. Marxist and Freudian themes can be traced from his ideas, Morris names him as an influence in NEWS FROM NOWHERE, and the notion of uniting the interests of capitalist and worker in one form of common association is picked up in much later writing (see COOPERATIVE CITY; FREELAND; LOOKING BACKWARD; LE CORBUSIER). His vision of a network of interconnected city states certainly also influenced the garden city movement. More directly, some of his followers began a journal in the early 1830s (*La Reforme Industrielle*), and from the 1840s onwards many North American 'transcendentalist' utopian communities (BROOK FARM, the North American Phalanx, the Clarkson Domain and so on) claimed inspiration from his ideas, initially popularized in the US by Ralph Waldo Emerson (see also WALDEN). A Fourierist newspaper, *The Harbinger*, was published in 1845–9, initially at Brook Farm and later in New York City.

FRATERNAL SOCIETIES, see FRIENDLY SOCIETIES, MECHANICS' INSTITUTES

FREELAND Theodor Hertzka (1845–1924), a Viennese economist, published *Freiland* in 1890 (translated as *Freeland: A Social Anticipation* in 1891) and used it to put forward a number of practical suggestions for economic reform. Just as he hoped, inspired by the ideas put forward in this UTOPIA, an International Freeland Society was created which attempted to develop land in what was then British East Africa, now Kenya. This was not a success, but other communities were inspired by the book, such as 'The Brotherhood of the cooperative Commonwealth' in Washington State USA which changed its name to Freeland in 1904 (see also FREE STATE PROJECT). Hertzka was what was termed in Germany and Austria a 'Manchesterist', who believed in the principles of free trade and laissez-faire economics. David Ricardo's ideas about competition were central to his beliefs, together with a LIBERAL or libertarian conception of human freedom (see also NOZICK). Unlike Bellamy's LOOKING BACKWARD published two years earlier, and the state SOCIALISM satirized in his contemporary Eugene Richter's DYSTOPIA *Pictures of a Socialistic Future* (1891), Hertzka's model was to minimize the state as much as possible.

The capital of Freeland, 'Eden Vale', is a spacious town, with each house having ten thousand square feet of garden around it. Transport is provided by cars and boats powered by springs, and all industry is organized so as to minimize pollution in residential areas. Freeland is a place where there is a free MARKET in all goods and services, and small COOPERATIVE units undertake production. Any worker is free to leave or join any cooperative. Since these decisions are based on an estimate of the shared profitability of the unit, efficiency and good ideas are rewarded. However, in order to prevent the growth of monopoly, the problem of rents, and asymmetries of information, in Freeland no land is privately owned, all capital is owned by the state, and all information about new technologies and working practices has to be made public. A committee of the International Free Society is responsible for Governance. The old, the disabled and single women are looked after by the state, which collects a small tax from all cooperatives to meet these costs. Over time taxes have been gradually falling as the major capital projects needed for Freeland's success are completed. Personal objects, houses and gardens are treated as private property.

Though there are some naïve assumptions about equilibrium at work in Hertzka's utopia it also neatly shows the connections between libertarian ANARCHIST ideas of freedom from various forms of constraint, SOCIALIST ideas about collective COMMONS (see also, GARDEN CITIES) and right-wing conceptions of unfettered markets. Clearly (as Adam SMITH recognized) markets can enable certain sorts of freedoms, and combining them with forms of SMALL-scale production makes *Freeland* seem a curiously modern book. (Though the assumptions about women's labour, and the subjugation of the local Masai population, reflect some rather elderly assumptions.) It is also worth noting the similarities between Hertzka's ideas and those put forward by the 'Ricardian Economists', or English Labour Economists, Thomas Hodgskin, William Thompson and John Francis BRAY. All were writing in the 1820s and 1830s, and putting forward the idea of a COOPERATIVE market alternative to capitalism. Though they had some influence on MARX, the development of much radical thought after Marx developed in much more statist directions (see WELLS), a point clearly indicated by so many of the DYSTOPIAS that mark the twentieth century.   105

Hertzka's book was also claimed as an influence by Theodor Herzl, who published his utopia *Altneuland* ('Oldnewland') in 1904 and describes a Zionist state with religious tolerance and socialist forms of organization (see KIBBUTZ).

FREE SCHOOLS There are a number of free or DEMOCRATIC schools across the world, many linked together in decentralized networks in order to share skills and knowledge. One of the best-known is SUMMERHILL in the UK. Free schools seek to operate independently of state education controls and are often self-funded which means, in most cases, charging fees to students. The movement can be seen as part of the ANARCHIST tradition and many look back to the inspiration of the Spanish anarchist educationalist Francisco Ferrer who established independent progressive schools in Spain in the nineteenth century in defiance of the church and state. BOOKCHIN argues that Ferrer's schools have been an important influence on radical educational thinking ever since (see also FREIRE, ILLICH,TOLSTOY). In general, free schools promote self-reliance, critical thinking, COMMUNITY responsibility and personal development. In most cases they are run on non-hierarchical, anti-authoritarian principles, with the students able to decide which lessons they attend and to participate directly in the running of the school (see also AUTO-DIDACTICISM).

FREE STATE PROJECT A libertarian (see ANARCHISM; LIBERALISM) attempt to establish a 'minarchist' government in New Hampshire, a state of the USA. In 2001, Jason Sorens argued in *The Libertarian Enterprise* that libertarians needed to concentrate their efforts in one area, and New Hampshire was chosen because of its low population, conservative culture (its motto is 'Live Free or Die') and prosperous economy. Once the number of members reaches twenty thousand, they have all pledged to move to New Hampshire and attempt to reduce levels of taxation, regulation and dependence on Federal funds. By 2005, nearly 7,000 people had signed up, under the motto 'Liberty in our Lifetime'. The FSP obviously reflects AMERICAN anti-state and pro-liberty traditions, but takes no particular political position on social or economic issues. It can safely be assumed that there are connections with white right-wing militia politics, but this is not a necessary feature of libertarian politics (see also FREELAND; NOZICK). Other, smaller attempts to establish libertarian states also exist – the Free West Alliance, Free State Wyoming, and the European Free State Project.

FREIRE, PAULO A radical Brazilian educator born in 1921. Trained in law, Freire began his working life in secondary schools, but in 1946 was appointed Director of Education for the state of Pernambuco. There he began to develop radical ideas, influenced by MARXism, concerning the relationship between formal education, literacy and the poor illiterate peasantry. In 1961 he was appointed to a post at the University of Recife, the city of his birth. Until the military coup of 1964, his ideas were being applied more widely by the state, but the coup resulted in his imprisonment and exile. Working successively in Bolivia, Chile, the USA (as a visiting Professor at Harvard) and Switzerland (for the World Council of Churches) he eventually returned to Brazil in 1979. He joined the Workers' Party, and was appointed Education Secretary for São Paulo in 1986. He died in 1997.

Known primarily for his work on 'critical pedagogy', Freire developed ideas about the form and content of schooling that stressed the relationality of teacher, learner and curriculum. In his most famous book, *Pedagogy of the Oppressed* (1970) he focuses on the idea of providing an education which does not elevate the teacher into being another oppressor, a representative of the dominant class, but allows teachers and students to learn from each other. This means that education should be informal and popular, not formal and élitist, and that ideas of dialogue should replace conceptions of the pre-established curriculum. Rather than 'banking' knowledge into an empty mind, critical pedagogy should generate knowledge collectively. Such knowledge would then have relevance to the practices of educator and educated, and help in raising their consciousness of the possibility of transforming those practices. This might also mean using pictures and drawings, in order to begin to help the illiterate participant think through their relationship to education, COMMUNITY, teacher and so on.

Such ideas have been influential in a variety of ways, particularly in thinking through the class and power relationships embedded in classrooms (see FREE SCHOOLS, SUMMERHILL). Though he doesn't go as far as ILLICH in advocating a 'de-schooling' of society, his analysis of political participation and literacy is also crucial to a post-colonial (or MARXIST) understanding of subaltern knowledges. That being said, it has often been noted that Freire's Christian metaphors are sometimes rather baffling for readers who do not share his tradition, and his simple oppressor/oppressed binary is rather difficult to apply neatly (in terms of the relations between gender and class, for example). Freire provides an inspiring model of education as a lived and shared experience with political consequences, a long way from the temporary period of MONASTIC socialization that is still dominant in most First World states.

FRIENDLY SOCIETIES Have their origin in the British tradition of working-class self-help or EMPOWERMENT, alongside COOPERATIVE and MUTUAL improvement societies, and TRADE UNIONS. The current legal definition of a Friendly Society in the UK, as stated in the 1992 Friendly Societies Act, encapsulates the fundamental purpose of these bodies, unchanged for several centuries. This is that such societies comprised a number of persons who join together to achieve a common financial or social purpose. Each society is governed by a set of rules which members agree to abide by and which can be changed DEMOCRATICALLY by a majority of members. Although some historians look to the medieval craft GUILDS as precursors of Friendly Societies, they did not appear until the late eighteenth century, growing rapidly from 1760 alongside the development of an identifiable working class in Britain. They can be seen as a spontaneous and COLLECTIVE response to working-class needs, one that became so successful that it was eventually incorporated and controlled by the liberal-capitalist state.

Members of the first friendly societies paid a small weekly or monthly contribution into a common fund, and then paid out benefits when members needed them, including during periods of unemployment or sickness. Funeral expenses were also provided. Members met once a month in a local public house to transact business but also to drink beer and socialize. An annual feast was held and funerals were invariably followed by a supper. A system of fines was used to ensure that members stuck to the rules. These rules typically covered attendance at meetings, conduct during social events, and malingering. Thus Friendly Societies were 'friendly' in two senses of the word; first, they supplied financial support in the new and precarious world of work. Second, they provided a place to belong and a source of conviviality in the frequently isolating environment of the town and factory. In the Society, men were members or brothers with a say in how its affairs were governed.

The middle decades of the nineteenth century were characterized by revolt and protest by the emerging industrial working class and the predictable response was repression of their organizations and institutions. Trade Unions and Friendly Societies were very similar in organization and function. In both, ceremony and ritual was an important part of the daily lives of members. There were open-air processions with bands, banners and uniforms on public occasions. Each had its own secret (often mystical) symbols and objects (see Freemasons; SECRET SOCIETIES). Officials had mysterious titles and their own regalia. Most worryingly for the ruling class, membership of both involved swearing secret oaths that sought to ensure that the primary loyalty of members was to each other (see MAFIA). From 1799 to 1824, the Combination Acts made the swearing of such oaths illegal.

Friendly Societies were not entirely outlawed, and the 1793 Friendly Society Act sought to control them through a registration scheme. Many societies did not register, preferring an illegal independence. As Friendly Societies were never persecuted in the same way as trade unions were, illegal union activities were often carried on under a front of Friendly Society respectability. The most famous case was when, in 1834, six members of the Tolpuddle Friendly Society of Agricultural Labourers were found guilty of swearing an illegal oath and were transported to Australia for seven years. The 'Tolpuddle Martyrs' received large scale public support and were released in 1836. The Trades Union Congress still holds an annual festival and memorial service in Tolpuddle. By 1815 they had around 925,000 members. By 1872 they had 4 million, compared with only half a million trade union members. By 1892 it is estimated that 80 per cent of male industrial workers were members. Affiliations were not fixed and groups of lodges regularly split off to form their own federations or swapped affiliation at the behest of their members.

As the societies grew they handled large amounts of money for millions of members and so developed the actuarial and accounting systems that were adopted by both the insurance industry and the welfare state. In 1911 the National Insurance Act created a welfare insurance system based on compulsory contributions for employers and employees. This scheme was administered by the Friendly Societies. The Friendly Societies declined once the services they offered were either subsumed by government or became part of the profit-making insurance sector. Many societies survive now as social or charitable bodies or as some of the few remaining mutual building societies. The Friendly Societies have been an extraordinarily successful example of GRASSROOTS collective organization for the purposes of mutual aid. They live on in the form of LETS, microcredit banks (see GRAMEEN) and CREDIT UNIONS.

G

GANDHI, MOHANDAS K. A charismatic leader whose philosophy of non-violence helped bring Indian independence from British colonial rule in 1947; he was assassinated the year after. Hailed in India as the father of the nation, he has been an inspiration for activists and campaigners worldwide; revered by many as the 'Mahatma' or 'Great Soul'. Born of a Hindu family in 1869, he was influenced early in life by the principles of non-violence to living beings, fasting for self-purification, and tolerance. Gandhi trained as a barrister in London and went to work as a lawyer in South Africa. It was there that he became involved in political activism and developed his tactics of NON-VIOLENT RESISTANCE and CIVIL DISOBEDIENCE in response to the humiliation and oppression faced by Indian immigrants. He called on fellow-Indians to defy discriminatory laws and to suffer punishment for doing so, rather than retaliate with violence. The protesters were met with severe state repression but the campaign of non-violent resistance eventually brought a public outcry that led the South African government to negotiate with Gandhi.

Returning to India in 1915, he joined the Indian National Congress and launched a series of campaigns to protest against British colonial rule. For example, he called for a boycott of all British goods and institutions (education, law courts, and government positions), inviting Indians to resign from government employment, and to refuse to pay taxes. He also urged all Indians to wear *khadi* (homespun cloth) rather than clothes made from British textiles and to spend time each day spinning in support of the independence movement. His campaigns were widely followed but led to the arrest and imprisonment of thousands. Gandhi himself was imprisoned several times. He also famously used fasting as a political weapon, not just against the colonial government but to call for an end to violent clashes between Hindu and Muslim communities, and the oppression suffered by the 'untouchables'. In 1934, he became disillusioned with what he saw as the Indian National Congress's lack of commitment to non-violence and resigned. Having tried to keep peace and cooperation between Muslim and Hindu communities during the fight for independence, Gandhi watched the partition between the Indian and Pakistani states with despair. In 1948, he was assassinated by a Hindu radical who held him responsible for the weakening of the new Indian government by insisting on payment to Pakistan.

Gandhi called his philosophy of non-violence *satyagraha*, 'the way of truth', and was influenced by his Hindu upbringing and beliefs, as well as by TOLSTOY's Christian ANARCHISM and Thoreau's writing on civil disobedience (see WALDEN). Besides the promotion of non-violent resistance, Gandhi's 'way of truth' has political, economic, moral and spiritual dimensions that have informed twentieth-century movements. For example, its emphasis on the diffusion of power to the GRASSROOTS and the development of self-reliant communities based on the traditional VILLAGE suggests some similarity with anarchism. His promotion of non-violence to all living things and his insistence on the need to live simply have found some resonance in ENVIRONMENTALISM. Gandhi's ideas and life have been a source of inspiration for many social movements, not only in India (see CHIPKO) but also globally in the peace movement, civil rights movement, the anti-nuclear movement and more recently the ANTI-CAPITALIST campaigns.

GARDEN CITIES Ebenezer Howard (1850–1928) was the author of *To-Morrow: A Peaceful Path to Real Reform* (1898), a book reprinted in 1902 as *Gardens Cities of To-Morrow*. Although English, Howard had spent time in the USA where he was influenced by the paternalist planning found in Bellamy's LOOKING BACKWARD. Morris's NEWS FROM NOWHERE, published eight years earlier, also contains similar ideas about the urban and rural, even if the vision is much less 'planned' than what we find in either Bellamy or Howard. Howard's vision of the town in the country had a huge influence on English suburban design, even if its radicalism eventually became more aesthetic than political. He felt that the benefits of the city and the country (see ARCADIA; CITY STATE) needed to be combined. The variety of opportunities found in the town could be fused with the clean air and beauty of the countryside, producing a new sort of settlement – a radially planned medium-sized green town, zoned into residential and industrial areas, and surrounded by a belt of agricultural land (compare to CITY OF THE SUN; FOURIER). The centre would be green space surrounded by a glass arcade called 'Crystal Palace', and then the concentric rings of the city spread outwards, cut through by grand boulevards. This would be a place that lacked the sweatshops and high rents of the town, but avoided the isolation and insularity of the country. All industry was powered by electricity, preventing smog, and the railway was kept to the periphery of the town. It was also intended to be an experiment in self-governing communities, since the garden cities would own their own land (including the 'green belt' around them) and be governed by and for their citizens. Once a population of about 32,000 had been reached, it would spawn a new garden city, connected to the old one by an inter-municipal railway but separated by the green belt, and in this way create an entire network of new cities which would supersede the old.

Though the overall plan was grand, individual tastes were supposed to shape the different houses found within the city, and Howard's ideas led directly to the foundation of the Hertfordshire towns of Letchworth (in 1903) and Welwyn Garden City (in the 1920s), and to the north London district of Hampstead Garden Suburb (in 1907), as well as many smaller examples across the country. The cottage and country house aesthetic of Letchworth was indebted to the ARTS AND CRAFTS movement, and the emphasis on physical health was reflected in a ban on the sale of alcohol that lasted until 1958. 'First Garden City Ltd' owned the land, and all citizens were shareholders in this company, hence allowing them to shape the development of the town. After problems that arose from an attempt at a hostile takeover in the early 1960s, this body became a statutory corporation in 1962, and in 1995 an Industrial and Provident Society with charitable status and officers appointed by local residents. The better-known industrial paternalist examples were Cadbury's 'factory in a garden' (see BOURNVILLE), Lever's PORT SUNLIGHT, Vickers' 'Vickerstown' near Barrow-in-Furness (1901), Joseph Rowntree's 'New Earswick' near York (1904), and ONEIDA's 'Kenwood' in the USA. George Cadbury and William Lever were members of Howard's 'Garden Cities Association', established in 1899, and the first conference held at Bournville in 1901. Via Georges Benoit's *La Cité Jardin* (1904), Howard's ideas also influenced LE CORBUSIER's attempts at city planning, though the latter was critical of what he saw as the low-rise sprawl of the proposed garden cities: he described his own creations as vertical garden cities. Garden cities have since been built outside Paris (1912), Tokyo (1918), Moscow (1923) and elsewhere.

Since the 1960s, the very idea of grand urban planning has been under attack for its technocratic paternalism, but garden cities have been enduring models for a certain kind of middle-class suburban idyll in which any leafy development could have the word 'garden' appended. They were also instrumental in bringing about the much more mundane sense of planning permission that now dominates the development of most developed urban settlements (see CHRISTIANIA). Perhaps most importantly, for Howard the early vision of garden cities represented a new and more communal way of thinking about COLLECTIVE living, which relegated the crowded selfishness of the old city to the history books. This was not merely urban planning, but a 'social REVOLUTION' which placed COMMON ownership and COMMUNITY at the centre of human life.

GILMAN, CHARLOTTE PERKINS, see FEMINIST UTOPIAS; HERLAND

GODWIN, WILLIAM Born into a family of DISSENTING ministers, Godwin (1756–1836) served as a Calvinist minister before becoming involved in British radical politics. His other claim to fame was his marriage to Mary Wollstonecraft, one of the founding mothers of FEMINISM. Godwin is often considered to have established a philosophical foundation for ANARCHISM and his work made him a prominent figure in the decade following the French REVOLUTION. *An Enquiry Concerning Political Justice, and Its Influence on General Virtue and Happiness* (1793) deals with a wide range of issues from equality to justice, rights, private judgement, government, freedom of speech, theories of law and punishment, and property. Some of these themes are picked up in *Things as They Are, or the Adventures of Caleb Williams* (1794), a fictional continuation of the political project started in *Political Justice* that offers a portrayal of aristocratic despotism, property monopoly and enclosures, and the manipulation of public opinion. A central theme of his work is government as a social evil, perpetuating dependence and ignorance, and corrupting the capacity for reason and moral judgement. Godwin extended this critique to all other institutions. Private property, marriage, organized religion, political parties, the law, and criminal punishment all lead towards mental enslavement and keep people from exercising private judgement. Godwin based his faith in rational self-government on the belief that reason would lead us to recognize the truth about what end was good. The full and free exercise of reason in private judgement and public discussion would displace the need for government and provide the foundation of morality. Godwin articulated a vision of morality based on utilitarianism, whereby moral judgement should be guided by the achievement of the greatest good. His vision of an ideal society was one which, having dispensed with all forms of authority and rule, left individuals free to act according to their private judgement; unfettered by institutions, individuals would be guided by reason to provide for the common good.

Godwin's radical ideas influenced many of his contemporaries, including a whole generation of ROMANTICS. But by the end of the eighteenth century, the political scene Godwin had been part of disintegrated under the pressure of repressive legislation and the growing nationalism fuelled by the war between France and England. Godwin fell into obscurity, writing history and children's books under the pseudonym of Edward Baldwin to support himself. However, he was rediscovered by nineteenth-century UTOPIANS – OWEN, KROPOTKIN and TOLSTOY all read his work. Certainly Godwin's extolling of the value of individual AUTONOMY against all forms of authority, particularly that of the state, anticipates a central theme of anarchism. However, his rejection of COOPERATION sits uneasily with the work of later anarchists, especially those who defend COMMUNITARIAN forms of anarchism and emphasize the values of voluntary association, solidarity and MUTUAL help.

GOLDEN AGE In many traditions, there is an account of a time when people were happy, wealthy and wise. Then, due to some sin, the action of gods, or the movement of history, the age is lost and humanity falls into some sort of darkness. The key element here is time, unlike the contemporary but geographically distanced legends of El Dorado and Shangri-La, as well as most post-Renaissance utopias. Probably the best-known city state version of a golden age is Atlantis. In Celtic and English mythology, King Arthur's island of Lyonesse (with its City of Lions and 140 churches) plays a similar function. A more Arcadian version of the golden age can be found in Christian accounts of Eden, but a classical E u ropean tradition goes further back than the Bible. According to the Greek poet Hesiod (c. 750 BCE), the golden age flourished during the reign of Cronus. People did not age, and lived in peace in an Arcadian paradise. This age was replaced by the declining values of (respectively) the silver age, bronze age, heroic age and iron age. We live in the latter, and will some day be destroyed by Zeus. A more cyclical chronology can be found in the Hindu epics. The Krita Yuga was the first age of the world, an age when people lived for four thousand years, and worshipped one god. There followed a decline to the present and fourth age, the Kali Yuga, a temporary state of affairs that will eventually lead to the coming of another age of righteousness.

The idea of a golden age can be an inspiration for political action, as in the accounts of primitive COMMUNISM within some versions of MARXISM, of the medieval within the ARTS AND CRAFTS movement, and often in various versions of environmental activism (DEEP ECOLOGY, for example). Yet, paradoxically, in some sense the golden age is really about the future, since its loss is the tragedy which must be overcome before human beings can live happily again, or reach their highest stages of social development. However, it can also be a repository for feelings of unrequited nostalgia, and (if part of a teleological account of history) might merely provoke the quietism of emptiness or anticipation. At its most minimal, some conception of a potential golden age is necessary for all UTOPIAS, and perhaps for any form of political action. Some idea of progress, or of the reduction of present sufferings, must mean that the KINGDOM OF HEAVEN ON EARTH that faces us is better than the world we leave behind. That idea, however flawed and corrupted, ties together most of the entries in this dictionary.

GOLDMAN, EMMA

'If I can't dance, it's not my revolution'.

An ANARCHIST activist and thinker (1869–1940), she was a leading figure in the development of revolutionary politics in the USA and was described by J. Edgar Hoover at her deportation hearing as 'one of the most dangerous women in America'. The founder of anarcho-FEMINISM, she developed the most trenchant libertarian critique of the marriage contract since GODWIN. Goldman was born in 1869 in a Jewish ghetto in Russia. The family moved to St Petersburg to escape persecution in 1882 but she left school a few weeks later and began work in a factory. In St Petersburg she came into contact with radical students and was introduced to both nihilist and left-libertarian literature. Her father disapproved of her turn to radical politics, attempting to whip them out of her. He then tried to marry her off at fifteen. Failing in both endeavours he sent her to live in AMERICA with her half-sister. Goldman learnt how the American poor lived at first hand, working in sweatshops as a seamstress and living in a slum. In 1886, four American anarchists were hanged on the flimsiest evidence for TERRORISM in Chicago. This event persuaded Goldman, by this time influenced by KROPOTKIN, that a revolutionary anarchism was required to overthrow the current order. At the age of twenty and already married, she moved to New

115

York, beginning a lifelong relationship with Alexander Berkman, and living in a *ménage á trois* with the artist Fedya, rejecting traditional sexual mores as outdated and authoritarian. Goldman was to take lovers of both sexes during her lifetime, applying the principles of sexual libertarianism that were the subject of much of her writing.

Temporarily embracing political violence, in 1892 Goldman planned an assassination with Berkman, for which he was imprisoned. In 1893 she was imprisoned for urging the unemployed to 'expropriate' bread if they were hungry. Her speeches at her trial gained her national notoriety as an advocate of atheism, free love and revolution. She was also conducting lecture tours, editing *Mother Earth*, a radical literary and artistic magazine, and developing her own writing. Falsely implicated in the assassination of President McKinley in 1901, she was imprisoned for a short period. She later served a sentence for distributing birth control literature and in 1917 was again imprisoned for two years for organizing rallies against the First World War. She and Berkman were deported to Russia in 1919. Goldman was at first enthused but quickly became disillusioned with the stifling of free speech, the corruption of the COMMUNIST Party and the growing persecution and use of forced labour. The last straw was Trotsky's use of the Red Army to crush strikes by the workers and sailors of Kronstadt. In 1921, Goldman and Berkman left for Europe. Goldman settled for a while in England where her very early criticism of SOVIET Russia made her as unpopular with the Left as she already was with the Right. In 1936 she travelled to Barcelona to join the struggle against Franco and fascism. She was made responsible for rallying support for the anarchist CNT–FAI in Britain (see SPANISH ANARCHIST MILITIAS). She continued to support the party despite her misgivings over their participation in the coalition republican government – she was (justifiably) nervous about the role in the coalition of the Soviet-dominated communist party. After the victory of Franco and the spread of fascism she settled in Toronto and died in 1940.

Many of Goldman's ideas are close to Kropotkin's anarcho-COMMUNISM. Her most original contributions are her defence of individuality and her creation of a feminist dimension to anarchist theory. Drawing on STIRNER and Nietzsche, she argued that society cannot be freed simply through mass action; it also requires liberated individuals. She was sceptical of the revolutionary potential of the masses having directly experienced the intolerance and prejudice of ordinary Americans. This said, she was no élitist individualist, as she simultaneously argued for 'a society based on voluntary cooperation of productive groups, COMMUNITIES and societies loosely FEDERATED together, eventually developing into free communism, actuated by a solidarity of interests'. She remained committed to SYNDICALISM and the revolutionary potential of DIRECT ACTION, industrial sabotage and the general strike. Although an early advocate of revolutionary violence, she later revised her views, insisting that methods and means cannot be separated. Social revolution required the transformation of individual consciousness, not just external social and economic relations. Goldman remained a firm believer in the need for revolutionary change but thought that it was more likely to be achieved through example and education. She thus herself lived in defiance of convention and published her experiences in her frank autobiography *Living My Life* in 1931. She was also a supporter of the work of Francisco Ferrer and the FREE SCHOOL movement.

Goldman's opposition to suffrage isolated her from the feminists of her own day but led to her growing influence on feminism in the 1970s. Whilst entirely agreeing that women were entitled to the vote as much as men, she sought a far more fundamental transformation of relations. Again she felt that personal EMPOWERMENT and a change of consciousness on the part of women was required. She railed against marriage, considering it a form of economic and sexual slavery. She was also a strong advocate of women's rights to control their own bodies, fertility and sexual behaviour on the basis of love and desire rather than convention. Despite her advocacy of free love this was not simply a call for libertarian promiscuity. Writing of her own feelings, she said: 'My love is sex, but it is devotion, care, anxiety, patience, friendship, it is all....' Her overriding conviction was that all human beings should be free to follow their own desires within voluntaristic COMMUNITIES. Revolution might bring about a communist society, but should not stop there. It must also end ways of thinking that limit and oppress the individual.

GRAMEEN BANK

'*Unless we create an environment that enables us to discover the limits of our potential, we will never know what we have inside of us.*'
Appalled by media images of the 1974 famine in northern Bangladesh, Muhammad Yunus, an economics professor at the University of Chittagong, began to take what he called a 'worm's eye' view of poverty in a village called Jobra, near the university campus. Based on his observations of the difficulty of getting credit for small business activities, and his own small loans to people in the village, he and colleagues established the 'village

bank' as a research project at the university. This was a bank owned by the poor, which lent to the poor. The success of the project meant that by 1979 Grameen had received some government support and was spreading across the country, becoming an independent bank by 1983. In 1989, the 'Grameen Trust' was established to replicate the microcredit approach on a worldwide basis. At the time of writing, Grameen has over 1,500 branches across Bangladesh, and has branched out into a variety of profit and not-for-profit activities, including housing loans, no-interest loans to beggars, mobile phones and internet to distant rural villages, a textiles plant, an alternative energy company and so on.

Like FRIENDLY SOCIETIES, MUTUALISM and CREDIT UNIONS, microcredit banks such as Grameen are attempts to reimagine the structure of finance in a more COLLECTIVE manner. The principal of 'microcredit' involves making loans for amounts that are too small for ordinary banks to be interested in, and at very low interest rates. Loans are usually made to 'solidarity groups' of five people, with the penalty that no member of the group is given any further credit if one person defaults. This has meant that Grameen's bad debts have been very low. Of considerable importance, the vast majority of the loans have been made to women.

The Grameen project has been massively successful, and it has (to date) lent well over £3 billion to nearly five million people. It has also encouraged the development of many other similar approaches aimed at the 'pre-bankable' poor, including various state and NGO funds that are available to support microcredit banks. It has gained increasing acceptance from a variety of sources, and the United Nations claimed 2005 as the 'International Year of Microcredit'. Small-scale investment, it is claimed, develops more enduring pathways out of poverty than the donation of aid. Grameen leaves the way open for new forms of COMMUNITY banking and lending that are not directly concerned with issues of profitability. For example, the 'Ripple Project' is an internet-based attempt to establish a global system of borrowing and lending based on countless direct trust relationships between friends. In principle, large financial institutions would then become redundant, since (like informal *hawala* or *hundi* systems of trusted financial intermediaries used in parts of Africa and Asia) there is no need for a lender of last resort. Everyone who has relationships of trust with anyone else can act like a bank. That being said, even Muhammed Yunus recognizes that microcredit is not, on its own, the answer to the problems of poverty. It is difficult to see how, for example, Ripple could build and run schools or railways unless organization was radically decentralized on a global basis. Nonetheless, as a GRASSROOTS attempt to solve the problem of credit within a capitalist context, it has been remarkably successful.

GRASSROOTS Movements of ordinary citizens organizing to change the conditions within which they live. They emerge out of a distrust of authority and hierarchy, whether vested in the state, large corporations, institutions, or the MARKET, and favour participative DEMOCRACY over representative democracy. Power is kept as close as possible to those affected by its operation. As a result, grassroots movements tend to privilege struggles rooted in local COMMUNITIES, although these LOCAL movements can be connected through NETWORKS that establish solidarity between different struggles. For example, People's Global Action is a network that grew out of an international ZAPATISTA gathering in 1998 to coordinate actions between grassroots movements worldwide that share an opposition to capitalism and a commitment to DIRECT ACTION. In grassroots movements, the methods for bringing about social change and the goals of social change are not easily distinguishable. By definition they are committed to direct action as a means of bringing change, and direct action already constitutes part of social change towards greater citizens' participation in, and control over, the construction of their lives and communities.

One key issue for grassroots activism is to ensure that people have the means to define and control the terms and nature of their participation. Education and the constitution of knowledge are important concerns here that have been addressed, for example, through consciousness raising as well as the development (or reappropriation) of local knowledge (see APPROPRIATE TECHNOLOGY, FREIRE). Another consideration is to challenge structures such as sexism or racism that prevent some members from participating. In order to take control over their lives, people also need to have access to means of production, whether land (MST) or capital (COOPERATIVES; CREDIT UNIONS; GRAMEEN BANK). Grassroots movements are not associated with any particular political perspective and they have emerged in relation to many issues and campaigns. An emphasis on decentralization, LOCALIZATION, and self-management, however, has made grassroots organizing a central principle of movements such as ANARCHISM, some versions of ENVIRONMENTALISM, and ANTI-CAPITALISM. (See, for example, BATTLE OF SEATTLE, CENTRI SOCIALI, CHIPKO, COMMUNITY-SUPPORTED AGRICULTURE, DISOBBEDIENTI, ECO-VILLAGES, LETS, VIA CAMPESINA.)

GUERRILLA The term (literally 'small war' in Spanish) was first used to refer to the actions of irregular Spanish troops who fought Napoleon's French army using hit-and-run tactics. However, these tactics can be traced back to the writing of Sun Tzu, a Chinese military strategist who lived over 2,000 years ago, and they were deployed against the Roman empire. Guerrilla warfare has played a significant role in modern history, notably in liberation and nationalist movements in South-east Asia and South America. Guerrillas follow a NETWORK model; they operate through small, decentralized, mobile and flexible cells (see also SECRET SOCIETIES). As a strategy, guerrilla warfare avoids mass confrontation and instead relies on protracted campaigns of SMALL operations that aim to gradually wear down the enemy. Guerrillas compensate for their inferiority in terms of numbers and equipment by their flexible style of operation and swift actions. Their tactics are based on intelligence, ambush, deception, sabotage and espionage, rather than the use of brute force. The principle is to prevent enemy forces using their full might by dispersing the struggle across multiple points of action. Dispersion makes them difficult to locate and contain. These characteristics of guerrilla warfare are aptly captured by Robert Taber's metaphor of 'The War of the Flea'. 'The flea bites, hops, and bites again, nimbly avoiding the foot that would crush him. He does not seek to kill his enemy at a blow, but to bleed him and feed on him.... All this requires time.... The military enemy suffers the dog's disadvantages: too much to defend, too small and agile an enemy to come to grips with.' In addition, many writers on guerrilla warfare stress the importance of establishing a civilian base and support. Both Ché Guevara and MAO TSE-TUNG argued that guerrilla success rested on getting the people on their side.

Guerrilla tactics have been deployed by insurgent groups against stronger powers throughout history. Notable examples in contemporary history include various national resistance movements during the Second World War, and later in China and CUBA. The Vietcong commanded by Ho Chi Minh in North Vietnam provide some of the most powerful images of guerrilla warfare, and succeeded in defeating the much stronger AMERICAN army. Separatist groups such as the IRA in Ireland and ETA in Spain and France have also relied on guerrilla tactics, as have Chechen separatist groups against Russian rule. Many movements who have linked their struggle for justice or liberation to ANTI-CAPITALISM also rely on guerrilla tactics (see for example BLACK BLOC, ZAPATISTAS). Finally, many groups in the Arabic world have deployed guerrilla tactics against the US-led coalition.

At this point, it should become clear that whether a particular struggle using violent tactics is described in terms of guerrilla warfare, freedom fighting or TERRORISM is contentious. Some have tried to distinguish guerrilla resistance and terrorism by suggesting that whilst terrorism instils a reign of terror by targeting indiscriminately the regime it opposes, civilians as well as soldiers, guerrillas target their violence at the enemy's armed forces. This argument would fit guerrilla theories that emphasize the importance of building and drawing upon popular support. However, this line of distinction quickly becomes blurred when one considers attacks on civilians working for or supporting the enemy's regime (as when the French resistance movement targeted collaborators during the Second World War). Thus how violent struggles are described depends on perspective, and maybe on their degree of success in overturning the status quo. Many modern states rest on foundations built through guerrilla warfare (Cuba, China, Algeria), and many contemporary protest movements using force have been condemned as 'terrorist', particularly in the aftermath of 9/11.

GUILDS Guilds controlled economic relationships throughout the Middle Ages and into the seventeenth century. Merchant guilds appeared in the late eleventh century and consisted of the merchants and traders in a town. As trade grew, these merchant guilds eventually split into craft guilds that were organized on the basis of particular activities. By the fourteenth century, tradespeople like silversmiths, goldsmiths and jewellers would have developed their own organizations, having previously been part of a single guild. Ironmongers, blacksmiths and armourers followed the same pattern of development. Parents, having decided on the future occupation of a male child, would send him to live with a craftsman of the appropriate guild as his 'apprentice'. In return for menial labour and food and lodging, the apprentice would be taught the skills of the trade. If, after about seven to nine years, suitable progress had been made, the apprentice would transfer to 'journeyman' status. He would now receive wages and be deemed eligible to go into partnership with another journeyman or master. At this point, the journeyman also secured full membership of the guild. To achieve the position of 'master', the guild member was required to submit his best piece of work to the guildhouse. Here other masters would determine whether the work was of sufficient quality to designate master status.

Masters played an important role in the governance of the guild and in administrating its numerous activities. Guilds are sometimes viewed as the forerunners of TRADE UNIONS in representing the collective interests of their members and SYNDICALIST unionism was sometimes called 'guild SOCIALISM'. Guilds also attempted to regulate the market by protecting it from outsiders and those who tried to undercut prices; they worked to maintain the uniform quality of goods, and they organized training. Entrance to the guild was controlled through specific interventions concerning approved hours of work, methods, number of employees, prices and so on. The use of new innovations was prohibited unless available to all. The intention was to maintain strict equality between guild members. Masters constituted guild 'courts' where judgement was made on those accused of transgressing policy and arbitrated in disputes between members. Guilds also had a religious and social function. They offered support to widows and orphans and those guild members unable to work (see FRIENDLY SOCIETIES).

Guilds remained powerful and prominent into the sixteenth century, but the Reformation brought suppression. In Britain thousands of guilds were 'audited' and those with strong religious purposes were disbanded. The remainder who were able to demonstrate exclusive craft purpose were required to pay large fees to continue to operate. By the seventeenth century the power of guilds had declined significantly in Protestant countries. Although they remained strong for a time in Catholic nations, France abolished guilds after its REVOLUTION and Napoleon proceeded to disband guilds in occupied countries thereafter. FREEMASONRY is probably a cultural relic of guild organization in terms of a particular pattern of bourgeois association. (WS)

GULLIVER'S TRAVELS Between 1714 and 1726 Jonathan Swift (1667–1745) wrote this extraordinary series of fictional travels which mostly satirized Hanoverian England, but also opened the possibility of different ways of living that might be kinder and more rational. Earlier satires like Bishop Joseph Hall's *Mundus Alter et Idem* (*Another World and Yet the Same*, 1605) had contained slapstick parodies of countries populated by fat people or drunks, but Swift's book is really the first serious DYSTOPIAN novel. When complete the book contained tragicomic accounts of Lemuel Gulliver's visits to various islands, usually by means of a shipwreck. Most of the visits are written as thinly disguised accounts of Swift's world. The pomposity of the minute Lilliputians (and their enemies in Blefuscu) exposes the self-importance of the English in their pointless battles with the French. The grand perspective of the gigantic inhabitants of Brobdingnag shows Gulliver's world as small and verminous, even if the Brobdingnagians' contempt for human beings betrays their own self-importance. In Laputa, the flying island, and its fiefdom Balnibarbi, the fetishisms of technology and abstract speculation are shown to be so much hot air (a likely target of Swift's satire here was the Royal Society, see NEW ATLANTIS). Glubb-dubdrib provides an opportunity to see that the grand figures of human history are just as sordid as its present ones, whilst Luggnagg's long-lived Struldbrugs show why it is better that human beings die rather than live forever.

Yet, at the same time, there are elements to these worlds that are often rather praiseworthy. The Lilliputians not only punish bad behaviour (with particularly severe penalties for lying and breaking trust) but reward people who have never committed any offences. They also have public nurseries and little sex distinction in education. The Brobdingnagians have a system of knowledge and law that only values pragmatic application and clarity, and they are contemptuous of the sophistries of the academics and lawyers that Gulliver describes. This UTOPIANISM becomes clearest in the last voyage, to the land of the Houyhnhnms, a race of calm and rational horses who use primitive people (Yahoos) as slaves. These horses have no words in their language for lying, power, government, war, law, punishment, and so on, and hence they are appalled by Gulliver's increasingly critical account of his Yahoo 'civilization'. This is not because they blame their Yahoos for being Yahoos – that is their nature, after all – but that these Yahoos who claim reason should fail so badly in being reasonable suggests a greater corruption. The Houyhnhnms live a simple ARCADIAN and egalitarian existence and practise a form of voluntary eugenics by choosing mates who will result in a desirable mixture of characteristics. They educate foals virtually the same, regardless of sex, value exercise and athleticism, and make decisions through four-yearly assemblies. (They do keep the Yahoos as slaves, however, and even consider exterminating them.)

In general, human beings do not come out well in Swift's worlds. It would be easy enough to classify him as a witty misanthrope, and certainly not a utopian in any simple sense. However, what the stylistic cleverness of *Gulliver's Travels* reveals neatly is the utopian impulse buried in dystopian accounts. Swift may be endlessly disappointed by the present state of human beings, but he appears to hope that they learn something from the distorting mirror that he usually presents them with, and cultivate their kinder and more rational aspects. Gulliver's inability to live amongst his family of Yahoos when he returns from his final voyage suggests that he, at least, has been changed. Perhaps the lonely misanthrope is the only one able to be realistic about the possibility of social change, unlike the relentlessly cheerful utopians who present a tidy final solution to all social problems, often without much reference to how we get from the dirty world of 'here' to the completed utopia over 'there'. Paradoxically, then, dystopians needs more optimism than utopians, because they know how difficult the journey will be.

H

HAYDEN, DOLORES Born in 1945, now Professor of Architecture, Urbanism and American Studies at Yale University, Hayden has written social criticism that demonstrates how the physical environment constitutes social life. She has not simply theorized from a distance, but been actively involved in political and artistic interventions to explore how the spatial might be lived differently. This combination of theory and practice provides a keystone in her analysis of how UTOPIAN experiments bring their theories and ideals into concrete forms and everyday practices. In doing this, she charts the material construction of significant INTENTIONAL COMMUNITIES: the balance between individual, sub-group and collective; the constitution, integration or separation of 'productive work', 'domestic work', leisure and worship; the nature of gender relations and the gendered division of labour; and, in all of these, the operation of power, control and autonomy within the formation and maintenance of COMMUNITIES.

Hayden's major work is *Seven American Utopias: The Architecture of Com - munitarian Socialism 1790–1975* (1976). In this she examines how seven utopian communities turned their beliefs into built forms: the SHAKERS, Mormons, FOURIERISTS, ONEIDA Perfectionists, Inspirationists, Union Colonists, and LLANO Colonists. Hayden explains her work as being about the relationship between the members of these experimental communities, their forms of social organization, and the complex, collective environments they created. She contrasts the creative practice of designing and building these communities with the dreary extravagance of much utopian writing. Central to the creation of community, she argues, is that a group must achieve a balance between authority and participation, community and privacy, uniqueness and replicability.

Just as the utopian communities diverged from one another in ideals, so they developed different built forms for the expression of these beliefs. For example, the Shakers developed a series of differentiated spaces to separate off the sexes, along with graduated levels of participation in the community. Different activities were separated, often through a gendered division of labour, and thus contact between members of different groups was limited. Yet within the religious meetings these constraints were largely removed, creating different experiences of 'earthly' and 'heavenly' spaces. In these ways, the Shakers constructed their community as a 'living building'. In contrast, the Fourierist community of New York State, established in 1843, was designed to bring community members together in varied social interactions and activities. The members had to fight off designs for buildings intended to give a grandiose exterior expression of Fourierism. These plans were promulgated by influential supporters of Fourier's ideals who were not part of the community. The members themselves believed in participation in the design process, allowing buildings to be developed gradually as an expression of community, and carrying out the building themselves rather than using external labour. They constructed their own, locally inspired, versions of the 'Galleries of Association', with communal spaces balanced with individual rooms and provision for families to build private cottages.

Utopian communities also learnt spatial principles from each other. Hayden's comment on the multiple spaces of the ONEIDA Community of Perfectionists is that they had borrowed socio-petal designs from the Shakers and socio-fugal ones from the Fourierists. Although a religious community based on principles of 'Bible Communism', the Oneida Community was thoroughly radical in regard to personal and sexual relations. Its system of 'complex marriage' sought to prevent the exclusivity of long-term pairings, and this was institutionalized through forms of spatial control. For example, they developed a pattern of 'mixed use' spaces, where communal areas such as sitting and dining rooms were interspersed with bedrooms. This increased sociability and prevented loneliness, but also acted as a form of surveillance to maintain complex marriage. Bedroom doors were visible from sitting rooms, discouraging exclusive relationships, and the bedrooms themselves were designed so they could not facilitate the splitting of small groups as an alternative to the deliberately designed communal spaces. In contrast to this form of peer surveillance the Shaker community embodied and enacted the discipline of the community, whilst simultaneously negotiating the importance of the individual. Not only clothes but also furniture was made to measure for the individual, using community skills. There was a strong emphasis on the design and innovation of tools and materials to fit the exact purposes of the community. Thus members were surrounded physically by the work of other believers.

In *The Grand Domestic Revolution* (1981), Hayden turns her attention to

FEMINIST UTOPIAN ideals, and a largely forgotten project within feminism. The 'material feminists' of the nineteenth century saw the home as a source of exploitation for women through the physical and economic separation of the public/private spheres. Whereas feminist literary utopias have largely turned to the creation of alternative spaces where a different form of womanhood or gender relations may be lived out, and the COMMUNITARIAN utopias built isolated communities, for over sixty years the material feminists tried to develop their utopian ideals within ordinary, everyday spaces. Thus, as well as the first call for the remuneration of domestic work, there were long-lived utopian experiments with communal kitchens and their converse, the 'kitchenless house' (see HERLAND). Melusina Fay Pierce advocated 'cooperative housework', and there was the development of neighbourhood nurseries, housewives' cooperatives and community dining clubs, thus moving out from the single-family dwelling to the redesign of residential areas. A number of social forces contributed to the difficulty of sustaining these utopian plans, such as the development of domestic consumerism combined with a growth of women's employment outside the home. When the second wave of feminism developed in the 1970s, it had forgotten the insights of the material feminists that spatial design reinforced gender inequality, and instead turned towards extracting women from the home, into public spaces still constructed and dominated by men, not recognizing the need to transform either space or the relations between them. (KD)

HERLAND A FEMINIST UTOPIA written by Charlotte Perkins Gilman (1860–1935), US writer and editor of a progressive journal, *The Forerunner*. In *Woman and Economics* (1898) Gilman also wrote about the sexual division of labour and kitchenless houses (see HAYDEN). *Herland* was published in 1915, and is the best-known of three utopian novels she wrote, the others being *Moving the Mountain* (1911) and *With Her in Ourland* (1916). *Moving the Mountain* describes an America in which men and women have learnt to live a SOCIALIST life together, but *Herland* describes a utopia with no men at all. Three male explorers hear tales of a strange woman land. They locate it at the top of a plateau in the middle of a fecund jungle, accessible only by a collapsible aeroplane they have brought with them. The novel unfolds as these three Victorian men (one a chauvinist adventurer, one a poetic fantasist, and the narrator a fairly reflexive 'sociologist') explore the isolated society that they discover. The best elements of the UTOPIA concern the quiet puzzlement and lucid intelligence that the women express at the men's illogical ideas concerning gender and social organization.

Herland is populated by women who lack the insecurity and desire to please that Gilman suggests is characteristic of most women. Two thousand years previously, the men of their race killed each other, and the isolated women began to reproduce parthenogenetically. These people are athletic, short haired, healthy and practise a gradual form of social improvement that is focused on their intense collective responsibilities to their children and the cultivation of their largely ARCADIAN land. Certain women are permitted to be mothers, but a limited division of labour means that education is carried out by different specialists, agriculture by others, counselling by others and so on. Whilst Gilman's vision is sometimes curiously nationalistic in its version of the matriarchal river of life, her superb characterization of women who do not measure themselves against men is often revealed in the eloquence with which they speak these new lives. The ECOFEMINIST and SUSTAINABILITY themes, too, are surprisingly modern. The sequel, *With Her in Ourland*, tells of the travels of the sociologist and his new Herland partner in the world beyond, and (despite similar racist and nationalist undertones) continues the theme of an ironic questioning of the varied class and gender inequalities that they find.

I

ILLICH, IVAN

'... the fraud perpetrated by the salesman of schools is less obvious but more funda-mental than the self-satisfied salemanship of the Coca-Cola or Ford representative because the schoolman hooks his people on a much more demanding drug.'

A radical educationalist and social thinker, Illich was born in Vienna in 1926, and died in Bremen in 2002. He began as a catholic priest in New York, and then became vice-rector of the Catholic University of Puerto Rico. In 1961 he founded the increasingly radical Centro Intercultural de Documentación in Mexico. After facing hostility from the church, it was eventually closed in 1976, by which time Illich had already resigned his position as a priest. He spent the rest of his life concentrating on teaching and writing. His first and most famous book, *Deschooling Society* (1971), a rgued for the replacement of prison-like institutions for education by life-long learning webs (see WIKIPEDIA). Even alternative schools like SUMMERHILL were not radical enough for Illich, who was consistently anti-institutional in his outlook, coming closer to older ideas about AUTO-DIDACTICISM than contemporary forms of democratic schooling (see also FREIRE). His other major polemical work was *Medical Nemesis* (1974), an attack on the medical profession and their institutions that questioned professional conceptions of health and illness and coined the term 'iatrogenesis' – illnesses created by hospitals.

His hostility to the institutional structures of the Catholic Church, to the organizations that govern work and economic life, and the sexual division of labour (in *Gender*, 1982) made him a genuinely heterodox thinker. He questioned the dependency that we have on 'experts', and re-described professions as knowledge monopolies that create passive consumers. Yet his work was not merely negative. In place of the conservative institutions of power he stressed human creativity, COMMUNITY and hospitality – and NETWORKS rather than hierarchies (see LETS). To a certain extent this represented a faith in the traditional, 'vernacular' skills of ordinary people in SELF-SUFFICIENT, pre-industrial economies – hence his life-long interest in the 'development' of the economies of the global south. Perhaps paradoxically, he also had considerable faith in the potential of new technology to DEMOCRATIZE the ownership of information. Best described as an ANARCHIST with similarities to the work of BOOKCHIN, Illich's ROMANTICISM also has nostalgic and conservative elements. However, his writings are elegant and inspirational.

INDUSTRIAL DEMOCRACY By analogy with political or state democracy, a description of democratic practices as applied to workplaces. There are two major ways of thinking about this concept. The first involves some LIBERAL conception of representative structures (see DEMOCRACY) that allow workers to have influence over decision making, responsibility and authority. The extent of such influence can vary substantially, from an employer's 'suggestion scheme', through workplace methods such as 'teamworking', up to the various forms of consultation and co-determination exemplified by KALMAR, Semco or the JOHN LEWIS PARTNERSHIP and the QUALITY OF WORKING LIFE movement. Whilst these examples provide illustrations of alternative forms of organizing, they all largely rely on the idea of EMPOWERMENT as something which MANAGEMENT does to workers. In other words, management and owners still have the ultimate sanction, and could withdraw democratic privileges if they wished.

The more radical way of thinking about industrial democracy would be in terms of WORKER SELF-MANAGEMENT. In this case a COOPERATIVE or an employee share ownership plan (ESOP) would mean that all those working for an organization would have a direct share in its profits and losses. As a result, they would have a clear interest in participating in democratic mechanisms to elect or deselect those who coordinate organizational activities; to dictate strategy; to take profits or reinvest, and so on (see MONDRAGÒN; SUMA). Both forms of industrial democracy have been credited with increasing the motivation and commitment of workers, as well as increasing productivity and decreasing labour turnover. Whilst advocates of the liberal version might suggest that these were good things to achieve because they can increase shareholder or owner value, for the radicals all these would be secondary to the idea that labour might escape alienation in a MARXIST sense. In other words, liberal ideas about job satisfaction are pale reflections of the conception of work as a form of human expression (see FOURIER).

Forms of TRADE UNIONISM may be relevant to both aspects of industrial democracy, though in the former they would largely be restricted to being a pressure group for democratization or a representative for workers 'interests' through collective bargaining. There is a grey area here, of course, because forms of representation can be radical in themselves, such as the idea of 'worker directors' put forward in the UK 'Bullock Report on Industrial Democracy' (1977). This report advocated trade union representation equal to shareholder representation on the boards of any companies that had more than 2,000 employees. Despite the wide publicity given to the report at a time of considerable industrial unrest, employers were clearly hostile and unions ambivalent. The report's recommendations were never implemented, though EU initiatives are now raising similar ideas on an Europe-wide basis. Anarcho-syndicalist trade unions (see ANARCHISM, SYNDICALISM) or GUILD socialists such the US 'Industrial Workers of the World' (IWW, or 'Wobblies') and the Spanish 'Confederación Nacional del Trabajo' sponsor a vision of radical industrial democracy based on overthrowing the capitalist system through a general strike and establishing an industrial form of COMMUNISM. The IWW's 'wobbly shop' model presumes the election of managers by workers, and the ending of the 'wage system'.

A phrase like 'industrial democracy' should be used with care. It has a wide range of meanings, with the liberal managerial ones now particularly dominant, and a wide range of built-in assumptions. One should not uncritically assume that democracy, in itself, is a pre-eminent value; or that the workplace, in itself, is a crucial site for democratic practice. Democracy may not matter everywhere and all of the time, and good work may not always be democratic (see BUREAUCRACY). In addition, it is quite possible to imagine a cooperatively owned organization or trade union with highly anti-democratic practice, and paternalistic owners who employ democratic practices. That being said, any conception of alternative organization must in some way reflect the interests and aspirations of alternative organizers, and it is difficult to see how some version of industrial democracy could ever be completely irrelevant to such a project.

INDUSTRIAL WORKERS OF THE WORLD, see INDUSTRIAL DEMOCRACY

INDYMEDIA (INDEPENDENT MEDIA CENTRE) A global alternative news forum that has been closely associated with the ANTI-CAPITALIST movement. It was founded in November 1999 in opposition

to government and corporate sponsored media to provide coverage of the
BATTLE OF SEATTLE. Indymedia developed into a decentralized NETWORK of
local centres (160 in 2005). Each operates independently once accepted
within the network and is expected to develop its own editorial policy and
form of self-governance. Indymedia strives to be non-hierarchical, although
some forms of hierarchies based on access to resources have been difficult
to avoid and there is great variety between different centres. One of the
defining features of Indymedia, and the foundation of its independence,
is its open publishing policy. This means that anyone with internet access
can participate in the process of news making and decide on the content
and nature of news coverage. Indymedia offers a forum for independent
and DEMOCRATIC DIY journalism. For similar web COMMUNITY
programmes see the financial 'Ripple Project' (see GRAMEEN BANK), OPEN
SOURCE SOFTWARE and WIKIPEDIA.

INTERMEDIATE TECHNOLOGY, see APPROPRIATE TECHNOLOGY

INTENTIONAL COMMUNITY Like COMMUNE, a general term for
a residential COMMUNITY which has in some way been more or less
consciously designed in order to encourage certain forms of interaction (see,
for example, BROOK FARM, CRYSTAL WATERS, FINDHORN, ONEIDA, TWIN OAKS).
These might include enviromental awareness (see ECOVILLAGE), forms of
religious or spiritual affiliation, personal growth, or radically DEMOCRATIC
decision making and egalitarian economic governance. Whether the term
includes planned settlements which are larger, and perhaps more diverse
(see AUROVILLE, CHRISTIANIA, GARDEN CITIES) is questionable, as is the
question of CULT homes and communities, and perhaps older religious
settlements (see AMISH). Definitionally, it would be difficult to exclude these
cases, but the term more often refers to SMALL communities that develop
an egalitarian, eco or gender politics – though not all would have these
qualities.

INTERNATIONALS Four organizations that sought to coordinate a
variety of left-wing political groups, parties, and TRADE UNIONS. This was
based on the notion of building a FEDERATED working-class organization
capable of fomenting and coordinating the transition to SOCIALISM or COM-
MUNISM. 'The International Workingmen's Association', more commonly
known as the First International, was founded in 1864 in London. *The*

Communist Manifesto was written by Marx and ENGELS to provide a political programme for the International. Membership included a number of left-wing groups, among them trade unionists, ANARCHISTS, socialists and left-republicans. In 1872 the anarchists were expelled after a fierce dispute between BAKUNIN and Marx. The split seriously weakened the organization and, after moving to AMERICA, it disbanded in 1876. The anarchists re-founded their own First International at the Berlin Congress in 1922, but meanwhile the Marxist and socialist elements had founded the Second International in 1889. Although it pursued international socialism, the Second International was perhaps the least committed to revolutionary politics of any of the Internationals, attempting to work largely through the electoral politics of the state. This difference was reflected in the fact that it was made up of established parties with a national membership base.

At its founding congress in Paris, the principles of the First International were formally adopted by delegates from 20 countries and MAY DAY was declared an international working-class holiday. Engels was a key member through his involvement with the German Social Democratic Party, and was made honorary president of the Second International in 1893. By 1900 the Russian Social Democratic Party (including LENIN) was a powerful influence. Conflict between Marxists and anarchists continued, with the anarcho-SYNDICALISTS within the 'Industrial Workers of the World' (see INDUSTRIAL DEMOCRACY) being opposed by the social democratic parties. In 1907 there were 884 delegates to the Stuttgart Congress that included the First International Conference of Socialist Women. The final congresses took place in 1912 and 1915. Although unanimous opposition to the war was avowed, many member parties supported the governments of their nations once hostilities broke out. A serious split developed between these parties and those who saw the war as something that all socialists should oppose. A last-ditch attempt to create a united front in 1915 failed but it did bring together and further radicalize the 'Left' of the Second International, laying the foundations of the Third International. In 1923, in the aftermath of the First World War and the Russian Revolution, the Second International became the Socialist International – largely an umbrella organization for dialogue between various centre-left social DEMOCRATIC parties such as the British Labour Party. It continues in this form to this day.

The Third International or Comintern was founded in 1919 by the Russian Communist Party, led by Lenin and Trotsky, with the aim of fomenting an international revolution that would ultimately lead to stateless communism. It described itself as 'the General Staff of the world revolution'. The Comintern held seven World Congresses and encouraged the formation of national Communist Parties, encouraging many revolutionary political parties to rename themselves as communist. For a party to join the Comintern it had to accept a number of policies that drew a clear distinction between revolutionary communism and reformism. From 1926 Stalin turned the Comintern into an instrument of SOVIET policy, with national Communist Parties expected to follow its instructions. This sometimes placed these parties in difficult positions – as with the suppression of SPANISH ANARCHIST MILITIAS during the Spanish Civil War, or the sudden opposition to fascism in the Second World War. In 1935 the final Congress repudiated the aim of world revolution, leading Trotsky to condemn it and to call for a Fourth International. This would carry on the original aims of the Third and oppose the increasing Stalinization of the communist movement. The Comintern was dissolved by Stalin in 1943 in order to help convince the allies that the Soviet Union had abandoned its revolutionary ambitions.

The Fourth International was founded in 1938, in Paris, to oppose Stalin's policy of 'socialism in one country'. Trotsky argued for a 'permanent revolution', required because global capitalism could only be overthrown by an international resistance. In 1939, with the outbreak of war, the headquarters of the International Secretariat moved to New York where it became heavily involved with the US Socialist Workers Party. The war made life extremely difficult. Many of its affiliated parties were wiped out by the Nazis or Japanese; others were suppressed by the allies. Despite this, the movement did manage to carry on until peacetime, incorporating the British Trotskyists. Serious splits developed after the war between those who argued that Trotsky's theory of post-war capitalist disintegration was about to be fulfilled and those who foresaw the rise of welfare states and the revival of capitalism. There were disagreements over how to regard the countries of the Eastern bloc, and disappointment concerning the tendency for revolutions to result in alliances with the Soviet Union rather than moving in an internationalist direction. By 1951, with tiny numbers, many members of the Fourth International were arguing that their future lay in joining Stalinist or Social Democratic parties and influencing them from within. This policy was bitterly opposed by those who were not willing to abandon the project. In 1953 these disagreements led to a major split, leading to a number of organizations and groups of parties claiming the title of Fourth International.

The history of the Internationals demonstrates that groups determined to bring about UTOPIAN changes could build federated international organizations to oppose the might of capitalism. The current dominance of corporate-led neoliberal globalization would seem to require a similar response. However, it might be that the era of such mass movements is over and that, in any case, their frequent slide into either fragmentation or authoritarianism has discredited them fatally.

ISLAMIC FINANCE According to the Qur'an (as well as quite a few other orthodox religions) earning money through interest on lending (*Riba*) is a sin. Money may be lent or given to the poor (see ZAKÂT), but living off the labour of others, or gambling, are both regarded as unethical (see also MUTUALISM). As a result, an alternative conception of finance, economics and banking has grown since the 1980s which attempts to partially reconcile Islamic law and custom (*Shari'a* or *Shariah*) with contemporary economics. This growth has also been driven by the increasing influence of cash-rich Muslim oil-producing countries. Economically, its objective is to promote efficiency and equity while also promoting the stability of the financial system. While modern capitalism treats money as a commodity with a market price (an interest rate), the Islamic financial system treats money only as a medium of exchange.

The basic principle is that money is given with zero interest, but in order to reflect the time value of money, several different devices are employed. These include *Mudharabah* (profit-sharing), *Musharakah* (partnership), *Murabah* (mark-up transactions), *Ijarah* (leasing), *Istisnaa* (industrial financing), and *Salam* (agricultural financing). The *Mudharabah* is a contract between an entrepreneur and a bank. The two parties agree on a profit-sharing ratio. In case of loss, the entrepreneur loses his efforts and time, while the provider of funds bears the financial loss. In a different kind of transaction, if a loan is requested for an item, the bank may buy the item on behalf of the customer but own it until the last agreed instalment is paid and the ownership then transfers to the customer. (Often there are no additional penalties for late payments.) In both of these cases, the principle is that the risks and the benefits should be shared. This encourages lenders to lend wisely, and borrowers to use wisely or spend judiciously, and hence neither to hoard nor squander their money. The Islamic system allows financial risks to be shared among the parties, and not largely shifted to the borrowers, as is often the case within a capitalist system. People who

135

deposit their money with Islamic banks are also not given interest, since the bank is seen simply as a place of safekeeping (*Wådiah*), and not somewhere that gambles with customers' money. However, people are usually rewarded with a gift (*hibah*) as thanks for allowing the bank to use their money.

Conventional individual insurance is prohibited, but an arrangement called *Takaful* allows for the risks of many people to be combined, in the same way that ZAKÂT allows for a form of social insurance (see also CREDIT UNIONS, FRIENDLY SOCIETIES). One of the differences between this and conventional commercial insurance is that, while the latter is owned by the shareholders with a pro fit motive, *Takaful* is owned by the policy holders with the objective of minimizing cost and loss. There is also a considerable emphasis on what would be called 'ethical investing'. Islamic banks' lending and investment strategies stress that firms must not have debts, cash or creditors that are excessive, because this again would be too much like gambling. Trading is not permitted with firms that deal in alcohol, pornography, gambling or pork, or are involved with any other activities deemed to be contrary to the spirit of Islam. Another important financial intermediary in Islam is the *Waqf* (charitable endowment foundation). This occurs when a privately owned property is endowed for a charitable purpose. It emphasizes that people's economic activity may not always be purely motivated by profit, but sometimes to serve the social interest or welfare of others. *Wåqf* plays a crucial role in providing essential services such as health, education and other municipal services at no cost to the government but through voluntary donation.

It has been suggested that such practices are making Islamic states and organizations uncompetitive with regard to capitalist ones, or that Islamic finance has more to do with Islamic identity than economics. However, even some commentators in the conventional financial system have come to agree about the potency of an interest-free system. In any case, the Islamic system has only been effectively established for forty years, and is growing rapidly, so any judgements may be premature. It is quite possible to argue that both religious and radical views on social justice and wealth redistribution are given concrete expression in the Muslim prohibition on *riba*. Interest systematically transfers wealth from the poor to the rich, widens inequalities, negates social solidarity, and creates an idle class of wealth owners. Rather than capitalism, red in tooth and claw, where anyone and everything can be traded, Islamic banking clearly illustrates the co-implication of MARKETS, ideas about COMMUNITY and moral and political principles (see also GRAMEEN BANK). (HM/IU)

ISLAND

'Nobody needs to go anywhere else. We are all, if only we knew it, already there.'
(The Raja's *Notes on What's What*)

Like FOURIER's 'Harmony', Aldous Huxley's *Island* (1962) is a place where rationalism and naturalism come together to produce a UTOPIA which reflected some of the more radical ideas that were to shape the counterculture of the West during the 1960s. In some sense, the novel is a mirror image of his DYSTOPIAS *Brave New World* (1932), and *Ape and Essence* (1948) as well as a response to Skinner's utopia, WALDEN TWO (1948), which itself used certain ideas from Huxley's dystopia. All these books describe very similar techniques for producing happy people, but underpin them with radically different justifications.

Pala is an island that cut itself off from the influences of both capitalism and COMMUNISM, instead developing a society that is shaped by a rationalist use of Eastern spiritual practices. The narrator (a cynical and damaged journalist) is shipwrecked on an island that (like the one in Diderot's SUPPLEMENT TO BOUGAINVILLE'S VOYAGE) seems to be much more innocent than the urban world he has left behind. Yet, as he discovers more about their way of life he begins to admire their sophistication, and regret his minor role in the oil-inspired invasion that threatens Pala at the end of the novel. Pala's story begins when a doctor successfully treated the Raja of Pala with a combination of hypnotism and surgery at the beginning of the nineteenth century. Together they decide to reform the island with an evolving set of beliefs summarized aphoristically in the reforming Raja's *Notes on What's What*. The spirituality of Pala is essentially Taoist, an acceptance of the world and everything in it, combined with an intense practical attention to states of mind and body. This includes teaching the 'yoga of love', as well providing medication to suppress personalities that are likely to cause harm to themselves and others.

Birds have been taught to parrot the word 'attention' in order to continually remind the Palanese of the need to be mindful. The use of meditation, visualization (or 'destiny control'), occasional hallucinogenic drugs, and scientific enquiry helps to train people in the practical things that they can do to deal with the suffering of the world, and gradually improve the society that they live in. Organizationally, this is a

137

FEDERATION of self-governing units with no state, army or church, where crime is being treated through therapy. The richest are allowed to be only four or five times wealthier than the average; the Palanese encourage temporary work placements, and discourage overproduction (except in the case of particular export goods). Producer and consumer COOPERATIVES are backed up by CREDIT UNIONS, and the population self-controlled to limit the strain on resources. Children are taught techniques to help crops to be more productive as well as eugenic methods of improving the Palanese race through artificial insemination. Sexual exploration (of any form) is encouraged, and children are parented within a Mutual Adoption Club of about twenty families. The word 'mother' is the name of a temporary function, not a permanent relationship, and various forms of behavourial conditioning (see WALDEN TWO) are used with young children to help them learn a generous attitude towards the world. Whatever the topic, the Palanese are resolutely anti-dogmatic, delivering contraceptives to every-one by post every month and using all and any physical or mental technique that they believe might be useful to improve their world.

Pala is invaded because of capitalism, combined with its own pacificism. Its survival (like utopian literature itself) was only possible in a simpler age, though Huxley leaves enough ambiguity to suggest that its beliefs might not be extinguished that easily. Like most twentieth-century utopias (see THE DISPOSSESSED, WOMAN ON THE EDGE OF TIME) *Island* is a complex book which can be read in many different ways. Like *Brave New World*, this is a book about happiness, the difference being that *Island* presents happiness as awareness, not sedation or dogmatism. It lacks the breathless optimism of earlier utopias, but presents a vision of a society in which issues of mental training are given as much attention as practical organization. Huxley's book helps to remind the reader that the organization of alternatives is unlikely to succeed if it concentrates solely on either mind or body.

ISLE OF PINES Henry Neville (1620–94) published this short book in 1668. An oddly subversive patriarchal 'pornotopia', the book was trans-lated into several languages, and probably had an influence on ROBINSON CRUSOE. The ROMANTIC idea of the 'noble savage' was, in many ways, a highly sexualized one (see Diderot's SUPPLEMENT TO BOUGAINVILLE'S VOYAGE), and Neville allows his imagination to wander. The story is told as the account of a Dutch trader, Henry Cornelius Van Sloetten, who discovers an ARCADIAN island with an English-speaking semi-naked population of two thousand people. The King, William Pine, gives Van Sloetten a copy of his grandfather's diary. This recounts how, in 1569, George Pine was shipwrecked on an island with only four women for company: his master's daughter, two servants, and a black slave. Free from moralizing and institutions, he sets to work and dies with over 1,700 hundred descendants. The book is replete with details of the efficiency and organization of Pine's work, though he could only manage the black slave woman at night when he didn't have to look at her. There were no predators, the weather was always balmy and food easy to find. The incest taboo appeared not to be a problem, but by the time Pine was sixty (with great grandchildren), it became possible to re-introduce it, as well as the observation of Christianity and Bible readings.

The second part of the narrative tells rather a different story. William Pine tells how, after his grandfather's narrative ended, the four families who were descended from each matriarch began to engage in wanton incest and rape, and the Bible fell into neglect. The family who were descended from the black slave were the worst offenders, and it was hence required that 'good and wholesome laws' needed to be passed (mostly involving the death penalty) to prevent adultery, blasphemy, rape and so on. Despite the cautionary aspect of the second part of the tale, Neville concludes with some general praise for the Isle of Pines, which if it were cultivated by European methods, would be equal in civilization to anything found in the civilized world. It is almost as if he can't quite convince himself that a 'state of nature' could surpass the organized COMMONWEALTHS from which the travellers come. Like his contemporaries More (see UTOPIA), Bacon (see NEW ATLANTIS) and Harrington (see OCEANA), he must conclude that UTOPIA really needs laws, not the subversions of innocence.

J

JOHN LEWIS PARTNERSHIP When the English retailer John Spedan Lewis joined the family business at the age of 19 in the early twentieth century he began to question the inequalities that enabled his family to draw more in profit each year than the entire staff received in pay. Gradually taking on responsibility for managing the two London department stores, he developed his ideas about changing the business and bridging the gap between workers and management. After his father's death he transferred his interest in the businesses of John Lewis and Company and Peter Jones Ltd to the workers, present and prospective, and the John Lewis Partnership was formed. The securities that comprised the payment for the transaction were subsequently surrendered to the Partnership. From the very beginning he described the Partnership as an experiment in INDUSTRIAL DEMOCRACY with progressive social aims.

In 2005 the Partnership owned 27 department stores and over 130 Waitrose supermarkets. It has a turnover in excess of £5 billion. It employs 59,000 partners, all of whom have a say in the way the business is run and receive a share of the profits. The organizational structure, strategy, and decision-making processes are still closely aligned to those laid down in 1929. The aim is that partners should not just profit financially from the business but that they should enjoy all the benefits of ownership including 'the sharing of gain, knowledge and power'. The Partnership is governed by a written constitution which is subordinate to the two settlements in trust establishing that the Partnership was to be owned in trust for the benefits of its members, who are partners from the day they are employed. The chairman and other directors are charged with upholding the constitution.

The ultimate purpose of the John Lewis Partnership is defined in its constitution as 'the happiness of all its members through their worthwhile, secure and satisfying employment in a successful business.' The co-ownership character of the Partnership is reflected in the balance of authority between the chairman, the central board, and the elected Partnership council. Each partner is based in a single constituency and given a single vote. In addition, the chairman may appoint the holder of a particular Partnership post to the council, subject to there being at least four elected members for every one he appoints. The influence of the Partnership council is wide in scope, even to the extent that if the Council judges the chairman to have failed to fulfil the responsibilities of his office it may pass a resolution to dismiss him. The central board consists of the board of directors and five partners elected by the central council. The Board has ultimate responsibility for issues of policy and for allocating financial resources. The elected partners may seek the council's opinion on any proposal that comes to the board unless the chairman argues that to do so would significantly damage the interests of an organization or person outside the Partnership.

The chairman is charged with ensuring that the Partnership retain its democratic vitality. The constitution requires the chairman to 'actively seek to share power with subordinates, delegating as much responsibility and encouraging as much initiative as possible'. The Partnership encourages partners to challenge management decisions openly both in branch council meetings and in the *In-House Journal* which is published weekly. In October 2005 the Partnership announced a review of its democratic processes following feedback from partners who felt that the democratic bodies were not effective. The Partnership is currently piloting a number of different democratic arrangements, and John Spedan Lewis's experiment in industrial democracy continues. (See also SCOTT BADER COMMONWEALTH; SUMA, TOWER COLLIERY). (AC)

JOURNEYMAN'S GUILDS, see GUILDS

K

KALMAR Whilst there have been many claims about the humanizing of capitalist work organizations, the Volvo Kalmar and Uddevalla plants provide rare examples. It has been common, since 'Human Relations' supposedly displaced 'Taylorism', for MANAGEMENT apologists to suggest that job enrichment, enlargement and rotation, or teamworking, could begin to reverse the trend to unemployment and deskilling that is generally associated with the introduction of new technology. By the 1970s it was beginning to be suggested that mass production did not necessarily involve degrading workers, partly because newer technologies combined with 'post-Fordist' (customized) production and consumption made 'up-skilling' jobs possible. So, reversing a historical trend, work was to be made more complex and AUTONOMOUS, hence enhancing the QUALITY OF WORKING LIFE.

Scandinavia, with its traditions of worker management co-determination, was one of the places where these ideas took root. Under the leadership of Per Gyllenhammar, Volvo had a tradition of experimenting with the 'socio-technical' aspects of production and a concern with the relationship between work and dignity. The Kalmar plant was completed in 1974, and was partly stimulated by the need to attract workers into an industry that was increasingly perceived as dirty and demeaning. In addition, in a high-wage, high-employment economy like Sweden's at that time, the high turnover of staff was having a considerable effect on the quality of the cars being produced, and costing a considerable amount in recruitment and absenteeism. The new plant was constructed as a series of bays with separate entrances for teams of 15–25 workers, with large windows and access to a rest area with comfortable chairs, coffee and telephones. The part-finished cars moved between the bays on Automated Guided Vehicles and each team was responsible for a general aspect of the car (wiring, upholstery or whatever) and was given discretion in how they achieved it. This included coping with absent members by exerting social pressure for equity, and hence learning conflict resolution and stress reduction techniques. A second plant at Uddevalla was begun in 1987 and opened in 1989, with the idea that each team would construct a complete car, pretty much reversing the fragmentation of craft work that industrialists like Ford had exploited.

Though there are varying accounts of this, and historical variations too, it seems that the costs at Kalmar and Uddevalla were about 30 per cent higher than comparable plants, and worse if compared to 'lean' production plants. (Though other authors have suggested that this depends on what costs and losses are taken into account.) Further, by the 1990s the tight labour market conditions that (in part) stimulated their development no longer held. As a result, in 1993, both plants were closed and production was transferred to conventional plants outside Sweden. Nonetheless, the idea of team responsibility certainly spread throughout the 1980s and 1990s, though it was often under the banner of 'total quality management', 're-engineering' or 'EMPOWERMENT'. As the Kalmar and Uddevalla experiments showed fairly clearly, a genuine attempt to humanize production organizations is unlikely to be successful if power is 'given' to workers under such specific and temporary circumstances. For power to be meaningful, it cannot to taken away when management decide to change their strategies, and it must involve the capacity to challenge those strategies themselves. Worker–management councils might be the beginning of a process, but the innovations described above did not include forms of COOPERATIVE ownership or WORKER SELF-MANAGEMENT. Whilst it is not possible to prevent managerialists from using words like 'empowerment' to describe replacing sticks with carrots, the reality of such ideas can be contrasted productively with organizations where power is shared and negotiated in much more complex ways.

KIBBUTZ This Hebrew word means 'communal settlement', one founded on a combination of ambitions for a Jewish homeland and SOCIALIST doctrine regarding equality of ownership, responsibility and reward. Theodor Herzl's UTOPIA *Altneuland* (1904) (itself inspired by Theodor Hertzka's FREELAND) is sometimes mentioned as an inspiration too. The first kibbutz is said to have been established in 1910 on Lake Galilee by Jewish immigrants to Palestine, the biblical location of Eretz Israel. The kibbutzim were central to Jewish settlement of Palestine, fuelled by the increasing persecution of Jews in Europe, and in absorbing immigrants. Kibbutzim also played a prominent part in defending the settlements against Arab opposition to the Zionist campaign, through staffing GUERRILLA armies like the Haganah and providing storage for weapons. Numbers of kibbutzim grew during the 1920s, and after more than a hundred years of Jewish settlement in the area, 268 kibbutzim, with 115,600 members (1.7 per cent

143

of the population of Israel), existed by the end of 2002. Most are located in the north and south of the country.

This form of alternative organization is based on horizontal COLLECTIVISM: shared ownership of property, including the means of production; DEMOCRATIC management and decision making; the principle of 'from each according to their ability, to each according to their needs', so that contribution to the COMMUNITY and recompense are divorced; a rotating allocation of work on the basis of SELF-SUFFICIENCY to avoid any extraction of surplus value from hired hands; an emphasis on the spiritual, political and moral value of work, especially of the physically demanding, agricultural variety; no compulsory retirement age; no gendered division of labour; COMMUNAL free provision of childcare from birth, so that children are brought up in specially designated houses amongst their peers by trained nurses, not in the family home by their parents; and the administration of education, food, healthcare and clothing on the same basis. Many kibbutzim are now the size of VILLAGES, though no public roads run through them and in legal terms each is private. Most have developed along similar lines, so in the middle are the shared facilities – schools, dining room, children's houses, medical centre, laundry and meeting rooms. Sleeping quarters surround the centre, and adjacent to these are stables and cattle sheds, with agricultural fields and orchards around the perimeter.

Since 1967 kibbutzim have also welcomed some 15,000 volunteers a year. The impetus behind the programme was to offer an opportunity for young Jewish people to explore their cultural identity, although volunteers today are mainly non-Jewish. They do unskilled labour typically for between 3 and 6 months, in return for food, accommodation and pocket money. Kibbutzim have never been homogeneous – there have always been variations in their individual tendency to emphasize Zionism over socialism or vice versa, their size and their economic activities. However, a number of developments have changed the face of the kibbutz at a macro level. These include Israel's own capitalist and individualist trajectory and the fact that, in line with changes in the wider economic context, kibbutzim shifted their activities from agriculture to industry (they now manufacture 9 per cent of Israel's industrial output). From inside the kibbutz, members have demanded greater freedom in, for example, choices regarding childcare arrangements, access to higher education and selection of work (both inside and outside the kibbutz). Also significant is the economic decline of many kibbutzim over the last two decades, due to an imbalance between investment, income and consumption.

These various pressures have resulted in a process of 'decommunaliza-tion'. Kibbutzim now regularly hire outside workers as well as allowing kibbutzniks to work outside the community – even encouraging them to set up small businesses to sell services like childcare, overnight accommodation or meals to the outside world. Indeed kibbutzniks are now expected to take responsibility for finding their own employment, and the focus has shifted to activities that are economically profitable. Children spend the day with their peers in the children's house but nights with their parents at home. Many communal services – the laundry, the kitchens, aspects of healthcare– have now been privatized so that members are charged for their use, for which they pay with a centrally administered consumption allowance according to their own discretion. There is also more hierarchy, with a proliferation of MANAGERIAL roles, a shift towards valuing 'mental' labour over 'manual' and a recoupling of contribution and reward – payment for overtime, for example, and differential wages based on the particular contribution of each job. In the larger kibbutzim, direct democracy is being replaced by a representative form, with boards responsible for health, housing, production and culture standing in for the general assembly. Numbers joining kibbutzim since the mid-1990s have also been outstripped at a ratio of approximately 2:1 by those leaving. The contemporary kibbutz is very different from its historical predecessor – so much so that the question of whether it still represents an alternative organization is perhaps an important one.

KINGDOM OF HEAVEN ON EARTH This Jewish and Christian concept was described by WELLS as 'one of the most REVOLUTIONARY doctrines that ever stirred and changed human thought'. The basis for this claim is the way that this idea has inspired the dispossessed to claim that the realization of heaven should be brought to pass in the present, just as Christ preached it as something that was 'at hand' and that constantly broke into and disrupted the prevailing order of things. Various MILLENARIAN sects – such as the CATHARS, the DIGGERS and the LEVELLERS – all attempted to actualize the Kingdom of Heaven. Millenarians claimed that they were the chosen people whose actions were to bring the dawn of a thousand-year heavenly kingdom in the here and now. Others invoked the idea by seeking a return to the GOLDEN AGE of EDEN and its supposed egalitarian innocence, as with the slogan of the PEASANT'S REVOLT 'when Adam delved and Eve

145

span, who was then the gentleman?' It could be argued that revolutionary SOCIALISTS, COMMUNISTS and ANARCHISTS, including MARX and ENGELS, were drawing on the same cultural tradition; reinterpreting the longing for an earthly PARADISE into rationalist political terms.

The appeal of the Kingdom of Heaven to the poor is perhaps not surprising when one considers that Christ and St Paul described it as a place where violence and oppression have come to an end; where bondage and slavery, inequality, and distinctions between the sexes are no more; where the Adamic curse of living by the sweat of one's brow is replaced by comfort and ease (see COCKAIGNE). Authorities throughout the ages have been insistent that it should be firmly placed in the future, safely beyond life in this world. Nevertheless, the longing for the Kingdom of Heaven and the belief that God's will guaranteed that it would happen certainly gave many UTOPIAN groups the confidence and determination to act in the pursuit of a different world.

KROPOTKIN, PETER A geographer, writer and revolutionary COMMUNIST (1842–1921). The foremost theoretician of ANARCHISM in the nineteenth century, attempting to find affinities between the principles of an anarchist society and tendencies found within the natural world. His major contribution was in his theorizing of MUTUAL aid which gave anarchism a philosophical basis and political programme at a time when the movement threatened to become irrevocably associated with TERRORISM in the public mind. Kropotkin was born into the higher ranks of the Russian aristocracy, developed a love of geography and wished to devote his life to his studies. The Tsar was favourably impressed by the young Kropotkin and had him enrolled at an élite military academy. However, Kropotkin continued with his private studies in literature, philosophy and, increasingly, in science. He shone at the military academy and became personal page to the new Tsar, Alexander II. Kropotkin was at first impressed by the initially liberal tendencies of the Tsar, who liberated the serfs in 1861, but the administration became increasingly authoritarian, propelling Kropotkin's views towards REVOLUTIONARY politics.

After Kropotkin graduated he went to eastern Siberia as a military administrator for a Cossack regiment. He realised how little of the wealth he had been surrounded by since birth was really necessary and his contact with peasant COMMUNITIES impressed him with the virtues of solidarity, spontaneity and simplicity. He concluded that COOPERATION was as important a factor in evolutionary success as competition and that mutuality in nature provided a model for human society. Returning to St Petersburg in 1867 to continue his scientific work, the establishment of the PARIS COMMUNE provided him with an example of how a social and political revolution might lead to a COMMUNIST society based on anarchist principles. In 1872 he visited Western Europe, making contact with members of the FIRST INTERNATIONAL, led by BAKUNIN. The expulsion of the anarchists from the First International convinced Kropotkin that all forms of institutionalized authority were dangerous, even those that had the best of aims. On his return to St Petersburg, he became actively involved in radical politics. He was heavily influenced by the narodniks, a group of usually socially privileged Russians influenced by the nihilist movement and inspired by TOLSTOY's religious anarchism. The narodniks attempted to spread anti-authoritarian ideas amongst the peasants by living and working alongside them, calling for a society based on FEDERATED voluntary associations of producers using the traditional Russian VILLAGE as a model.

Although many preferred non-violent agitation, Kropotkin was a firm advocate of peasant uprisings and the forcible appropriation of land and property. He argued for a complete social REVOLUTION to be undertaken by workers and peasants, and fomented by the use of populist agitators and the construction of revolutionary organizations. In 1874 he was arrested and imprisoned in the notorious Peter and Paul fortress. After three years he made a dramatic escape and fled to England, hoping to contribute to what he believed was the coming revolution throughout Europe. For the next five years he devoted himself to the revolution, setting up the journal Le Révolté in 1879, which encouraged individual and COLLECTIVE acts of revolt, including political strikes in the SYNDICALIST tradition. Kropotkin was again imprisoned in 1882, this time by the French, but was released in 1886 after protests by prominent liberals. In 1887 he wrote a memoir of his experiences as a prisoner in both Russia and France, arguing that imprisonment was useless as a way of reforming anti-social conduct. He also argued in the article 'Law and Authority' that the law acted to promote the very behaviour it purportedly sought to eradicate because it was primarily aimed at the protection of private property and the institutions of the state. Kropotkin believed that a society without property or government would have little incentive to crime, other than crimes of passion, which the prospect of punishment would do little to discourage in any case. He argued that the most effective way of regulating conduct   147 was through a NETWORK of agreements and customs – the main means of cementing human societies together for most of history.

After his imprisonment Kropotkin returned to London where he forged friendships with many prominent anarchists and socialists, including MORRIS. He founded the Freedom Press Group (which continues to the present day) and was supposedly offered the post of Professor of Geography at Cambridge, which he refused because he wished to devote his life to his political activities. From 1890, Kropotkin began to withdraw from active politics, as MARXISM and parliamentary SOCIALISM began to dominate the British labour movement. He also moved away from his original support for revolutionary violence; although he remained a believer in the necessity of revolutionary social change, he came to believe that change was a result of the gradual development of individual consciousness. He therefore encouraged attempts to spread an anarchist sensibility by the small-scale collective self-organization of the activities of everyday life.

After the abortive 1905 RUSSIAN REVOLUTION, Kropotkin began to become involved once more in Russian politics and planned to return to Russia to support the cause. For some years he worked with the exiled Russian Social Revolutionaries in London, who allied themselves with the Bolshevik wing of the Russian Social Democratic Party. He also became increasingly concerned about the rise of German militarism, seeing it as a serious threat to the possibility of progressive politics. When war broke out he supported the allies, a position which brought him criticism from both fellow anarchists such as Malatesta and from the Russian revolutionary left. In 1917, however, he returned to Russia and was offered a cabinet post in the Provisional Government by Kerensky – which, as an anarchist opposed to all forms of state authority, he refused. When the Bolsheviks came to power he became dismayed at what he saw as the extension of BUREAUCRATIC state power. In Kropotkin's view a new authoritarianism was replacing the free operation of the autonomous SOVIETS of peasants and workers that sprang up after the revolution and which he hoped would form the basis for a communo-anarchist society. In 1919 he met LENIN and discussed these tendencies and the persecution of dissident political groups. Lenin agreed to attend to any injustices that Kropotkin might draw to his notice but quickly tired of the old man's frequent letters, and little notice was taken of Kropotkin's protests. When he died in 1921 the government offered to provide a state funeral but his family turned this down. His funeral procession proved to be the last time the red and black flag of anarchism was flown in the SOVIET UNION, as later that year the Bolshevik government suppressed the movement.

Kropotkin based his anarchism on the idea of the 'laws of nature' in much the same way that Marx sought to ground his socialism on the 'laws of history'. The determinism of this approach and its appeal to 'natural' laws appears simplistic but Kropotkin was seeking to counter the influential idea that individualist competition was legitimated by Darwinian evolutionary theory. In his most famous work, *Mutual Aid* (1902), he uses observations of the natural world to argue that cooperation and mutuality are the key factors in the most successful species. In *The Conquest of Bread* (1892), Kropotkin takes issue with the Hegelian idea, also utilized by Marx, that society progresses through conflict. Rather, Kropotkin argues, despite history largely being 'nothing but the struggle between the rulers and the ruled' progress only happens when conflict is resolved and cooperation becomes the guiding principle of society. The chief obstacle to the natural tendency of human beings to harmony and altruism is the state. In *The State* (1897) he argues that, despite the influence of the state, communities based on mutual aid continue to be the dominant way in which social life is sustained. Human beings seek to build federated communal structures such as the self-governing village, or the craft GUILD, or TRADE UNIONS, in order to pursue their freedom within collective institutions. Because of his hostility towards ruling élites who oppress the masses in the defence of their own privileges, Kropotkin was equally dismissive of the sort of transitional revolutionary governments advocated by Marxists. He believed that revolution is a bottom-up and spontaneous process. Any centralized political authority will thus become counter-revolutionary, resisting any development that threatens to transcend itself.

Kropotkin advocates a society based on networks of voluntary associations. The commune – linked by local interests, affinities and sympathies – will become the basic unit of society and will be entirely autonomous. Individual conduct will be governed by agreement and custom. Private property would be abolished, the wage system would cease to exist, and there would be common ownership of the means of production. Kropotkin saw underconsumption as the main problem with capitalist economies, so with higher rates of both production and consumption a leisured existence for all would be possible (see also, for example, FOURIER, LE CORBUSIER, LOOKING BACKWARD). Work and leisure would become artistic pleasures, and individuals would find their fulfilment as free members of free communities.

L

LE CORBUSIER Born Charles-Édouard Jeanneret-Gris in Switzerland, this architect, planner and self-publicist (1887–1965) adapted his grandfather's name as his pseudonym in 1920. Like the Italian futurists, Le Corbusier was fascinated by the streamlined designs of cars, aeroplanes and massive US grain elevators. Influenced by Howard's GARDEN CITIES, he put forward a modernist manifesto for better urban living conditions based on order, space and functional design (though using the vertical, rather then Howard's horizontal spread). His fondness for scale, uniformity and height have led to many of his buildings and plans becoming emblematic of the failures of modernism which have been so widely criticised from the 1960s onwards (see SOCIAL CAPITAL). However, his hostility to ostentatious ornamentation, dirt and disorder and his promotion of a fairly egalitarian version of planning echoes many UTOPIAN schemes, particularly the geometries of CHRISTIANOPOLIS, or the CITY OF THE SUN.

Le Corbusier's modernism was more than just aesthetic, but it was not initially revolutionary. With his designs for workers' housing (the glass box 'Dom-ino', a combination of the words domicile and innovation) and the 'Contemporary City Plan for Three Million' people, he intended to bring the efficiency and productivity of the factory into the city. Most of Paris was to be cleared, and replaced with twenty-four central gigantic skyscrapers for the élites, and Dom-ino housing near the factories for the workers. This, he thought, would prevent the revolution bubbling up from the disordered slums – 'architecture or revolution'. However, failing to find support from the capitalists for his vision of the future, he turned to technocratic SYNDICALISTS for a more DEMOCRATIC conception of industrial modernism (see SAINT-SIMON; LOOKING BACKWARD). His 'Radiant City' did away with the inequalities of his previous designs and provided sunlight and fresh air for everyone, with houses based on the size and needs of each family. The apartment blocks and roadways were elevated on piles, in order to maximise the green space within the city for pedestrians, sports and nature. The division of labour was extensive. Laundry and catering were dealt with in each block, specialized professionals carried out childcare, but most women would stay at home. This form of organization would save so much time that people would need to work only five hours a day.

This is a BUREAUCRATIC utopia, one in which the planners determine human needs, and the happiness of the residents is then guaranteed. Like many utopias, it is radically egalitarian for almost everyone apart from the planners and intellectuals themselves. Le Corbusier promised social harmony, and attempted to escape from the disorder of the masses by redeveloping the streets as a scientifically managed public sphere. In his *Vers Une Architecture* of 1923, he even suggests that you should not get undressed in the bedroom because it results in mess, and should always tidy away your possessions in the ample drawer space his houses provide. With no politics and no disorder (see CHRISTIANIA), the Radiant City places itself firmly in the tradition of the patriarchal and authoritarian CITY STATE, a dream that now looks more like a nightmare.

LE GUIN, URSULA see DISPOSSESSED; SCIENCE FICTION

LENIN, VLADIMIR ILYICH The leader of the Bolshevik Party, which later became the Russian COMMUNIST Party. Both a formidable theoretician of applied MARXISM and a dedicated REVOLUTIONARY activist, Lenin (1870–1924) developed the theory of 'Leninism', which he described as the application of Marxism to the age of imperialism. He was the chief architect of the 1917 October Revolution that replaced the discredited Provisional Government with rule by the SOVIETS, and the first Premier of the SOVIET UNION as a result.

Lenin was born in Simbirsk in Russia to liberal middle-class parents. In 1887 his eldest brother Alexander was hanged for plotting the assassination of Tsar Alexander III. The experience radicalized Lenin as well as convincing him of the futility of TERRORIST methods. He was arrested and expelled from University for taking part in student protests but continued his studies independently and qualified at law in 1891. Moving to St Petersburg in 1893 he became increasingly involved in the production of propaganda and the study of Marxism. In 1895 he was arrested and exiled to Siberia. In 1898 he published *The Development of Capitalism in Russia* which began his work of adapting Marxism to Russian conditions. Marx had assumed that revolutions would take place in the most industrially advanced states. Lenin set about reinterpreting revolutionary tactics for conditions in semi-feudal, economically backward Russia. He was released

151

from Siberia in 1900 and left for Switzerland, a haven for revolutionary and radical émigrés.

In 1903 a party congress of the Russian Social Democratic Party took place with the result that there was a split between two wings of the party, the Bolsheviks and the Mensheviks. The Mensheviks allied themselves with both LIBERALS and other social revolutionaries and intended to work towards a DEMOCRATIC parliamentary system. Lenin found himself in charge of what was rapidly to become an independent Bolshevik party. In 1905 the first Russian Revolution took place and the Tsar conceded a semblance of democracy and the formation of a parliament, the *Duma*. However, Tsarist absolutism quickly reasserted itself. Lenin took little public part, preferring to build the Bolshevik Party and to attempt to raise support for SOCIALISM. The Tsar's increasing suppression of political dissent meant that Lenin had to leave Russia and from 1907 until 1916 he lived as an exile. The First World War saw the collapse of the Second INTERNATIONAL over the issue of support for national war efforts. Lenin's opposition to the war did not stop him realizing that it might provide the preconditions for another revolution and the callousness of the management of the war indeed led to the February Revolution of 1917. The Provisional Government established was made up mainly of the Mensheviks, the Socialist parties and the middle-class party of the Cadets.

Lenin returned to Russia and published the *April Theses* designed to galvanize his party into a more radical position. He called for opposition to the Provisional Government, an end to Russia's involvement in the war and the transfer of power from parliamentary representative government to the SOVIETS that had grown up spontaneously in the wake of the Revolution. They were councils that ran a wide range of social units, from factories and army units to village COMMUNES and city neighbourhoods. The *Petrograd Soviet of Workers' and Soldiers' Deputies* was particularly important and provided Lenin with a base to argue that the dual government would not be able to work in the long term as the conflicting class interests represented would eventually lead to a struggle for dominance.

The Provisional Government gradually lost support due to its failure to bring about social and agrarian reform or to bring the war to an end. The soviets and the Bolsheviks grew in popularity and increasingly commanded the loyalty of ordinary people, including large numbers of soldiers and sailors. In October 1918 the Bolsheviks, with the almost complete support of the working class and poorer peasants, and with very little bloodshed, assumed complete power. The Provisional Government disintegrated. Russia had suffered enormous casualties and the destruction of its already weak economy so Lenin offered to negotiate with all the combatant governments. After being snubbed by the Allies, he made a separate but disadvantageous peace with Germany.

In 1919 Lenin met with revolutionary socialists from around the world and formed the Third International and the Bolshevik Party was renamed the Russian COMMUNIST Party. The work of reconstruction was brought to an abrupt end by the invasion of Russia by foreign armies seeking to 'liberate' the country from communism. By the end of 1919 it was obvious that the Red Army was able to defeat the invaders but much of the country lay in ruins. There was widespread famine in the towns and the soviet system had broken down in the countryside. The real danger signal for Lenin came when the Krondstadt Garrison mutinied and had to be suppressed in a bloody campaign that cost many lives on both sides. The 'red terror', when opposition parties were suppressed and suspected counter-revolutionaries executed, arose during this period as a response to the threat of complete collapse.

Lenin's response to growing discontent in the countryside and famine in the towns was to shift to a pragmatic approach that mixed small-scale private ownership with collective enterprise, attempting to harness individual self-interest to the building of a socialist state. His objective throughout was to foster peasant and worker AUTONOMY but he believed that ideology should come second to the needs of economic reconstruction. It was obvious by this time that, though the revolution had survived, the invasions had had the effect of stopping its spread. Lenin's main objective thus became the construction of a strong socialist state that could act as an inspiration to other workers throughout the world. In 1922 he retired from public life after two strokes that left him partially paralysed. However he published a number of papers which were critical of a number of leading figures in the Party, including Trotsky and Stalin. Despite his expressed wish that no memorials be created for him he became an icon. His body was embalmed and placed on permanent display in Moscow and the city of Petrograd was renamed Leningrad.

Lenin's greatest contribution to revolutionary socialism was his development of party organization and discipline, though arguably these structural features also made the revolution vulnerable to dictatorship by a single individual through the structure of the Communist Party. Lenin identified the need for a highly disciplined federation of activist cells united by a single set of ideas. He believed that the party needed to provide leadership because Russia lacked a middle class with a strong social democratic tradition. Marxism could only be inculcated amongst the workers and peasants through the example of party members. Some sympathetic observers were led to describe the outcome of the early stages of the Bolshevik programme as a form of SYNDICALISM as a result. Lenin also reinterpreted Marxism to take account of the preponderance of peasants in Russia, believing that the peasantry had revolutionary potential. His programme was based on their hunger for land and included a number of stages. First they must be united against Russian feudal landowners; next, the poorer peasants would combine to reclaim their fair share of land from landowners and wealthy peasants. Finally the peasants would be able to revive a modern version of the self-governed VILLAGE via large-scale COLLECTIVE farming supported by technical innovations. The disasters of the collectivization programme undertaken by Stalin may be at least partly attributed to his policy of brutal coercion. Lenin, however, insisted that the peasants themselves had to come to their own arrangements for achieving communism in agricultural production. This recognition of the revolutionary potential of the peasantry paved the way for most of the major revolutions of the twentieth century, particularly in China (see MAO).

Lenin's legacy is difficult to disentangle from the later disasters of Stalinism but to have preserved the Revolution in the terrible circumstances of 1917 to 1921 is a monumental achievement. It is one of history's great speculations as to what the outcome would have been if Lenin had not died so prematurely. However, well before the invasion of foreign armies, anarchists such as KROPOTKIN were expressing worries at the rise of authoritarianism. Even Lenin, as his health deteriorated, tried to warn his party comrades that Stalin was in a position to seize absolute power. The irony is that Lenin's own preference, on the grounds of efficiency, for individual responsibility had provided Stalin with this opportunity. If Lenin's design of the Communist Party and its tactics of top-down control made the rise of a new bureaucratic governing élite likely, it is still difficult to see what else could have been done when the avoidance of starvation for millions of Russians overrode all other considerations. Lenin had the misfortune to lead a revolution in the worst conceivable circumstances. It can be argued that the failure of the first worker's state has proved to be the greatest disaster to befall the cause of left UTOPIANISM in the history of the common people. On the other hand, out of the wreckage can still be salvaged the memory that, for a while, the dream of radicals for a fair society was almost within reach. In addition, the soviets provided an example of how the principles of self-organization, direct democracy and federation could work on a large scale. Without Lenin, even this brief glimpse of freedom for ordinary people would have never existed.

LETS (LOCAL EXCHANGE AND TRADING SCHEMES) Created when a group of people forms an association and establishes a local unit of exchange. Members then list their offers of, and requests for, goods and services in a public directory priced in the local unit of currency. Individuals decide what they want to trade, who they want to trade with, and how much trade they wish to engage in. The type of products and services typically traded ranges from alternative therapies, childcare, lifts, gardening, house maintenance, or business services, to food, or craft products. The value of products or services can be established on the basis of the time that goes into their production, irrespective of the skills or qualifications required (see also TIME BANKS), or through negotiations between buyer and seller, depending on the scheme.

The association keeps a record of the transactions by means of a system of cheques written in the local units. Every time a transaction is made, these cheques are sent to the treasurer who works in a similar manner to a bank sending out regular statements to the members. No actual cash is issued and no interest is charged or paid. The level of LETS units exchanged is thus entirely dependent upon the extent of trading undertaken. Neither does one necessarily need to earn money before one can spend it because credit is available and interest-free. As such, LETS are private associations for pursuing economically orientated COLLECTIVE self-help based on not-for-profit and COOPERATIVE principles. They operate in order to provide for needs and wants that are fulfilled neither by the private or public sectors nor by the INFORMAL WORK of the family, kin, neighbourhood and COMMUNITY.

The first scheme was developed in Canada's Comox Valley in 1983 as a way of keeping the local economy going during a period of industrial decline and high unemployment. Since then, LETS have grown worldwide with over 1,500 LETS groups in 39 countries. In the UK in 1999, the 303 LETS had some 22,000 members who were predominantly aged 30–49, women, from relatively low-income groups and either not employed or self-employed. Just 2 per cent join to use it as a means of gaining access to formal employment; the rest join either for ideological reasons such as to promote alternatives to capitalism (23 per cent) or to engage in complementary means of livelihood for economic and community-building reasons (75 per cent).

LETS have been seen as potentially revitalizing community economies by offering people excluded from conventional employment, financial systems and commodity markets the opportunity to develop alternative systems of work and exchange. But the extent to which these schemes provide alternatives to capitalism, and promote more equal forms of local community development, depends on the ability to attract a wider membership, and to tackle power inequalities between members. Their main value seems to lie in their ability to provide social support and MUTUAL aid. In terms of SOCIAL CAPITAL, they develop 'bridges' (bringing people together who did not know each other before) more than 'bonds' (bringing people who already know each other closer together), operating in a similar way to the FRIENDLY SOCIETIES. (CW)

LEVELLERS A disparate grouping of radical agitators that arose during the English Civil War and had support in the NEW MODEL ARMY. They differed from the Seekers, RANTERS, and QUAKERS, who were part of the religious DISSENTING tradition, because their aims were largely political and secular. Having said this, the DIGGERS, who called themselves the 'True Levellers', combined a fully worked out programme of COMMUNISM with a mystical pantheism. The term 'Leveller' was originally one of abuse, coined by the opponents of the egalitarian wing of the parliamentarians. The parliamentary leaders, mostly well-off gentry, were well aware of the risks they had taken in arming the common people and enabling them to hold positions of responsibility but they had little alternative if they were to defeat the King. The more radical hopes of the common people were tolerated because the promise of a more prosperous and equal society was a major factor in persuading them to fight. The Levellers harked back to what they saw as the pre-Norman conquest liberties of the common people, and hence saw the Civil War as a crusade to recover liberty and get rid of the 'Norman Yoke'. The Levellers were also very conscious of themselves as a social class, despising those who did not work for their living but who arranged the world for their own convenience and profit.

After the Royalists were defeated and Parliament became the sovereign power, the Levellers demanded their reward. They worked through agitation in the army, the publication of pamphlets, and petitions to Parliament. Leveller supporters often identified themselves by wearing green ribbons. Amongst their demands were universal male suffrage, biannual or annual elections (see OCEANA), complete religious freedom, an end to censorship, the abolition of the monarchy and the House of Lords, trial by jury, no taxation of the poor and a cap on interest rates. These demands seem relatively modest today, though many have still not been achieved. At the time they were considered extremely radical and threatened to 'turn the world upside down'. Leveller spokesmen became increasingly critical of Members of Parliament who they saw as appropriating the gains of the Civil War whilst the common soldiers were expected to return to a state of servitude.

For the senior officers and gentry (nicknamed the Grandees), Leveller support in the army was the most ominous feature of the movement. In 1647, after many regiments had elected Leveller 'agitators' to represent them, the Grandees agreed to hold debates over their demands. These became known as the Putney Debates, but further agreed meetings between the two sides resulted in the arrest of many Levellers and the punishment of Leveller soldiers. Despite a number of demonstrations, petitions and mutinies over the next two years, there was never enough of a concerted, widely executed campaign to prevent the Grandees tightening their grip. Eventually the chief spokesmen of the Levellers were imprisoned and some were executed; by 1649, the movement had effectively been crushed. Although the Levellers were defeated and seemingly achieved little, they came close to steering the English REVOLUTION in a direction that might have led to a very different form of society. The Levellers provide an example of the ability of common people, with none of the advantages of wealth and education, to organize and articulate their arguments and demands. They provide a link in the utopian tradition that joins the MILLENARIAN movements and medieval PEASANT REVOLTS to the Chartist and SOCIALIST movements of the nineteenth century.

LEWIS, JOHN, see JOHN LEWIS PARTNERSHIP

LIBERALISM The core belief that individual liberty is a natural right and any form of force that limits freedom is justified only if it is aimed at p rotecting the equal right to liberty for all. Indeed most of the philosophical, political and economic debates that have informed liberalism have been articulated around the question of what degree of political authority (especially of the state) can be justified. The idea of individuals having natural rights that not even kings could override can be traced back to the Enlightenment thinkers of the eighteenth century (for example Locke or ROUSSEAU) who insisted that natural rights to liberty were best secured through government by consent rather than coercion. Thus the development of liberalism needs to be seen as a reaction against conservatism and absolutist regimes, both of which were deemed to unduly restrict individual freedom.

The American and French revolutions of the late eighteenth century were the first large-scale experiments to put liberal ideas to the test and to demonstrate that people could govern their own affairs. Industrialization and the development of capitalism in the nineteenth century were both i n fluenced by liberal thinking (in particular the work of SMITH and Ricardo), but also shaped liberal debates by raising new questions. Indeed the accumulation of wealth by some was accompanied by the poverty and misery of many others who had flocked to the cities to sell their labour. The celebration of individual and MARKET freedom led to inequalities that seriously damaged the liberties of the most disadvantaged, raising questions about the role of the state in reconciling liberty and equality. The twentieth century raised new challenges for liberalism in the form of the various FASCIST regimes that emerged in Europe, as well as the rise of COMMUNISM. Far from being a unified political theory or position, liberalism is best seen as a tradition encompassing broad debates about the nature of human liberty, and the best economic, political and social systems to protect it.

One of the debates within liberalism is over the very conception of liberty. Some advocate 'negative liberty', which is simply the absence of coercion or interference from others (the state, traditions, religious fundamentalism and so on). On this view, favoured by libertarianism, the role of government is that of 'nightwatchman'; it should be limited to the protection of individual liberty – to ensuring, for example, that citizens do not coerce each other. A 'positive' conception of liberty, on the other hand, centres on the freedom to become oneself, to fulfil one's potential, and is often associated with an emphasis on rights to education and equal opportunities. Today this view characterizes what could be called 'social liberalism' and tends to support some form of intervention to protect the equal opportunities of the disadvantaged (for example by making laws banning sexual and racial discrimination – see liberal FEMINISM).

Another, related, dividing line within liberalism concerns the MANAGEMENT of the economy. In liberalism, private property, free markets and liberty are intimately connected. The freedom to hold and exchange property, as well as to sell one's labour, is seen as a way (and for some, the only way) of protecting individual liberty. The dispersion of power that results from a free market economy protects individuals against state power. For classical liberals such as Smith, the government should not interfere with markets since they coordinate the actions of self-interested individuals to deliver public good. This laissez-faire approach is the one still favoured by libertarians (or 'minarchists') such as NOZICK, RAND and neoliberals inspired by Friedman or Hayek. However, whilst all liberals are in favour of a market economy, some grew suspicious of its ability to protect and sustain a free society. Thinkers such as Keynes, Dewey, or Roosevelt argued that in order to protect all citizens' liberty, the state needed to ameliorate market mechanisms, for example by redistributing wealth through taxation. Government intervention, and in particular the development of the welfare state, was justified in terms of creating the conditions in which liberalism could survive against the threats of FASCISM and COMMUNISM.

Another important debate that has animated liberalism concerns the political framework and moral basis for the coordination of individuals' liberties. The free society envisaged by liberalism is composed of individuals all having their own, possibly incompatible, conceptions of the good life. The problem for liberalism is to provide a political framework within which citizens who disagree with one another can coexist. A first liberal answer is to leave questions of the good life to the private domain, and to promote neutral government. Since society is composed of people with different objectives and conceptions of the good life, it is best governed by BUREAUCRATIC principles that do not presuppose any particular conception of what is good. However, not all disagreements can be treated as purely 'private matters' and removed from the public domain. Some values or objectives (such as environmental protection) can only be pursued through coordinated efforts on a society-wide scale; moreover, one person's pursuit of the good life may threaten or offend another's. Liberalism resolves the question of coordination through the DEMOCRATIC process, constitutional government and the rule of law. However this still begs the question of how basic rights should be defined when citizens disagree about values and objectives. One possible answer draws on the notion of the social contract: a collectively enforced social arrangement made legitimate by the fact that the people who agreed it are subjected to it. RAWLS's appeal to 'public reason' to establish a core set of political principles subject to consensus among all reasonable citizens is the modern embodiment of the social contract.

The legacy of liberalism for the modern world is profound and can be seen in the notion of universal human rights; the defence of civil liberties and the freedom of speech and press; pluralism and multiculturalism; representative democracy, constitutional government and the rule of law; the free market and free trade; the transparency of government; popular sovereignty; privacy and the idea that government should not intervene in the private affairs of citizens; and equality before the law. The meanings and applications of these ideas continue to be debated and contested, but they have become deeply engrained and taken for granted in many modern societies.

LIBERTARIANISM A radical combination of ANARCHISM and LIBERALISM (see also FREELAND; FREE STATE PROJECT; NOZICK).

LLANO DEL RIO A colony established in California in 1914 with the aim of providing equal wages, education and social benefits to members. It can be seen as following the American utopian experiments of the nineteenth century (such as BROOK FARM, ONEIDA, NEW HARMONY). Its main founder, Job Harriman, a lawyer and member of the SOCIALIST Party, had become disillusioned with trying to implement social change through the political system, and together with other socialists decided that change could best be achieved by giving people the opportunity to experience socialism first hand. They raised capital by selling stock to members and acquired land in the Mojave Desert north of Los Angeles. The cooperative settlement was soon thriving; by 1916 it had drawn over 1,000 people and was largely self-supporting. It produced most of its food, had established several businesses from a tannery to a barber shop, and set up its own school, library, community hall and journal. The cooperative continued to prosper until its water supply was diverted by an earthquake fault and it went into receivership in 1917.

Two hundred of the original settlers moved to Stables, a defunct lumber town in Louisiana, which they renamed New Llano. For over twenty years,

New Llano continued to apply the cooperative and socialist principles of Llano del Rio, and became a landmark for social and economic experiments. Besides its SELF-SUBSISTENCE agricultural activities, New Llano became renowned for the production and quality of its food and manufactured goods, opened one of the first Montessori schools in the USA, and provided fertile ground for cultural and political activities including an orchestra, a theatre and a nationally distributed socialist paper, *The American Vanguard*. It experimented with what were at the time innovative social programmes: a minimum wage; low-cost housing; maternity leave and childcare provision; universal heath cover and social security systems.

New Llano was badly hit by the Depression and, like so many other AMERICAN businesses, faced financial ruin. The settlers tried different ways to get out of debt but the colony eventually went into receivership in 1939. Like many other UTOPIAN experiments, Llano del Rio and New Llano went down in history as 'failures', but together the two experiments lasted for 25 years, which is far more than many conventional businesses, and inspired the lives of thousands of residents or visitors. New Llano also anticipated many of the social reforms, such as minimum wage, family leave, health cover, that were to form the basis of later welfare states.

LOCAL EXCHANGE AND TRADING SCHEMES, see LETS

LOCALIZATION Reversing the trend of globalization by discriminating in favour of the local, thus increasing COMMUNITY and/or state control over the economy. The argument for localization starts with a critique of the comparative advantage thesis often put forward to support trade liberalization. According to this thesis, nations should specialize in products that they can produce more efficiently and cheaply than other nations. Rather than trying to meet their own needs by producing everything, they should export products for which they have a comparative advantage, and import the rest. However, localization advocates point out that this thesis does not take into account the fact that some countries become dependent on exports whose prices they don't control, and on imports for meeting their own basic needs; nor does it take into account transportation and environmental costs. They argue that trade liberalization does not hold the promise of increased prosperity for all, as the theory of comparative advantage would have it, but rather the increased inequality of wealth and power between rich and poor nations. For example, developing nations that have shifted their agricultural production away from subsistence crops towards cash crops for export MARKETS have seen the prices of the products they export come down whilst becoming increasingly dependent on imports for their subsistence.

Supporters of localization want to maximize communities' SELF-SUFFICIENCY and promote more SUSTAINABLE and equitable forms of development. Thus they go along with SCHUMACHER's suggestion that 'Production from local resources for local needs is the most rational way of economic life, while dependence on imports from afar plus the consequent need to produce for exports to unknown and distant peoples is highly uneconomical and justifiable only in exceptional cases and on a small scale'. What constitutes the boundaries of the local depends on the types of goods or services and may range from VILLAGES for some food products, to nation states for some industries, or even groupings of nations for large industries such as airplane production. But whatever the boundaries, the aim is to start from the principle of encouraging local production for local consumption, and to move towards SMALL-scale production.

Several measures are envisaged to promote the development of local economies. One would be the (re)introduction of PROTECTIONISM, in the form of for example tariffs on imports or quotas, to provide safeguards for rebuilding local economies. Measures could also include tax and accounting regulation that seeks to limit transfer pricing within multinational corporations and the shifting of profits to where corporate taxes are lowest. Controls on capital movements across nations are also deemed important to ensure that money stays local, as are various forms of LETS and CREDIT UNIONS, and COMMUNITY-SUPPORTED AGRICULTURE and FARMERS' MARKETS. Increased taxes on fuel to reflect the environmental costs of transportation would also increase the cost of international trade. But localization is more than simply a series of economic and financial measures. Advocates of localization also demand a shift of decision making towards citizens. Localization is imagined as a way towards greater economic and political DEMOCRACY; people would become more actively involved in the decisions affecting them. Finally, it is important to note that those who support localization tend to draw a distinction between globalization and internationalism; whilst they oppose globalization and its disempowering effects, they support international COOPERATION through the flow of information or technology that aims to protect and rebuild the local.

LOCAL MONEY, see BARTERING; LETS; TIME BANKS

LOOKING BACKWARD Edward Bellamy's (1888) million-selling industrial COLLECTIVIST utopia had a huge contemporary influence on US political opinion on the left, and also later on Ebenezer Howard's GARDEN CITY movement in the UK. (Howard was instrumental in getting the book published in Britain.) Against the individualism of either ROMANTICISM or MARKET capitalism, Bellamy turned to a strong state as his model, embellishing it with ringing phrases about the brotherhood of man and the solidarity of the race. In *Looking Backward 2000–1887* a wealthy Bostonian falls into a hypnotic trance and wakes 113 years later. At the end of the novel, he dreams that he is back in the unfair and dirty world of 1887, and is massively relieved to wake again in this new present. The novel is largely taken up by his introduction to the world of 2000, free from the strikes and unrest that characterized the Boston that he left behind.

Some time early in the twentieth century, all the warring companies had been peacefully consolidated into nationalized industries, and the nation was now itself being run as a SYNDICALIST monopoly from which all members benefited (see INDUSTRIAL DEMOCRACY). With the nation as employer, all the citizens became employees, and a complex BUREAUCRATIC structure ensured that the work and profits were shared with all members of society, including the physically or mentally incapable. All citizens are educated until the age of 21, when they join the 'industrial army' until the age of 45, after which they are free to do what they wish (though women become exempt on becoming mothers). Apart from three years of directed labour, citizens can choose the trade that is most attractive to them. Since everyone is paid the same, via a public credit card, imbalances of supply in the labour market are dealt with by having shorter hours for the less popular jobs (see also WALDEN TWO). This impressive solution does not prevent people from choosing trades that they find worthwhile, but allows for centralized planning of production and distribution. Similarly, the personal shares that each person has in the national wealth can be spent as the individual wishes, but since all have the same income, there is little need for conspicuous consumption (or motive for crime and war) and no attempt to sell products via advertising (see also COOPERATIVE CITY). Instead, shops have single samples of products that can be delivered from central warehouses.

The Commander-in-Chief of the industrial army is elected by all the retired members, but government is carried out by a MANAGERIAL élite who all carry military titles and are appointed on a meritocratic basis. They are motivated to rise through the ranks by the status that it provides, as well as (rather oddly) 'special privileges and immunities in the way of discipline'. Most importantly, their role is to run the vast bureaucratic apparatus which evaluates the abilities and piecework output of the workers, and rewards them with re-gradings and public honours (such as a red ribbon) for those who serve the people well. Religion is tolerated, though rare. If a group of citizens wish to spend their allowance on the wages of a clergyman, or the rental of a place for worship, they are free to do so. Authors and artists are also allowed freedom of expression, and (again rather oddly) are entitled to any royalties on their work. However, if someone does not accept the authority of the state, they become a non-person who is imprisoned or hospitalized – pitied and treated rather than punished.

Reading Bellamy now, after MAO, Stalin and the excesses of managerialism, provokes a more DYSTOPIAN reaction. Morris's NEWS FROM NOWHERE was probably the first of these criticisms from the left, but Eugene Richter's *Pictures of a Socialistic Future* (1891) neatly summarizes the contemporary LIBERAL reaction (see also FREELAND). Nonetheless, *Looking Backward* provides many cogent arguments and powerful images in favour of industrial COMMUNISM. Bellamy's faith in new inventions also reminds us that technical progress (such as the transmission of concerts by telephone) can and does provide resources for social improvement, and not simply deskilling. Most interestingly, he embeds these within an atmosphere of cultural liberalism and professional freedom that is more bourgeois than state communism generally encouraged, and a series of military disciplines that now appear more FASCIST than communist (see also BUREAUCRACY, VOYAGE TO ICARIA, WELLS). Like so many other authors of his time, he also follows some eugenic arguments, noting that women now choose men on the basis of their natural abilities, not their wealth, and that this helps to improve the race. Bellamy's utopia is a strange mixture of civil religion based on an elaborated division of labour, a MARXIST political economy, and the middle-class US tastes of the 1880s, but in places it can almost be read as prophecy rather than fiction. In his postscript to later editions of the work, he concludes by articulating the connections between UTOPIAN fiction and social change.

All thoughtful men agree that the present aspect of society is portentous of great changes. The only question is, will it be for the better or the worse. Those who believe in man's essential nobleness lean towards the former view, those who believe in his essential baseness to the latter. For my part I hold to the former opinion. *Looking Backward* was written in the belief that the Golden Age lies before us and not behind us, and is not far away. Our children will surely see it, and we too, who are already men and women, if we deserve it by our faith and by our works.

LUDDITES A term commonly used to describe an irrational opposition to progress and technology, thus perpetuating the propaganda of the opponents of the original Luddites. They consisted of three slightly different groups of English workers, mostly involved in textile manufacture, in the opening decades of the nineteenth century. The SECRET SOCIETY that they developed, and the beginnings of an identifiable industrial working-class consciousness opposed to the interests of employers, have identified them as forerunners of modern TRADE UNIONISM as well as later working-class movements. Luddism first appeared in 1811 when threatening letters, purportedly sent from the mysterious 'General Ludd' appeared in Nottingham. Bands of knitting machine operators gathered under the cover of darkness and then broke the machines of a number of selected employers who the Luddites accused of using new technology to drive down wage rates. This type of action then spread through the hosiery and lace-making districts of Nottinghamshire and adjoining counties. There were further outbreaks in 1812, 1814 and 1816. In Yorkshire, cloth croppers destroyed newly installed shearing frames in 1812. In Lancashire, rioters attacked cotton mills that had installed steam-powered looms.

Despite the shared tactic of machine breaking in the three areas, aims and organization varied. Nottingham stockingers were concerned with wage reductions, the rents they paid for use of the machines, the use of unskilled workmen and the introduction of inferior-quality but cheaper alternative products. They were not opposed to new technology as such, only to those employers they saw as using it to dismantle customary wage rates and employment practices. In Yorkshire, the croppers were highly skilled and well paid, and were justifiably worried that new technology would destroy their position in the aristocracy of labour. In Lancashire, the Luddites were mainly handloom weavers being made directly unemployed by the substitution of their domestically based work with power looms in factories. There is still some difficulty in knowing exactly how the Luddites organized themselves or how numerous they were, as they made extensive use of pseudonyms, secret oaths and covert meetings. The government certainly took them seriously, sending more troops against them in 1812 than Wellington deployed against Napoleon in the Peninsula War.

It is difficult to assess whether they represented a REVOLUTIONARY threat or were simply a few well-organized bands skilled at propaganda. It is clear that night raids, where the efforts of sometimes over a hundred men were coordinated and sent against armed defenders, involved a high degree of planning. The reluctance of local people to assist the authorities in their enquiries also indicates a high level of popular support. Luddism has been described as COLLECTIVE bargaining by riot, a method of bringing pressure to bear on employers. The authorities responded to Luddism with repressive measures, making machine breaking a capital crime. Wherever there was any evidence of participation Luddites were shown little mercy. They were either hanged or transported. Luddism was thus crushed or swept away by the sheer pace of the industrial revolution, but their methods of organization contributed to the wider development of working-class radical movements.

LUXEMBURG, ROSA

'Freedom is always the freedom of the dissenters.'

A Polish-born German REVOLUTIONARY and SOCIALIST theorist (1870/1–1919). Although she was active in Poland it is for her contribution to German socialism that she is best known. Luxemburg joined a left-wing Polish party, 'The Proletariat', in 1886 but fled to Switzerland in 1889 to avoid detention. She attended Zurich University, coming into contact with socialist intellectuals and becoming increasingly opposed to the nationalist tendencies of the Polish and German socialist parties, believing that revolution must be aimed at the overthrow of international capitalism. She did not think that this aim was consistent with the idea of national self-determination, a view that later brought her into conflict with LENIN. She founded the Social DEMOCRATIC Party of the Kingdom of Poland to work towards international revolution, remaining its chief theoretician even after moving to Germany and joining the German Social Democratic Party in 1898. There she worked to counter the parliamentary politics that had become dominant in the party, despite its revolutionary rhetoric. She attempted, both within Germany and within the Second INTERNATIONAL, to persuade the socialist parties to oppose the imminent world war, calling for a general strike and a refusal to obey orders. When war did come, and the Second International parties supported national war aims, she left the party and founded the Spartacus League in order to continue to pursue revolutionary politics and her opposition to the war. This opposition led to her imprisonment for two and a half years from 1916. Though over-whelmingly supportive of the RUSSIAN REVOLUTION, she was critical of the Bolsheviks, fearing what she saw as the imposition of centralized authority.

After the war, Luxemburg found herself released from prison and part of the ruling party, following an uprising by soldiers and sailors in Kiel in 1918 which helped to bring the Independent Social Democratic Party (USPD) into power. The Spartacus League had affiliated themselves with the USPD as one of the other breakaway parties that had opposed the war. Eventually the coalition fell apart over how far the revolution should compromise with the German middle classes and capitalism. When a second wave of revolutionary activity broke out, aimed at a complete takeover by the workers' parties, Luxemburg tried to discourage it as she feared that a right-wing backlash would result – which it duly did. Luxemburg was captured by nationalist militia in Berlin, battered to death with rifle butts and her body thrown into a river.

Luxemburg's theorizing was generally Marxist, calling for a party-led class struggle for a socialist revolution which would eventually result in communism. However, she also incorporated some ideas more usually associated with ANARCHISM. These two strands to her thinking were termed the 'dialectic of spontaneity and organization'. The spontaneity would come from bottom-up class struggle and self-management on the part of the workers and peasants. The organization would come from the structure provided by a revolutionary party. The party's role would be to aid and develop the spontaneity and capacities of working people rather than to lead them and dictate what form the revolution should take. Luxemburg believed that both elements were essential for the development of communism and was critical of the Bolshevik Party for elevating the latter over the former.

LYCURGUS, see PLUTARCH

M

MANAGEMENT The celebration of this occupational group, social practice and academic domain has been a remarkable act of organizational colonization over the past century. This dictionary is an attempt to put management in its place, as one organizing principle amongst many others. The etymology of the word 'management' reflects this gradual expansion of its claims to importance. It seems to be derived from the Italian *mano*, hand, and its expansion into *maneggiarre*, the activity of handling and training a horse carried out by *maneggio*. From this, very specific, form of manual control, the word gets expanded into a general activity of training and handling people. The later development of the word is also influenced by the French *mener* (to lead) and its development into *ménage* – household, or housekeeping – and the verb *ménager*, to economize. So an intimate technology of the hand or of the household grows to become a technology of the workplace, and eventually of the state too. As a result, it is very difficult to 'define' management clearly. In some usages it is a synonym for 'organization' itself, as if all organizations were necessarily managed, or were the result of the activity of management.

Such a conflation is clearly unhelpful. As the MULTITUDE of entries that surround this one demonstrate, the historical and geographic diversity of real and imaginary forms of human organization cannot be reduced to one word. To do so is simply to reproduce assumptions about the three senses of management that so many alternative and UTOPIAN organizations contest. First, that all organizations require a specialized and permanent cadre of organizers who are given higher status and reward than everyone else in the organization. Second, that any form of organizing, patterning, arranging of people and things must be done by 'managers'. Third, that such organizing constitutes a specialist body of knowledge that some have and others do not – either by credentials or disposition. Of course, each of those assumptions is interlinked, but they add up to a powerful legitimation for the collective social mobility of one particular occupational group. So too do they ensure that the activities engaged in by universities, consultants, gurus, publishers and after-dinner speakers are lucrative ones.

That being said, many versions of utopian thinking have certainly echoed assumptions about a class of rulers. From Plato's REPUBLIC to WELL's *Modern Utopia*, the idea of an élite who govern on behalf of the common people has been something of a golden thread. Further, the corporatist elements of these ideas stretch back to SAINT-SIMON'S meritocracy of experts, and Bellamy's managers of the industrial army (see LOOKING BACKWARD). Importantly, the idea of management was itself a bourgeois challenge to conceptions of royal, religious or military privilege. If the arrogance of absolute and inherited power was the context, then no doubt the idea of a technocratic élite was a radical, possibly even revolutionary, suggestion. The connections between management and a LIBERAL version of society underwritten by BUREAUCRATIC forms of organization are important, but the key point here is that management does not have a monopoly of liberal ideas about freedom, or bureaucratic notions of due process. Indeed, it could be argued that contemporary senses of management are hostile to the careful impartiality of bureaucracy, and the sorts of freedom being discussed usually involve temporary and limited 'EMPOWERMENT' (see KALMAR; QUALITY OF WORKING LIFE) and not a radical attempt to think about ownership and decision making (see ANARCHISM, COOPERATIVES, WORKER SELF-MANAGEMENT).

MAO TSE-TUNG Born to a farming family in 1893, Mao was active in the creation of the Chinese Communist Party (CCP) in the 1920s, and became chairman of the party from 1945 until his death in 1976. Under Mao's leadership, the CCP took power and formed the People's Republic of China in 1949, with Mao as Chairman of the Republic until 1959. He is remembered for freeing China from foreign domination, for forging and later breaking the alliance with the SOVIET UNION, for his economic experiments, and for the Cultural Revolution he launched in 1966. He was also a political thinker and adapted Marxism-Leninism to a country dominated by the peasantry; his ideas were widely circulated with the publication of *Quotations from Chairman Mao Tse-Tung*, better known as 'the little Red Book'. Whilst a personality cult was created around him, he has also been widely criticized for economic policies that led to the deaths of millions of Chinese, for the establishment of one-party dictatorship, and for the social and economic chaos unleashed by the Cultural Revolution.

Mao met with MARXISTS whilst working as a library assistant in Beijing, and became involved in the CCP from its inception in 1920. In the late

1920s, with half of China under the control of the nationalist Kuomintang, Mao took to the countryside, where he assembled a small army and mobilized against the landlords. After gaining support from the peasants in the south-east of the country, he helped establish, and became chairman of, the Chinese Soviet Republic in 1931. In 1934, under increasing pressure from the campaigns of the Kuomintang forces, Mao and his GUERRILLA army began the Long March, a legendary retreat from the south-east to the north-west of China, that covered nearly 10,000 kilometres and cost tens of thousands of lives. In 1937, Japan declared war on China, which gave the CCP cause to unite with the nationalist forces. After defeating the Japanese, China went through a period of civil war between the CCP (supported by the Soviet Union) and the Kuomintang (supported by the USA). On their victory in 1949, the Communists founded the People's Republic of China, with Mao as chairman of the Republic. Whilst in power, Mao launched a vast programme of reforms including the redistribution of land from landlords to peasants, the COLLECTIVIZATION of farming into producers' cooperatives, and the simplification of Chinese characters to increase literacy.

Following Khrushchev's denunciation of Stalin in 1956, relations between China and the USSR deteriorated rapidly. Khrushchev and Mao accused each other of straying from true Marxist doctrine, and in 1960 Russian technicians and economic aid were withdrawn. In 1958, Mao launched The Great Leap Forward, a programme of economic development through which China would attempt to do in a decade what the Soviet Union had done in four. This was to be an alternative model of economic growth based on rural SMALL-scale industry, organiZed in COMMUNES. At first the programme met with some success, but it soon proved disastrous. The mobilization of peasants towards steel production, combined with adverse natural conditions and the cancellation of Soviet support, led to a famine in which up to 30 million people died. As a result, Mao was demoted from the post of Chairman of the People's Republic, although he remained chairman of the CCP.

In 1966, he launched the Cultural Revolution 'to criticize reactionary bourgeois authorities in science, to criticize the ideology of the bourgeoisie and all other exploiter classes ... to transform all areas of the superstructure mismatching the economic base of socialism, to promote the strengthening and development of the socialist system'. The Cultural Revolution was aimed against the emergence of a privileged class of intellectuals and

BUREAUCRATS. In support of his purge, Mao mobilized an army of young people, the Red Guards, whose authority surpassed that of the official army, police or law. Inspired by *Quotations from Chairman Mao Tse-Tung*, the Red Guards ruthlessly opposed and attacked revisionism, careerism and bureaucracy, sending their victims to forced labour camps to 'learn from the peasants'. Possession of the Little Red Book became an unofficial requirement for all Chinese citizens.

Mao was also a prolific writer and political thinker. He wrote extensively on Marxism and guerrilla warfare. Mao's political thinking draws on Marxist-Leninism, but stresses the role of the peasantry in bringing about the revolution. It was the mobilization of rural COMMUNITIES in the 1920s and 1930s that brought the Chinese Communist party to power. Mao's political thinking also concerned military strategy and guerrilla warfare, which he considered central to the revolutionary struggle. In Maoist thought, power comes from the barrel of the gun and requires the mobilization of the masses in guerrilla warfare; it is an act of violence by which one class overthrows another. Maoist thinking also stresses the continuous nature of the class struggle throughout the socialist period. The class struggle does not end with the revolution; even when the proletariat has seized power there remains the danger that the bourgeoisie will seek to restore capitalism.

Although Maoism remains the official ideology of the CCP, and it is still prohibited in China to publicly question its validity, its role in shaping China's politics has faded. Indeed there is a widespread perception that more pragmatic leaders have abandoned his thinking. The line of the CCP is that whilst Maoism was necessary to break China from its feudal past, it led to disasters and excesses. China now faces economic and political conditions unforeseen by Mao and requiring different solutions. Some remain nostalgic for the idealism of revolutionary Maoism, and regret that guaranteed employment, education and healthcare are now lost in the new MARKET-driven economy. Maoism has influenced communists around the world, in particular in Latin America and Asia; there are also parties created in Europe and the USA in the 1960s and 1970s that continue to support his ideas.

MARKETS In *The Wealth of Nations* (1776), Adam SMITH notes what he describes as a 'certain propensity in human nature ... to truck, barter and exchange one thing for another'. Out of this emerges the division of labour and the market. But against Smith's account of this 'natural' emergence of the market runs an alternative narrative. In England, throughout the eighteenth century, there are accounts of bands of ordinary men and women holding up merchants and wealthy farmers on their way to market, or visiting them at their homes, and demanding the right to buy bread at what they considered a 'fair' price (see also DIGGERS, PEASANTS' REVOLT). These groups were defending a 'moral economy', regulated by custom, which allowed members of the 'lower orders' to satisfy basic needs against an encroaching economy which celebrated *laissez-faire*, self-interest and profit-maximization: it was a clash of value systems. Frequently, such popular price-setting actions passed off peaceably. Other actions were less peaceful and the 'food riot' was also a common occurrence in eighteenth century England.

Two centuries later, across the global South, ordinary people resist International Monetary Fund (IMF) and World Bank policies directed towards the creation of free markets that allow private companies to charge whatever they wish for grain, or to export or store it even in times of dearth. These are policies that involve the privatization of essential utilities such as water and electricity and the enclosure of COMMON land which forces people to join, and thus create, a labour market. From Cairo's 'bread riots' of 1976, to the anti-IMF uprising in Algeria in 1988, to the ZAPATISTA rebellion which marked the first day of the North American Free Trade Agreement in 1994, to ongoing struggles against water privatization in Bolivia, markets have been contested. In all these examples, the state has responded with brutal force. In the new millennium, a bitter struggle over intellectual property rights to 'immaterial' products has begun (see INDYMEDIA, OPEN SOURCE SOFTWARE, WIKIPEDIA). What are at stake here are markets in music, film, software, drug formulae and so on. The full weight of global governance is brought down on those governments that have dared to manufacture generic drugs without paying the 'appropriate' licensing fee, while teenage music downloaders risk dawn raids by police. The point is that the market does not emerge 'naturally'. It is nearly always created and must nearly always be imposed on reluctant populations, who in turn nearly always resist.

Like Smith, Friedrich Hayek, theorist of economic LIBERALISM, believed the market emerges as the result of spontaneous evolution. But Hayek's understanding of the market is nevertheless interesting. For Hayek, the market is an immanent mechanism for the coordination of individual plans.

Production is, of course, social. As individuals living within society, we depend upon COOPERATION with others in order to satisfy most of our needs, and Hayek's market order includes not only private individuals, but also the *relations* between them. Because individuals are private, their expectations and plans do not necessarily match and may even conflict. The matching of these expectations can be the result of two alternative ordering principles: either an authoritarian ordering principle, which must be introduced from outside the system; or a spontaneous principle, such as the market. For Hayek the spontaneous order is superior because the nature of knowledge is fragmentary, dispersed and frequently contradictory. The market coordinates individual knowledge, but in such a way that each individual remains ignorant of the overall outcome. For Hayek, competition is a 'discovery process'. Through the market individual agents discover 'which goods are scarce goods, or which things are goods, and how scarce and valuable they are'. They discover the 'minimum costs of production' or what the desires and attitudes of consumers might be. Thus scarcity of goods and services, for example, is not *given*, as in mainstream economic theory, but is rather produced as a result of market interaction.

Markets thus constitute a communication system which enables dispersed knowledge to be utilized. Price signals focus the attention of individuals on what is worth producing and what is not. The knowledge which markets organize is thus not only the *know-how* necessary for production, but also a social force that makes it *necessary* to produce certain products in certain ways for certain purposes. For Hayek, one outcome of market order is *efficiency*: the market ensures that whatever is produced is produced at its lowest possible cost. But this efficiency cannot be achieved without coercion. Private individuals *must* follow the common indicators provided by the market which functions through rewarding some and punishing others. From the market emerges a system of prices, which are *norms*: those producers who can *beat* the norm and produce at a lower price are rewarded; all others must *meet* the norm, or they are punished. The system is dynamic since the effect of any individual beating the norm is to change the norm itself. All are compelled to continually 'improve' and we can thus understand the market as a 'disciplinary mechanism'.

If the market is characterized by continuous compulsion, 'movement for movement's sake', as Hayek put it, what are the alternatives? Take the ANTI-CAPITALIST mobilization against the G8 summit in Gleneagles in July 2005. This counter-mobilization involved a NETWORK of thousands of individuals cooperating over a period of up to two years. Needs and desires were openly expressed and all decisions were taken on the basis of consensus. Over the period of the mobilization, enormous wealth was produced, both material in terms of the physical infrastructure of the temporary 'convergence centres' in Stirling, Edinburgh and Glasgow, and immaterial in new knowledges and skills, new models for sharing skills and making decisions, new relationships. We can, in fact, understand this counter-mobilization as a distributed coordinating machine, functioning to organize heterogeneous human plans. In other words, an alternative to the market. (DH)

MARX, KARL The most influential political and philosophical thinker of the modern age. Although he rejected the ROMANTIC UTOPIANISM of some of his contemporaries, his critique of capitalism as unjust and alienating, and his vision of COMMUNISM, have inspired numerous attempts to bring about social REVOLUTION. As a result, Marx's ideas may be seen as a major force behind the history of the twentieth century and remains an inspiration to social movements across the world. Marx was born into a wealthy Jewish family in Trier, Prussia in 1818. Marx went to the University of Bonn to study law in 1835, but after a year his father made him transfer to Berlin. There he came into contact with the left-Hegelians, including the ANARCHIST STIRNER. Hegel's philosophical method and the radical uses to which it was put by this group were to set Marx on the path to many of his most important insights, particularly that of dialectical materialism.

The Prussian state, never a model of tolerance, became even more repressive after the accession of Friedrich Wilhelm IV to the throne in 1840. Political dissent was suppressed and Marx was forced to abandon his academic career, shortly after obtaining his doctorate. He took a post editing the LIBERAL newspaper *Rheinische Zeitung*, but the paper was shut down in 1843, partly as a result of conflict with government censors. Marx scraped a living as a freelance journalist but struggled to publish due to his growing reputation as a seditious writer. He accepted an invitation to co-edit a radical German journal published in Paris and there met many prominent radical thinkers, including PROUDHON and BAKUNIN. Most importantly, Marx met Engels, already a committed communist, who persuaded Marx of the importance of class relations in understanding social development and revolutionary politics. His stay in Paris went badly in terms of earning his living. He quickly fell out with his fellow editor, Ruge, and the journal was soon banned in Prussia. The Prussian authorities announced that Marx was to be arrested if he ever returned because of his numerous attacks on the monarchy. Eventually the French King ordered that Marx be expelled and he left for Brussels in 1845. For the next few years Marx and Engels moved between Belgium and London engaging in research and political activism. They co-wrote *The German Ideology* and *The Poverty of Philosophy*, Marx's critique of Proudhon. Both of these paved the way for *The Communist Manifesto*, published in 1848 for the Communist League, the forerunner of the First INTERNATIONAL.

Marx was invited back to Paris by a new republican government but it collapsed in 1849. He then moved on to Cologne to set up the *Neue Rheinische Zeitung* but was expelled after a year by the authorities as a brief spell of LIBERAL democracy was suppressed. Left penniless in the aftermath of closing down the paper, Marx and his family settled in London. For most of his remaining years his household experienced hardship and ill health, with three of his children dying in infancy. Other than some occasional income from journalism and lectures, Marx was to remain financially dependent on Engels for the rest of his life. He attempted to carry on his leadership of the Communist League, transferring its headquarters to London, but dissent led to its transfer back to Cologne. Marx was left to concentrate on his theoretical work, particularly the writing of *Capital*. In 1864 Marx returned to active politics when he was invited to sit on the General Council of the International Working Men's Association, also known as the First INTERNATIONAL. Despite his renewed political involvement, the first volume of *Capital* was completed and published in 1867. By 1872, however, the International was disintegrating in the wake of the defeat of the PARIS COMMUNE in 1871, the expulsion of Bakunin, and the failure to recruit the larger British TRADE UNIONS. Marx again withdrew in order to concentrate on completing *Capital*, although his increasingly poor health prevented him from making much progress. Marx died in March 1883 and was buried in Highgate Cemetery in London. In 1893 and 1894 Engels published volumes 2 and 3 of *Capital*, completing Marx's most comprehensive statement of the workings of capitalism.

Marx's thought covers three major areas that broadly coincide with different stages of his life: philosophy; a historical analysis of social relations; and a critique of capitalism derived from the political economy of writers such as Ricardo and SMITH. In all three areas his concern was to provide SOCIALISM with what he saw as a scientific basis that would enable a

175

successful transition to communism. He was thus opposed to what he saw as the nostalgic or impractical forms of utopian SOCIALISM and ANARCHISM that were dominant in the movements of his day. Following the Bolshevik Revolution of 1917 the triumph of his ideas (or at least their interpretation by LENIN and Trotsky) seemed complete. The subsequent lapse of the SOVIET UNION into totalitarianism and the eclipse of socialist politics during the latter part of the twentieth century have led some to write Marx off as outdated or inaccurate. Others have sought to revise and modify Marx's ideas but remain convinced that his analysis of capitalism is still essentially valid. His own beliefs are difficult to untangle from those of his later followers and detractors, and the very nature of his writing makes it nonsensical to try to adopt a neutral position. Even Marx himself is known to have commented in exasperation at some self-styled Marxists, 'If that is Marxism, then I am not a Marxist.'

It was from Hegel that Marx derived the notion that history should be interpreted as progress towards a desirable form of society. For Marx, the engine that drives progress is conflict between classes: between those social groups who acquire a powerful position and seek to defend it, and those who are dispossessed as a result. History can thus be divided into stages, each of which is characterized by a different form of economic organization. Transitions between these stages occur as class conflict eventually brings about change. Marx argued that economic systems are made up of a particular combination of what he called the *means of production* (the material resources required for production) and the *relations of production* (the social organization of these resources). Together, the means and relations of production form a distinctive *mode of production*. Marx argued that European societies had moved from a feudal mode to a capitalist mode when the labour of individuals itself became a commodity and the only possession that the working class could bring to the MARKET to trade. The culture and ideology of a society was the result of its underlying economic organization.

Marx argued that within capitalism the dominant class is the *bourgeoisie*, the property-owning employing class. He regarded them as a highly significant class because of their capacity to constantly enhance production through re-investing profits. Marx foresaw that the global development of capitalism was in the process of sweeping away all previous social and economic forms and was capable of enormous growth and dynamism. This was not least because of the ability of the bourgeoisie to determine the dominant beliefs of society. He argued that the ideology of the ruling class tends to become that of society as whole, functioning to protect that class by persuading the working class (or *proletariat*) that their interests are the same. He believed that this was an instance of *false consciousness*, as ideology prevented the working class from becoming aware of its own interests. Despite the dominance of the peasantry throughout most of Europe at the time, Marx argued that only the proletariat could challenge capitalism. He believed that the proletariat had the historical destiny of bringing about the end of capitalism and of leading mankind into a communist society. Despite capitalism's immense capacity to adapt, Marx thought that it contained the seeds of its own destruction. Capitalism is prone to periodic crises such as recessions or wars over resources and territory. In addition, the factory system brings together large numbers of the working class, living in close proximity to one another in densely populated cities. These factors, Marx thought, would induce a proletarian consciousness of itself as a distinctive class with its own interests and forms of organization. Eventually this consciousness would develop into a revolutionary movement.

Marx argued that at the heart of capitalist production was a simple act of theft. Each worker must produce enough to pay for his/her own wages plus the costs of materials and the production process itself. Beyond this, the worker produces profits for the capitalist. This additional labour Marx called surplus value, a measure of the amount of labour that was done purely to support the consumption of the bourgeoisie and to provide additional capital to reinvest. In turn improved technology enabled even more surplus value to be extracted from the workers, causing their share of total wealth to decrease. Marx believed that the result of this process would be a polarization between classes. This development of class-consciousness would be aided by the tendency of capitalism to increasingly remove from the worker any control, ownership or involvement. Marx thought that the bourgeoisie would fiercely resist any move towards socialism, using the full resources of the state. This belief was borne out by the behaviour of both the liberal democratic and absolutist governments of Marx's time. The conclusion Marx drew was that only a well-organized international revolution, itself prepared to utilize physical force, could overthrow capitalism. Although he believed that historical forces made a revolution inevitable eventually, he was no political quietist. He theorized and took part in working-class struggles and revolutionary organizations in the belief that a revolution could be brought about more quickly through both action and scientific understanding.

177

Marx has been criticized by supporters and opponents. Historically the peasantry, not the proletariat, has been important in the overthrowing of capitalist governments. Marx predicted that the most advanced capitalist economies ought to be those that were most susceptible to revolution. In practice, it has been in much less developed economies, such as Russia and China, that revolutions have broken out. Anarchists and some Marxists were also critical of Marx's insistence that the existing institutions of the state would have to be retained in a transitional *dictatorship of the proletariat* before full communism could be achieved. The rise of BUREAUCRATIC authoritarianism in the Soviet Union and China appeared to confirm fears that such an arrangement would lead to one form of oppression being replaced by another. Marx's elevation of class as the most significant factor in social relations is also questioned in a number of ways. For example, many FEMINISTS would see the domination of women by men as a more fundamental form of oppression than that of class.

For those hostile to Marxism, usually on the political right, such criticisms amount to a complete refutation. For others, Marx's work is a living tradition that requires modification and development but still has a powerful explanatory and ethical significance. In the last few decades even this work has been declining in the face of a resurgent MANAGERIAL neoliberalism and, within the radical camp, attacks by thinkers who question many of the assumptions on which Marxism is founded (see AUTONOMIA). Without doubt his work has had an enormous influence on the modern world and has inspired the most significant utopian projects in human history. However, Marxist political movements, particularly in the West, have been declining for many years. The recent ANTI-CAPITALIST movement has not adopted Marxism as its prevailing theoretical and tactical framework. That said, without Marx, contemporary movements would almost entirely lack a language for its critique. Yet many within the movement are suspicious of what they see as the inherent authoritarianism of a single 'official' idea. It is unfair to traduce Marx because of the way in which his work has been used as a justification by followers. What is genuinely surprising is not so much the inevitable weaknesses in his work that have emerged over the past century and a half but the extraordinary relevance of it. No more compelling set of ideas has emerged to replace Marx as a way of understanding the workings of global capitalism or of exposing the violence, exploitation and injustice upon which it is founded.

MASSACHUSETTS BAY COLONY The various DISSENTERS who left England in the 1620s and 1630s established a series of theocratic UTOPIAN communities, initially in what is now 'New England', USA. Perhaps the best-known of these was the Massachusetts Bay Colony (MBC), initially formed as a profit-making venture in 1628. In 1629 the members of the company signed the 'Cambridge Agreement', which effectively turned a business into a stockholding COOPERATIVE with all shares owned by emigrants. John Winthrop, a staunch Puritan, and 1,000 colonists arrived in 1630 to what he described as 'city on a hill', echoing Augustine's *City of God*. About 200 died in the first winter, and 200 returned to England the following year, but over the next ten years about 20,000 Puritans established a series of settlements along the north-eastern coast. The MBC was a more inclusive version of Calvin's Geneva (see CHRISTIANOPOLIS; CITY STATE) with voting rights being conferred on 'freemen', that is to say, members of the church. They believed themselves to be members of the chosen few, the 'elect' who had been selected by god to avoid eternal damnation. That this new 'promised land' had been kept secret until now was a further proof that this was a new exodus, the last chance at redemption. The price of such a position was eternal vigilance, about one's own behaviour and that of one's neighbours. Like many other Protestant groups (see AMISH, ANABAPTISTS), they believed that responsible men (not women, not servants) entered directly into a relationship with god, without interference from either the church or state back in the countries from which they came. This belief that 'conscience' was a reasonable defence for action effectively meant that the diverse range of Puritan sects (see CULT) exemplified one or both of two tendencies: authoritarian intolerance and assumption of 'manifest destiny', or an insistence on personal responsibility and independence (see OCEANA). The MBC's charter was taken away in 1684, but the influence of Puritan beliefs on the subsequent growth and industrialization of the USA is usually regarded as considerable (see AMERICA).

MECHANICS' INSTITUTES and **MUTUAL IMPROVEMENT SOCIETIES** Both institutions grew in nineteenth-century England, reflecting the determination of adults to educate themselves despite a complete lack of provision, and closely related to the long tradition of AUTO-DIDACTICISM. Mechanics' Institutes were firmly in the hands of the middle-class philanthropic patrons who established them. Few 'mechanics' took part

179

in the governance of the institutes. The London Mechanics' Institute was set up in 1823 and was followed by similar institutes in all the main industrial towns. The original purpose of the institutes was to provide scientific education for artisans but, in practice, the main users of them were clerks, shopkeepers and members of the lower middle class. They preferred more artistic and literary subjects and the curriculum was modified accordingly. The largest Mechanics' Institutes, such as those in London and Manchester, went on to become universities. Essentially, then, the Mechanics' Institutes represented education *for* the working classes rather than *by* them.

Mutual Improvement Societies are much less well-known as they did not leave scores of impressive stone-faced buildings scattered across England. They were, however, much closer to the people they served. A society would consist of a small number of members who met together in each other's houses or in a hired room. Members arranged a set of rules, a programme of lectures, essay readings and discussions. Books were bought over time to build up a small library. Members contributed a small weekly subscription to fund the society and its main aim was to promote basic literacy – although in some instances the subjects were extended to geography, history, French and chemistry. They also provided an opportunity for working people to acquire skills in public speaking and debating. Samuel Smiles observed that, by 1847, there was scarcely a town or village in West Yorkshire that did not have such a society. They were frequently attached to pre-existing bodies such as chapels, Sunday schools, FRIENDLY SOCIETIES or Chartist branches. If they occurred in places where there was already a Mechanics' Institute, working people tended to prefer the Mutual Improvement Societies because they controlled what was taught and how it was taught, despite the much lower level of financial resources. Mutual Improvement Societies also allowed the discussion of political and religious subjects, frequently banned in the Mechanics' Institutes. Just as the Societies were spontaneously and MUTUALLY created, so they tended to die out when the school system began to cater more for working people. Yet some, such as the Workers' Educational Association, continued – and provided an education for much of the leadership of the labour movement in the twentieth century.

MICROCREDIT, MICROFINANCE, MICROLENDING see

CREDIT UNIONS GRAMEEN BANK

MILLENARIANISM A diverse set of religious DISSENTING groups operating mainly in medieval Europe. Some were involved in social dissent and UTOPIAN projects and the remarks below refer generally to such groups. They were known as millenarian because they believed they could bring about the thousand years of the KINGDOM OF HEAVEN ON EARTH that, within Christian doctrine, is believed to precede the final judgement. To dissent from the core doctrines of the medieval church was to place oneself outside society – and so religious dissent was frequently, though not always, tied to social protest. Frequently, the various millenarian sects and communities arose amongst the poor and dispossessed. Their poverty was not the voluntary poverty of MONASTICISM and they lived lives of extreme hardship and chronic insecurity. The way in which these sects often operated was an expression of their desire to control their own lives, find meaning in them and sometimes resist the control of others. CATHARISM, through not strictly millenarian, demonstrates similar features. Often millenarian movements were violent, ANARCHIC, and, at times, REVOLUTIONARY. In some cases millenarian sects were avowedly utopian, aiming at the overthrow of existing hierarchies and attempting to replace them with something approaching COMMUNISM. The millenarian tradition is of more than simply historical interest. The idea that all men and women were equal and that a GOLDEN AGE was possible through human action has been a powerful influence on subsequent movements. Millenarian beliefs were evident in the English PEASANTS' REVOLT and passed from them to groups such as the LEVELLERS, DIGGERS and RANTERS, and so into Chartism and thence to SOCIALISM. Other millenarian groups of note include the Flagellants, the BRETHREN OF THE FREE SPIRIT, the Taborites and the ANABAPTISTS.

MINARCHISM or **MINIMAL STATISM**, see ANARCHISM; LIBERALISM; MUTUALISM, NOZICK; RAND

MODERN UTOPIA, A, see WELLS, H. G.

MONASTICISM A feature of a number of world religions, including Buddhism, Christianity, Hinduism and Jainism. Christian monasticism formed an important part of medieval society and took on various forms in the Orthodox, Eastern Orthodox, and Catholic churches. It has declined markedly in modern times but is still significant within the Roman Catholic Church. All forms of monasticism share one central characteristic: members

181

renounce their participation in day-to-day life and devote themselves to the pursuit of their religion. COMMUNITIES tend to be self-governing but follow a 'Rule', a set of precepts established at the founding of a particular order but sometimes modified over the history of the order.

In most cases becoming a monk or nun requires a renunciation of worldly possessions and the taking of vows of voluntary poverty. Frequently chastity is also a requirement and some orders cut themselves off completely from contact with the outside world. This is particularly true of some Buddhist and Orthodox Christian orders. Others, such as the Christian Dominican Friars, have been mendicant, going out into wider society to preach and tend to the spiritual needs of the laity, whilst also pursuing a life of contemplation, worship and prayer. Other monasteries provided a wide range of services, including healthcare and education, to the surrounding community. In medieval Europe, monasteries assumed great importance in the economic as well as spiritual affairs of society. Most scholarly activity, until the emergence of the universities, took place in monastic libraries and scriptoriums. Over time they tended to accrue wealth and land through bequests and so became major landowners and employers, sometimes wielding significant political power. The Abbots of monasteries formed part of the feudal hierarchy, often already being members of noble families and thus able to combine spiritual and secular power. The sometimes luxurious lives of medieval monks drew much criticism (see ABBEY OF THELEME); there were frequent calls for reform and a return to the more austere demands of the original rule. New orders such as the Cistercians or the Franciscans were often founded as a result of such demands from within the Church.

The UTOPIAN appeal of monasticism has a number of aspects. First, though they were by no means libertarian, members entered them voluntarily and submitted to the rule by choice. Second, monastic communities have often been highly successful organizational units, able to guarantee the material needs of their members and to provide a degree of security. Third, though the hierarchy within the monastery often reflected that of wider society, it provided a degree of opportunity for the marginalized to obtain a respected position. Finally, monasteries have frequently been COMMUNITIES imbued with a sense of belonging and MUTUALITY when compared with the competitive insecurity of normal life. Many alternative communities share the features of COMMUNAL life first developed through monasticism. They frequently combine an explicit spiritual, political or social purpose with

SELF-SUFFICIENCY and collective organization. Like monasteries, they also provide a retreat from the demands of a seemingly harsh and atomized society.

MONDRAGÒN A network of worker COOPERATIVES established in the 1950s in the Basque region of Spain under the inspiration of Father José Maria Arizmendiarrieta. At the end of 2004 *Mondragòn Corporaciòn Cooperativa* linked 228 cooperatives in the industrial, retail, financial and educational sectors employing 71,500 workers, with operations in 23 countries. The Basque country suffered both economic deprivation and political persecution under the Franco regime (see SPANISH ANARCHIST MILITIAS) and Father José Maria sought to revitalize the area by promoting educational, cultural and economic activities. In 1943 he set up a technical school, and five of the students set up a cooperative called Ulgor (later to become Fagor) to manufacture oil stoves and lamps. As Ulgor flourished, other cooperatives were established alongside it, either as a spin-off, or as autonomous ventures. When access to capital became a problem, Father José Maria proposed the creation of a cooperative bank, the *Caja Laboral Popular,* set up in 1959 to channel MUTUAL savings into cooperative development. In 1967, a cooperative social security system was developed to provide pension and welfare to worker-members. The various cooperatives officially federated in 1986 under the *Mondragòn Corporaciòn Cooperativa,* a coordinating body for all the worker-owned cooperatives in the Basque community, including a research company, a technical college, a cooperative bank, and a network of supermarkets.

Father José Maria died in 1976, and although he never had a direct hand in the MANAGEMENT of the cooperatives he helped establish, his sense of DEMOCRACY, EMPOWERMENT and self-reliance continues to be reflected in the cooperative's values and principles. As a cooperative, Mondragòn adheres to the principles laid down by the International cooperative Alliance. Members, on being hired in a cooperative, lend a set amount of the cooperative's capital. The dividends that accrue from their shares of the capital are re-invested and members can only cash their dividends when they leave the cooperative or reach retirement. This means that the majority of profits are reinvested, whilst 10 per cent is earmarked for social services and COMMUNITY development. All worker-members have the right and responsibility to participate in the management of their cooperative. In practice, democracy in Mondragòn works through indirect participation. 183

A team of managers is appointed for a fixed term (usually four years) by the supervisory board, which is in turn accountable to the General Assembly of all the members. Mondragòn also promotes cooperation between co-operatives through the creation of profit-pooling sub-groups of coopera-tives, as well as the transfer and training of worker members of cooperatives in crisis to other cooperatives within the FEDERATION. In addition, Mondragòn has a policy of wage solidarity that imposes a maximum pay differential of 6:1 between the top and bottom of the pay scale, a ratio that has increased since the 3:1 ratio set initially, but remains lower than in the private sector.

Mondragòn has become mythologized as the success story of the cooperative movement and has managed to reinvent itself to survive social and economic changes. Yet it has also been criticized for failing to remain true to its initial principles. As Mondragòn expanded and internationalized, the distance between managers and workers has increased. Yet Mondragòn continues to offer a successful alternative to neoliberal capitalism and provides a living example of how a community can gain control of its own development and encourage WORKER SELF-MANAGEMENT, while contributing to the wider Basque community development.

MORE, THOMAS, see UTOPIA

MORRIS, WILLIAM, see NEWS FROM NOWHERE; ARTS AND CRAFTS

MST (MOVIMENTO DOS TRABALHADORES RURAIS SEM TERRA)   Brazil's Landless Workers' Movement was officially founded in 1984 to support and co-ordinate the struggles for land that had taken place all over Brazil since the late 1970s. Sem Terra has become one of the largest GRASSROOTS social movements in Latin America. Its aim is to reclaim unproductive land and redistribute it to people for whom land provides both food and dignity. In doing so, it is only trying to exercise a right inscribed in Brazil's constitution, the right to use unproductive land for a 'larger social function'. The main tactic used has been the occupation by landless families who plan the invasion and set up camp on the land. Once occupied, a judge (eventually) decides whether to expropriate the land and give it to the occupying peasants. Those involved come from all shades of the political spectrum; they operate in decentralized groups with no membership or leader, and privilege DIRECT ACTION over party politics. As MST has no membership, it is very difficult to assess its size. Anyone who is landless and does something about it is part of MST. In 1985 MST organized 35 land occupations, mobilizing 10,500 families. By 2005, MST had won land titles for more than 250,000 families in 1,600 settlements, and 200,000 encamped families were awaiting government recognition. In fighting for more equitable land ownership, MST has also joined other movements in Brazil and globally to challenge neoliberal economics and the corporate takeover of agriculture. Through its campaigns, direct action and educational programme, MST seeks to promote SUSTAINABLE, SMALL-scale farming. It is part of the international farmers' movement VIA CAMPESINA that campaigns for food sovereignty and land reforms.

MULTITUDE Originating in the writing of Hobbes and Spinoza, the term multitude has more recently been adopted by political theorists within AUTONOMISM, particularly Hardt and Negri, to evoke the potential for radical transformation that rests within our being drawn into the web of global capitalism, or Empire. The notion of the multitude draws upon a critical reading of MARX's analysis of the relationship between capital and the proletariat. In some way, the multitude serves the same role in Autonomist thinking as the proletariat did in classical Marxist analysis. However the notion of the multitude moves us onto a later stage of capitalist development, where labour is no longer confined socially to 'the working class' nor spatially to the factory or office. Rather, labour has become dispersed through the fabric of productive, reproductive, affective and intellectual life; and the factory-office has dissolved into society. Industrial labour has been replaced by 'immaterial labour' that includes intellectual labour such as the production of ideas, knowledge, images, and emotions. By extending production to include all these forms, global capitalism has also drawn us all into its net. In our various social roles and activities as workers, homemakers, students and consumers we are all folded into Empire, contaminated by it, part of it. Thus multitude is defined in relation to this late stage of capitalist development where capital has turned all our various activities into subjects of production and objects of exploitation, a position no longer reserved for wage labourers directly employed by capital.

But if multitude refers to our common position and participation in the grip of Empire, it also gestures towards the counter-power that comes with this position. In classical Marxist analysis the proletariat was seen as existing in relation to capital and as having power to overthrow it. For Autonomist writers the very participation of the multitude in Empire opens up the possibility of liberation. Thus the multitude contains potentiality, it is a form of immanence that lives in the revolutionary potential of each and all of us as repositories of immaterial labour within global capitalism. But by moving away from the proletariat to the multitude as the agent of radical change, we lose the unity that allegedly defined the 'working class'. The multitude is not defined by its unity but as a COMMUNITY of differences, a movement made of incommensurable singularities. Unlike the notions of 'the mass', 'the populace', 'the working class' or 'the people', the multitude is not defined as an organized unity but as a NETWORK of differences with REVOLUTIONARY potential that has had strong resonance within the ANTI-CAPITALIST movement.

MUTUAL AID/IMPROVEMENT SOCIETIES, see FRIENDLY SOCIETIES, MECHANICS' INSTITUTES

MUTUALISM A term that refers (in a restricted sense) to a particular organizational form, or (in a more general sense) to a principle that underpins a libertarian form of ANARCHISM. The origins of this word are in the ideas of mutation and changeability. In terms of its use as organizing principle, it suggests that all the parties in an association are subject to the same changes – in other words, that there is no hierarchical organizer who benefits differentially from the association (see also NETWORK). A mutual company is owned by the people that do business with it (that is, it has no issued stock or shares). In this restricted sense, whilst mutual organizations are similar to COOPERATIVES, the term tends to refer to financial sector companies rather than those that deal in production or distribution. As a result, the members of co-ops tend to be the employees, whilst the members of mutuals include anyone who has an account with them. In principle, since they do not need to pay dividends to shareholders, all members should benefit through lower rates on borrowing and higher rates on lending.

With its origins in the early FRIENDLY SOCIETIES, mutualism tended to be concentrated in the areas of insurance, housing and funeral services, with the aim being to provide cheap services to the working classes. In the UK, Building Societies, Money Clubs, Sick Societies and Burial Societies were formed from the middle of the eighteenth century onwards as means of providing a form of insurance. They usually brought together members of the 'respectable' working class sponsored by the philanthropic middle classes and based around schools, NON-CONFORMIST chapels, inns or specific occupations (see GUILDS). They were underpinned by a sense of morally based self-help, often articulated as a sense that the large industrial towns were becoming a breeding ground for discontent and that financial discipline might result in a better sense of citizenship. By the twentieth century, mutuals dominated their respective markets in the UK and US (where they were sometimes also called 'Savings and Loans'), but since the 1990s a wave of demutualization has hit the sector, driven by the supposed 'need' to raise finance capital (though for the opposite tendency, see CREDIT UNIONS, GRAMEEN BANK).

Leaving aside specific organizational forms, the idea of mutualism has been central to certain formulations of anarchist theory. PROUDON's reformulation of the labour theory of value suggested that property is theft when it is earned through living off the labour of others (see also ISLAMIC FINANCE, for a similar position on the payment of interest). To live off charging more than the costs of a product was hence unethical, since it implied having some sort of coercive power over others which would make them pay more than the thing was actually worth. This led to libertarian or individualist anarchist positions in which SMALL-scale producers might unite in voluntary associations. KROPOTKIN also made the idea of self-interested reciprocity, which he called 'mutual aid', central to his ideas, stressing that cooperation was a more basic principle than competition. Like many twentieth-century utopian thinkers (see COOPERATIVE CITY, FREELAND, LOOKING BACKWARD), Kropotkin put forward the idea that mutualist systems of wealth production would only require that people worked half as long as they did under a capitalist regime. This was because they were no longer producing the surplus value that allowed the parasitic managerial and aristocratic classes to live off working people's labour.

The key point about mutualism, in anarchist theory, is that it is a MARKET-based form of association that is entered into freely, and that it benefits all. A division of labour that allowed for specialization and which produced a complex product would hence be legitimate if all benefited equally from the labour time that they spent. However, if association was not needed, then it would not happen – in the case of family farms, for example. An early example of this sort of mutualism was Josiah Warren's highly successful Cincinnati Time Store, that lasted from 1827 until 1830. Warren (an ex-member of OWEN's 'New Harmony', and sometimes described as the 'American Proudhon') insisted that price should be based on cost, and since cost could be measured in labour, they could trade 'labour for labour'. He set up a system of labour notes that measured how much labour had gone into particular commodities, and based these on the value of pounds of corn. One hour of labour was worth twelve pounds of corn, though different sorts of labour were also recognized. Contemporary versions of this sort of small-scale mutualism would include BARTERING, CREDIT UNIONS, Community Currency, LETS and TIME BANKS. In theoretical terms, mutualism could be described as a sort of radical COMMUNITARIANISM or COLLECTIVISM, in which individuals are tied to others through a variety of economic and social links (see SOCIAL CAPITAL), but it is more usually viewed as an anarchist form of LIBERALISM, in which the freedom of the individual is the first principle. What ties both interpretations together is a hostility to large-scale coercion, most particularly that associated with the capitalist BUREAUCRATIC state; a faith in small-scale market mechanisms; and a refusal to imagine that a violent REVOLUTION will bring about a fair alternative economic structure (see also BRAY).

N

NETWORK This word has been applied to transportation, media, biology, technology, mathematics and human societies. In its essence, it suggests a non-hierarchical web of connections (or ties) between organizations and/or people and/or objects. Such a web would have communication nodes but no controlling centre. In principle, unlike a hierarchy (see BOOKCHIN, BUREAUCRACY), the network does not need centralized direction, and hence could still operate even if parts of it were not functioning. It thus has something in common with 'cellular' or 'bottom-up' methods of organizing (see GRASSROOTS, GUERRILLA, WIKIPEDIA). However, the metaphor is an elastic one, since some 'nodes' can be conceptualized as more important than others (in terms of establishing rules for the rest of the network), and some connections can be seen to be more important than others (if their information is particularly valued). In other words, networks can easily begin to look like hierarchies if there is a great deal of distinction between the elements of the network. Further, since networks have been conceptualized as being 'weak' or 'strong', then it is possible to imagine a hierarchy of networks, or even (in the most conventional case) the word 'network' functioning a little like the term 'informal structure' (or COMMUNITY) in relation to the formal structures of organizations. The utilitarian use of the term 'networking' appears to have this meaning, as does the production of 'sociograms' through 'sociometry' as practised by US social network analysis sociologists from the 1950s onwards.

Thus the radically non-hierarchical potential of this word has been degraded considerably over the last fifty years. At its worst, it has even been used (by Manuel Castells) as a general description of an information society. However, since this 'network society' contains forms of organization and economy that are clearly hierarchical and exclusionary, it is difficult to see what distinctiveness the word actually has in this context. Rather like EMPOWERMENT or MANAGEMENT, it is a word that has now been so overused that any precise meaning is difficult to pin down. Nonetheless, many of the forms of alternative organization in this dictionary, and some of the

UTOPIAS, are informed by a sense of organization as distributed and DEMOCRATIC. So too are some ANTI-CAPITALIST movements. The work of making a net could be hierarchically controlled, or broadly coordinated, but it could proceed through the autonomous activities of each of the nodes. This could be an imagined state of social order (see THE DISPOSSESSED, WOMAN ON THE EDGE OF TIME), a political philosophy (see ANARCHISM, FEMINISM), a technological practice (see INDYMEDIA, OPEN SOURCE SOFTWARE) or a located political practice (see AUTONOMIA, ECOVILLAGE). All of these ideas, and many more, seem to provide the potential to make the word 'network' mean something else again.

NEW ATLANTIS

'The End of our Foundation is the knowledge of Causes, and secret motions of things, and the enlarging of the bounds of Human Empire, to the effecting of all things possible.'

Francis Bacon's (1561–1626) mysterious UTOPIA borrows the ancient name of ATLANTIS to imagine a place of great learning and scientific progress. It was written in 1624, and published posthumously in 1627 (Bacon supposedly died after contracting a cold while stuffing a chicken with snow to test the preservative effect. *New Atlantis* is really a fragment, perhaps the beginning of a larger project. What Bacon describes is only the quasi-MONASTIC college of learning, 'The House of Salomon' (perhaps inspired by Tycho Brahe's research community at Uraniborg on the Danish island of Hven). There is little detail concerning the social or political institutions of Bensalem, though we know that it has been a monarchy for 3,000 years, and that its rules were established by King Solamona 1,900 years previously. Bacon is often credited with the 'invention' of the modern scientific and experimental method. This is certainly an exaggerated claim, but in *New Atlantis* he is the first utopian to show science at the centre of social planning. But (perhaps unsuprisingly for an English politican of the time) this is a science that is a SECRET and élite form of knowledge, a state-sponsored knowledge aimed at satisfying the material wants of human beings, and one based on technology as the source of power ('the effecting of all things possible').

The travellers arrive at Bensalem by ship, lost and crying to their god to save them. Whilst King Solamona has forbidden exchange with foreigners (like PLUTARCH'S Lycurgus), he did institute a law that mandates kindness to those who arrive. They are taken to the 'Strangers' House' and allowed to stay for six weeks. Over time they learn a few details. Directly commenting on More's UTOPIA, Bacon insists that couples are not permitted to judge each other naked before marriage, but friends can report back after having seen their intended swimming naked. There is much emphasis on the strength and vitality of the faithful union, and a general abhorrence of promiscuity and homosexuality. There are also massively detailed ceremonies for men who have produced thirty children, which the mother is allowed to watch though she may not be seen.

But all this is a precursor to the accounts of King Solamona's main achievement: the establishment of Salomon's House, or the 'College of Six Days Works'. This is a scientific institution on a massive scale. We are first told that in order to gain knowledge about the world, the isolation of Bensalem is relaxed every twelve years in order that two ships can be sent to discover foreign secrets. The three brethren of the house aboard each ship are sent ashore in disguise until they can be collected again, and we are not allowed to know where they are or what they are doing. This secrecy (and slight sense of paranoia) suffuses the entire book, with many conversations ending prematurely, or intentions being veiled in various ways. Despite these mysteries, we are left in no doubt that the House of Salomon is a place of incredible wonders – deep caves for making new materials, telescopes, perfumes which can imitate any smell, new sorts of food, perpetual motion, elixirs that prolong life, half-a-mile high towers, submarines and so on. These are produced not only by spying on the rest of the world, but by a division of labour that separates different processes of knowledge generation into a sequence that begins with reviewing what is already known and ends with axioms that have a general truth. Even then, the brethren of the house can decide whether or not to release their knowledge to the state.

Unlike CHRISTIANOPOLIS and CITY OF THE SUN, Bacon's technocracy seems very modern and materialistic, and perhaps rather AMERICAN in its faith in material progress (see LOOKING BACKWARD). But, like many other utopias, this is a perfected state that endlessly requires devout reference to its earthly and spiritual makers in order to legitimate its absence of history and politics. A GOLDEN AGE in the past is used to legitimate a golden age in the future. As Condorcet noted two hundred years later in his *Fragment sur l'Atlantide*, despite the faith in science, innovation almost seems to have stopped in Bensalem. Nonetheless, the development of the Royal Society of London (1662), the leading English scientific institution, was sponsored by Bacon's disciples, and adopted the motto of Salomon's House as its own (see GULLIVER'S TRAVELS for a later satire). As Susan Bruce puts it, Bacon makes 'the relation between empire and empiricism' perfectly clear.

NEW DISCOVERY OF TERRA INCOGNITA AUSTRALIS

Les Aventures de Jacques Sadeur dans la Découverte de la terre Australe was published anonymously in 1676. Its author, Gabriel de Foigny (c. 1630–1692) was a French priest who (like Campanella, author of CITY OF THE SUN) enjoyed a turbulent relationship with the authorities. Initially relinquishing his Catholicism to move to Geneva (see CHRISTIANOPOLIS), he spent the rest of his life escaping from various accusations of impropriety (vomiting drunk in front of the communion table, seducing servants, and so on), as well as of blasphemy. The Australians that he writes about in the second half of his book (this unknown land having just been 'discovered' by Europeans) have no need of either religions or inequality, and are probably best thought of as rationalist ANARCHISTS.

Jacques Sadeur, a French sailor, is shipwrecked in Australia and (after fighting some 'monstrous Fowls') is admitted into the society of Australians. They are eight feet tall, reddish in colour, and hermaphrodites (which is lucky, because for some reason so is Monsieur Sadeur). The Australians are most distinguished by what they do not have compared with Europeans – laws, rulers, private property, families or priests. Even speaking of religion is considered improper, since it can only lead to speculation and disagreement, and prayer is deemed impious since it implies that 'the Incomprehensible Being' does not know our wishes. The same prohibition applies to sex, and Sadeur notes that though Australians have a responsibility to replace themselves with a child, they never discuss where it comes from. Their land is as flat as their society, which is uniform in all respects ('Tis sufficient to know one quarter, to make a certain judgement of all the rest') and has a population of over 100 million but no central city. They live in communal houses ('Hiebs') and schoolhouses ('Hebs'), both built from glass, and their education does not finish until the age of 35. They are also vegans, or more precisely fruitarians, who eat largely in secret, sleep very little, and wear no clothes.

Most radically, this ARCADIAN utopia is one in which rationalism, transparency and the public good are valued above all. If there are disputes, they are debated at their regular morning meetings (see AGORA). If someone makes a discovery or invention, they share it. All are educated and treated equally. In a discussion about freedom which has strong echoes of Kant, the Australians insist that no irrational constraint on anyone's behaviour is tolerated on the grounds that being human means being free, not being a slave. That includes being a slave to sexual urges, which is why the Australians consider Sadeur not fully human, a 'half-man'. This eventually leads to his downfall, since he proposes mercy for some women from a neighbouring people who were brutally exterminated by the Australians after an attack. Their rationalism is shown to lead to a lack of compassion, and they condemn Sadeur to death for his sympathies by eating a fruit that kills 'with all the signs of the greatest joy and pleasure in the world'. He eventually escapes, carried back by a huge bird.

Like ROUSSEAU, Foigny appears to reject the doctrine of original sin, believing instead that people were born reasonable and good. His 'savages' have many noble characteristics that stem from their not being contaminated by the apparatus of civilization. Yet, like Swift's Brobding-nagians and Houyhnhnms in GULLIVER'S TRAVELS, there is a certain coldness to their rationalism. Sadeur's weaknesses are all too human, yet regarded as incomprehensible by the haughty Australians who, despite caring for freedom, in the end seem to despise the mechanisms of life itself.

NEW HARMONY, see OWEN, ROBERT

NEW JERUSALEM The Englishman Samuel Gott (1614–71) published *Novae Solymae* anonymously in Latin in 1648. It was not translated into English – as *Nova Solyma, The Ideal City; or Jerusalem Regained* – until 1902, when it was initially and erroneously attributed to Milton. A very early example of a UTOPIA set in the future, it describes a time when the Jews have been converted to Christianity. This metaphorical New Jerusalem is built on the ruins of an older city, with twelve great brass gates, each inscribed with the name of the patriarch of one of the twelve tribes of Israel. The city is a model of efficient commerce and austerity, full of improving slogans and statues of famous men. The education of the young is accorded high value, and is carried out with particular attention to the cultivation of a good temper, self-control and moderate appetites. Schools have no windows to the street, and pupils are hardened by various tests and encouragements (see also PLUTARCH). Sometimes this involves allowing the children to gorge on delicacies until they are disgusted, or shunning those who lie, and whipping the sluggish. Girls, however, are not educated at all. Gott was particularly influenced by Andreae's 'humanist' attitude to education in CHRISTIANOPOLIS, but it is difficult for contemporary readers to imagine Nova Solyma as anything but DYSTOPIAN.

NEW LANARK Founded by David Dale in 1785, this Scottish mill town became strongly associated with the social reformism of his son-in-law Robert OWEN. It was established with involvement from the industrialist Richard Arkwright in a gorge on the River Clyde, a location that took advantage of the power of the water from the nearby falls. By 1800 there were four mills, making New Lanark the largest cotton-spinning complex in Great Britain. Social aspects were established from its inception. Housing was provided for workers in three- and four-s t o r e y blocks of superior quality and a school was provided for over 500 pupils. At this time New Lanark had a population of around 2,000 people, 500 of whom were children from the poorhouses and charities.

Dale went into partnership with Owen in 1799. Initially Owen concentrated on introducing new systems of production and MANAGEMENT, but in time he began to extend the welfare provisions of the town. Having to overcome opposition from business partners, Owen decided to seek other, more sympathetic support. In 1813 he circulated a pamphlet called *A New View of Society* and proposed that 5 per cent should be paid on capital and the remaining surplus given to education and other social improvements. With support from various partners (including Jeremy Bentham), Owen took control and became free to put into practice his philosophies. Despite initial resistance, his methods were advanced for the day and maintained efficient production. Welfare policies also yielded commercial benefits; his cheap village shop helped raise real wages and fund the infant school, which allowed mothers an early return to work. In 1816 Owen's 'New Institute for the Formation of Character' was established, which included space for nursery, infant, and adult education as well as community rooms and public halls. New Lanark attracted much interest and many notable visitors from across Europe and was known at the time as a 'model VILLAGE'. A dispute with his partners over methods of education led to Robert Owen leaving New Lanark to establish a community in New Harmony, Indiana. Production of various types continued until the late 1960s, and concerted restoration of the town followed the establishment of the New Lanark Conservation Trust in 1974. The village remains largely intact and was declared a world heritage site in 2001. (WS)

NEW MODEL ARMY The 'new modelling' of the British parliament's professional army was encouraged by Oliver Cromwell in 1644. The 'Self-Denying Ordinance' removed the existing military command and the New Model Army Ordinance was passed the following year. Parliament's rationale was to enforce strict discipline but to ensure regular payment. The first Lord General of the army was Sir Thomas Fairfax, with Oliver Cromwell taking control of the cavalry. Fairfax produced a disciplined and motivated force in which officers were promoted on merit. The New Model Army was soon instrumental in defeating Royalist forces and expediting the end of the English Civil War. Parliament attempted to disband the army but failed to settle pay arrears. The rank and file became increasingly politicized, LEVELLER influence grew and representatives called 'agitators' were appointed. An army council was formed consisting of two agitators and two officers from each regiment. A constitution was produced and a representation of discontent was issued to Parliament.

A series of debates followed in Putney in 1647 and Whitehall in 1648. The Putney meetings discussed 'The Agreement of the People'. This was a programme for a new system of government which set out key principles: the abolition of the aristocracy and the creation of a House of COMMONS to be elected by 'all free-born Englishmen' every two years; private property; equality before the law; the abolition of titles; and the election of sheriffs. The New Model Army also advocated religious tolerance. There was a strong sense that the principles and identity of the army outweighed religious principles. This realization was something that could be extended to society as government for the people rather than for pursuing the will of Kings. Following the execution of Charles I in January 1649, divisions in the Army were placed under greater pressure. Cromwell, Fairfax and others did not intend to tolerate the radical demands of the agitators. A number of mutinies occurred but were put down, with a number of leaders either killed in battle or executed. Thereafter the more radical elements of the army began to dissipate as Cromwell's campaigns rolled into Ireland and crushed the Scottish Royalist invasion of England. Throughout the period of the COMMONWEALTH, the New Model Army played an important policing role in England. With the death of Cromwell and the eventual restoration of the monarchy, however, the regiments of the New Model Army disbanded – with the exception of that commanded by General George Monck, which evolved into the Coldstream Guards. (WS)

NEWS FROM NOWHERE William Morris (1834–96) was a remarkable polymath who combined artistic, commercial, literary and political activity. His 1890 UTOPIA *News from Nowhere* reflected his evangelical conversion to SOCIALISM in the early 1880s. Earlier in his life he had founded Morris & Company ('The Firm') which specialized in decorative arts and textiles, and was very strongly driven by RUSKIN's ideas concerning craft p roduction and the ARTS AND CRAFTS political aesthetic. He also wrote highly successful narrative poetry, and was offered the posts of Professor of Poetry at Oxford and Poet Laureate, both of which he declined. He was a member of the Second Pre-Raphaelite Brotherhood, founded the Society for the Preservation of Ancient Buildings in 1877, the Socialist League in 1884 and the Kelmscott Press in 1891. On his death, his doctor remarked that the illness was simply 'having done more work than most ten men'.

In *News from Nowhere*, the time traveller William Guest (a thinly disguised version of Morris himself) falls asleep and wakes up about two hundred years in the future. His journey down the Thames through London, and then up the Thames into the country, involve him having endless conversations of the 'well dear traveller, since you ask' variety. We discover that, in the 1950s, there was a bloody REVOLUTION that resulted in a huge movement from towns to the countryside. Through this 'clearing of misery', cities have given way to woodlands and whilst many London landmarks are still there, having been saved by a 'queer antiquarian society', they have been converted for better use. Trafalgar Square is now an apricot orchard, and the Houses of Parliament are used to store dung. The population is described as healthy and robust, the weather seems permanently perfect, and the entire social system is based on freedom. Goods are given freely in colourful open air markets, and there is much emphasis on crafts and quality. There are neither legal nor prison systems, because stealing is pointless and violent crimes are punished through the guilt of the transgressor. There is no education system, because children learn what they want, when they want – whether that be thatching a cottage, or book learning. Marriage and divorce is a matter for the partners concerned, and consensual DEMOCRACY is practised through local 'motes' which return to controversial issues repeatedly until they are solved.

News from Nowhere is, in part, a reaction to Bellamy's LOOKING BACKWARD and shares with it the element of travel into the future. Where Bellamy was lauding a strong state BUREAUCRACY, Morris is describing an English utopia of VILLAGES, rivers and an ARCADIA of small market towns. (He described Bellamy's book as a 'Cockney paradise', perhaps a DYSTOPIA for Morris.) The title may have been inspired by Samuel Butler's anagram EREWHON, yet Morris's book is not a philosophical satire but primarily a reaction against industrialism in favour of a new medievalism in which production and ownership are COMMUNAL. Like FOURIER (whom he cites in the novel) Morris wants work to be desired, to be a natural part of the human condition. People gather together in 'banded workshops' to enjoy the exercise of their craft, but there is no compulsion to work. Such compulsion would simply produce ugly objects and debased people. Indeed, the journey up the Thames (in the second half of the book) is motivated by the desire to join the haymaking, and haunted by the worry that it will be finished before the protagonists arrive, and the wider fear of a 'work famine' in the future. Morris wanted this book to be a message from the future, and the most beautiful parts of the novel are precisely about Guest's longing when he realizes that he cannot stay here, in this long English summer.

Morris's nostalgic 'merrie England' doesn't include the plague, deprivation or feudalism. The women are pretty, and enjoy serving food and putting flowers on the table. The economic system is barely described at all, technology is dealt with by vague reference to something called 'force' (too complex for the author to understand), and Morris's continual sneering at 'Cockneyfication' betrays a deep class paternalism. Nonetheless, *News from Nowhere* has often been described as the archetypal ANARCHIST ECOTOPIA (see also ISLAND) and describes a complex future that is still (to some extent) in process within the novel itself. This is a future which is producing a new kind of people, freed from relations of repression, not merely a new set of institutions. Morris's enjoyment of the solid detail of everyday things and his deep love for the countryside manage to lift the novel above mere sentimentality. Furthermore, and perhaps rather tellingly, unlike Bellamy's utopia, Morris's is still well known over a century later, implying that this vision of a proto-COMMUNIST 'second childhood' has been attractive to readers. Even the later technicist socialism put forward by H. G. WELLS had to justify itself in response to Morris's 'ripe and sunny' vision, which Berneri thought was one of the few 'living dreams of poets' (like Diderot's SUPPLEMENT TO BOUGAINVILLE'S VOYAGE).

NON-CONFORMISM A term used to describe various English religious DISSENTING groups, which implies a refusal to conform to established doctrines, laws or conventions. Currently the term is used purely to denote Protestant denominations such as the Methodists and QUAKERS, who are outside the Anglican Church, but in the seventeenth century such dissent often had serious political overtones. The phrase originates with the 1662 Act of Uniformity. Those who refused to conform to the official church were unable to take part in many aspects of public life, including the professions, and were excluded from most forms of higher education. Earlier dissenting groups are also referred to as non-conformists and suffered similar forms of official repression. The effect tended to be the forging of strong COMMUNAL identities, as well as pushing them towards various forms of political radicalism. This took its most developed form during the English Civil War. Such groups included the ANABAPTISTS (see also AMISH), the DIGGERS, the Muggletonians, the Familists, the LEVELLERS, and the RANTERS. Their exclusion from the professions led both to the development of the AUTO-DIDACTICISM of the DISSENTING ACADEMIES and to a turn to private enterprise in pursuit of alternative respectable livelihoods (see QUAKERS). The British labour movement has always had a strong association with non-conformity, particularly Methodism, although historians such as E. P. Thompson argue that Methodism acted more as a brake on than an incitement to political radicalism. The development of Christian ANARCHISM also owes something to the long historical tradition of non-conformity (see TOLSTOY).

NON-VIOLENT RESISTANCE A DIRECT ACTION strategy for achieving political or social change that rejects the use of physical violence (at least against persons; violence against properties seems to be a more controversial issue). It includes a large number of tactics that include hunger strikes, pickets, vigils, sit-ins, demonstrations, blockades, BOYCOTTS, and various acts of CIVIL DISOBEDIENCE such as a refusal to pay tax or to be drafted. The latter can be traced back to Thoreau's influential essay on *Civil Disobedience* (see WALDEN), and TOLSTOY's Christian pacifism. Civil disobedience relies on a particular conception of power that sees even the most totalitarian regimes as being dependent on the cooperation of the 'ruled' (see MULTITUDE); hence non-violent resistance seeks to undermine the power of the rulers by withdrawing this cooperation. Non-violent resistance is not merely a set of tactics; it is grounded in a position of respect and love for all others, including one's opponents, that has sometimes been articulated along religious lines. It also rests on the belief that a peaceful society cannot be achieved through violent means.

Non-violent resistance has a long history and has been used by TRADE UNION, peace, ENVIRONMENTAL (see CHIPKO) and civil rights movements as well as in more recent ANTI-CAPITALIST protests. It has also been an important element in fights for independence from colonial rule (see GANDHI) or against oppressive regimes (for example the 'revolutions' in the SOVIET states in the 1980s and early 1990s largely relied on non-violent resistance). Whilst some critics see non-violent resistance as a form of resigned passivity or apathy, supporters claim that many non-violent campaigns have relied on taking action to deprive a ruling regime of financial income, or of the cooperation necessary to run the country, and have required having the courage to face the consequences of non-cooperation.

NOZICK, ROBERT A US libertarian political philosopher (1938–2002), whose *Anarchy, State and Utopia* (1974) put forward a direct challenge to RAWLS's influential LIBERAL conceptions of state-sponsored fairness and equity. Nozick is a radical conservative who draws on ANARCHIST ideas in order to defend what he sees as the most important right – the absolute liberty of all persons to do as they will with their bodies and property as long as it does not interfere with the rights of others. The key principle here is non-interference, which disallows anyone, or any institution, from limiting the freedoms of others. However, Nozick does not advocate the complete dissolution of all COLLECTIVE institutions, but advocates a 'minarchist' or 'nightwatchman' state. The state would be limited to 'the narrow functions of protection against force, theft, fraud, enforcement of contracts, and so on'. Treating such a state as merely a 'protection agency' that results from MARKET transactions between free individuals and different potential agencies, he proposes that this form of association can then be asserted as the only legitimate monopoly. Any extension of the state (and the state is always in danger of expansion, often for good DEMOCRATIC reasons) would infringe individual freedom.

Nozick's UTOPIA (unlike Rawls's liberal state) is one in which inequality and unfairness are simply the result of free transactions between consenting adults. He suggests that attempts at forced redistribution (through taxation for example) demean people as rational and competent beings. It results in placing some in a state of dependency, and punishes those who have done well. *Anarchy, State and Utopia* has been an influential book for free market liberals (see also Hertzka's FREELAND), but has drawn much criticism from SOCIALISTS and COMMUNITARIANS. The assumption that

199

individualism is a particular virtue or even a primitive state of being denies the MUTUALISM of human beings in societies and COMMUNITIES. Further, Nozick must require an 'original position' of equality for his inequalities to be seen as legitimate. If this was not the case, then inequalities might merely reflect the inheritance of financial or social capital, and this would violate the freedoms of those who were unlucky enough to be born poor. Nonetheless, Nozick is one amongst many who are suspicious of the role of the state. Many twentieth-century DYSTOPIAS (and actual states) have shown how individuality can be threatened by BUREAUCRATIC regimes, and many utopias (from Plato's REPUBLIC to Bellamy's LOOKING BACKWARD) appear oppressive simply because they assume that the state is the answer to all our ills. These are not merely questions of scale (because they also involve questions of 'rights'), but they certainly raise issues of proximity and responsibility that can easily be lost when organization becomes too distant from everyday practice.

OCEANA James Harrington (1611–77) was a broadly republican English political philosopher who found little favour with Cromwell and the parliamentarians. The publication of his 'political romance' *The Common-Wealth of Oceana* was prohibited in 1655, but it appeared in 1656 with an unlikely dedication to Cromwell himself. Harrington's formation of the 'Rota' club in 1659, and publication of *Rota: or a Model of a Free State* in 1660 (pushing for the rotation of public offices, see LEVELLERS) meant that, after the restoration of the monarchy, he was arrested on conspiracy charges in 1661. Upon his release he did not take part in public life again. *Oceana* has little literary merit, and is really a dry description of the operation of certain principles of an ideal COMMONWEALTH, partly inspired by his study of the Venetian republic. Harrington's UTOPIA is an egalitarian property-owning DEMOCRACY in which land is the principal basis of power, not inherited title. There is freedom of religious expression (though not for Jews), and all priests are also members of the national universities in the towns of 'Clio' and 'Calliope'. Like Lycurgus in Sparta (see PLUTARCH) the lawgiver Olphaus Megalater (a thinly disguised Cromwell) has established this ideal state, with a capital called 'Emporium'. In Oceana landowners are limited to holdings that earn less than £3,000 per year, and all authorities are elected for a maximum of three years – and then cannot hold office again for three years. This means redistribution of land amongst 'freemen', and controls on inheritance. (None of these reforms apply to servants.) Harrington also put forward the important idea of two chambers of parliament, one for debate (or 'invention') and one for voting (or 'judgement'), based on the idea that too much eloquence provided a danger for democracy by swaying opinion in a populist direction (see AGORA).

The massive detail of Harrington's work (on salaries, ceremonies, censuses, civil marriage ceremonies, tax-relief for families with children, free education, and so on) later led to it later being derided as a handbook for BUREAURACY. It is based on the assumption that, as Harrington himself put it, 'we are certain never to go right, while there remains a way to go wrong', and hence all the loopholes need to be closed in order that 'people can have no other motion than according to the order of their common-wealth' (in Davis, 1993: 26–7). The relationship between procedural BUREAUCRACY and LIBERALISM becomes crucial in evaluating such a consti-tution, but the influence of *Oceana* was substantial. There was a Harrington-ian party in Parliament, and the states of Carolina, Pennsylvania, New Jersey and MASSACHUSETTS had constitutions which were substantially influenced by his ideas – so much so that there was a formal proposal to change the name of Massachusetts to Oceana. In its detail, *Oceana* reads startlingly like a description of the modern state, even if its feudal distinctions of land ownership no longer make much sense to a contemporary reader. The book reads more like a statement of public policy than a utopian fiction (which one might expect to have some sort of plot), but there are many other utopias that share Harrington's faith in total organization (see CHRISTIANOPOLIS; CITY OF THE SUN; LOOKING BACKWARD; VOYAGE TO ICARIA, WELLS).

ONEIDA

'*God reigns over body, soul and estate, without interference from human govern -ments.*'

An INTENTIONAL COMMUNITY founded by John Humphrey Noyes (1811–86) near Oneida, New York, United States of AMERICA on land that originally belonged to the Oneida branch of the Iroquois. Based on a form of Christian COMMUNISM (see also TOLSTOY) that Noyes called 'perfectionism', the COMMUNITY was established in 1848 (consolidating earlier experiments from 1840 onwards, and influenced by the ideals of the SHAKERS). In its early years it spawned several short-lived smaller communities in the region. By 1878, the main community had over 300 members. It was based on the ethic of 'communalism' over both property and people, hence every member was (in principle) married to every member of the opposite sex ('complex marriage'). Men and women were formally equal, with collective childcare (from the age of 1 to 12) in the 'Children's House' to allow both sexes to work, and parents allowed to see their children once or twice a week. Women (radically, for that time) wore a short skirt over trousers in order that their mobility to work was not restricted. Job rotation was also practised, so that all members of the Oneida 'family' shared in all elements of its labour. The central logic of Oneida was that possessiveness was a sin, and perfection could be attained by learning to share all the pleasures provided by God without jealousy or guilt.

In order to avoid unwanted pregnancies men were encouraged to practise 'male continence' – not ejaculating during sex. This meant that 'amative' relationships were largely to replace 'propagative' ones. In practice there was a great deal of social engineering in any relationship at Oneida. Noyes attempted to encourage infertile liaisons between younger men and post-menopausal older women. Following the principle of 'ascending fellowship' he also insisted that the 'Central Members' (of either sex) had first responsibility to provide sexual and spiritual guidance for younger members. From 1867, potential parents also had to be vetted by a 'stirpiculture' committee which considered their moral perfection before making proposals for who should conceive with whom. Moral perfection was to be attained by a great emphasis on education, and a continual process of (almost exclusively negative) 'mutual criticism' which was voiced at community meetings (see THERAPEUTIC COMMUNITIES for later developments of this idea). The overall governance of the community was carried out by a BUREAUCRATIC system of 21 committees and 48 departments. They dealt with moral and educational matters, as well as organizing the various elements of small-scale craft production that had allowed the community to become SELF-SUFFICIENT. Every day there was a meeting at the Mansion House in which all members were encouraged to participate.

Noyes himself was not usually subjected to criticism, since he believed that perfect leaders were already untroubled by jealousy or guilt. Perhaps this was also why he insisted that his seniority of fellowship meant that he had the first responsibility to initiate spiritual and sexual intercourse with girls from the age of fourteen. Partly because of parental objections to this practice, as well as Noyes's attempts to hand over the community to an atheist son, in 1879 the community voted to abandon complex marriage and began to dissolve. However, there was a substantial amount of buildings and stock, together with established production and markets in fruit canning, silk, horse carts and chains, and cutlery. As a result, in 1881, most of the members formed a company, 'The Oneida Community Limited', which was effectively established as an Employee Share Ownership Plan (ESOP), with stock distributed to the 226 remaining men, women and children. The company had a reputation for being progressive, and a woman, Harriet Joslyn, was on the board of directors and superintendent of the silk mill.

For a century, initially under the stewardship of Pierrepoint Burt Noyes (one of the stirpiculture children), Oneida was a major producer of tableware (particularly cutlery). It and the Kenwood residential estate (see GARDEN CITY) were heavily influenced by ideas of paternalist INDUSTRIAL DEMOCRACY (see also BOURNVILLE, ROWNTREE) until the 1940s at least. In 1987, it again vested 15 per cent of its (now dispersed) shares in a new ESOP. However, by 2003 it had begun closing its US factories, and now exists only as a brand for products made elsewhere. Oneida was a radical experiment which re-thought notions of family, education, property and equality (see also BROOK FARM, LLANO DEL RIO, and OWEN's 'New Harmony'). It is now remembered largely for certain sexual practices, but may as readily be understood as a long-lasting and highly radical attempt to put elements of FOURIER's ideas into practice.

OPEN SOURCE SOFTWARE Software that comes with permission for users to have access to the software source codes. 'Open' in this context does not necessarily mean free of charge, but refers to users' freedom to adapt and improve programs. Thus software could be distributed for free but remain 'closed' or proprietary if the source codes are not disclosed. Open source software has its roots in the hacker culture of the 1960s and 1970s, but a significant landmark was Richard Stallman's announcement about the GNU project in 1983 (http://opensource.org/). Stallman explained his motivations in the 'GNU Manifesto', one of which was to 'bring back the COOPERATIVE spirit that prevailed in the computing COMMUNITY in earlier days'. The goal of GNU was to give computer users freedom by replacing software which had restrictive licensing terms with free software. The starting point was the development of an operating system to rival, but compatible with, the copyright Unix. In order to prevent GNU software from being turned into proprietary software, free software licences were developed based on the idea of 'copyleft'. Copyleft uses copyright law to serve the opposite of its usual purpose. Instead of being a means of privatizing through MARKETS, it becomes a means of retaining software as part of an intellectual COMMONS. It gives everyone permission to run, copy, modify and distribute the program (or modified versions), but not permission to add restrictions of their own.

If Stallman's motivation was primarily a political one that stressed users' freedom, the open software movement also uses commercially oriented arguments that put forward the superior nature of the NETWORK development process when users are also involved as co-developers. The two terms 'free' and 'open' source software are sometimes used to index these two different motives, political and pragmatic respectively, although the distinction is hard to maintain in practice. The movement has inspired g reater openness and participation in other media and communication fields, including open licences for published material, and open publishing. Open publishing breaks the barriers between information producers and consumers and enables users to publish and edit news or information, and act collectively in a decentralized way. Examples include WIKIPEDIA, INDYMEDIA CENTRE and the 'Ripple Project' (see GRAMEEN BANK).

OPERAISMO, see AUTONOMIA

OWEN, ROBERT Born in 1771 to a sadler and ironmonger in New-town, Wales, he found a position in a large drapery in Stamford, Lincolnshire. Moving to Manchester in 1788, in 1792 he was appointed manager of the Piccadilly Mill. The failure of a partnership project led to Owen leaving Piccadilly and establishing the Chorlton Twist Company with two local businessmen. Owen was introduced at this time to the daughter of David Dale, owner of the NEW LANARK mills in Scotland and learned that Dale wished to sell the mills to someone willing to continue his humane policy towards the children employed there. In 1799 Dale agreed both to the sale of New Lanark and the marriage of Owen to his daughter. It was through New Lanark that Owen established his reputation as a philanthropist. Owen improved and expanded the living conditions in the village and established a number of public buildings. His belief was that character was formed by the influence of the environment on the individual, and that therefore education was vital to the development of 'rational and humane character'. During this time, he also became involved in public affairs. His first published work was his *The First Essay on the Principle of the Formation of Character* (1813). This was combined with three further essays to produce *A New View of Society* which remain the most coherent statement of Owen's principles.

For Owen, in a market economy, mechanization created 'a most unfavourable disproportion between the demand for and supply of labour.' This produced a decrease in consumption and economic depression as manufacturers responded to decreased demand by reducing output and laying off labour. The depression following the Napoleonic wars appeared to confirm his analysis. Owen advocated practical remedies for these problems. His National Equitable Labour Exchange attempted to value goods and reward labour in terms of time, and labour bazaars were instigated in which the products of labour were exchanged using notes valued though hours of labour. He proposed a 'new moral world' of COOPERATIVE communities protected from the MARKET, in which members would contribute according to ability and consume according to need. These communities would consist of about 1,200 persons living on 1,000 to 1,500 acres and 'should increase in number, unions of them FEDERATIVELY united shall be formed in circles of tens, hundreds and thousands, till they should embrace the whole world in a COMMON interest'.

In 1824 he left New Lanark and sailed to the United States of AMERICA. Eventually he bought a plot of land in Indiana from an earlier Rappite community (see SHAKERS). New Harmony became the best known of 16 COMMUNITIES established through Owen's influence between 1825 and 1829. It used a system of 'labour notes' as a sort of TIME BANK, but none of the communities lasted more than a few years. There were financial difficulties and the motivation of members was sometimes lacking, many being far from 'industrious and well-disposed.' Disagreements persisted about their structure and the status of religious beliefs. Soon their COMMUNAL principles were abandoned, though other later communities were certainly influenced by these experiments (see BROOK FARM, ONEIDA). Owen returned to England in 1829, having lost four-fifths of his fortune on the project.

Democratic SOCIALISM had developed in Great Britain during Owen's absence: cooperatives, labour exchanges and TRADE UNIONS were becoming more popular. From 1833 Owen helped found the first British unions, including the Grand National Consolidated Trades Union. Although they were well supported by workers they were strongly opposed by employers, the government and the courts. But Owen's ideas had become influential and a number of enterprises were established based on cooperative forms of ownership. Many failed due to insufficient funds, but in 1844 the ROCHDALE PIONEERS Cooperative Society was founded and proved the first widely successful movement organized along these lines. In the 1840s, Owen established a new community at Queenwood Farm in Hampshire intended to support 500 people. The project was always short of capital, however, and never had more than ninety COMMUNITARIANS. In 1841, Owen secured capital to build a mansion, Harmony Hall, to house a school that would train Owenites. After a turbulent few years, in 1844 the annual Owenite Congress rebelled against his control of community policy. He continued his missions to Europe and North America, and to organize public meetings proclaiming his views. Robert Owen died in 1858 in the Bear Hotel, next door to the house in which he was born. (WS)

P

PANTISOCRACY, see ROMANTICISM

PARADISE An ARCADIAN utopia, from a Persian word referring to hunting parks and walled pleasure gardens. It was borrowed to refer to the Christian EDEN, and in medieval Europe was commonly believed to be a place where death and decay were unknown, and that still existed somewhere on earth (see KINGDOM OF HEAVEN ON EARTH). In Irish and Welsh mythology, Mag Mell ('plain of joy'), and Tir na nOg ('land of the young') are islands or places at the bottom of the ocean with a similar mythical function. See also ATLANTIS; EL DORADO; SHANGRI-LA.

PARIS COMMUNE In March 1871, the Central Committee of the National Guard, representing 300,000 armed Parisians, took power in what became a radical, if short-lived, experiment in working-class rule. The French–Prussian war started in July 1870 but rapidly ended with Paris under siege. The gap between rich and poor had widened, and food shortages and the continuous bombardment were adding to an already widespread discontent. In order to defend the city, many tens of thousands of Parisians became members of a militia known as the National Guard which provided fertile grounds for the development of SOCIALIST ideas. On 18 March 1871, following the signature of a peace treaty with Bismarck, and worried about the radicalization and increased authority of the Central Committee, the government ordered regular troops to seize the cannons held by the National Guard. Many of the troops refused to obey instructions and joined the National Guard in a quickly spreading rebellion. The government fled to Versailles, leaving the Central Committee as the only effective government in Paris. It almost immediately abdicated its authority and called for a free election of a COMMUNAL Council to be held on 26 March.

The 92 elected members of the Council included skilled workers, several professionals (such as doctors and journalists), and a large number of political activists. All members were delegates rather than representatives of the people, recallable, and paid an equal wage. Whilst the majority were reformist Jacobins and Republicans, there was also a minority of socialists and ANARCHIST followers of PROUDHON. The Council proclaimed Paris AUTONOMOUS and sought to recreate France as a FEDERATION of communes. In a symbolically significant gesture, it adopted the red flag and reclaimed the republican calendar developed in the aftermath of the 1789 French Revolution. Despite differences, the Communal Council agreed on policies on free education, and the right of employees to take over and run enterprises deserted by their owners. By May, 43 workplaces were WORKER SELF-MANAGED. In addition, many of the organizations set up to deal with the siege (those providing food and nursing, for example) continued to operate at district level and constituted a NETWORK of directly DEMOCRATIC neighbourhood assemblies. Perhaps the most celebrated achievement of the Commune was the initiative demonstrated by ordinary workers and citizens in managing public life, and in assuming responsibilities normally reserved to state administrators, MANAGERS or professional specialists.

But these achievements were short-lived. On 21 May 1871, the government launched a counter-attack. Following a week of vicious fighting (referred to as *la semaine sanglante*, or the bloody week), the last resistance fell and the government was restored. During this week over 30,000 *communards* were killed, many more were shot in later reprisals, and 7,000 were exiled to New Caledonia. Although the Commune was only short-lived, it is regarded by many COMMUNISTS, socialists and ANARCHISTS as a model of a liberated society. Both MARX and LENIN saw the Paris Commune as a living example of the dictatorship of the proletariat, whilst anarchists such as BAKUNIN and KROPOTKIN praised the spontaneous self-organization that led to its creation, even though they felt it did not go far enough in eliminating the state and encouraging workers' COOPERATIVES.

PARTNERSHIP, see COOPERATIVES; ESOP; JOHN LEWIS PARTNERSHIP; MONDRAGÒN; SCOTT BADER; TOWER COLLIERY

PASSIVE RESISTANCE, see NON-VIOLENT RESISTANCE

PEASANTS' REVOLT This rebellion (one of many across Europe around this time) began in 1381 in the VILLAGE of Fobbing in Essex, England, where a royal tax commissioner was enquiring into tax evasion.

The Black Death had reduced the population significantly and labour shortages had raised wages. Landowners responded by legislating to protect their interests; the 1349 Statute of Labourers attempted to push wages back to pre-plague levels. Nonetheless, the poll tax of 1380 was three times higher than that of the previous year and taxed rich and poor at a flat rate. Resistance to efforts to collect unpaid tax spread to adjoining villages and then to other counties. Throughout Kent, Suffolk, Hertfordshire and Norfolk, armed bands of villagers attacked manor houses and churches. Wat Tyler assumed control of the Kentish rebels and with associates from Essex led by Jack Straw marched on London. The preaching of John BALL provided the peasants with a religious and political justification of their actions in terms of the restoration of pre-Norman-conquest liberties, a characteristic of English radicalism that was to persist through to the LEVELLERS in the seventeenth century.

On 13 June, the rebellion arrived in London. The authorities were ill-prepared and, joined by some of London's poor, the rebels began to attack buildings. They burned down the Savoy Palace, home of Richard II's uncle, John of Gaunt, opened prisons, destroyed legal records and stormed the legal offices of the New Temple. The following day saw a meeting between King Richard and the peasants at Mile End. The rebels pledged their allegiance to the King and submitted a petition for labour based on free contracts and the right to rent land. The King submitted to these demands. On the same day, a group of rebels gained access to the Tower of London and executed those hiding there, including the Archbishop of Canterbury, the Lord Chancellor and the Lord Treasurer. It is believed that these men were so unpopular that the Tower guards simply let the rebels through the gates.

There was another meeting with the King on 15 June. The peasants demanded an end to feudal serfdom and for Church property to be dispersed among the populace. Following a dispute, Wat Tyler was fatally stabbed and a surprise ambush was able to control the rebels. From this point the London revolt ebbed away. In the months following, the authorities were able to regain control in all the regions that had experienced uprisings. A judicial enquiry was appointed and the King visited affected areas. Whilst concessions were revoked and there were many reprisals, the revolt served not only to begin to articulate ideas about freedom but also to make medieval peasants more aware of their market value as labourers. (WS)

PERMACULTURE A system for creating ecologically, socially and economically SUSTAINABLE human settlements. The development of permaculture stems from mounting concerns over production and consumption in the global north, and their increasing burden on the environment. The term was coined by two Australians, Bill Mollison and David Holmgren, in the mid-1970s, and is a contraction of PERMAnent and agriCULTURE, but also permanent and culture. For Mollison, this extension from agriculture to culture is essential if we are to build systems that provide for human needs. Permaculture privileges household and community self-reliance in food, but recognizes that this can only be achieved by considering the economic and social systems within which production takes place. 'Self-reliance in food is meaningless unless people have access to land, information, and financial resources. So in recent years it has come to encompass appropriate legal and financial strategies, including strategies for land access, business structures, and regional self-financing. This way it is a whole human system' (Mollison, 1991: vii).

Permaculture is based on the idea of COOPERATION between human and natural systems, and is articulated in terms of three principles. *Care of the earth* suggests that we have no more right to survive than any other species and that we should seek to preserve all natural resources (soil, atmosphere, water, forests, all animal and plant species). *Care of people* means that all should have access to the resources necessary to their existence. *Fair share* suggests that we only take the natural resources necessary to cover our basic needs. This involves setting limits to our consumption so as not to overtax ecosystems, nor deprive other people (including future generations) of necessary resources, as well as redistributing surpluses to those under-supplied (Whitefield, 2000: 6).

In practice, permaculture points to certain principles for building sustainable systems. A central tenet of permaculture is the idea of 'minimum effort for maximum effect'. Human intervention should be kept to a minimum as it tends to drain natural resources and energy flows. For example, current systems of food production consume around 10 calories of energy (on such inputs as fossil fuel, machinery, chemical fertilizers, pesticides) for every calorie of food. This could be replaced by production systems that use less energy and fewer non-renewable resources, and instead reproduce the relationships between plants, or between plants and soil, observed in nature (using cover crops to work and feed the soil, for example, rather than heavy machinery and chemical fertilizers). Thus

211

permaculture is information- and imagination-intensive rather than energy-intensive. Emphasis is placed on relative location and connections so as to maximise the potential cooperation between elements of a system, and on the recycling of energy.

In practice, permaculture has been associated with the LOCALIZATION of production and consumption, as this limits transport and provides the necessary conditions for the observation of natural systems and the impact of our actions on them. Thus permaculture not only lends itself to but also promotes many localization systems such as COMMUNITY-SUPPORTED AGRICULTURE, or LETS.

PHALANX or PHALANSTERY, see FOURIER

PIERCY, MARGE, see WOMAN ON THE EDGE OF TIME

PIRATE UTOPIA Plato might have believed that a ship at sea requires one captain and an obedient crew, but the history of pirate communities tells a different story. During the golden age of piracy seventeenth- and eighteenth-century pirate COMMUNITIES operating from free ports created an upside-down world of high living and DEMOCRATIC forms of self-governance, or pirates' UTOPIAS, amidst a lawless existence plagued by constant danger of death. During the emergence of competing colonial powers in the sixteenth century, state-backed practices of piracy (also referred to as privateering) were used by competing nations to raid each other's trade routes. The dividing line between privateering and unauthorized piracy was quite blurred and often changed with shifting political alliances. In time, the benefits of stable trade routes become more evident, leading to both a rejection of piracy by polite society and a rejection of society by pirates' communities. Huge numbers of seamen, many pressed against their will, found themselves caught between war, a disease-ravaged Europe and the possibility of a modicum of control of their own destiny through the lawless roving way of life.

Pirate havens tended to form around voids created by national contests for the control of territories, and shifted between bases in North Africa, the Caribbean, and the coast of Madagascar. The ongoing existence and success of pirates in disrupting trade posed a great threat to imperial stability. Peter Lamborn Wilson also documents massive conversions to Islam, particularly centred around North African cities such as Rabat-Sale in

Morocco. Pirate utopias were characterized by an egalitarian distribution of booty and forms of governance that embodied an ethic of liberty, equality, and freedom over one hundred years before the French REVOLUTION. There are tentative hints that practices of pirate MUTUAL aid, culture, and perhaps even a language emerged.

Linebaugh and Rediker argue that pirates' communities developed democratic organizational forms not as representatives of a people but rather as a developing maritime proto-proletariat. They argue that during this early period of accumulation, piracy functioned as a strategy of class struggle where tactics of mutiny and desertion were employed. Piratologists argue that an instrumental relation to violence was held, where fiercesome displays of force and scimitar waving were favored in hope of causing fear-induced surrender. Pirate utopias existed as a multi-ethnic melting pot of ongoing CARNIVAL composed of drop-out wage labourers, escaped indentured servants and slaves, and mutineers, many of whom mixed with native communities in North America and Madagascar. There are also tentative suggestions of influxes of political exiles such as RANTERS and DIGGERS from the radical wing of the English revolution. To this day the use of pirate imagery retains a good deal of cultural resonance and appeal and has continued to be used by ANTI-CAPITALIST organizers to symbolize their desires to push beyond the world of capital.

PLATO, see ATLANTIS; REPUBLIC

PLUTARCH Mestrius Plutarchus (CE *c.* 45–*c.* 120), known in English as Plutarch, was Greek by birth and educated in Athens, but lived in Rome for a time. The collection of fifty biographies in his *Parallel Lives* is structured by comparing great ancient Greeks in his past with Romans in his present. At least two of those lives have had a considerable influence on UTOPIAN writing since – that of Lycurgus, the law-giver of Sparta, and Solon, the founder of Athens.

Lycurgus probably lived in the ninth century BCE, but most of Plutarch's account is difficult to verify in any detail. Plutarch tells us that Lycurgus seized power in a *coup*, and immediately introduced a 28-man senate to balance the power of the two kings. An assembly meeting in the open air ratified the senate's decisions. He then proceeded to redistribute land equally between all 9,000 (male) Spartan citizens (excluding the helots, or slaves) and replaced silver and gold with heavy iron money. This was to ensure that the hoarding of money was almost impossible, and that luxuries could not be purchased from abroad. Through a variety of measures, Lycurgus hardened the Spartans into a state of total readiness for war. Citizens were forced to eat at common tables, and (except under special circumstances) forbidden to eat at home. They were not allowed to use anything apart from the crudest tools to make and furnish their homes, making opulence impossible. The family unit was broken up, with men visiting their wives in the evenings for sex, and both sexes being encouraged to seek partners with whom they could produce the best children. If the elders deemed that a baby was not strong it would be thrown into a deep cavern. In addition, mothers washed their babies in wine to discover whether they were weaklings who would be harmed by such treatment, or strong enough to thrive.

Girls were educated by sport, to strengthen their bodies rather than their minds, and took no part in the running of the state. The education of young boys was militaristic and violent, again with an emphasis on toughening the character, not filling the mind with more than was necessary. At the age of seven, they were taken from their parents and subjected to the discipline of older boys. They were allowed one piece of clothing per year, went barefoot with shorn hair, and were often forced to steal to get rations in order to develop the arts of scavenging. Sometimes they also killed helots, for martial practice and for sport. Though Plutarch was critical of this particular practice, in general he was impressed by Lycurgus and notes that his reforms produced a society that lasted for 500 years. Because there were few distinctions in property, wealth or land, the Spartans sought distinction through virtue. Plutarch tells us that it was because Lycurgus had travelled and had compared different states 'just as physicians compare bodies that are weak and sickly with the healthy and robust' that he could design this totalitarian COMMUNIST state so effectively. (Though it should be remembered that all manual labour was carried out by the helots, so this was a communism of the slave owners, not for the slaves.) Despite Lycurgus's cosmopolitan experiences, he did not wish to pollute Sparta with outside influences, so he only allowed visitors who had a compelling reason to come, and restricted Spartans from travelling abroad (see NEW ATLANTIS).

Another of Plutarch's lives concerns Solon (c. 638–558 BCE), supposedly the founder of Athens and one of the seven sages of Greece whose motto was 'know thyself' (see also Plato's REPUBLIC). He introduced laws that covered the four main classes of the population, and codified military obligations, taxation, trial by jury and systems of representation.

His laws were written on wooden cylinders and kept in the Acropolis. Though many of his reforms were reversed by the tyrant Pisistratus, enough were kept to make Solon a legendary figure in terms of the writing of a 'constitution' for a state. Lycurgus and Solon were later echoed in UTOPIAN fiction as the lawmakers who founded particular CITY STATES – King Utopus in UTOPIA, Sol in CITY OF THE SUN, King Solamona in NEW ATLANTIS, Olphaus Megalater in OCEANA, and so on. As with many 'classical' texts, the influence of Plutarch's work is partly in its description of a GOLDEN AGE that many later writers would use to criticize the failings of their present. Yet these lives also tell us something about the enduring notion of the figure of the charismatic founder, and the idea of a designed society.

POLIS The first example of the CITY STATE, and the form of political organization characteristic of Ancient Greece between the eighth and fourth centuries BCE. It refers to an AUTONOMOUS political unit centred on a city and its surrounding territory. One of the significant features of the polis was its relatively small size; this allowed for a certain amount of experimentation in structure and participation. Whilst most poleis started as monarchies, by the sixth century BCE, they began to settle around two forms: oligarchy and DEMOCRACY. Oligarchy (rule by the few) was the most common form of government in the Greek poleis. The oligarchs were usually drawn from the noble classes or the wealthiest citizens, although various forms were invented, including having members chosen by lot, elected, or rotating among members of a certain class. In addition, many oligarchs ruled in conjunction with other political structures. For example, in Sparta (see PLUTARCH) the oligarchy ruled with a council and assembly. The second alternative that emerged was democracy: the most famous of which was in Athens centred on the AGORA. This was very different from modern democracy; the relatively small size of the polis allowed all citizens to participate in decisions through public discussion, rather than rule indirectly through representatives. Another important difference was the way in which citizenship was defined, because only citizens had political rights and duties and could participate in government. And citizenship was limited, defined by descent, and excluded slaves, foreigners, women and children.

The overwhelming influence of the polis on Western political thoughts and structures is revealed by the etymology of the term 'political' itself. But as the origins of the term suggest, 'political' had a much broader meaning than in modern usage. It was not restricted to forms of government but pertained to the affairs of the polis, touching upon all aspects of life, as well as the very condition of human existence. This broad understanding is clearly articulated in Aristotle's *Politics*. Aristotle traced the emergence of the polis to practical concerns for survival; humans have to associate in order to meet the basic needs of life. But if human relationships are born out of the bare necessity of life, they also provide the arena for the good life. It is in these COMMUNAL relationships that humans can realize their 'political nature'. This is based on human capacity for language and moral judgement and can only be realized within a COMMUNITY, a polis. Thus, the polis is not only about the handling of practical affairs, but a form of association that enables human beings to realize their nature as human beings, and as such is the most natural form of political organisation.

The polis, especially in its Athenian version, has become a powerful trope in the political imagination. Unlike nation states that may consider citizens first and foremost as subjects of state administration, city states such as classical Athens consider citizens as communities of equals who can rule themselves. This idea has resurfaced at many points in history, for example in the European city states in the Renaissance, or in the Paris Commune in 1871. More recently, some have invoked an alternative geopolitics (with a more inclusive definition of citizenship) to oppose the power not only of nation states, but also of global capitalism. Bookchin, for example, was inspired by Aristotle's writing in his articulation of libertarian municipalism (see Social Ecology), a model of face-to-face democracy in which citizens' assemblies making decisions about public life counter the power of the nation state and capitalism.

PORTO ALEGRE This city of over one million inhabitants in Brazil has become an international symbol of participative DEMOCRACY through its experiment in budgeting and its hosting of the WORLD SOCIAL FORUM in 2001 and 2003. Through the participatory budget, citizens are involved in decisions regarding public expenditure and investment priorities. It began in 1989 with the left-wing coalition led by Brazil's Workers' Party winning the local election, and has since been replicated in many other cities in Brazil and South America. The system works through the implementation of GRASSROOTS mechanisms for decision making based on general assemblies organized by district (see PARIS COMMUNE). The city is divided into 16 districts, and thematic areas were established to ensure the representation of particular issues (urban development, transport, health and social services, education, culture and leisure, economic development and taxation). Every year, there are two general assemblies for each district and theme. The first round of assemblies accounts for the investment plans approved the previous year, and makes public policy and spending open to citizens' scrutiny. In the second round, citizens define their investment priorities and elect delegates and board members for the forthcoming year. All citizens can participate in the assemblies, either directly or through informal groups or associations. Interspersed between these two general assemblies are several thematic and district meetings in which all citizens can discuss and debate the allocation of resources and investments.

The delegates elected by the assemblies constitute a forum that acts as an intermediary between the general population and the municipal board. The municipal board is constituted of two elected representatives for each district and theme, and acts as a legislative body. Board members defend the priorities and choices of their district or theme to the executive. Finally the executive formed of the elected mayor and administrative bodies works with the municipal board to propose the budget and implement it. The participative budget has challenged the growing gap between citizens and leaders characteristic of representative democracy, as well as the traditions of corruption that had permeated the political culture of the city. Several mechanisms are in place to ensure that delegates and municipal board members do not become detached from their roots, and do not seize power. Board members are elected every year and cannot be re-elected more than once; they can be recalled; and their action is open to public scrutiny in the general assemblies.

By opening up policy Porto Alegre has challenged the notion that MANAGEMENT is best left in the hands of professional experts. Whilst participative democracy has often been challenged for being inefficient, its success in Porto Alegre has become internationally acclaimed, even by the International Monetary Fund and the World Bank. Particularly notable achievements include the improvement of the city infrastructure, the extension of heath and education provision, and the creation of economic opportunities through the promotion of small enterprise. Nonetheless, many challenges remain to be addressed. In particular, the participation rate of citizens remains limited, although it has increased and it does includes marginalized groups such as women, the young, and the working class. But even if it remains open to improvement, Porto Alegre provides a living example of an alternative way of practising democracy.

217

PORT SUNLIGHT In 1885, William Hesketh Lever and his brother James founded Lever Brothers to make and sell soap. The Lever family were NON-CONFORMISTS and followed strong principles of 'self-improvement'. As a young man Lever had formed reading groups with his friends to develop his education, and his primary inspiration came from Samuel Smiles's *Self-Help* (see AUTO-DIDATICISM). He wished to pursue these principles through his business, believing that given fair conditions 'all men could improve themselves'. For Lever, 'The truest and highest form of enlightened self-interest requires that we pay the fullest regard to the interest and welfare of those around us.'

He purchased a site four miles across the River Mersey from Liverpool in order to build a 'model' factory and village. By the end of 1889 the factory was complete as well as 28 cottages for workers. Over the next eight years a further 278 cottages were built, laid out along wide, tree-lined avenues. Lever involved himself heavily in the development of the village and travelled to find new ideas of town planning. Port Sunlight (named after one of his soap brands) became an important example of the work of the GARDEN CITIES movement (see also BOURNVILLE, SALTAIRE). In 1914 it was to host a congress of the International Garden Cities and Town Planning Association. By 1909 there were 700 houses occupied by Lever Bros workers. The village also had a theatre and concert hall, a library, a swimming pool, a gymnasium and an institute providing classes for adults. The residents were to be models of respectability and so there were no public houses. Rents were controlled to about a quarter or fifth of the weekly wage. Lever published a company magazine called *Prospect* that not only publicized local events, but also served as a vehicle for promoting his philosophies. Whilst he earned something of a reputation as a benevolent dictator, contemporary accounts found high standards of health and a strong sense of COMMUNITY. The properties in the village remained company-owned until 1980, when they were sold on the open market. Unilever (the successor to Lever Bros) handed over the management of the village to the Port Sunlight Village Trust in 1999. The entire village is now designated as a Conservation area. (WS)

PROTECTIONISM An economic policy of protecting local industry by placing taxes on imported goods or services, or subsidizing domestic producers. The earliest forms of protectionism were primarily concerned with SELF-SUFFICIENCY during a potential conflict, but by the nineteenth century advocates of free trade, often relying on Ricardo's theory of 'comparative advantage' (that different states should specialize in different sorts of production) established the idea that protectionism prevented the MARKET from working properly. During the early decades of the twentieth century, protectionism was the dominant strategy for international trade. At the present time, most of the key players in global political economy officially regard protectionism as a bad thing, but in practice this often depends on who is being protected. Institutions like the World Trade Organization, the International Monetary Fund, and the World Bank often attempt to 'open up' Second and Third World markets to competition, but are rarely quite so zealous if the interests of first world industry and employment might be harmed.

For the LIBERAL p roponents of free trade, open global markets are essential in order that the best goods can be produced at the best prices. From this point of view protectionism merely supports inefficient producers, and disadvantages new producers from innovatively attempting to exploit new markets. As a classic example, the British 'Corn Laws' were an example of protectionism that simply benefited the powerful (wealthy landowners) and their repeal by the *laissez-faire* 'Manchesterists' in 1846 is usually seen as a victory by liberals (see FREELAND). Contemporary attempts to block foreign imports or prevent the 'off-shoring' of jobs are often criticized on similar terms, as impediments to the free market which will (if left to its own devices) provide jobs and reduce poverty in the global South. This assumes that markets operate to create the greatest good for the greatest number, and that (through a certain tendency to equilibrium) wealth 'trickles down' to the poor.

However persuasive some of these arguments might be in abstract terms, the reality of 'free' markets has largely been that they benefit the players who are already powerful – first world states, and their banks and corporations (see FAIR TRADE). The marketplace for global trade is massively skewed in favour of those with purchasing power, and against those who are already in debt. To this it should be added that older forms of protectionism (import tariffs) not only protected LOCAL producers but also raised revenue for the state, hence reducing the local tax burden. Combining these arguments suggests that protectionism could be a highly rational strategy, but (because of financial and political pressure) it is one that it is difficult for any indebted Third World state to pursue.

One radical response would be to suggest that assumptions about global   219 trade are damaging in themselves, and that there should be a much greater emphasis on local SUSTAINABILITY. Others might suggest that this would breed nationalism and isolationism, when a cosmopolitan spirit of internationalism is likely to be much more helpful in solving global problems (compare LIBERALISM and COMMUNITARIANISM). Freedom of exchange might also mean freedom to do other things too, with the corollary being that restrictions on exchange might result in less everyday AUTONOMY and more state control. On a much smaller scale, many INTENTIONAL COMMUNITIES and UTOPIAS have tended to be isolationist, but this is often to protect the purity of local beliefs and practices. In practice, complete freedom to trade is unlikely since this would mean that there would be no protection against anything or anyone being sold. Assuming that the sale of child sex workers will be prohibited in most cultures and that people don't usually want to buy poisonous food, then the real questions are how much protection, and who enforces it?

PROUDHON, PIERRE-JOSEPH The first person to claim the title of ANARCHIST. He was a major influence on the development of SOCIALISM, anarchism and COMMUNISM. Although MARX became a critic of Proudhon, he was heavily influenced early on by his ideas. Proudhon was also a major influence on BAKUNIN and KROPOTKIN, though he proposed a MUTUALISTIC form of individualism based on peaceful social REVOLUTION rather than their full-blown anarcho-communism. Born in 1809, at sixteen he entered the local college but poverty meant he had to scrounge books from better-off friends. At nineteen he became a printer and later supervised the printing of FOURIER's work. His proofreading of ecclesiastical texts gave him an opportunity to educate himself, but also resulted in his becoming a firm atheist. He began to write his own social theories and in 1838 was granted a small pension by the Academy of Besançon to further his studies.

Around 1839 he went to Paris to continue his research, coming into contact with socialist ideas. In 1840 he published his first and most famous work *What is Property?* to which question he gave the answer 'property is theft'. In 1843 he moved to Lyon and became involved with the workers' movements. In 1846, he was tried for sedition for the publication of *Warning to Proprietors*, but was acquitted. Also in 1846, Proudhon began to criticize Marx for what he saw as his centralist ideas regarding the organization of the socialist movement. Proudhon published the *Philosophy of Poverty* during the same year, to which Marx responded with his famous rebuke *The Poverty of Philosophy*. Though he felt that the abortive French revolution of 1848 was premature, he threw himself into writing and editing revolutionary newspapers. Having been elected as a member of the new National Assembly, Proudhon attempted to found a 'people's bank' that would offer credit without interest. This venture failed completely but provided the basis for the later development of CREDIT UNIONS.

During a prison term for championing DIRECT ACTION he wrote *The General Idea of the Revolution in the Nineteenth Century*, which includes a detailed account of his agrarian theories. Though constantly harassed by the French authorities during the 1850s, he lived quietly for a number of years until the publication of his book *Of Justice in the Revolution and the Church* in 1858, when he had to flee to Brussels. This book contained Proudhon's mature social philosophy, developing his ideas of a pluralist society in which order is achieved through a mutual respect for human dignity, nurtured in the family and reinforced by active participation by all in community affairs. In 1862 he began to sketch out his ideas for a world FEDERATION, publishing *Of the Federal Principle* in 1863. In 1865 he played a part in the founding of the First INTERNATIONAL and published his last book *On the Political Capacity of the Working Classes*, describing how workers and small farmers could liberate themselves from capitalism. He died in Paris that same year.

Proudhon's thought changed and developed throughout his life and is often inconsistent. In his earliest writings he defines his problem as 'to find a state of social equality which is neither community, nor despotism, nor parcelling out, nor anarchy, but liberty in order and independence in unity'. In *What is Property?* Proudhon develops a forceful critique of private property and its enforcement by the state, leading to his self-description as an anarchist. He defined anarchism as 'the absence of a master, of a sovereign', envisaging a society where force gives way to reason. Despite these very radical pronouncements, Proudhon did not in fact completely reject private property and government, merely their operation as part of capitalism. In particular he objected to the way in which income is earned by some as a result of the labour of others. Proudhon argued for direct exchange of products by free associations of workers, with value being determined by the cost of production and the amount of labour time. He later argued that this would need the support of free credit and a system of mutual guarantees, implying a minimal role for government. In essence he retains competition, markets and private property but within an egalitarian and non-monetary framework.

Initially he thought that the government could be reformed so as to largely abolish its own role as the promoter and protector of capitalism (see BRAY). His contact with Bakunin and Marx was to change this view, as was his stay with the Lyon Mutualists, a revolutionary COOPERATIVE workers' organization. This group argued that workers had to take charge of their own interests by associating together into NETWORKS of cooperatives, eliminating capitalism and ensuring independence and security for their members. The conclusion that both Marx and Bakunin drew from the 1848 revolution was that class conflict was an inevitable feature of revolution but Proudhon was still committed to the reconciliation of the classes and the avoidance of further bloodshed. He hoped that the bourgeoisie might be persuaded to capitulate if they saw that the revolution was an historical inevitability. The core organization of such a society would be the worker's COMMUNE that would take care of the welfare, educational and social needs of its members as well as organizing production. He is less consistent on the issues of representation to larger coordinating bodies that he sees as being governed by the principle of majority rule rather than the non-binding delegatory democracy favoured by many other anarchists. Proudhon deals with this problem by insisting on the freedom of individuals and groups to disassociate from existing bodies whenever they please, forming new ones with which they have more affinity. His three underlying principles are competition, free credit and equivalent exchange, to which he devoted much of his thought. The negative aspects of competition were to be nullified by the actions of a central credit bank. His attempt to combine MARKET mechanisms with socialist economics has been criticized but the twentieth-century version of welfare capitalism owes a good deal to his framework.

Proudhon finally arrived at the conviction that only the working classes could free themselves by rejecting bourgeois institutions and politics. He called for an alliance between the proletariat and the peasantry and for the transformation of society through direct action that would build class consciousness and political strength. SYNDICALISM and the French TRADE UNION movement still owe a great deal to his influence. After his death Proudhon's followers formed the core of French socialists in the First International, under the leadership of Bakunin. Many of the Proudhonites were to be killed or scattered after the crushing of the PARIS COMMUNE in

1871 and they were further weakened by the split between Marxists and anarchists. It should also not be forgotten that within his own lifetime his reputation was immensely greater than that of Marx or Bakunin. Though much less consistent than Marx, he did pay much more attention to how a socialist society might actually work, and his ideas on mutualism energize the ANTI-CAPITALIST movement today.

Q

QUAKERS The Religious Society of Friends was established in the seventeenth century. Its origins are complex but George Fox is often seen as the movement's founder. Fox, one of a number of religious DISSENTERS preaching during Cromwell's COMMONWEALTH, denounced many of the practices and institutions of the time as being inconsistent and obstructive of true faith. He was critical of wider society and in particular what he saw as the misuse of authority. Early members were widely persecuted. The name 'Quakers' was coined when a group including Fox was tried for blasphemy in 1650 and Fox claimed that the judge should 'tremble at the word of God'. The judge sarcastically dubbed the defendants Quakers in response. They were similar to other movements of the time, including the Seekers, RANTERS and the LEVELLERS, and drew followers from such movements. Throughout the 1660s and 1670s Fox worked to establish a more formal organization by forming a network of 'meetings'. In 1678 the London (now British) Yearly meeting was established as the representational head of the movement.

Quakers refer to each other as 'Friends'. The name 'Religious Society of Friends' was not used until the eighteenth century and there are a small minority of members who prefer to omit the word 'religious' (see also SHAKERS). Indeed, although they are largely a Christian movement, there are members who do not subscribe to particular religious beliefs because the movement does not hold a universal set of doctrines. Their central concept is that of the 'inner light' or 'that of God within'. Early Quakers saw this light as deriving from Christ but later Quakers portray it as a guiding force existing within each person. Since Friends believe that everyone contains this light, our task in life is to try and understand what it is saying. This is an ongoing process known as 'continuing revelation'.

Over the years a set of basic beliefs held by Friends did emerge. These remain today as a series of 'testimonies' regarded not as fixed statements but as a shared understanding of how Friends relate to God and the wider world. The Peace Testimony rejects the use of violence to resolve conflicts as it is assumed to be always violence against God within. The Testimony of Equality reflects the belief that since all people share the same inner light they deserve equal treatment. Early Quakers refused therefore to bow or remove their hats to 'superiors' and were also leading campaigners in the women's rights and anti-slavery movements. The Testimony of Integrity (or the Testimony of Truth) states that integrity is derived from being led by the Spirit. Quakers therefore emphasize the importance of taking responsibility for actions and striving always to deal honestly with others. Finally, the Testimony of Simplicity refers to the lack of significance that should be given to material possessions. Quakers have traditionally adopted simplicity in their appearance and attempt to restrict consumption to need; this now echoes ENVIRONMENTAL concerns.

Quaker meetings are without formal organization. Members sit together in silence in 'expectant waiting' until a member feels a need to speak. Then they will rise and give 'ministry'. Meetings of 'business' are conducted on the basis of consensus; there is no voting since there is the commitment to reach agreement that is consistent with the guidance of the 'spirit'. A decision or the 'sense of the meeting' is eventually reached. Sometimes those who disagree will 'stand aside' but much effort will be spent hearing the concerns of these members. Adversarial debate is avoided and members are expected to speak only once on a subject.

The beliefs of the Society of Friends have always strongly emphasized action. The guidance of the Spirit should, they maintain, be translated into action which, in turn, leads to greater spiritual understanding. This is seen in the manner in which Quakers have acted upon the guidance of the testimonies by establishing organizations pursuing different social causes. Initially barred from higher education and the established professions, Quakers played a significant role in the NON-CONFORMIST involvement in business. Quaker businesses were highly regarded for the principles on which they operated, which included not only fair prices and quality products, but also a commitment to social philanthropy. They were instrumental in founding both Amnesty International and Oxfam and businesses such as Cadbury (see BOURNVILLE), ROWNTREE, Lloyds Bank and Clarks Shoes. Today over 25,000 attend meetings in the United Kingdom and there are 600,000 members worldwide. (WS)

QUALITY OF WORKING LIFE (QWL) A North-Western European LIBERAL reformist movement based upon industrial psychology and sociology. The term originated in the US in the 1960s, but it built on

a substantial amount of Northern European work on 'socio-technical systems', much of it done at the Tavistock Institute in London. Rather than designing work around machines for maximum efficiency, the socio-technical systems approach was to treat the human and the technical as intimately related. This approach was developed by the Oslo Work Research Unit within the Norwegian INDUSTRIAL DEMOCRACY Programme. Scandinavian traditions of codetermination were influential, summarized in the Swedish slogan 'From Consultation to Codetermination' and the 'Leadership, Organization and Codetermination' programme in the 1980s. Other important initiatives were the German 'Arbeit und Technic' programme and the French 'Agence Nationale pour l'Amélioration des Conditions de Travail'. By the 1980s, QWL was an international movement of consultants, personnel managers, academics and sympathetic TRADE UNION officials (though other trade unionists have been hostile to these initiatives, treating them as a distraction from collective bargaining). Like the 'human relations' movement in the 1920s, the central idea was that the worst effects of deskilling through 'scientific management' could be ameliorated through the use of job redesign, job rotation, enlargement or enrichment, (semi-) autonomous working groups, team working, and worker-management consultation and participation.

Ideas about the humanization of MANAGEMENT have been common since the 1960s, though their consistent application is rare (see KALMAR). As many critics have pointed out, QWL-type initiatives (often now called 'EMPOWERMENT') are often a way to get workers to resolve intractable control problems and hence improve profitability. In addition, adding one boring and degrading job to another does not necessarily make either job less boring and degrading. In any case, such schemes rarely survive if the economic environment becomes hostile. QWL does not radically alter the terms upon which management and workers share power (see WORKER SELF-MANAGEMENT), and almost never includes a serious attempt to consider issues of ownership (see COOPERATIVES; MONDRAGÒN; SUMA). Workers might gain considerable improvements in their conditions through QWL practices (see also SYNDICALISM), but whether they can be classified as radical forms of alternative organization is doubtful.

R

RABELAIS, see ABBEY OF THELEME

RADIANT CITY, see LE CORBUSIER

RAND, AYN US philosopher and writer (1905–1982) probably best known for her polemical novels *The Fountainhead* (1943) and *Atlas Shrugged* (1957) where she seeks to present aspects of her 'objectivist' philosophy. This is most explicit in *Atlas Shrugged,* where the novel's main protagonist, Dagny Taggart, is introduced to a hidden valley in America's Rocky Mountains. In 'Galt's Gulch', she is able to witness a society built upon 'rational selfishness', rampant individualism and apparently completely unfettered capitalism. In this 'UTOPIA of Greed' man is truly free – free to act in his own self-interest. All relationships are contractual – the only word forbidden is 'give'. Her heroes, heroic of both mind and body, are able to ceaselessly innovate, both creating staggering new inventions and demonstrating man's mastery over nature as the earth yields its riches to their new techniques. This outpost of bountiful riches and elegant (but simple) living is contrasted with the world outside that is rapidly becoming a DYSTOPIA, as 'looters', exploiting notions of fairness and charity, appropriate the wealth generated by business owners. As their entrepreneurial spirit is stifled, business owners flee to 'Galt's Gulch' and, in their absence, the achievements wrought by man steadily disintegrate leaving AMERICA a starving wilderness. Redemption is only achieved when people finally realize that entrepreneurs are essential to a functioning society and welcome them back on terms imposed by the business leaders.

Rand's work draws upon the Austrian School of economics and most notably Ludwig von Mises' *Human Action*. In essence, she states that there is an objective world and that individuals can gain knowledge of it through reason. Reason also dictates that the only moral objective is the pursuit of one's own happiness, and the only place that this can take place is under a LIBERAL MARKET system. Unsurprisingly, then, the utopia in *Atlas Shrugged* is not a generous one and Rand has no sympathy with those who do not succeed (see also FREELAND; FREE STATE PROJECT; NOZICK). (GL)

RANTERS A radical group active from the late 1640s to the mid-1650s, during the period of the COMMONWEALTH. Many of the leading members had been members of Cromwell's NEW MODEL ARMY, including Laurence Clarkson (aka Claxton), Jacob Bauthumley and Joseph Salmon, and the group developed partially out of the decline of the LEVELLER movement. Their name is the insult thrown at them by their critics, and they were considered heretical by the established Church. Ranters believed in the concept of the indwelling spirit and in this respect had origins in the medieval heretics, the BRETHREN OF THE FREE SPIRIT. Their pantheist beliefs led them to reject the authority of the church since 'spirit' was believed to reside in every man. Regarded as religious libertines, they believed that whatever was done in the name of the indwelling spirit was acceptable – as everything came from nature, everything was justifiable.

Whilst the movement was relatively small, it attracted growing attention as members of the establishment began to report on its activities. Such accounts were preoccupied with the 'extreme' activities of alleged Ranter members and many acts of disorder were attributed to the movement. Ranters were accused of indulging in wife swapping, excessive drinking, illicit sex and other immoral behaviour. They were particularly associated with nudity which they may have used both as a form of social protest to shock and as a visible rejection of worldly goods. The government began to view Ranters as a threat and some leading members were arrested, imprisoned and forced to recant. Clarkson's pamphlet, *A Single Eye All Light. No Darkness*, in which he outlined his view that sin was a concept devised by the ruling class to keep the poor in order, was seized and burned. His associate Abiezer Coope was also imprisoned. The growing notoriety of the Ranters prompted Parliament to pass the Adultery and Blasphemy acts of 1650 which were directly aimed at controlling perceived Ranter excesses.

Many Ranters became QUAKERS after the restoration of the crown. At the time both were considered of similar backgrounds and were accused (usually falsely) of direct association. Some modern historians have alleged that the Ranter movement was a myth created by conservatives to create a moral panic in defence of traditionalism. Whilst is generally considered that a radical core did exist, the movement's influence was probably exaggerated. In the nineteenth century the term Ranters was revived to describe primitive Methodists because of their enthusiastic preachers and congregations. (WS)

RAWLS, JOHN This US political philosopher (1938–2002) published his highly influential *A Theory of Justice* in 1971. In it, he put forward a series of arguments which have been variously understood as supporting a state LIBERAL or even SOCIALIST position. Adopting elements of Immanuel Kant's moral philosophy, and the social contract theory of ROUSSEAU and others, Rawls put forward a thought experiment which is usually called 'the original position', or 'the veil of ignorance'. He suggests that we imagine a society, a UTOPIA perhaps, that we will have to live in. However, we do not know in advance what position in that society we will take. In other words, we do not know our race, ethnicity, gender, sexuality, socio-economic class, religion, state of health and so on. Rawls argues that the rational society to choose would be one that maximized fairness and equality, and not a society which rewarded the few for whatever reason.

He distilled these ideas down into two principles - the liberty principle and the difference principle. First, that each person would have the same rights and freedoms, but that these do not include the 'freedom' to tie a person into a contract of some form. These freedoms are not, in themselves, negotiable, but they can be partially traded off against each other. That is to say, some restriction on collective liberty may be accepted in return for collective safety, as long as everyone's liberty and everyone's safety are still the same. The second principle is that inequalities or differences (of social and economic kinds) are only legitimate if they benefit everyone. In other words, if the society decides it needs doctors, and people will only train as doctors if they are paid more, and qualified doctors treat everyone equally, then it is legitimate that doctors should be paid more. If we apply this argument to MANAGERS, we can see that their high pay and status in contemporary societies would fail several of Rawls's tests. These arguments are aimed at refuting utilitarian arguments that would suggest that 'the greatest good of the greatest number' might mean that some suffer for the benefit of the majority, and argument which would allow managers to be paid highly even if their activities caused harm to many members of society.

Rawls's ideas have been attacked by the left and the right. For right-wing LIBERTARIANS like Robert NOZICK (as well as some individualist ANARCHISTS), his attachment to using the state as a mechanism for determining the public good is already a violation of the most elementary freedoms. On the other hand, despite its radicalism, for some SOCIALISTS and COMMUNITARIANS, Rawls's thought experiment is too liberal, placing the primary value on freedom rather than COMMUNITY. Rawls's later work certainly develops more in liberal rather than radical directions, discussing (in *Political Liberalism*, 1993) the 'overlapping consensus' that is needed to forge agreements on fairness and equity within a pluralistic DEMOCRACY.

REPUBLIC, THE

'Justice, we say, is the attribute of an individual, but also of a whole city, is it not?'
'Certainly'
'And is not a city greater than an individual?'
'It is' (...)
'Now' I said 'if in our argument were we to watch a city in the making, should we not see its justice and injustice in the making also?'

Plato's UTOPIA *The Republic* (*c.* 360 BCE) probably owes more to the influence of Spartan forms of organization (see PLUTARCH) than it does to Athenian ones. (Though the rational Pythagorean COMMUNITIES of what is now southern Italy in the six-century BCE may have also influenced his ideas.) The independent citizens of Athens had been defeated by the collective discipline of Sparta during the Peloponnesian war (431–404 BCE), and much of Plato's authoritarianism undoubtedly reflects the triumph of this stern militarism. Unlike the Sophists, Cynics and Stoics (all schools of Greek thought that celebrated freedom, equality and conscience) Plato wished to build enduring institutions that would ensure a long-lasting CITY-STATE. In the *Timaeus* and the *Critias* he describes the GOLDEN AGE of ATLANTIS and its competition with ancient Athens as established by Solon the lawgiver (also described by Plutarch), whilst in the *Laws* he compares the historical institutions of Crete and Sparta.

The Republic begins as an attempt to define the nature of personal justice, but rapidly becomes a discussion about how rulers can be just. Plato's enduring assumption is that people cannot govern themselves, and hence that they need to be ruled by a special class of people who are intellectually and morally superior. But how to ensure the goodness of the rulers? Plato suggests that they must be selected, intensively trained and tested to be 'warrior athletes' (capable of dealing with internal dissent and external threat), and they must have the character of philosophers in order to be able to distinguish clearly between the good and the bad. It is only after years of such training, at the age of fifty, that they can take their turn in ordering the city. In order to secure the position of these guardians, Plato proposes the propagation of a 'noble falsehood' which would explain the necessary order of things to the common people. The people will be told that when God was making them, he placed gold in some, and silver, iron and copper in others. The people will also be told that if silver, iron or copper ever rules the city, it will perish.

A philosopher king presides over the republic, but his men of gold are not allowed to be rewarded in gold. Instead, no guardians have any private property or marriages, both men and women must eat in common and they must live in houses that are open to all. Female and male guardians are treated equally, and are expected to be temperate and logical in their behaviour. This unity is reinforced by having eugenic principles of reproduction (disguised as a lottery system), and children reared in common nurseries (in order to break up the family). At every turn, Plato is keen to ensure that there are few reasons for dissension and fragmentation, and hence engineers both the structure and ideology of the republic to be simultaneously hierarchical and COMMUNAL. That is to say, hierarchical for the lower orders (which included slaves), and communal for the guardians. The question of the division of labour becomes particularly important for the lower orders, because the larger and more complex the republic becomes, the more different trades are required to support it. Plato clearly prefers a smaller, simpler republic, but recognizes that if people want luxuries then the city and its territories will need to grow (though he warns that such growth can lead to war).

In order to prevent the contamination of the ideology of the republic, Plato is keen that there should be strict controls on its music, stories and songs; and poetry is to be banned altogether. Continually using metaphors of health and illness, he suggests that the healthy city must be guarded against unhealthy ideas, and that it is the philosopher who can see this most dispassionately. Almost any change in teaching or culture is prevented in the interests of the common people. *The Republic* is one of the earliest European utopias, but like so many (see More's UTOPIA, for example) it seems very DYSTOPIAN to twenty-first century eyes. Plato describes a socially engineered élite (see also Wells's A MODERN UTOPIA), who know what is best. In order to achieve this, they are given totalitarian powers that reflect the worst excesses of FASCISM or state COMMUNISM. Oddly, there is very little detail about the economic and legal systems that apply to the lower orders. It is as if Plato assumes that these are trivial matters that will all follow from the cultivation of the élite, and their enforcement of a rigid division of labour and prohibition on social mobility. Yet, as he is also clearly aware, if the lower orders knew the true principles behind their social order, they would rebel.

As Berneri (1971) comments, it is unlikely that Plato's *Republic* could have been written in the republic he imagines. He may have been disappointed with Athenian DEMOCRACY, but he places a huge faith in the character of his educated guardians. They may not have been tyrants in their motivation, but they have been given tyrannical powers. As Aristotle later observed, Plato has really described two states in one, and it is difficult to imagine that this would not breed dissent. However, *The Republic*'s influence has been substantial, and many spartan city state utopias have borrowed its central organizing principles (see, for example, CHRISTIAN-OPOLIS; CITY OF THE SUN). Plato's attempt to reason his way to a comparative study of different states represents a key beginning for reflective social thought, and opens the possibility that the future does not have to be like the past. Perhaps, as Kumar (1991) suggests, *The Republic* is better considered as a guide to the character of the virtuous person, and not an ideal COMMONWEALTH, since (as Plato notes) that does not exist anywhere. Building utopia inside us is perhaps a much more modern strategy. It allows for the ideal city to become much more portable, and become less a place, and more a set of practices.

REVOLUTION This word is commonly used to refer to a sudden overthrow of the status quo and its replacement by an entirely different state of affairs. That the word is also used for the turning of a wheel conveys this sense of social arrangements being turned upside-down. Many believe in the necessity of revolution for a fundamental reformation of society. The argument is that existing political and social institutions must be swept away if better ones are to emerge. Democratic SOCIALISTS and the reformist left prefer the idea of change achieved gradually by an incremental transformation of society, mirrored by changes in individual consciousness and behaviour. Finally a revolution may be conceived not as a deliberate strategy so much as the emergent effect of other social, political and economic changes, as in the industrial revolution.

Revolution has often been pursued as a part of a strategy for bringing about a new society, led by revolutionaries organized into parties dedicated to the overthrow of existing states and institutions. LENIN's political strategy rested upon his determination to turn the more radical elements of the Russian Social Democratic Party into an effective and dedicated revolutionary organization. MARXIST revolutionaries typically see themselves as a vanguard acting on behalf of the masses; in other cases revolutions have been brought about by small groups in pursuit of their own interests. For example, it might be argued that the English Revolution of 1642–53 merely replaced monarchical rule with that of the Whig Grandees. The historian Christopher Hill argues that the real revolutionaries of the period, radical groups such as the DIGGERS, RANTERS and LEVELLERS, were initially encouraged in order to mobilize mass support and then ruthlessly suppressed when Whig aims had been achieved. This has been a common fate for revolutionaries: many surviving Bolsheviks were purged early on in Stalin's consolidation of power over the SOVIET UNION.

It was the French Revolution of 1789 that provided the archetypal model for revolutions that were to follow and that demonstrated the rising power of the middle classes as opposed to the authority of the crown and nobility. The slide of the French Revolution into repression also provided a warning of what was to come in many later revolutions. The revolutions that took place during the long revolutionary century from 1840 to 1970 were inspired predominantly by the UTOPIAN hopes of LIBERAL reformers, SOCIALISTS, ANARCHISTS and COMMUNISTS. Following on the European industrial revolution, the rapidly expanding middle classes demanded more political influence. The result was a wave of largely unsuccessful 'bourgeois' revolutions from 1848 onwards. At the same time the newly created industrial working classes were beginning to organize themselves into TRADE UNIONS and revolutionary parties inspired by the leadership of revolutionaries such as BAKUNIN and MARX. The result was that bourgeois revolutions often paved the way for attempts to bring about more radical social change from below.

In 1905 there was a failed liberal revolution in Russia that paved the way for the socialist revolution of 1917. In 1918 the Kaiser was overthrown in Germany by a popular revolution which resulted in the establishment of the short-lived Weimar Republic. This was followed by an abortive socialist revolution led by LUXEMBURG and Karl Liebknecht in 1919. The Xinhai Revolution in China overthrew the Qing Dynasty, establishing the Republic of China in 1911. By 1949 this had been overthrown by a socialist revolution led by MAO's peasant armies. The 1936 Spanish Revolution quickly went beyond the establishment of a republic as a result of the action of both anarchists and socialists, until crushed by Franco. The pattern was repeated again in CUBA where the last major socialist revolution took place in 1959 following the establishment of a discredited liberal democratic administration.

The Cold War between the Soviet bloc and Western capitalist states led to a number of attempts to sponsor 'revolutions' throughout the developing world or to oppose such revolutions with pro-Western counter-revolutions. Such revolutions were often only nominally communist or liberal democratic. The concept of 'permanent revolution' also arose in the twentieth century to describe a constant and dynamic transformation of society towards full communism following partial socialist revolutions. The phrase, most associated with Trotsky, originates in the idea that socialism must develop on an international scale because it could not survive within state boundaries. MAO instigated the 'cultural revolution' from 1966 to 1976 in a bid to transform Chinese society at a more fundamental level rather than simply changing the institutional and political structures of the state. In retrospect this has come to be seen as a disastrous measure that discredited communism both within and outside China. Since 1960 there have been many further revolutions, some claiming an affinity with socialism and others with bourgeois liberalism, particularly in the ex-colonies of the great nineteenth-century powers. In many cases these have turned out to be no more than *coup d'états*, a simple replacement of one ruling élite with another. The year 1968 saw a wave of protests and near-revolutionary conditions in many Western states, most notably in France, but this seemed to mark the end of the revolutionary decades rather than a new era of radical political change.

This is not to argue that revolutions are no longer a feature of contemporary politics. Revolutions in Iran (1979) and Afghanistan (1996) established fundamentalist Islamic states. The satellite communist parties of Eastern Europe were largely overthrown in bloodless revolutions such as the 'velvet revolution' in Czechoslovakia in 1989. Since the rise of neo-liberalism it could even be argued that MARKET capitalism has become a revolutionary movement backed by the crusading right-wing ideology of the US translated into military force. There are also still some revolutionary movements on the left, such as the ZAPATISTAS in Mexico, but most ANTI-CAPITALIST organizations work through protest and more LOCAL forms of DIRECT ACTION.

Revolution may be seen as an emergent process that arises naturally through other changes. The terms 'industrial revolution', 'scientific revolution' or 'technological revolution' all capture this sense of the rapid transformation of everyday life, just as the 1960s have been described as a 'sexual revolution'. Though not entirely uninfluenced by the political aims and interests of various groups, such revolutions tend to occur in an unforeseen way through complex combinations of social, economic, technological and political factors. Often this form of change interacts with deliberate political revolutionary attempts. Those on the Left have generally moved away from the idea of violent and sudden political revolutions. This is partly because the political scene appears much less likely to give rise to revolutionary opportunities and partly because the 'failure' of many revolutions has left many much less confident that this is an effective method to bring about a better society. Left reformers now tend to support engagement with existing institutions in the pursuit of incremental political change. The problem with this strategy is familiar. Attempts to bring about significant reform tend to be resisted by powerful vested interests. It should be noted that revolutionary and reformist change are not necessarily incompatible. The two may be pursued as part of a single strategy: reforms may produce an appetite for more radical change. However, in practice, reforms often reduce the pressure for more significant change. Many Marxists have argued that the rise of the welfare state and sectional forms of trade unionism has stabilized the capitalist system.

The desirability of revolution is one of the biggest dividing lines between utopians. Many anarchists and Marxists would agree that those currently in power will not let go of it without the resort to violence. Therefore, they argue, it is a sad necessity that violent revolution will be necessary in order to bring about any progress towards a free society. One of the major disagreements between revolutionary anarchists and Marxists has concerned whether a revolution should be followed by a transitional period in which the old institutions of the state are retained in order to achieve full communism gradually. Anarchists, including KROPOTKIN and Bakunin, have worried that retaining these institutions leads to the re-emergence of a hierarchical society. Other radical utopians would argue that there is a close link between ends and means, and that trying to achieve freedom through violence is always doomed to failure. Only NON-VIOLENT RESISTANCE and a revolution in personal consciousness can hope to change society in ways that will not lead to new forms of oppression. There is currently no way to resolve such a debate. That future revolutions would need to be different from those of the past, and that the prospects for them seem much more uncertain, is less contentious.

RIPPLE PROJECT, see GRAMEEN BANK

ROBINSON CRUSOE Whether Daniel Defoe's 1719 novel is a UTOPIA (or even a DYSTOPIA) is a questionable point. Apart from the native 'Friday', Crusoe is shipwrecked alone on the island, and is largely occupied with recreating the civilization he has left behind. There is no pre-existing social structure to be described, and the only perspective we have is that of Crusoe himself. Though there are many different readings of the novel, the majority would focus on Crusoe's conquest of nature, and his construction of a small scale ARCADIA. Defoe may well have been influenced by Neville's ISLE OF PINES, but in its turn the influence of Defoe's book was huge, producing an entire sub-genre of 'Robinsonnades' in the following two centuries. Some were largely derivative versions of industrious Europeans surviving in various forms of wilderness, often accompanied by homilies on simplicity and hard work, such as Johann Wyss's *Swiss Family Robinson* (1813). Others, with more radical intent, began to develop the ROMANTIC idea of the 'noble savage' and the original state of nature which fitted so neatly with accounts of EDEN and the idea of a GOLDEN AGE, and which had been prefigured in de Foigny's NEW DISCOVERY OF TERRA INCOGNITA AUSTRALIS (1676). Books such as Swift's GULLIVER'S TRAVELS (1726), and Diderot's SUPPLEMENT TO BOUGAIN-VILLE'S VOYAGE (1796) contained ideas about travel to 'virgin' islands where people and creatures were found who showed the manners, politics and institutions of Europe in a distinctly negative light. They were closer to simplicity than their conquerors, like innocent children who ask the most awkward (and revealing) questions.

ROUSSEAU's suggestion that the education of his pupil in *Emile* (1762) should proceed through a reading of *Robinson Crusoe* (in preference to the classical education assumed at the time) underlines the idea of 'natural man' being born free, but everywhere being placed in chains. However, the common development of such ideas towards the celebrations of male individualism, and a racist contempt for the 'natives', is hardly surprising. MARX, in the *Grundrisse*, notes precisely that point. Crusoe is better understood as a fable about heroic Western man, not a yearning for lost COMMUNITY. Nonetheless, in terms of its influences, *Robinson Crusoe* marks a point at which Europe begins to come to terms with certain limits, and the contingency of its social and technical organization begins to be seen more clearly.

ROCHDALE PIONEERS Often considered as the first successful COOPERATIVE enterprise, as well as a continuing source of inspiration for the modern movement, the Rochdale Equitable Pioneers Society was founded in 1844 by a group of 28 artisans working in a cotton mill in Rochdale, in the north of England, with the aim of creating a store that would sell affordable and unadulterated food to its members. By pooling their savings (£1 per person), the men assembled enough capital to rent the ground floor of a warehouse. The members bought staple food (initially only 4 items: flour, sugar, butter, and oatmeal) in large quantities, and sold these to each other at low prices. But what the Pioneers established was far more than just a shop. In a room above the warehouse they opened a school and a library for members and their children, effectively operating as a MUTUAL IMPROVEMENT SOCIETY. The Pioneers also became missionaries of the cooperative movement, encouraging the development of other societies, and broadening the scope of their organization to include p roduction, insurance, wholesaling and education. This led to the formation of the Cooperative Wholesale Society (CWS) in 1863, which became the contemporary 'Coop' in the UK, a chain of supermarkets, banking and insurance services.

The Rochdale Society was not the first cooperative in Britain, but what made the achievements of the Pioneers so influential was their develop-ment of, and adherence to, what became known as the Rochdale Principles of Cooperation. These included voluntary and open membership, DEMOCRATIC control on the basis of 'one member one vote', the provision of education, the return of surplus to members in proportion to their contribution (the dividend or 'divi') and, quite radically for the time, equality of the sexes. Whilst the Pioneers' ideas have been updated, they remain the main influence behind the seven principles of cooperation more recently articulated by the International Cooperative Alliance.

ROMANTICISM

'*Bliss was it in that dawn to be alive, / But to be young was very heaven!*' (*The Prelude*, X, 692–3).
William Wordsworth's famous exclamation in his epic autobiographical poem *The Prelude* emphasizes the link between the UTOPIAN aspirations of English Romanticism and the drama of the French REVOLUTION. Indeed, as the poet goes on to relate, events in France appeared to enable those who hoped for a better world to find it –

Not in Utopia – subterraneous fields,
Or some secreted island, heaven knows where –
But in the very world which is the world
Of all of us, the place in which, in the end,
We find our happiness, or not at all. (X, 723–7)

Many observers understood the French Revolution not only as an extension of the spirit that had already inspired the revolution in AMERICA but also as an enacting of the Biblical schemes of apocalypse and revelation (or as a secularized version of such narratives). As Robert Southey commented, 'a visionary world seemed to open upon those who were just entering it. Old things seemed passing away, and nothing was dreamt of but the regeneration of the human race.' Revolutionary enthusiasm stimulated a significant amount of utopian writing in the 1790s, perhaps most notably Thomas Paine's *Rights of Man* (1791–2) and William GODWIN's *Enquiry Concerning Political Justice* (1793). According to some, the subsequent descent of the Revolution into violence and imperialism prompted further relocations of the utopian impulse as writers turned inwards to the 'imagination' or away from politics to 'nature' as the sites where they could find 'happiness'. Wordsworth, for example, found his own version of utopia in Grasmere in the Lake District, an ARCADIAN place that provided him with:

… the sense
Of majesty, and beauty, and repose,
A blessed holiness of earth and sky,
Something that makes this individual Spot,
This small abiding-place of many men,
A termination, and a last retreat,
A Centre, come from wheresoe'er you will,
A Whole without dependence or defect,
Made for itself, and happy in itself,
Perfect Contentment, Unity entire.
(*Home at Grasmere*, 161–170).

Other poets continued to engage with the question of how society could be reordered, frequently wrestling with the problem of whether or not violence was necessary to this process. Percy Bysshe Shelley produced the most ambitious vision of a cosmic utopia, *Prometheus Unbound*, an epic poem in which he combines Greek and Christian narratives to explore the centrality of love to the transformation of both the physical earth and the nature of man, imagining a state in which:

... man remains
Sceptreless, free, uncircumscribed – but man;
Equal, unclassed, tribeless, and nationless,
Exempt from awe, worship, degree; the king
Over himself; just, gentle, wise – but man.
(*Prometheus Unbound*, III, iv, 197–201).

While the revolutionary fervour of the early 1790s and the subsequent processes of disappointment and displacement were major factors, another can be found in the increasing industrialization of the period. BLAKE's desire to build Jerusalem in 'England's green and pleasant land' is perhaps the most famous expression of the nation's utopian potential as structured against the 'dark satanic mills'. His *Songs of Innocence* celebrate through text and image a pastoral GOLDEN AGE that may already be lost, as is suggested by the pairing with *Songs of Experience*, which includes the poet's DYSTOPIAN vision of the metropolis 'London'. Blake's poetic visions of a rural utopia have some parallels with the 'back to the land' schemes of the period, such as those of Thomas Spence who advocated the abolition of private property and who produced his own work of utopian writing, *A Supplement to the History of Robinson Crusoe*. This is one of the many rewritings of the two most important novels for British utopianism in the eighteenth century, ROBINSON CRUSOE and GULLIVER'S TRAVELS.

In addition to utopian projects for Britain, many writers of the Romantic period looked to distant lands, particularly the Americas and the East, as possible locations for alternative systems of organizing society. The 'new' world became a significant imaginative space for those in the old. For example, following the failure of their hopes for the French Revolution, the poets Robert Southey and Samuel Taylor Coleridge conceived in 1794 the idea of a 'Pantisocratic' COMMUNITY to be established on the banks of the Susquehanna river in Pennsylvania in which all property could be shared. The scheme never materialized due to political and personal disagreements. Nearly three decades later, Lord Byron celebrated the Kentucky of Daniel Boone as a state of 'Nature' (opposed to 'Civilization') and a 'young, unawakened world [that] was ever new' (*Don Juan*, VII, 515). More frequently, Byron looked to the East for the settings of his poems and, like Shelley and Thomas Moore, he used the locations of his oriental romances to offer a seductive alternative world and reflect critically on the West. These oriental works were produced during a period in which Britain was significantly expanding its empire and there is a complex relationship

239

between the imperial project and the vogue for exotic utopias. It is significant that in *Frankenstein* Mary Shelley parallels the utopian aspirations of the scientist with those of the explorer, suggesting that the masculinist, idealistic and self-glorifying ambitions of both figures are destructive not only of themselves but also of domestic values. Finding its moral centre in the values of the home and family, *Frankenstein* stands as a powerful critique of the utopian aspirations that are central to Romanticism. (SB)

ROUSSEAU, JEAN-JACQUES

'No citizen should be rich enough to buy another, and none so poor that he is obliged to sell himself.'

Perhaps the key philosopher of radical ROMANTICISM, he was born in Geneva in 1712 and died near Paris in 1778. A musician by training, he was influenced by the Calvinist traditions of the CITY STATE of Geneva (see CHRISTIANOPOLIS; CITY OF THE SUN) and his earliest publications were for Diderot's *Encyclopédie* (see SUPPLEMENT TO BOUGAINVILLE'S VOYAGE). During a turbulent and vagabond life, his work (both fiction and political philosophy) was banned in France and Switzerland, but his reputation grew after the French REVOLUTION.

Central to his ideas was the concept of the 'noble savage' (see ARCADIA), and the famous aphorism 'Man is born free but everywhere placed in chains'. Rousseau suggested that civilization is double-edged – it both corrupts innocent human beings and is necessary to prevent selfish conflicts. His writings on education (*Emile*, 1762) stress a humane movement from the child-animal to the reasonable adult, and he recommended ROBINSON CRUSOE as reading which would assist such an education. (Though this was for boys only, since the duties of girls did not require such a separation from animal nature.) According to the entirely speculative anthropology he deploys in his *Discourse on the Origin of Inequality* (1754) 'natural man' is degraded by property and competition. In *The Social Contract* (1762) Rousseau argued that some form of 'society' is certainly required, but the actually existing societies that he observed around him were based on inequality, fear and jealousy. In order to recapture the GOLDEN AGE of human association, the social contract needs to become the will of all, and not merely a corruption which is of benefit to the rich and powerful. Government by magistrates would replace authoritarian and monarchical regimes. However, Rousseau was also hostile to systems of representative

DEMOCRACY, which has caused considerable debate as to whether his ideas about the COMMUNITY of the 'general will' could be applied to units larger than the city state.

Rousseau's attacks on the idea of original sin, and on private property, have led to his being seen as a major influence on COMMUNIST and SOCIALIST thought. His influence on radical humanist conceptions of education is also significant (see FREIRE). His suspicion of majority rule echoes many of the central tenets of LIBERAL and ANARCHIST ideas, and his nostalgia for primitive innocence and preference for the country echo many elements of ENVIRON-MENTALISM. His legacy is a paradox: is it possible to be free and still accept restrictions? Rousseau's life, and his very modern and reflective sense of self, would suggest that he would have found this a difficult question to answer.

RUSKIN, JOHN English author, poet, artist, art critic and social critic, born in 1819. During a prolific life, Ruskin argued passionately for an anti-modern form of SOCIALISM and an aesthetic based on passion and authenticity (see especially *Unto This Last*, 1862). Born into a wealthy family, Ruskin's key insight (following FOURIER and the early MARX) was that work can and should be a creative and affirming act. The theme that runs through his extensive writings is the conviction that Victorian society was immoral, materialistic and exploitative, but that good art (produced by good people), has redeeming characteristics. Or, as he came to articulate it later, in order to produce great art, it is necessary to change society. His defence of the ROMANTIC and naturalist Pre-Raphaelite movement was both aesthetic (in the sense of being anti-formalist), and political (in the sense of the later developments of Chartism). His attacks on the political economy that naturalized poverty as the operation of scientific laws directly influenced William Morris (see NEWS FROM NOWHERE) and the ARTS AND CRAFTS movement, but he spent the last sixteen years of his life in semi-seclusion at his house, Brantwood, in the English Lake District.

When Slade Professor of Fine Art at Oxford, he convinced his students that their studies were not incommensurable with road digging, and participated himself. (WELLS derided this as 'the Olympian unworldliness of an irresponsibly rich man', and noted that 'it proved the least contagious of practices'.) Through his monthly digest *Fors Clavigera: Letters to the Workmen and Labourers of Great Britain* (1871-84) Ruskin sponsored a UTOPIAN vision of a mock-medieval 'gothic' England where art and life

241

were one, and work was organized according to a GUILD structure. His 1871 'Guild of St George' was based on the idea of good men giving a tithe of their income in order to buy and develop some land (see GARDEN CITIES), but without employing any modern technology. The guild was to be led by an elected master (initially Ruskin). Three classes of members were envisaged. The 'Companions Servant' (wealthy men who devoted themselves to the guild), the 'Companions Militant' (workers directed by the master to achieve the guild's aims), and the 'Companions Consular' (who acted as friends of the guild, giving income and pledging to live simply). Despite Ruskin's assumption that the guild would rapidly become a popular social movement, by 1878 its membership was still the original 32 people. Nonetheless, there were short-lived communal experiments at Barmouth in Wales and Totley in Sheffield, a working man's teashop in London, and an attempt at communal street sweeping – in all of which he was directly involved. In addition, his ideas inspired a commune called 'Ruskin' in Tennessee which lasted from 1894 to 1899. Ruskin's influence was primarily intellectual. A religiously inspired reformist and a florid writer, he was a moralizing radical who inspired many, but achieved little himself.

S

SADE, MARQUIS DE Though this French writer never actually published a worked-through UTOPIA, his *Philosophie dans le Boudoir* (1795) is an early example of sexual LIBERALISM combined with republican rationalism that marked much of the subsequent development of alternative organization, particularly from the 1960s onwards. De Sade (1740–1814) insists that freedom and equality should be central to both public and private life. This meant that the 1789 REVOLUTION that toppled the monarchy should be followed by a revolution in thinking that topples the church, and that makes the legal system effective and not moralizing. Free citizens should not have their ideas imposed on them by priests and judges, and in the area of sexual ethics he was particularly clear upon this point. In a way that amplified the English development of utilitarianism, de Sade insisted that there was nothing immoral about pleasures of any sort, providing they were engaged in by free individuals (compare with Neville's earlier ISLE OF PINES). He suggested that women in particular suffer from repression and hypocrisy, and that all people should be freed from the bonds of monogamous marriage (which reduced people to property) and allowed to explore their sexuality as they wished. He proposed the establishment of state brothels for this purpose, both for men and for women.

Of course, in many of his other books, *120 Days of Sodom* (1785) and *Justine* (1791) for example, De Sade's sexual pornotopianism is extreme, and much more difficult to articulate as pro-FEMINIST because of its sheer patriarchal violence. Even in *Philosophy in the Bedroom*, the prostitution of women or girls into his state brothels was to be enforced by law, meaning that logical and political contradictions abounded. Gentler forms of sexual liberalism can be found later in FOURIER, MORRIS and WELLS but not until the 1960s in a form so challenging. Despite his nobility and service as an army officer (where he was brutalized by scenes of carnage), he was first imprisoned for various sexual offences in 1777. Though released from the Bastille in 1789 (where he had been imprisoned for five years in the 'Tower of Liberty') even the revolutionaries found him too much and he spent time in various prisons. In one, over 1,800 people were guillotined outside

243

his window during a month. He was eventually determined insane, and his work was either published elsewhere, or not until a century later. On one reading De Sade, like Diderot in the SUPPLEMENT TO BOUGAINVILLE'S VOYAGE, is a ROMANTIC naturalist who follows ROUSSEAU's aphorism that we are born free but everywhere placed in chains. A more extreme version would be that he is a Nietzschean egoist, who believes morality to be an excuse for the weak. Whichever interpretation is preferred, De Sade's powerful thought deserves a response, and comparison with the terrors inflicted by his contemporaries.

SAINT-SIMON, CLAUDE-HENRI DE ROUVROY, COMTE DE Born into an ancient aristocratic family in Paris in 1760, Saint-Simon was driven by a sense of his own importance and destiny. He refused communion at the age of 13, was imprisoned and then escaped. He acted as an officer on the AMERICAN side during the American revolution, fought at the battle of Yorktown, and was again imprisoned. During the French REVOLUTION, despite renouncing his title, he was again imprisoned for a while, and spent the rest of the time speculating in land in order to form a gigantic bank to support his various undertakings (which included what is now the Panama canal). It was said that his valet had orders to wake him with the phrase, 'Remember, monsieur le Comte, that you have great things to do.' By his forties, he had squandered his fortune on various schemes, and began to write, though his work attracted little notice until a few years before his death in 1825.

Saint-Simon was an instinctive rebel, but his mature SOCIALISM was also tempered by witnessing the brutality of the mob during the French REVOLUTION. What society needed, he thought, was a stable social order in which the chiefs of industry would control society. These men of science, by virtue of their intelligence and training in philosophy, science and engineering, would be able to rule with the best interests of everyone in mind. Saint-Simon's general theory of history suggests a progressive development towards larger units of 'association' and away from 'subjection'. This 'spontaneous harmony' was a result of industrialism, and might even result in a European state with homogeneous institutions (perhaps led by England). Though his writings are confused and contradictory, in *Du Système Industriel* (1821) and *Catéchisme des Industriels* (1824), he puts forward a meritocratic hierarchy in which science is used to produce things which are useful for all. New institutions, such as the chambers of 'Invention',

'Examination' and 'Execution' would organize public works and festivals. Politics would disappear, and become a branch of economics since efficiency and production would be all that mattered in the new order. In the unfinished *Nouveau Christianisme* (1825), he adds a Christian ethics to his society, suggesting that the industrial chiefs and trained *savants* would become priests of a new humanist religion.

After his death, several of his disciples (particularly Barthelemy-Prosper Enfantin and Saint-Amand Bazard) established a short-lived journal (*Le Producteur*) and attempted some experiments in COMMUNAL living, incorporating radical ideas about 'free love' and the equality of the sexes. But it was Saint-Simon's collaboration with Auguste Comte on the journal *L'Organisateur* from 1819 that was crucial in developing his reputation more generally, since Comte's rather mystical faith in scientific progress almost entirely echoed Saint-Simon's ideas. In some sense, he is perhaps best seen as the grandfather of MANAGEMENT, since his faith in a technocratic élite finds clear echoes in later utopias (see LOOKING BACKWARD; WELLS) as well as ideas about the importance of the welfare state and BUREAUCRACY. His ideas about socialism as a science also influenced MARX, though Marx condemned Saint-Simon's UTOPIANISM (as well as that of FOURIER and OWEN). Saint-Simon was certainly a radical, and hostile to inherited privilege, but his bourgeois 'socialism' was of a patrician kind. Science, being a firm and certain kind of knowledge, a 'religion of Newton' or 'cult of Reason', essentially plays the key role in his grand schemes for social engineering. Science would 'shift the Earthy Paradise and transport it from the past into the future' (see GOLDEN AGE).

SALTAIRE A 'model' industrial village built by the wool producer Sir Titus Salt. His intention was to establish 'a paradise on the sylvan banks of the Aire, far from the stench and vice of the industrial city'. It survives in well-preserved form, within five miles of Bradford, England. Titus Salt joined his family's wool business in 1824 and became Mayor of Bradford in 1848. Finding little sympathy for his plans to relieve the town's pollution problems, he decided to move his operations away from the city. A site was acquired with excellent water supplies and transportation links, and with sufficient space to bring almost the entire production process under one roof and to establish housing and amenities for his workforce. Work began on the massive Salt's mill in 1851 and when opened in 1853 it was one of the largest and most advanced industrial complexes of the age. Salt then turned towards building a settlement for his workers. Between 1854 and 1868 over 800 high-quality dwellings were built, laid out on a gridiron pattern and supplemented with a range of 'improving' facilities such as a school, hospital, two churches, bathhouses and a park (see also BOURNVILLE, PORT SUNLIGHT).

The Salt family lost ownership of the mill in 1892. Following several changes in ownership, the mill ceased production completely in 1986. The surrounding village, although held by the Bradford Property Trust since 1933, inevitably suffered. However, the establishment of the Saltaire Village Trust in 1984 and the purchase of Salt's Mill by local entrepreneur Jonathan Silver led to regeneration. Salt's mill now is a major cultural centre housing the world's largest collection of works by the Bradford-born artist David Hockney. The village itself was declared a UNESCO world heritage site in 2001 as an important example of the 'integration of industrial, residential and civic buildings within a unified design, created on a greenfield site away from the parent city, by means of planned dispersal'.

SCHUMACHER, E. F.

Born in Germany in 1911, this heterodox economist became renowned for his promotion of SMALL and SUSTAINABLE systems for social and economic development. Schumacher came to Britain to escape Nazism, and after the Second World War worked as an economic adviser to the British Control Commission charged with rebuilding the German economy. From 1950 to 1970, he served as chief economic adviser to the National Coal Board, and died in 1977. Through these experiences he came to believe that modern economic policies, with their emphasis on large-scale technology, growth and profit, were failing people and the planet by creating ENVIRONMENTAL degradation and dehumanizing labour conditions. Large institutions, multinational corporations, unlimited economic growth and ever-increasing consumption were considered symbols of progress. In *Small is Beautiful: Economics as if People Mattered*, a seminal collection of essays published in 1973, Schumacher denounced the human and environmental damage caused by this 'idolatry of gigantism', and outlined alternatives based on LOCALIZATION.

One of the essays in the book, entitled 'Buddhist Economics', reflects Schumacher's experience as an adviser to the government of Burma. In this essay he imagined what an economy based on Buddha's idea of 'Right Livelihood' would look like, and described a system regulated by concerns for permanence, equality, the reduction of desires, the alleviation of suffering, respect for beauty, and the dignity of work. To Schumacher it was logical and natural to produce, consume and organize as locally as possible, which inevitably meant on a smaller scale. Schumacher also founded the Intermediate Technology Development Group in 1966. The idea of Intermediate or APPROPRIATE TECHNOLOGY privileges the development of user- and environment-friendly technologies that can be developed and managed cheaply within local communities. Complementary to his interest in Intermediate Technology was his involvement in sustainable agriculture. He became President of the Soil Association, a UK-based body regulating and promoting organic food and farming. A college named after him based in Devon, is devoted to ecological studies; the Intermediate Technology Development Group he set up is still going; Schumacher UK and the E. F. Schumacher Society in the USA are both engaged in spreading Schumacher's ideas; and *Resurgence,* a magazine for which Schumacher wrote regularly, continues to examine the 'small is beautiful' ethos.

SCIENCE FICTION A form of speculative fiction suspended somewhere between utopias, fantasy and sociology. One definition of science fiction (SF) is that it involves systematically altering technological, social or biological conditions and then attempting to understand the possible consequences. Hence it could be argued that the science fiction of the last century has often involved thought experiments of a UTOPIAN or DYSTOPIAN variety. H. G. WELLS, for example, produced examples of both, and some novels (such as Aleksei Tolstoy's journey to Mars to establish a COMMUNIST state in *Aelita*, 1924) are difficult to classify as either one or the other. The pre-history of what we now call SF is satirical and/or utopian travel writing, which exaggerates or inverts certain aspects of the author's world for comic or political effect (see, for example, EREWHON; GULLIVER'S TRAVELS; NEW ATLANTIS).

Though much SF writing over the past century has involved relocating cowboy plots into spaceships, or constructing fantasy worlds which retell ancient myths, some has involved thought experiments of an extremely challenging kind. For example, one stream of SF has explored radical philosophy, with authors such as J. G. Ballard, Philip K. Dick, Kurt Vonnegut and Greg Egan (see his 1994 *Permutation City*) exploring the connections between technology, progress and consciousness. Other work has been more 'political'. On gender, for example, Ursula Le Guin's *The Left Hand of Darkness* (1969) and Marge Piercy's WOMAN ON THE EDGE OF

247

TIME are examples of work that has proposed FEMINIST UTOPIAS. In Le Guin's novel, a society with only one sex is described. Reproduction is achieved when one person goes into the monthly cycle of Kemmer as either male or female, and stimulates another to take the opposite sex. For the rest of the time, everyone is asexual, and Le Guin explores what this might mean in terms of psychology and social institutions. On race and ethnicity, Octavia Butler's Xenogenesis trilogy reimagines origins and evolution from a African American perspective, whilst Le Guin's *The Lathe of Heaven* (1972) has everyone turn grey as a 'utopian' solution to the problem of racism. Le Guin's THE DISPOSSESSED, as well as Robert Heinlein's (1966) *The Moon is a Harsh Mistress*, James P. Hogan's (1982) *Voyage from Yesteryear*, Greg Egan's (1995) *Distress* and Mack Reynolds's *Lagrange 5* series, all consider the possibility of various ANARCHIST societies.

With honourable exceptions, the majority of this sort of 'political' science fiction has been dystopian, of the nature of a warning concerning present tendencies. Ray Bradbury's *Farenheit 451* (1953) is concerned with censorship and the loss of freedom. Harry Harrison's *Make Room! Make Room!* (1966) warns of overpopulation. Margaret Atwood's *The Handmaid's Tale* (1985) links a male technocracy with women being used as wombs in a future in which most people are sterile. David Brin's *Earth* (1990) depicts ecological collapse (though see also ECOTOPIA). A fair amount of recent science fiction, sometimes termed 'cyberpunk', has focused on the domination of technology and corporations, with versions of consumption, MANAGEMENT and organizational life usually being diagnosed as dehumanizing in various ways. The work of William Gibson, Neal Stephenson and Bruce Sterling is often cited, but another more recent example is Richard Morgan's (2004) *Market Forces* in which corporate executives duel with each other in armoured sports cars.

So, in some sense, much interesting science fiction is allegorical. It presents fables that we can learn from, or be inspired by. It is hardly surprising that many radicals (whether counter-cultural or political) have found in SF a mirror for their own longings. The line between escapism and the radical imagination is a very fine one. As Mannheim put it:

> Wishful thinking has always figured in human affairs. When the imagination finds no satisfaction in existing reality, it seeks refuge in wishfully constructed places and periods. Myths, fairy tales, other-worldly promises of religion, humanistic fantasies, travel romances, have been continually changing expressions of that which was lacking in actual life. (1960: 184)

SCOTT BADER COMMONWEALTH Created in 1921 in the UK by Swiss-born Ernest Bader (1890–1982), this company's experiments in INDUSTRIAL DEMOCRACY and common ownership were acclaimed by SCHUMACHER in his influential book *Small Is Beautiful*. The company manufactures synthetic resins, gel coats and polymers from five sites across four continents and by the beginning of the twenty-first century employed nearly 700 employees. Bader was a committed Christian (he became a QUAKER) and believed that business should help build a better world. After running the company as a family business for 30 years, he was eager to find a way of distributing capital more equitably, and to act on his belief that labour should hire capital. In 1951, the Bader family took the radical decision to entrust ownership to a charitable trust, the Scott Bader COMMONWEALTH, which holds the shares of the company in perpetuity. This structure guarantees independence as its shares cannot be bought or sold by external shareholders and provides for COMMON ownership of the company by employees, all of whom are expected to become members. Membership entitles employees to participate in the direction and MANAGEMENT of the company by exercising their voting right in the General Meeting, and through elected staff representatives who sit on governing bodies including the Board of the Scott Bader Company (see COOPERATIVES, ESOP, JOHN LEWIS PARTNERSHIP).

The company practised socially responsible business long before the term became popularized, and made its social purpose explicit when it published its values in the early 1950s. These values include avoiding involvement in weapons of war, caring for the environment, recognizing and fulfilling the company's responsibility to the wider COMMUNITY, and contributing to the development of employees. The constitution of the Commonwealth also stipulates that a proportion of profits gets redistributed to the wider community through various charitable activities (see ZAKÂT). Indeed one of the conditions attached to the creation of the Commonwealth was that whatever members award themselves in the form of bonus must be at least matched by payments to charitable causes.

SEATTLE, see BATTLE OF SEATTLE

SECRET SOCIETIES A general term that covers a wide range of o rganizations that disguise their existence, or conceal aspects of their internal functioning. Much is often made of their initiation ceremonies, rituals and secret signs. However, this is not by any means a watertight definition. Most business organizations and virtually all states protect secrets which they wish to keep from competitors, citizens or 'enemy powers'. In addition, many business organizations and most states engage in forms of espionage which are aimed at discovering the secrets of others, and such activities themselves require forms of concealment. This description becomes even more confused if we consider that many secret societies appear to be acting on behalf of elements of the state, or in order to build semi-legal or illegal business activities (see PIRATE UTOPIA), or both. In fact, the connotations that come with the idea of a secret society tend to conceal how widespread forms of disguise and concealment are in organization more generally.

Perhaps the best-known secret societies are those associated with organized crime, political organizations termed TERRORISTS, GUERRILLAS or freedom fighters, and various religious organizations with beliefs contrary to the state (see CULTS, DISSENTERS). In these cases, forms of cellular, NETWORK and covert organization are employed in order to evade detection by the state or hostile groups. In 1799, in the wake of the French REVOLUTION, the English state passed an Unlawful Societies Act, which prohibited secret organizations in case they fomented dissent (see LUDDITES, TRADE UNIONS). The same would also be true of contemporary ANTI-CAPITALIST protesters, and some coordinated forms of DIRECT ACTION. However, not all secrecy is aimed at concealment from the state. There are also many secret societies that (it is claimed) reflect the interests of powerful players within the state, such as Yale University's 'Skull and Bones' society, the Freemasons, and the many other university and social clubs associated with the wealthy and powerful and sometimes expressed as 'the old boys' network'. Related to these groups are pro-capitalist associations such as the 'Bilderberg Group', the 'Council on Foreign Relations' and so on. Whilst the existence of these groups is not denied, their activities are mysterious and have inspired many conspiracy theories on both the Left and the Right. Some of these theories may well be accurate, such as the various covert activities of the US (see AMERICA) during the Cold War, whilst others shade off into esoteric stories about ATLANTIS, or paranoid accounts of the global Jewish world order. There is also, of course, a considerable trade in historical accounts of secret organizations that tie together the Pope, the Rosicrucians, the Illuminati, and so on.

In summary, whilst the idea of a secret society may seem something that should not really belong in a dictionary like this, the properties of secrecy are crucial to understanding both the operations of the powerful and the powerless. The contemporary popularity on the Left of accounts of Sub-comandante Marcos of the ZAPATISTAS is paralleled by a fear of a global conspiracy run by corporations, or wars being fought over oil interests, or drug dealing and the control of gambling in Las Vegas. The blurring of the boundary between these legitimate questions of politics and organization with unlikely racist and esoteric conspiracies has the potential to defuse the importance of these issues more generally. To use the phrase popularized by the TV show *X-Files*, if 'The Truth is Out There', we might discover the difference between wild speculation and a cool understanding of actual organizational strategies.

SELF-MANAGEMENT, see WORKER SELF-MANAGEMENT

SELF-SUFFICIENCY Consists in providing for one's own needs without outside aid or exchange; and involves producing one's own food, energy, clothing and so on (see also SUBSISTENCE WORK). Whilst self-sufficiency (or self-reliance) was widespread in agrarian societies, it was largely eroded by the joint processes of industrialization and the enclosure of the COMMONS. Many have suggested that the model of the self-sufficient VILLAGE provides a more harmonious mode of organization (see GANDHI, TOLSTOY). Today, self-sufficiency is being reclaimed as one alternative to global capitalism and is central to the articulation of some contemporary UTOPIAS (see ECOTOPIA) within ENVIRONMENTALISM and ANTI-CAPITALISM. Arguments for global capitalism and free MARKETS rely on the comparative advantage thesis: nations should abandon self-sufficiency and specialize in the production of commodities for export. However, many critics have pointed out that trade liberalization has drawn producers from the global South into unequal competition with heavily subsidized, capital-intensive producers from the global North. As a result, the South has become dependent on the vagaries of world prices, placing under threat the livelihoods of millions of subsistence farmers and small producers in the South. A return to local self-sufficiency is thus seen as a way of addressing the problems created by global capitalism.

Self-sufficiency, just like LOCALIZATION and SMALLNESS, is also sponsored on both socio-political and environmental grounds. For some, self-sufficiency is a precondition of EMPOWERMENT and DEMOCRACY; these terms can only be meaningful if people have control over their means of livelihood. This line of argument is central to VIA CAMPESINA's articulation of food sovereignty: the right not only to to have enough to eat, but also to define the way in which one's food is produced. The environmental argument for self-sufficiency rests on the close relationship it establishes between local COMMUNITIES and the ecosystem on which they rely. It reduces the environmental cost of long-distance transportation and encourages practices, knowledge and technologies that are in harmony with the local environment and ensure long-term SUSTAINABILITY.

Self-sufficiency is a concept that can be applied to different levels and different spheres of production. At an individual or household level, it may involve people growing and preserving their own food, producing their own medicine, household items and energy, or building their own houses with recycled or renewable materials, using APPROPRIATE TECHNOLOGY or PERMACULTURE design. At a community level, self-sufficiency may involve some of these practices, as well as developing forms of local exchange where needs are met by local producers (COMMUNITY GARDENS, COMMUNITY SUPPORTED AGRICULTURE, ECOVILLAGE, FARMERS' MARKETS), sometimes using local currencies (see LETS, TIME BANKS). Finally it can also be applied at national levels, for example for industries or as a PROTECTIONIST principle underlying national policy. CUBA's agricultural policy following the break-down of trade relations with the Soviet Bloc in 1990 provides an example of a successful conversion towards food self-sufficiency. The government launched a national effort to transform the nation's agriculture from a high-input system relying on imported fuel and chemical products, to low-input small farming relying on local resources and appropriate technology. By 1995, Cuba had overcome its food shortage and almost reached self-sufficiency.

Finally, it should be stressed that few advocates of self-sufficiency would argue for complete self-provisioning or autarky. Instead, self-sufficiency to cover basic needs (food being a prime example) is often imagined in conjunction with the creation of networks of cooperation and FEDERATION between communities (see for example SOCIAL ECOLOGY).

SEM TERRA, see MST

SHAKERS A Christian COMMUNIST SECT, the Shaking Quakers split from the English QUAKERS in the early eighteenth century, and were named because of their ecstatic form of worship that was understood as sin leaving the body. Under the leadership of Mother Ann Lee ('The Bride of the Lamb'), nine Shakers left for AMERICA and established a settlement in Watervliet, New York State, calling themselves the 'United Society of Believers in Christ's Second Appearing'. From the late eighteenth century onwards new COMMUNITIES were established in New Hampshire, Massachusetts and other states, but the Shakers began to decline in numbers from the mid-nineteenth century onwards. Their peak of 6,000 members and eighteen communities is now reduced to one COMMUNITY with a handful of members.

The Shakers (like many similar communities – the Rappites, the Amana Colonies, the Zoarites and so on) stressed COMMUNAL values concerning property, insisted that celibacy was the purest state, and modest simplicity the best way of life. Their teachings involved sex segregation but equality based on the idea of a bisexual god, a rejection of lust, celebration of hard work, racial equality (there were black and native American members) and pacifism. Houses were divided, with separate staircases for each single sex 'family', and surveillance to prevent physical contact during shaking worship (see HAYDEN). As a result, new Shakers had to come through conversion or adoption – though children were given the option to leave at 21. Like the AMISH Anabaptist sect, or the ONEIDA community (see also BROOK FARM, and OWEN's 'New Harmony') there was a considerable emphasis placed on the virtues of hard work and a MONASTIC lifestyle. As a result, the Shakers have become well known for the quality of their crafts, the simplicity and elegance of their architecture, and their innovative music and dance (often involving native American motifs). All had a considerable influence on forms of 'form follows function' modernism in the USA and later Europe from the early twentieth century onwards (see LE CORBUSIER). Engels also praised them as the 'first people in America, and indeed in the world, who brought into realization a society based on the community of property'.

SHANGRI-LA A fictional Himalayan utopia described in the novel *Lost Horizon* by James Hilton (1933). This is a contemporary ARCADIAN paradise in a valley, based on a Buddhist MONASTERY and isolated from the outside world, which reminded our hero 'very slightly of Oxford'. It has excellent libraries, and almost no crime because everyone has what they want. It also has no government beyond the senior lamas who believe that 'to govern perfectly it is necessary to avoid governing too much'. Northrop Frye described it as 'a neo-Kantian kingdom of both ends ... with Oriental wisdom and American plumbing'. (The baths are made in Akron, Ohio.) It is loosely based on the Tibetan Buddhist idea of Shambhala, a mystical Kingdom beyond the snowy peaks of the Himalayas. See also ATLANTIS; COCKAIGNE; EDEN; EL DORADO.

SITUATIONIST A stream of ideas and organizations in the twentieth century that have attempted to blur the distinction between art and politics. These were movements which were responding quite directly to mass communication, and often employing much of its emerging rhetoric and aesthetic in order to either exceed or invert modern industrial culture. One such group, the Situationist Internationale (SI) was founded in 1957 by a small band of artistic and political activists in a bar in the Italian village of Cosio d'Arroscia. It was disbanded in 1972 following the failure of the revolutionary uprisings in Paris in May 1968 in which the SI played an active role. The SI was inspired by and elaborated upon the theory and practice of three avant-garde art movements; Futurism, Dadaism, and Surrealism. It shared with these movements the desire to enjoy an immediate experience of the world and transform everyday life into a reality desired by all those who live it.

This overcoming was to be achieved by a radical restructuring of social relations dominated by images, by subverting the banality of everyday life through realizing the artistic expression within it. In the MARXIST parody of SI co-founder, Guy Debord, 'so far, philosophers and artists have only interpreted situations. The point now is to change them. Since individuals are defined by situations, they must have the power to create situations worthy of their desires'. The Situationist critique of both capitalist and COMMUNIST society insists that we live in the society of the spectacle – a kind of pseudo-reality in which all social relations are mediated by commodity fetishism and all spontaneity is suppressed. A key concept was unitary urbanism, which required the study and negation of the relationship between the material world and its subjective and emotional experience. Through techniques of *dérive* and psychogeography, architecture, decoration, and street layouts were exposed as a means of social conditioning and repression. Countering that, if one takes one's desires for reality, Situationists believed, everyone could 'live in their own cathedral'.

Situationists were less interested in organization than the practice of REVOLUTION itself. The SI claimed that it would 'only organize the detonation', precisely because they saw formal organizing as one of the ways in which ordinary people gave up control of their lives (see also **AUTONOMIA**). Revolution demands a critical perspective fostered by avant-garde art. But if, as Sanguinetti argued, 'all rebellion expressed in terms of art merely ends up as the new academy' then an entirely new form of expression is required. Fundamental to this project was the development of a fluid language based on the concept of *detournement* – a reversal of perspective. For example, economists and their critics insist that everything has a value. Therefore, Situationist groups would steal useless objects, create meaningless graffiti, engage in uncommodified exchange (potlatch) and acts of vandalism (such as decapitating the Mermaid in Copenhagen harbour) in order to challenge meaning in the context in which it arises.

The fate of Dada and Surrealism had taught Situationists that all forms of **DISSENT** occupy a position within the system they oppose, and that this exposes them to the danger of being incorporated, reduced to an advertising slogan. In response, Situationists attempted to build a critique that would not conform to the perspectives or classifications recognized by spectacular society. This task was to prove their undoing. They became so paranoid about the dangers of recuperation that most members were expelled for failing to stop the embezzlement of their revolutionary discourse by the state. With its abhorrence of hierarchy and its emphasis on spontaneity and negation, the Situationist movement exerted a strong influence on UK punk rock in the 1970s and French *Parkour* in the 1990s, as well as radical *pro-situ* political groups such as the Angry Brigade, Reclaim the Streets, Culture Jammers, Neoism, and the Surveillance Camera Players. (MC)

SLOW FOOD Set up in 1986 by Carlo Petrini in Italy to resist the onslaught of fast food and the standardization of taste. It aims to preserve local cuisine, traditional food products and know-how within eco-regions. In 2005, it was established in 50 countries and counted 80,000 members. Through its 'Ark of Taste', the movement seeks to rediscover and promote forgotten food and wine products threatened by industrialization or environmental damage. Its initiatives also include the development of a seed bank to preserve biodiversity, the protection of family and organic farming, lobbying against GM food, the promotion of environmentally friendly gastro-tourism, raising awareness of the risks of fast food and agribusiness, as well as linking producers and consumers through **FARMERS' MARKETS**, or gastronomic fairs. Slow Food describes itself as the 'eco-gastronomy faction' within the **ENVIRONMENTAL** movement. Its protest against the takeover of

255

food and wine production by agribusiness, together with its promotion of LOCAL cuisine has made it a close ally of the anti-globalisation movement; indeed it has been referred to as the 'culinary wing' of the movement. It is also inscribed within a broader 'slow movement' which in various forms has resisted the increasing pace of modern life since the onset of the industrial revolution and has urged people to seize back the control of time. To symbolize its celebration of taking time to enjoy food, Slow Food has adopted the snail as its icon.

SMALLNESS Beginning with Adam SMITH, theorists have long stressed that MARKET efficiency and self-organizing capacities are dependent upon SMALL enterprises competing in LOCAL markets on the basis of price and quality. No buyer or seller should be large enough to influence prices. From this perspective, multinational corporations – which use their financial power to manipulate prices, drive competitors out of the market and determine what products will be available to consumers – are distorting the market and robbing it of its self-regulating capacities. However, it is not mainly for its market efficiency that smallness has attracted the interest of those who are looking for alternatives to global capitalism. Smallness has also been defended on environmental and political grounds. SCHUMACHER, in his book *Small is Beautiful*, denounced the environmental and human devastation created by policies that emphasize economies of scale and growth. Instead he advocated the creation of localized economies geared towards meeting local needs. The idea of smallness has also been central to some parts of the ANTI-CAPITALIST and ENVIRONMENTAL movements. From an environmental perspective, it is argued that smallness causes less transportation, and concentrates production where its environmental impacts will be felt. SMALL STATES are also praised for their potentially democratizing effect, and ability to bring decisions closer to the people who will be affected by them. It is an essential principle behind many of the UTOPIAN theories and practices in this volume: for example, APPROPRIATE TECHNOLOGY, CITY STATES, ECOVILLAGES, LOCAL EXCHANGE TRADING SCHEMES (LETS), PERMA-CULTURE, SOCIAL ECOLOGY.

SMALL STATES The idea that size is a basic factor in the nature of states or other enterprises is one that has been propounded throughout history. The belief in the superiority of the small state has existed since Aristotle, Plato (see REPUBLIC), Sallust and St Augustine. In the small state they detected the virtues of DEMOCRACY, tolerance and *homonoia* – self-regulating balance – all of which were seen to be sadly lacking in larger states. In modern times this has led to the idea that salvation from the problems of the modern world lies in SMALLNESS. André Gide asserted his belief in the virtue of small nations and proclaimed that the world would be saved by the few. In the 1970s this idea came to be encapsulated in SCHUMACHER's famous phrase 'Small is Beautiful'. His belief in small units of organization was largely a reaction to a world that was increasingly dominated by superpowers and multinational companies. Schumacher was hostile to over-large organizations of whatever sort: he maintained that whenever something was wrong, it was usually attributable to size.

For Arnold Toynbee smallness was the ideal container for the flourishing of variety. To Jean-Paul Sartre smallness gave a welcome glimpse of what he termed 'the other' in all its varied facets. He contended that this had been lost behind the overwhelming power of centralism as typified by the French state. To Leopold Kohr smallness was the antithesis of the power that was the source of most of the misery in the world. Kohr believed that the central problem is that of lust for power and that it is invariably misused by those states which have become over-large. Central to this category are the self-proclaimed 'great powers' whose size engendered the idea of invincibility and encouraged aggressive behaviour. The central belief is that size, rather than mode of production and ideology, is the most important factor explaining state behaviour. A small state is more likely to be free from the delusions of grandeur inherent in the large state and so is more likely to act for the benefit of its people. In the small state the relationship between government and people will inevitably be a closer and more harmonious one.

Kohr maintained that the logic of all this was that a Europe consisting of small nations such as Scotland, Wales, Brittany and Catalonia, together with small existing states like Denmark, the Netherlands and Portugal, was more stable and desirable than one in which the erstwhile great powers such as Britain and France still vaunted their ambitions. While the idea of the small nation has proved to be particularly attractive in contemporary Europe, the ideas of the CITY STATE and the AUTONOMOUS region have also had their protagonists. Alongside small nations, they are seen as viable alternative political structures that have played a significant role in former times. Whatever the exact nature of its components, a small state world is usually imagined as some kind of FEDERATION (see KROPOTKIN). It is

257

contended that small states find it easier to remain members of such an organization than do large ones, because they are forced to recognize the limits of their power while large states are likely to have a more self-centred agenda. In reality, the tendency of federal groupings has too often been for power to be drawn to the centre and to be eventually monopolized by their larger components. The contention of those who support the small states solution is that the division into smaller political units makes it less likely that power will be concentrated and monopolized in this way. Notable historical examples such as Switzerland have been used to demonstrate this proposition. Since the 1990s this theory has proved particularly relevant. The small nations of Central and Eastern Europe made a vital contribution to the end of the Cold War and the fall of the SOVIET UNION, a state which was a major example of the problems arising from massive size. Their subsequent importance in the reshaping of Europe is testimony to their potential to contribute to the development of more devolved structures of power (see ALTERNATIVE GEOPOLITICS). (GP)

SMITH, ADAM A Scottish political economist and moral philosopher (1723–90) whose work has been influential in creating the academic discipline of economics and in providing the best-known rationale for economic LIBERALISM and capitalism. Today Smith's reputation rests on his explanation of how rational self-interest in a free MARKET economy leads to economic well-being. It may seem surprising that whilst for some Smith is an advocate of ruthless individualism, his first major work, *The Theory of Moral Sentiments* (1759), concentrated on ethics and charity, and particularly on sympathy in exercising moral judgements. But to Smith sympathy and self-interest were not antithetical; they were complementary. Thus in what became his best-known publication, *An Inquiry into the Nature and Causes of the Wealth of Nations* (1776), Smith asserted that 'Man has almost constant occasion for the help of his brethren, and it is in vain for him to expect it from their benevolence only.' Charity, while a virtuous act, could not provide the essentials for living. Self-interest was the mechanism that could remedy this shortcoming. In what has become a well-known quote, Smith suggested that 'It is not from the benevolence of the butcher, the brewer, or the baker, that we can expect our dinner, but from their regard to their own interest.'

For Smith, the free market would produce the right amount and variety of goods and it was competition, the 'invisible hand of the market' that would ensure self-regulation. Competition would drive people to produce goods valued by society at a price people were ready to pay. Shortage of a particular product would lead to price increase, which in turn would attract producers, and the shortage would be remedied. Equally, if one manufacturer tried to charge prices higher than their natural level, consumers would turn to cheaper manufacturers and force the manufacturers to price down. Through the mechanism of competition, the law of the market governs the conflicting interests of individuals and promotes the social good. In *The Wealth of Nations*, Smith also suggested that the main cause of prosperity was the increasing division of labour. Smith gave the famous example of pin manufacturing, and asserted that ten workers could produce 48,000 pins per day if each of the eighteen specialized tasks was assigned to particular workers, whilst one worker would be lucky to produce even one pin per day if there was no division of labour.

Adam Smith has sometimes been caricatured as someone who opposed all forms of government intervention in economic life. In fact, he believed that the government should enforce contracts and grant copyrights to encourage inventions and new ideas. He also thought that the government should provide public works that it would not be worthwhile for individuals to provide. He did oppose intervention in the form of PROTECTIONIST measures, as this would distort market mechanisms. However, he was equally opposed to other forms of market distortion, including monopoly; and was particularly suspicious of the 'rapacity' of the merchant class as well as of corporations. Smith wrote at a time when small producers and consumers dominated the market, and he did not anticipate the increasing concentration of economic power with the Industrial REVOLUTION. Ironically, his name is now invoked to defend economic policies that privilege corporate power. Whilst Smith was not the first to defend the free market, he provided arguments that were to influence generations of free trade economists from his close successors David Ricardo and John Stuart Mill to contemporary neoliberals.

SOCIAL CAPITAL A concept that stresses the importance of social ties for cohesion and involvement in public affairs. The central idea is that higher levels of social capital result in better health, educational participation and neighbourliness, and lower rates of crime and unemployment. The usual assertion is that, in 'developed' societies, levels of social capital are falling, causing fragmentation and alienation. In an obvious sense, social capital refers to something like a COMMUNITY or social NETWORK. However, community and network are vague words which imply a certain form of warm sociality, a sort of 'trust', without actually telling us much else. Proponents of social capital theory suggest that declines can actually be measured in terms of lower rates of participation in various associations and societies. In *Bowling Alone* (2000), a study that popularized the concept of social capital, Robert Putnam suggests that there are two main forms: 'bonding' capital, which ties similar people together, and 'bridging' capital, which ties disparate groups of people together. Putnam is keener on the second type, exemplified by choirs and sports clubs, because he claims that it holds many benefits for society at large. In contrast 'bonding' capital tends to be exclusive, being the property of distinctive groups such as the AMISH or the MAFIA.

For COMMUNITARIANS from the Right or the Left, these are attractive arguments, and the idea of social capital has become popular in both academic and policy circles. Putnam was certainly not the first to use it. From early beginnings in studies of schooling, the social critic Jane Jacobs began to use the term in the 1960s (see LE CORBUSIER) and the sociologists Pierre Bourdieu and James Coleman in the 1980s. It also has a history as a term within economics that is defined as the total stock of capital possessed by the tradeable and non-tradeable parts of an economy. Of course the use of the term 'capital' is interesting in several ways. First, because this is a capital that cannot be 'banked' in order to gain interest, but that becomes useful when it is used, and shrinks if it is not used. Second, because the term 'capital' implies that it is something that is useful in terms of what gains it can deliver (like the term 'human capital') and not for its own sake. This has undoubtedly been influential in terms of policy. For those who wish to address questions of social exclusion and DEMOCRATIC participation in the global North, or the endurance of development programmes in the global South, questions of community have become important. 'Third way' governments, and global institutions such as the World Bank and the Organization for Economic Cooperation and Development, have invested heavily in the concept. However, it is worth noting certain assumptions that are built into this interest. First, one should notice a nostalgic narrative of the decline of community that goes back at least a century. Further, the idea that community needs to be re-invigorated has echoes of a middle-class call for the working classes to behave as the middle classes do. This might imply that the 'other' of the economy should be b rought into alignment with the interests of the state (see SOCIAL ECONOMY).

As with the term community, it is not always the case that social capital implies a warm form of sociality. As the distinction between bridging and bonding suggests, social capital can be used in exclusionary ways, and it is difficult to see a clear distinction between one and the other. For example, when someone decides to join a COMMUNE, they are presumably bridging, but their continuing adherence to the organization could only be called bonding. Finally, the politics of the term are very flexible. It can both be a call for a nostalgic return to family values, or a radical call for an alternative to the marketization of all relationships (see COLLECTIVISM, MUTUALISM). The fact that some pro-MANAGEMENT writers are now suggesting that social capital (like organizational culture) enhances organizational performance illustrates the problem nicely. The concept is obviously useful but might obscure understanding of the ways in which capitalism and managerialism erode the bases of collective action in the first place.

SOCIAL CENTRES, see CENTRI SOCIALI

SOCIAL ECOLOGY One of the most influential currents within radical ENVIRONMENTALISM, closely associated with the work of BOOKCHIN and drawing upon ANARCHISM and SOCIALISM. For Social Ecology, environmental problems are firmly rooted in relations of domination between people. The domination and exploitation of nature is the product of domination within society, in particular authoritarianism and hierarchy. Whilst these relations of domination have been present for centuries, they have been exacerbated by the development of capitalism. By identifying capitalism as the main cause of environmental destruction, Social Ecology is offering a critique not only of capitalism, but also of other currents in the environmental movement that trace ecological problems to anthropocentrism or human presence on the planet. Social Ecology's perspective on environmental issues is grounded in a socialist critique of capitalism, rather than a ROMANTIC 'love of nature'. According to Bookchin, Social Ecology was born out of the problems of a MARXIST reliance on economic laws to envisage the downfall of capitalism. For Bookchin, it is not economic imperatives that will drive capitalism to its downfall but its impact on the environment, its plundering of the earth. This ecological imperative will drive capitalism into an irreconcilable contradiction with the natural environment.

Social Ecology not only provides a critique of capitalism, but also outlines the kind of society that could replace it. Here the key idea is that of LIBERTARIAN municipalism. Drawing on PROUDHON, BAKUNIN and KROPOTKIN, among others, as well as on historical examples such as the PARIS COMMUNE or the POLIS, Social Ecologists envisage a society where economic and political affairs have been decentralized to municipalities governed by citizens' assemblies and freely conFEDERATED into local, regional or international networks (see SMALL STATES). Thus the emergence of the new society would not rely mainly on changes in lifestyles or values (as for DEEP ECOLOGISTS, for example), but on institutional changes that would promote direct DEMOCRACY through popular assemblies where citizens would meet, debate and decide on matters of COMMON concern. The economy would be placed in the hands of citizens and organized according to the principle of 'from each according to ability, to each according to need'. Technology would be deployed so as to eliminate drudgery and give all citizens sufficient free time to participate in self-fulfilling activities as well as in public affairs. Whilst Social Ecologists are critical of the way rationality has been deployed in modern society, they have faith in human reason to organize life in ways that are ecologically and socially responsible, and governed by concerns for justice, cooperation and diversity.

Social Ecology has been criticized on several grounds. For example, Deep Ecologists, among others, have argued that a non-hierarchical society envisaged by Social Ecologists would not necessarily be ecologically responsible. Social Ecology has also been accused of idealism as its vision of libertarian municipalism lacks an analysis of how to challenge existing power structures. Moreover, history suggests that Social Ecologists' faith in human reason to develop a socially and ecologically responsible society may be misplaced.

SOCIAL ECONOMY The growing interest in the not-for-profit sector has brought to the fore the problem of how to define it. Economic activities that exist neither in the MARKET economy nor in the redistributive realm of the public sector mean that conventional public–private and state–market dualisms that dominate thinking no longer suffice. Instead, terms such as the 'third sector' have become increasingly popular. One useful approach is to appreciate the historical context of the three sectors and how their roles and functions have fluctuated over time. Until the collapse of feudalism in Western Europe, exchange between people was formed mainly in accordance with two principles: reciprocity and redistribution. It was only after this that the market began to play any real role. But the rise of the market in England during the early nineteenth century led to strong reactions. Workers formed TRADE UNIONS so as to restrict the free supply of labour and firms formed cartels or trusts to restrict production. Thus, the market had scarcely come into existence before attempts were made to control it. One consequence was the expansion of the public sector during the twentieth century. Even during the advent of industrialism the newly emergent market was dependent on the public sector as regulator and problem solver. Both systems functioned side by side (see SMITH).

Nor did reciprocity disappear with the rise of the market and the expansion of the public sector. Although it is often assumed that the main site where reciprocity occurs, the family, lost its productive functions with the advent of the market, there is little evidence that this was the case. Reciprocity has persisted in realms that the public or private sector has not reached (caring activities, for example) and this has complemented the private and public sectors. Indeed, the family and kinship NETWORK (and to a lesser extent neighbourhood and COMMUNITY networks) can still be identified as the carriers of the reciprocity principle. However, there is also a quasi-formal realm that this principle of reciprocity inhabits. This is the 'social economy', which addresses those needs and desires that neither the private nor public sectors, nor the informal networks of the family, kin, neighbourhood and community, have managed to fulfil. It is based on COOPERATIVE or MUTUAL principles and is not-for-profit in the sense that the initiative does not seek to expropriate a profit from its operations. It is private (non-public) in nature even if there is sometimes public sector involvement, and it produces and sells services of a collective interest.

Various views exist concerning the potential role of the social economy's The first, dominant approach is to view the social economy as an alternative. The emphasis is upon whether the social economy can be used as a means of creating formal jobs and improving employability so as to fill the gaps left by the public and private sectors. This stance is more often than not adopted by those whose normative prescription for the future of work and welfare is to return to the supposedly golden age of full employment and/or comprehensive welfare provision. The second approach is to view the social economy as an alternative to informal work. In this view, the problem is that many people are currently unable to engage in formal or informal employment. As such, the role of the social economy is to provide access to forms of meaningful and productive activity beyond employment. This approach thus seeks to harness the social economy to compensate for the deficits of both the formal and informal spheres so that 'full engagement', not full employment, can be achieved. (CW)

SOCIALISM Despite sharp disagreements, there are a number of characteristics of socialism to which most socialists subscribe. First, it is an ideology or system of beliefs about how society, and particularly production, ought to be organized for the COMMON good of all rather than for an élite minority. Socialism is usually also taken to mean the social ownership of the means of production, though this may take different forms from LOCAL ownership by COMMUNES to state ownership. This principle has often been extended to the complete abolition of private property and the COLLECTIVE ownership of all goods. In all cases the objective of common ownership is to bring about an egalitarian society in which individuals are not forced to labour using productive capacities owned by others who appropriate the greater share of the wealth produced despite a much smaller contribution of effort. As a result it is usually taken as axiomatic that socialism is directly opposed to MARKET capitalism.

The word socialism is thought to have its origin in the early nineteenth century, being used to describe the UTOPIANISM of OWEN in Britain and SAINT-SIMON in France. Socialism as a description of how COMMUNITIES actually organize themselves may be much older: many socialists, including Engels and KROPOTKIN, have argued that pre-modern society was effectively socialist. Indeed Christian socialists have sought such proof in the Bible, whilst some GUILD socialists sought to reinvent a medieval form of WORKER SELF-MANAGEMENT through SYNDICALISM. Nonetheless, it is in the development of working-class movements and struggle that socialism takes on its modern meaning. A major element was the development of TRADE UNIONS, which are thus usually taken to be a major part of the socialist project, and socialism was certainly the official ideology of most trade unions by the twentieth century. The working-class socialist movement has been characterized by an emphasis on collective solidarity rather than individualism, on COOPERATION rather than competition, and on struggles against the ruling classes and employers.

Within this broad shared definition of socialism a number of different strands have developed. By the end of the nineteenth century distinctions could be made between the utopian socialism of thinkers such as SAINT-

SIMON, OWEN and FOURIER; MARXIST socialism; and the various strands of LIBERTARIAN socialism associated with ANARCHISM. One has to be careful with this distinction, however, as Marx used the term utopian socialism in a derogatory sense to discredit the ideas of rivals. Utopian socialism might be defined as being concerned with how social and economic relations should be rather than planning how they will come about. Marxist socialism tends to stress how the conditions for the transition to socialism may be brought about. Marx and Engels attempted to understand 'scientifically' the workings of capitalism and the historical and economic preconditions needed for socialism to emerge through REVOLUTION. Though anarchists are split over whether a revolution is a necessary precondition for socialism, they are generally in favour of SMALL-scale DIRECT ACTION. They try to put socialist principles into effect in the here and now rather than waiting until the historical preconditions are met for the introduction of a complete socialist system. As such they have often been aligned with utopian socialism rather than traditional Marxism.

There has always been a strong internationalist aspect to socialism, particularly stressed by Trotskyists. They argue that socialism is only possible through international working–class solidarity and requires the dismantling of the system of competing capitalist nation states (see ALTERNATIVE GEO-POLITICS), recognizing that national interest is a poor basis for ensuring a better deal for the poor and dispossessed or for the solution of the collective problems facing humanity, such as ENVIRONMENTAL degradation. Differences between the strands of socialism tend to have more to do with the tactics that should be followed rather than disagreements over what a socialist society should be like. Some assume that socialism can only come about through a sudden seizure of power. Socialism would thus be characterized by the working classes forcibly taking over the existing instruments of the state and appropriating property and the means of production into collective ownership. MARX envisaged this form of socialism as a temporary state of affairs to enable full COMMUNISM to develop as a libertarian form of society very similar to that proposed by most anarchists. As communism developed, so state institutions would become irrelevant and would 'wither away', being replaced by a FEDERAL NETWORK of directly DEMOCRATIC communal assemblies. Anarchists often share the conviction that a revolution is required but believe that full communism needs to be established immediately without retaining the apparatus of the previous state. Other socialists such as Fabians or reformist Marxists believe that socialism is best achieved by incremental change, working within the structures of democratic states.

All of the above variations can be described as 'left' socialism, seeking a complete transformation in society, but there are also many who would describe themselves as socialists who seek more modest forms of social change. Such socialists believe in various combinations of regulated markets and socialized ownership. They sometimes describe themselves as market socialists, or even social democrats. They advocate the coexistence of state-regulated markets with socialized welfare provision by the state, the state ownership of key utilities and industries, and tax systems that limit the accumulation of private wealth and economic inequality. Thus, for some, the desired endpoint of socialism might simply be partial state ownership combined with representative democracy. Chinese socialism fits neither left nor market socialism. The Chinese Communist Party describes its approach as 'socialism with Chinese characteristics' but for many socialists it looks like a heavily state-controlled version of entrepreneurial capitalism. As can be seen, socialism is an umbrella term for a range of movements that have their origins in the nineteenth century. Most remain committed to a different form of society but have broad differences over how they envisage such a society and how it is to be achieved.

The final point to consider is whether socialism is facing a general decline. Many European socialist parties and trade unions have moved towards the right in recent decades and have become less ambitious in their aims. Formerly socialist parties, such as the British Labour Party, have altered course in the direction of encouraging free markets and away from regulation, taxation and welfare provision. In addition, socialist working-class mass movements are no longer the force they were. However, as this dictionary shows, calls for a more egalitarian society where the poor have more control over their own lives and receive a more just reward for their labour are still widespread. What is lacking is the confidence in the ideological and organizational structures provided by the socialism of the last two centuries, particularly Marxism.

SOVIETS The word originally referred to the peasant and worker councils that were a feature of life in both late-Tsarist and post-revolutionary Russia. Russia had a long tradition of VILLAGE self-management, with peasants to an extent deciding their own affairs through the village *mir* or council. Following the first REVOLUTION of 1905, soviets began to spring up spontaneously as industrial workers and peasants sought to run their own affairs. After the February 1917 revolution soviets emerged all over Russia and formed FEDERAL links with each other, sending many delegates to national congresses, led by the highly influential Petrograd Soviet. Both ANARCHISTS and the Bolsheviks saw the soviets as the basic COMMUNAL and productive unit of the new COMMUNIST society they were attempting to bring about. They combined the LOCAL direction of affairs through direct DEMOCRACY with the capacity for building large-scale federal institutions.

During Kerensky's Provisional Government between the February and October Revolutions, the soviets came to form an entire alternative system of government. They included anarchists, MARXISTS and other Left reformists and SOCIALIST revolutionaries. The Bolsheviks, seeing their potential, worked hard to win support and called for 'all power to the soviets', eventually winning majority support within the most influential large urban soviets. Action by the soviets was central to the successful seizure of power in October 1917. Though LENIN was determined to promote the autonomy of the soviets, their real influence began to decline as the Russian Communist Party centralized power, initially as a response to counter-revolution and civil war and then, after Lenin's death, in the furtherance of Stalin's aims for complete control. Though the new state was to be called the SOVIET UNION, ostensibly governed by its elected assembly of the Supreme Soviet, in effect appointments were made to the soviets through the hierarchy within the Party. The soviets became the opposite of all they had originally stood for, instruments of top-down authoritarian centralized control. Despite their later history, their early days demonstrate their effectiveness as organizational units and the ability of ordinary people to democratically participate in wider NETWORKS (see PARIS COMMUNE).

SOVIET UNION An officially SOCIALIST or COMMUNIST state founded in 1922 in the aftermath of the Russian REVOLUTION of 1917 and the civil war of 1918 to 1920. It was dissolved following the secession of its member republics and satellite states in 1991. From 1945 to 1991 it was considered one of the two global superpowers, and the politics of the post-war era largely revolved around the Cold War between Western capitalist states and the SU. The SU also provided the primary model and support for a number of other nominally communist states in the post-war period. It came into existence following the takeover of the Russian state by the Bolsheviks, supported by the SOVIETS, and led by LENIN. The Bolsheviks renamed their party the Russian Communist Party, which became the sole ruling party in the SU. It was Lenin's intention that the Russian state should dissolve into stateless communism where workers and peasants councils would take over. The desperate state of the country following revolution, the First World War, and a savage civil war largely created by an invasion backed by foreign powers, instead pushed the Party to extend state power under one-party rule. The Union that emerged from these circumstances was a FEDERATION of socialist republics, each ruled by the local national communist party, over an area broadly similar to that of the old Russian Empire. By 1940 there were 15 republics and a number of nominally independent states over which the SU had a decisive influence.

When Stalin succeeded Lenin in 1924, the policy of a strong state within the borders of the SU was pursued, rather than the internationalist line of Trotsky and Lenin. The centralized repressive structures of 'war communism' were retained and extended. The result was rapid industrialization and the establishment of an integrated and largely isolated economic and military state under the dictatorship of the ruthless Stalin. Many of the original revolutionaries and others who opposed Stalin's policies found themselves liquidated without trial as he consolidated his personal hold on the Party and the SU. The SU emerged from the Second World War with great prestige as a partner to the victorious Western allies. It was also still seen as a beacon of hope by many on the Left, providing an example of what was described as 'actually existing socialism'. The SU supported the independence movements of ex-Western colonies, most notably CUBA. For a while even many of its post-war opponents were convinced that the SU's methods of central economic planning would enable it to out-compete the West in terms of economic growth, technological development and military capacity, a view promoted within the SU by constant official propaganda.

Nontheless, it became increasingly obvious that the SU was an authoritarian regime and a betrayal of the hopes of the Russian Revolution. The Left largely viewed the SU as a 'degenerated workers' state' operating an economic policy of 'state capitalism', though some believed that it was still capable of developing further towards socialism. DYSTOPIAS such as Orwell's *Animal Farm* and *Nineteen Eighty-Four* powerfully convey the conviction that the SU represented a particularly modern form of totalitarianism: the complete control of institutions and political life by the party but also the manipulation of culture, individual behaviour and even individual consciousness (but see REPUBLIC). Further, it became increasingly clear that the SU was unable to sustain itself economically against the capitalist West, partly because the arms race was an enormous drain on its resources. Political repression, even though this eased following Stalin's death, created popular opposition fuelled by shortages of basic goods and the allure of Western consumer society. This opposition was particularly in evidence in satellite states that had sometimes attempted to break away from Soviet control, leading to military intervention (in Hungary in 1956 and Czechoslovakia in 1968). The SU's invasion of Afghanistan in 1979 in support of its communist party was disastrous. It weakened internal support because of the high casualty rates, placed even more strain on its ailing economy, demonstrated the weakness of its military capability and brought about the end of the relatively harmonious relations that had existed for some time with the non-Communist world.

In the 1980s Mikhail Gorbachev made a last effort to reform the SU by reducing official control of the media, pursuing economic LIBERALISM, and reducing control over the governance of satellite states and member republics. Though popular in the West, these policies led to even more rapid break-up as its constituent republics began to secede. This had always been a theoretical right under LENIN's original constitution, but had been prevented by military force. In 1991 the member republics signed new treaties to create the Commonwealth of Independent States following which the core institutions of the old Soviet Union, including the Red Army and the Supreme Soviet (the central parliament of the SU), were dissolved. The SU provides both an example of how UTOPIAN hopes could become reality and an object lesson in what can go wrong. It still provokes fierce debates regarding whether its eventual authoritarianism and failure were inherent in the very nature of the attempt or whether it came close to succeeding but was defeated by circumstances and the opposition of capitalist states. Its eventual failure accelerated the decline of socialism and left-wing political parties and it currently seems unlikely that any left-wing movements will seek to repeat the attempt on this scale again.

SPANISH ANARCHIST MILITIAS In 1936 General Franco led a rebellion against the republican government of Spain. ANARCHISM was the most influential REVOLUTIONARY political movement in Spain at the time and its SYNDICALIST tactic of general strikes was largely responsible for the radicalization of the Spanish peasantry and workers. The government was much less radical than many of its supporters and both SOCIALIST and

269

anarchist **TRADE UNIONS** were frustrated by its conservatism. Large areas of northern Spain had already been **COLLECTIVIZED** and many factories were **WORKER SELF-MANAGED**. The CNT, the main anarchist trade union, had been warning the government for some time that a military rebellion was being planned by the Right from military bases in Morocco. The government downplayed the threat and refused to give arms but the CNT found its own weapons by raiding an arsenal. Militias were formed and placed on alert days before the expected rising. These groups were central to the defence of republican Spain in the early days of the civil war. Where the anarchist militias were strong the rebellion was quickly crushed, as in Barcelona. However, the anarchist stronghold of Zaragoza was lost, a serious blow to the defence of Catalonia. Some argue that the republican government was culpable because it downplayed the threat and did not attempt to help defend the city. It was only the armed militancy of the socialist and anarchist unions that prevented the rebellion from succeeding elsewhere.

After the outbreak of war the militias continued to play an important role. They followed anarchist principles in their organization. They had no ranks and commanders were elected by the troops. Decisions were often arrived at through debate. Orwell describes the **DEMOCRATIC** nature of these militias in this book *Homage to Catalonia*. The most famous of the anarchist militias was the Durruti Column, led by Buenaventura Durruti. At its peak it had 8,000 men and was highly effective militarily. The Iron Column, composed of ex-convicts and other marginal members of Spanish society, was also a formidable fighting force. As the fascists advanced the government began to incorporate the militias into the regular army on the grounds of military efficiency. Many observers believed that this incorporation was more motivated by a desire to neuter them politically. Conventional military ranks and discipline were reasserted by 1937. In addition the growing influence of the **COMMUNIST** Party, due to dependence on the **SOVIET UNION**, meant that many anarchists and other non-party socialists found themselves imprisoned or executed by their own side. Anti-anarchist propaganda accused the militias of cowardice or helping the fascists. Those socialist and anarchist militia fighters who survived the defeat of the government formed a large part of the 200,000 liquidated by the Franco regime in the years immediately after the civil war.

SPARTA, see PLUTARCH

SQUATTING The practice of occupying unused properties or land without having a legal title. Squatters claim rights over properties by virtue of occupation, or use, rather than ownership. They oppose the principle of private property with the notion that property belongs to those who use it, a principle and practice that pre-dates formal property law (see ANARCHISM). Thus squatting rests upon a radical revision of property rights based on a rejection of the speculative use of property. Squatting is not only about getting 'free housing' but is also a political act that takes as its starting point homelessness (or landlessness) and the existence of vacant property; and asserts people's basic rights to shelter through DIRECT ACTION. In some countries, squatting is considered a crime whilst in others it is seen as a civil conflict between squatters and owners. Despite often facing threats of eviction, squatters do in some cases win legal rights to a building or land by putting forward the principle of adverse possession. This refers to the right to take ownership of property by virtue of living in it, or using it, for a certain period of time.

Squatting has a long history and has been used in rural and urban areas alike. For example, landless peasants from the DIGGERS to the MST have reclaimed unused land to grow their own food, whilst urban squats have been created to provide housing for the homeless as well as a base for popular organizations that cannot afford market rents (like radical magazines, women's centres or city farms and gardens). For contemporary examples of urban squats that have not only provided housing but also served as centres of political protest and a basis for the development of alternative community life and activities, see CENTRI SOCIALI, CHRISTIANIA.

STIRNER, MAX A German philosopher (1806–56) who was a major influence on the development of nihilism, existentialism and individualist ANARCHISM. Stirner attended university in Berlin and was taught by Hegel. In 1841 he joined the Young Hegelians, led by Bruno Bauer and including MARX, Engels, Ludwig Feuerbach and Arnold Ruge. Marx, Engels and Ruge became COMMUNIST REVOLUTIONARIES and broke with Stirner and Bauer. Stirner in turn was to rail against both SOCIALISTS and anarchists on the grounds that all political movements were essentially about self-gratification. In *The Ego and Its Own* (1844) Stirner proposes a radical anti-authoritarian and individualist critique both of modern Western society and its proposed cures of humanism, socialism, COMMUNISM and anarchism. All religions and ideologies, he argued, rest on empty concepts that serve

271

merely to conceal the self-interest at their heart. Recognizing the inherent self-interest in institutions such as the state, church or school destroys their claims for legitimate authority and power over the individual.

Stirner suggests that once these false claims have been exposed and the individual's drive for self-realization, or egoism, recognized as the only valid aim for a human being then freedom can be obtained. Released from the pursuit of empty ideas and from the shackles of obedience to authority, the self is free to choose its own way and enjoy itself while doing so. This does not imply complete solipsism. Stirner also advocates a 'union of egotists', an association freely entered into with others to enable each to realize their self-interest more effectively. Though often thought of as an individual anarchist, Stirner entirely repudiates anarchism as a collective movement and he also rejects revolution or any social movement aimed at reforming existing institutions. Stirner's rejection of all absolute concepts or fixed ideas leads to a nameless void, without meaning or existence, from which mind and creativity can emerge. For Stirner the power to create oneself comes from the dynamics of complete autonomy and the rejection of all pre-existing meaning structures.

Stirner's influence has been obscured by Marx's indictment of him, running to several hundred pages in the original version of Marx's *The German Ideology*. However, the challenge of Stirner's work was in itself an important influence on Marx's theory of the materialist basis of history. In addition Nietzsche is believed to have read Stirner's book, and his own nihilism resembles that of Stirner. The strong strand of individualism within anarchism, with its insistence on the primacy of individual AUTONOMY even within COMMUNAL social units, owes a good deal to his influence and is one of the contrasts with the more COLLECTIVIST spirit of communism. Although the notion that self-interest lies at the foundation of all social structures and values is highly unpalatable for most UTOPIANS, it may be a useful corrective to the rose-tinted view that so often underestimates the problems of accommodating the deep rooted self-interest of human beings within collective endeavours (see also RAND).

SUBSISTENCE WORK The unpaid household work undertaken by household members for themselves or for other members of their household. This non-exchanged work takes up over half of people's total working time in the North and more in the South. In the global North, subsistence work is sometimes caricatured as a 'peasant' form of production that has been replaced by commodified forms of production in which goods and services are delivered through monetary transactions by capitalist firms. There may be odd examples either of households where subsistence living is practised or 'downshifters' who attempt to engage in SELF-SUFFICIENT living, but, on the whole, such a mode of production is viewed as a minority practice and of little importance in understanding contemporary economies and societies. A key problem with this idea is that people and households cannot be effectively classified according to their reliance on one principal form of work. An understanding of how households combine different modes of production is important if the nature of work in the advanced economies is to be more fully understood.

Once subsistence work is conceptualized as part of a plurality of practices used by households, then a very different reading of such work emerges. Even if (most) goods production has moved out of the household, this is not the case with service production. Households still engage in a tremendous range of self-servicing activity from routine housework, cleaning windows, cooking, gardening, childcare and elder care through to car maintenance, home maintenance and improvement activity. The move of goods production into the marketplace, therefore, seems to have been followed only partially by the shift of service provision. Indeed, the common finding of studies of how people spend their working time in Western societies is that nearly half of all working time is spent engaged in subsistence work and that over the past forty years there has been no shift towards the paid sphere. Working life, therefore, is not becoming more dominated by paid work. Subsistence work is not only ubiquitous but households everywhere continue to provide many goods and services for themselves on an unpaid basis. Even if self-sufficiency is rarely achieved, self-reliance (the use of subsistence work as one of a plurality of economic practices) remains a ubiquitous strategy that opens up the possibility for enacting and imagining alternative futures for work beyond capitalism. (CW)

SUDBURY VALLEY SCHOOL, see SUMMERHILL

SUMA A worker COOPERATIVE that has been one of the pioneers in wholefood, FAIR TRADE and organic products distribution in the UK. It started as a one-person operation distributing wholefood in 1974. Thanks to rapidly growing demand, it soon employed seven people, who became the founder members of the co-op in 1977. At the time of writing, Suma employs 120 workers and has a £20 million turnover, making it the largest independent wholesaler of health food and wholefood in the UK. Suma considers itself a 'radical business' because it departs from conventional organizational practices, in particular the division of labour, the separation between MANAGEMENT and worker, and hierarchy. Suma is a living example of INDUSTRIAL DEMOCRACY and EMPOWERMENT in that it practices WORKER SELF-MANAGEMENT. All worker owners are invited and strongly encouraged to participate in the quarterly general meeting that decides on major strategic issues. The general meeting also elects six of its members as a management committee that meets weekly to implement the business plan and other decisions taken by the general meeting, and reports back to the general meeting. The management committee appoints company officers for different functions of the organization but these officers do not have voting power. Instead power rests in the elected management committee, and ultimately the general meeting. All these roles are typically performed on a job-share basis rather than by single individuals. In addition, there are no 'bosses' overseeing the work of the employees; employees work in flexible teams carrying out daily tasks but also taking responsibility for management.

Suma also encourages multi-skilling and job rotation; so drivers will work in the warehouse or in the office for two days a week; office workers will do manual work for one day a week. And, quite radically, all employees, from the company officers to the warehouse packers, are on the same wages. In addition, Suma runs its business according to ethical principles that respect the ENVIRONMENT and human rights. For example, it has always refused to stock GM products, and was one of the pioneers in developing fair trade products in the UK. The continuing success of Suma 30 years on provides a living proof that genuine industrial democracy and workers' empowerment are possible, and that there are socially and environmentally responsible alternatives to global capitalism (compare JOHN LEWIS PARTNER-SHIP, SCOTT BADER, TOWER COLLIERY).

SUMMERHILL A DEMOCRATIC school, originally founded in Hellerau near Dresden by A. S. Neill (1883–1973) in 1921. Neill was the headmaster at the Gretna Green school in Scotland, but left to pursue his idea that happy, free children are more likely to learn, and less likely to suffer the various problems associated with coercive education and emotional repression. Neill's approach was influenced by Reich and Freudian psychoanalysis, and for some time he offered 'private lessons', or therapy, with some of the children. After moving to Sonntagsberg in Austria, and then Lyme Regis in England, the school finally settled in Leiston, Suffolk in England in 1927. Pupil numbers gradually declined until the late 1950s, when a resurgence of interest in radical education and the publicity gained from Neill's books finally put the school on a firm financial foundation. It is now run by Neill's daughter, Zoe Readhead, taking fee-paying students between the ages of 4 and 19 on a day or boarding basis. Summerhill is based on the idea that children learn best when they are in control of their own learning (see AUTO-DIDACTICISM), but in fact the democratic control of the school goes much further than that. All lessons are optional, and students are free to use their time as they see fit. School meetings to decide on rules and sanctions are held four times a week, and staff and students have an equal vote.

Despite the fact that the whole Summerhill experience cannot simply be reduced to 'lessons', the school was inspected by the UK government's regulatory body for schools continually throughout the 1990s, and was eventually served with a notice of complaint for not having compulsory lessons. Faced with closure, or a radical change in the school's policy, Summerhill chose to contest the notice. In March 2000, faced with losing the case, the government offered a settlement that was accepted by the pupils. Summerhill represents an example of an extreme LIBERAL or ANARCHIST approach to education that stresses individual and collective decision making. The 'free range' children it produces are, according to critics, insufficiently disciplined, and an example of the problems created by a permissive society. For those who support the idea of Summerhill, the school produces mature citizens who choose rather than obey, and have a sceptical attitude towards arbitrary authority (see also FREIRE, ILLICH).

Whilst Summerhill was arguably the first, and the most famous, example of a FREE SCHOOL there are now many others. Dora and Bertrand Russell established the Beacon Hill school in Sussex in 1927, and Dora continued to run it after their divorce in 1935. The Russells offered important early support to Neill. At the time of writing, there are about 70 other democratic schools in existence. The Sands school in Devon, England, is a 'de-institutionalized' secondary school, as was Dartington Hall, also in Devon. The Sudbury Valley School, founded in 1968 in Framingham, Massachusetts, now has over 40 schools basing themselves on this model in eight countries. The 'Hadera' schools in Israel, Tokyo Shure in Japan, Tamariki

275

in New Zealand, and the Sri Aurobindo Ashram (see AUROVILLE) are based on similar principles. Neill's model assumes that command and control ideas are damaging both in education and in life. As he put it, 'the function of the child is to live his own life – not the life that his anxious parents think he should live, nor a life according to the purpose of the educator who thinks he knows best.' As many UTOPIANS have suggested, when work and play become separated, neither are done with any joy or meaning (see FOURIER; NEWS FROM NOWHERE; ISLAND). Sadly, as fee-paying schools with limited bursaries, democratic education is usually only available to the children of those with enough money to pay for it.

SUPPLEMENT TO BOUGAINVILLE'S VOYAGE In a short book that very much reflects its age, revolutionary egalitarianism is here joined with an ARCADIAN view of ROUSSEAU's 'noble savage', who is inevitably corrupted by contact with modern civilization. Like the endless island UTOPIAS written after Defoe's ROBINSON CRUSOE, it places utopia at the edge of the known world, both real and far away in time and space. Denis Diderot (1713–84) was a French writer and philosopher whose commitment to freedom of thought, religious tolerance and scientific enquiry led to his twenty years' work as editor of the *Encyclopédie*, a gigantic work which was formally banned in 1759, but completed secretly in 1772. The *Supplement* was written in 1772, but not published until 1796, when post-revolutionary politics made Diderot a far more acceptable figure.

Louis Antoine de Bougainville (1729–1811) was a naval commander who, after fighting against the British in Canada, circumnavigated the globe from 1766 to 1769, visiting Tahiti in April 1768. His book *Voyage Autour du Monde* was published in 1771, and described Tahiti as a PARADISE where happiness went hand in hand with innocence. People were welcoming and sex was easy to come by, even if the Tahitians stole everything that they could and the crew left several Tahitians dead and many more suffering from venereal disease. Diderot's *Supplement* is based around the idea that Bougainville suppressed certain parts of his description. It is structured as a dialogue between two people who have found the missing supplement, and allows Diderot to re-read the *Voyage* as a condemnation of property owning, sexual repression and imperialism. Because they are closer to the beginning of the world than Europeans, Diderot suggests, the Tahitians have a greater love for liberty, and the French can learn much from their innocence. In section two of the *Supplement*, 'The Old Man's Farewell', there is a speech given by an old Tahitian on the beach as Bougainville leaves to continue his voyage. In it, the old man condemns the French for their violence, and the assumption that places, things and people can be owned. By contrast, the Tahitians are described as strong and full of vitality, working only enough to SUBSIST and keep themselves clothed, and as most hospitable towards strangers. Diderot informs the reader at some length that they are also unashamed to show their bodies and enjoy generous sex once they have reached maturity. Other parts of the *Supplement* discuss the Tahitians' surprise at the prohibitions of religion and law.

Though it was popularized by Rousseau, the poet John Dryden coined the term 'noble savage' in 1672. For Diderot, and many others influenced by a ROMANTIC view of human nature, the idea captured a humanist critique of European expansionism and imperialism in the 'virgin' areas of the earth (see, for example, Neville's ISLE OF PINES, de Foigny's NEW DISCOVERY OF TERRA INCOGNITA AUSTRALIS or Swift's GULLIVER'S TRAVELS). It also captures something of the Judeo-Christian idea of a 'fall' from EDEN, or the more generalized conception of a GOLDEN AGE. Diderot's *Supplement* is heavily reliant on these ideas, and combines them with a particular interest in sexual liberalism which was common in radical France at that time (see SADE).

SUSTAINABILITY Although the term had been used within the ENVIRONMENTAL movement before, it acquired popular appeal following the publication of the Brundtland Report to the UN Commission on Environment and Development in 1987. The report defined sustainability in terms of meeting 'the needs of the present without compromising the ability of future generations to meet their own needs'. Another definition commonly deployed is that offered by the World Conservation Union in *Caring for the Earth* (1991), which sees sustainability as 'improving the quality of life while living within the carrying capacity of supporting ecosystems'. So sustainability involves ensuring both human and ecological well-being, finding ways of organizing human activities so that societies, now and in the future, can provide for themselves whilst preserving ecosystems. The idea of sustainability is based on the premise that the earth has finite capacity, and that the rate of economic growth pursued in the second half of the twentieth century, particularly in the West, will inflict irreversible damage on the planet, or reach 'natural limits'.

But beyond this broad agreement, sustainability is a highly contested term that has different priorities and implications for different groups. One of the controversial issues concerns the relationship between sustainability and economic MANAGEMENT. For some, sustainability entails finding ways of reconciling economic growth with the Earth's capacity by, for example, switching to green technologies (renewable sources of energy, recycling), establishing and enforcing environmental standards (as in the Kyoto agreement), introducing green taxes, developing more environmentally friendly transport policies, or simply relying on the forces of the MARKET (such as consumer pressures) to 'green businesses'. This 'weak' conceptualization has been captured under the notion of sustainable development, a term popularized by the Brundtland report as a framework within which environmental protection and economic development could be integrated. It has since become a key principle in national and international economic and environmental policy, as exemplified in Agenda 21, the global action plan for sustainable development signed by 173 national governments at the Rio Earth Summit in 1992.

Whilst the notion of sustainable development has done much to raise public debate and attention on environmental issues, many feel that it does not go far enough in challenging the practices that have led to environmental degradation. A 'strong' view of sustainability would hold that economic growth is incompatible with the earth's finite resources. From this perspective, the notion of sustainable development is a contradiction in terms, a smokescreen used by government and business to pay lip service to environmental issues whilst maintaining their commitment to economic development. This is the view adopted at the radical end of ENVIRON-MENTALISM, for example by SOCIAL ECOLOGY and DEEP ECOLOGY, and it is based on a more radical critique of global capitalism. For proponents of this view, sustainability entails a radical transformation of the economy, replacing the pursuit of material goods by focusing on equality, justice, human and ecological health, cultural and biological diversity, and participation. It has informed alternative models of economic and social organization with principles of LOCALIZATION, SMALLNESS or SELF-SUFFICIENCY, and is represented in practices such as ECOVILLAGES or PERMACULTURE.

Another controversial issue within sustainability relates to population growth and control. Some suggest that the current population of over 6 billion is already more than the planet can support and that action should be taken to limit the world population. However this raises concerns about human rights violation – in sterilization programmes, for example. At the heart of these controversies are questions about what is to be sustained. Sustainability relates to the interconnections between economic, social and ecological systems; but different perspectives privilege different dimensions. For example, many insist that addressing the problems of global poverty and injustice is a precondition for environmental sustainability, as evidence suggests that the world's poor bear the brunt of environmental degradation, and may be forced into further spoiling of the environment by eking out a living on marginal lands. By opening these issues for public debate, the concept of sustainability has called into question the economic policies of infinite growth characteristic of the industrial world for much of the twentieth century, and has encouraged thought about alternatives.

SYNDICALISM The term given to the aim of transforming capitalist society through working-class DIRECT ACTION, particularly through working-class industrial organizations. It contrasts with the other major strategy of working-class movements, political action through party organization. Clearly the two strategies are not incompatible, as in the case of GUILD socialism, though some ANARCHIST syndicalists do reject political parties entirely. Anarcho-syndicalism shares the principles of worker solidarity, industrial action for political aims and worker self-management, but also aims at revolutionary transformation towards an anarchist society. The main instruments of syndicalist action have been the TRADE UNIONS and the main weapons have been the various forms of industrial action, including work-to-rules, control over the labour process, industrial sabotage and, most importantly, the strike. Indeed traditionally the general strike for political aims has been the favoured approach in furthering more REVOLUTIONARY forms of syndicalism, and was used to great effect in 1930s Spain.

Syndicalism is more than simply a tactic to achieve REVOLUTION. It also provides a structure for organizing a new society once capitalism is overcome, as well as a position on the rights of labour over its own production and work. Most syndicalists argue that all participants in a trade or workplace should share equal ownership of production and therefore deserve equal earnings, benefits and control. Syndicalism, though essentially a form of SOCIALISM, does not necessarily imply COMMUNISM, however, as earnings may be privately retained, though equally shared within a syndicate. A syndicalist society would be based on WORKER SELF-MANAGED syndicates; these would federate with other syndicates and the exchange of goods and services would be negotiated between them. There are close affinities between the idea of the syndicate and the SOVIETS. Modern Continental European and the US trade union movements have been strongly influenced by syndicalism, and strikes for political purposes are still more common in Europe than in the UK, where political strikes were made illegal during the 1980s. Syndicalism may have had the perverse effect of weakening the power of organized labour in the US, the only developed economy in which no political party was founded to represent the interests of organized labour.

SWIFT, JONATHAN, see GULLIVER'S TRAVELS

T

TERRORISM Currently, the word is generally used in a pejorative sense to refer to the activities of non-state groups pursuing political, nationalist and/or religious goals that involve violence against non-military personnel. However, a simpler definition would be that a 'terrorist' is someone the speaker wishes to condemn, as opposed to the positive term 'freedom fighter', or the rather more tactical term GUERRILLA. Other more neutral terms include insurgents, miltants, rebels, those involved in liberation struggles and so on. Essentially, it is now a politically mobile term that describes a strategy of semi-covert violence that is not sanctioned by 'law'. (That is to say, within a war that has been declared by both sides and is therefore in theory subject to the Geneva Convention.) Some 'terrorists' have won the Nobel Peace Prize (Nelson Mandela, Yasser Arafat), whilst some states have engaged in terrorist means to achieve political ends (assassination, death squads) such as the US state's COINTELPRO operation against the Black Panthers. With these contradictions in place, there can be no likely agreement on what terrorism is, or whether it can be justified now or in the future.

The term originates in post-revolutionary France to describe the activities of the Jacobins, who murdered thousands at the guillotine in the name of the REVOLUTION. However, this 'state terrorism' was not how the word came to be used during the nineteenth and twentieth centuries since it was usually reserved for activists who were involved in 'anti-state' campaigns. For example, the Russian ANARCHISTS (see BAKUNIN) and Narodniks (populists) who were involved in the assassination of Tsar Alexander II in 1881; the Internal Macedonian Revolutionary Organization which assassinated Alexander I of Yugoslavia in 1934; and the Irish Republican Army that repeatedly bombed the United Kingdom during the second half of the twentieth century. Other examples are Action Directe; the Angry Brigade; the Japanese Red Army; the Red Army Fraction; the Red Brigades and Weather Underground. At the same time other groups, such as the Klu Klux Klan or anti-abortion activists in the USA, have engaged in terrorist activities without being labelled terrorists. More recently, the term has become even more charged as a result of the activities of Arabist groups (often claiming inspiration from Islam) such as Al-Qaeda, Hamas, Hezbollah and Islamic Jihad, which have conducted international operations against the USA and pro-US targets in the name of changing what they see as a pro-Western bias in global economics and ideology.

Terrorist groups are often organized on a 'cellular' structure, with semi-autonomous groups having few links back to a command hierarchy. The purpose is to ensure that the capture of particular operatives would not jeopardize the entire organization. However, this structure is not unique since it can also be found in guerrilla organizations (ZAPATISTA), state-sanctioned espionage (see SECRET SOCIETIES) and some ANTI-CAPITALIST organizations. It is also worth noting that organized crime groups such as the MAFIA engage in many of the practices that are associated with terrorism, but do so for private gain. However, terrorist groups may also engage in organized crime in order to fund their operations, and some individuals may engage in terrorist acts even though they are not part of a formal organization. (For example the 1995 Oklahoma City bomber, Timothy McVeigh, or David Copeland, who set off a nail bomb in a gay bar in London in 1999.) This complexity suggests that any attempt to define terrorism according to specific means and ends is likely to fail.

The espoused intention of terrorists is to gain publicity for their cause (or seek direct revenge for particular injustices) and thereby influence state policy and public opinion. However, it is also likely that terrorist groups believe that stimulating a disproportionate response will be likely to encourage others (who might share particular grievances) to take their side in a conflict. The radical interpretation of terrorism is that it is the result of a grievance that has systematically been ignored by those with the power to change matters. All other avenues for reform being closed, 'armed propaganda' aimed at revolution is then used as a strategy of last resort. Of course the state concerned will also deny its role as the cause of any conflict and many citizens of the state will harden in their attitudes towards those they see as responsible for the atrocities that kill 'innocent' people. Though in principle it is possible to see terrorism as a strategy for social change, it is difficult to argue such a case with much conviction. Periods of terrorism have certainly been followed by periods of desirable social change (in South Africa and Northern Ireland, for example), but the causal connection between the two is unclear and the legacy of violence left behind may take generations to heal (see NON-VIOLENT RESISTANCE). Ultimately, terrorism is a mirror image of the instrumentality of state violence, a brutal case of any means being justified. This necessarily suggests that economic and political issues of marginalization need to be addressed if a 'solution' is going to be found for grievances. At the present time, the prospects of such an analysis becoming a standard model for international relations do not look good.

THERAPEUTIC COMMUNITIES An attempt to use a hospital not as an organization run by doctors in the interests of efficiency, but as a COMMUNITY with the participation of all of its members. Therapeutic communities offer a radically different, group-based approach for a wide range of people suffering from emotional disturbance. The central philosophy is that people are active participants in their own and in others' treatment. Members tend to learn a great deal through the routine inter-actions of daily life and the experience of being therapeutic for each other. Collaborative and DEMOCRATIC style form an essential part of therapy, with members and staff COLLECTIVELY managing both the activities of and admission to the community. Participants are expected to contribute towards a safe environment with clear boundaries and expectations, to take part in group and individual psychotherapy, and to engage in creative and social activities. The aim is to encourage members towards a better under-standing of their previous behaviour and to enable them to improve their interpersonal skills.

In the UK, they were initially developed in the early 1940s to treat the psychological casualties from the Second World War (though see also ONEIDA). Therapeutic communities are now used in many settings – adult psychiatry, community-based mental health, voluntary sector, educational and penal provision. Communities may vary from small family-size groups to large hospitals. In AMERICA, they are often used in the context of drug addiction. Although (like COMMUNES) different types of therapeutic communities can be categorized in terms of degrees of adherence to the underlying principles, most place strong emphasis on the principles of democratization. Elections to the community and to positions within it, decisions about treatment and discharge, and many other decisions are taken through regular, often daily, meetings at which each community member has an equal vote, both staff and 'patients' (see also SUMMERHILL). However, there are also strict rules. Infringements are typically dealt with via emergency meetings that can be called at any time of the day or night, again with all having a say in the decisions. The emphasis on community decision making is seen as both contributing to and being the therapy – co-creating a culture of EMPOWERMENT, belonging and responsibility.

In the UK, three regional therapeutic communities were developed as the treatment of choice for people with severe personality disorders, following promising results in terms of psychological and behavioural changes during treatment, reduction of violent incidents, and significant improvements following treatment. Perhaps more cynically, but most influentially, research has since focused on the financial effectiveness of reduced service usage and savings following discharge. Cost issues aside, therapeutic communities represent an attempt to democratize and de-institutionalize some elements of state healthcare (see ILLICH). (JC)

THOREAU, HENRY DAVID, see WALDEN

TIME BANKS Forms of local currency where the unit of exchange is time rather than money. In this sense they are similar to LETS, the main difference being that in Time Banks, everyone's contribution is valued equally (a principle that may or may not hold true in LETS). Early beginnings can be traced to Josiah Warren's Cincinnati Time Store (see MUTUALISM) and the work of OWEN, but the idea was developed by Edgar Cahn in the 1980s under the name of Time Dollars. It has since taken hold in different countries. For example, there were 79 schemes running in the UK at the start of 2006, and another 34 schemes being developed. In Time Banks, participants earn credits for giving each other services or help. One hour of one person's help entitles that person to one hour of another participant's help. Time is exchanged through a broker who keeps a list of the services offered by participants and records of the transactions. The types of services and help exchanged are wide-ranging: child care, music lessons, computer assistance, home repair and decorating, cooking and meal delivery, running errands, tutoring, hairdressing, house cleaning, translating.

Time Banks aim to challenge social exclusion and inequality by starting from the premise that everyone has something to offer. One hour of grocery shopping is worth the same as one hour of website design. Thus, unlike 'real money', anyone can earn credits and have access to services they might not otherwise be able to afford. Through INFORMAL WORK they are also seen as contributing to local economies and community regeneration, not only by tackling problems of social exclusion and inequality, but also by helping to develop webs of support and SOCIAL CAPITAL.

TOBIN TAX, see ATTAC

TOLSTOY (or Tolstoi), **LEO** *'I know a commune where the people earn their living themselves. One of the members of this community was more educated than the rest; and they require him to deliver lectures, for which he has to prepare himself during the day, that he may be able to deliver them in the evening. He does it joyfully, feeling that he is useful to others, and that he can do it well. But he grows tired of the exclusive mental labour, and his health suffers accordingly. The members of the community therefore pity him, and ask him to come and labour in the field again.'* WHAT SHALL WE DO? (1886)

Count Leo Nikolayevich Tolstoy (1828–1910) moved from being a novelist with social concerns to being a Christian ANARCHIST who wrote polemics. (Though he did not use the word anarchist about his own thought, because of its violent connotations at that time.) Perhaps the most consistent strain in his later writing is a hostility to any sort of institution, most particularly the state. In this he was influenced by PROUDHON (whom he met), though he added to Proudhon's materialism the spiritual conviction that God is within everyone. Still best known for his novels *War and Peace* (1862–9, the title also borrowed from Proudhon) and *Anna Karenina* (1875–7), he was born into an aristocratic Russian family. His early politics displayed a paternalist interest in improving the conditions of the peasantry, and considerable enthusiasm for gambling and prostitutes. After fighting in the Crimean war and travelling, he returned home. There he began to write school texts intended to help country people learn reading and arithmetic, and organized an early example of a FREE SCHOOL. Above its entrance was the motto 'Enter and Leave Freely'.

Though his novels are clearly realist explorations of politics and history, his various polemics made his mature politics clear. In *A Confession* (1879) he described his 'conversion' to an anti–institutional Christianity based on the primacy of selfless love. In *What Shall We Do?* and *How Much Land Does a Man Need?* (both 1886) he attacked the money economy, private property, and the parasitic professional and aristocratic classes. *The Kingdom of God is Within You* (1894) developed ideas of non–violence and pacifism (see NON-VIOLENT RESISTANCE) based on Jesus's metaphor of turning the other cheek, and was influenced by Thoreau's essay on civil disobedience (see WALDEN).

In *What Is Art?* (1897) he demanded that religion and social purpose should be the prime meaning of art, and denounced work that merely produced beauty for money, including his own earlier 'sentimental' novels. Tolstoy's insistence that the highest form of reason is love, and the highest form of love is reason, implied that the state (along with patriotism) would eventually wither away. It would eventually be replaced by COMMUNES and COOPERATIVES of rational and loving individuals, people who would not need external authority to ensure that they lived well.

Essentially Tolstoy's anarchism is individualist, in the sense that he believes that the choice to live ethically will produce a better person, and eventually a better society. But this is not to defer a promise of social change to the future. His point is precisely that the 'the kingdom of god is already within us', if we choose to look for it, and that we do not need organized religion to help us find it. Tolstoy's better world would tend to embrace the values of the VILLAGE, the domestic, the spontaneous and the family – authentic nature rather than artificial culture (see ROMANTICISM). Rather like RUSKIN and Morris (see NEWS FROM NOWHERE), he also believed that manual labour was improving, and that the division of labour was a perversion of human nature. In matters of sex and gender, he was generally of the view that sex was not in itself a sin (though chastity was the highest ideal), marriage was an unnecessary institution, and that household tasks and child rearing should be shared between the sexes. Tolstoy was also a vegetarian and a supporter of the model world language 'Esperanto'. In later life he was also extremely eccentric, giving large gifts to beggars, inviting destitute peasants back to his house, and finally dying shortly after deciding to become a wandering ascetic who had renounced his own wealth entirely.

Tolstoy's influence, as both novelist and social thinker, became very substantial in his later life. Despite being a thorn in the side of the Russian authorities, and often censored, he was too well known to be persecuted (though he was excommunicated from the Russian Orthodox Church in 1901). Even his financial and public support of the Doukhobors (a pacifist religious minority) was tolerated. The post-revolutionary SOVIET UNION embraced him as one of their own, even though his anti-institutional Christianity could not possibly be called state COMMUNIST. A distant relative, Aleksey, later became a well known SCIENCE FICTION novelist who wrote *Aelita* (1924) – the description of a journey to Mars to establish a communist

UTOPIA. KROPOTKIN said of Leo Tolstoy that, despite his Christianity and his pacifism, he was an inspiration to anarchist thinkers. His correspondence with GANDHI concerning passive resistance to oppressive power meant that Gandhi (and later, Martin Luther King) cited him as a major influence on their ideas about NON-VIOLENT RESISTANCE. Tolstoy argued, perhaps more strongly than any other thinker, that Christianity was a moral version of socialism, and that socialism without Christian selflessness would simply reproduce new structures of power. Though many might not agree that Christianity is the only moral basis for such selflessness, the history of the Soviet Union certainly justifies an anarchist hostility to those who place their faith in the dictatorship of the proletariat.

TOWER COLLIERY Having struggled for over 140 years to control their own destiny, in 1995 the coal miners at Tower Colliery in South Wales finally came to own both their own labour and the colliery they work. Under the pretext that the mine was uneconomic, it was closed in 1994. In response, relying initially on the miners' redundancy payments, a group of TRADE UNION activists organized a buy-out and it reopened as a workers' COOPERATIVE. These days, there are six elected working board members and each worker owner holds one share and casts one vote. This DEMOCRACY has persisted for ten years ,while both employment and output have risen by over 40 per cent. Tower's success is also reflected in the best terms and conditions of employment ever enjoyed by miners: developing their own training programmes for apprentices and prospective board members; a responsive management process; annual profits of around £4 million on an average turnover of £24 million; and the emergence of Tower as a beacon of regeneration in a blighted region. It has institutionalized direct employee participation in policy decisions, operates through 'teamwork', genuinely values its human resources and is continuously involved with its COMMUNITY stakeholders – many of whom are also shareholders. But nothing is ever quite as it seems and, both as an experience and as a 'case study', Tower is difficult to accommodate within existing theory.

Perhaps curiously, operational management and work organization appear almost unchanged from the 'old days'. This is partly because MANAGEMENT structure is subject to legal regulation and partly because mining technology imposes a division of labour that restricts experimentation. There is little scope for 'direct control' over work organization although elected underground 'shift captains' regularly liaise with surface technical

287

managers on how work will proceed (but this latter practice also occurred under the previous regimes of private and public ownership). While Tower employs technical managers and a formally trained finance director, other managerial specialists – in marketing, purchasing, personnel and the control room – are all ex-miners. Authority in the cooperative is diffuse and has to be continuously negotiated. The charisma of Tyrone O'Sullivan – the radical union activist who led the buy-out team – sits uncomfortably alongside the authority of expert managers and that of owner-worker shareholders. Daily authority is exercised by the elected board, who also have to take account of a continuing union presence. The coexistence of this complex mix of legitimations can be bewildering. In particular, given worker ownership and cooperative articles of association, some might argue that there is no longer a role for unions. This is not the view at Tower. There is 100 per cent union membership and, although the unions' influence is now less central, they continue to negotiate terms and conditions and changes to work organization. From the outside, the 'authority to act' might seem ambiguous but it troubles no one at Tower. They are deeply experienced pragmatists and, while these seeming paradoxes do not go unremarked, few care to offer anything more than a rhetorical explanation: 'It's how we do things here.'

And, perhaps, this is the *only* point one needs to grasp. The overall impression emerging from the WIRC research is that Tower has shown us how to manage 'without management' (see WORKER SELF-MANAGEMENT). The metaphor of 'how we do things here' is refracted in an abiding antipathy to any form of management authority and a deep mistrust of formal politics. Both attitudes stem from an historical experience in which the only institution that can be trusted is the union. For the worker owners at Tower, it seems to be their fierce historical commitment to an almost forgotten tradition of SYNDICALIST values which has permitted them to articulate their own alternative collective and political identity while simultaneously creating both the financial and SOCIAL CAPITAL to ensure the maintenance of their worker-owned space. (WIRC)

TRADE UNIONS Associations of wage earners formed by them to represent their interests. Many would extend this concept of competing interests to incorporate social class, and see trade unions as representing working-class interests. The main weapons of unions have been strikes backed by picketing, demonstrations, working to rule, 'go-slows', boycotts, and sometimes industrial sabotage. They emerged, along with a number of other working-class self-help organizations, in the wake of industrialization in the eighteenth century. Many of their functions were at first indistinguishable from those of FRIENDLY SOCIETIES, MUTUAL aid and fraternal societies. All used subscriptions to provide benefits to members in distress due to unemployment, ill health or old age, and for funeral expenses. As many of these aspects of social welfare were taken over by the state in the twentieth century, unions have become more focused on COLLECTIVE bargaining with employers. Trade unionism has also always been one of the major strands of the labour movement and has often had avowedly political aims, generally derived from forms of SOCIALISM, including ANARCHISM and MARXISM. In the SYNDICALIST tradition, trade unionism is seen as the main mechanism for the transformation of society through politically motivated industrial action and, in particular, the general strike. According to syndicalists, trade unions would also enable the formation of self-governing FEDERATED workers' councils that would be the basic COMMUNAL unit of society (see INDUSTRIAL DEMOCRACY, WORKER SELF-MANAGEMENT).

From the eighteenth century in Western Europe, industrialization created a new class of wage earners for whom it became increasingly obvious that their COLLECTIVE interests were opposed to those of their employers. There is some debate as to whether medieval GUILDS provided the precursor to unions but, although there are some similarities, the guilds were primarily professional associations that attempted to control trade and standards. They were dominated by employers rather than by the lower ranks. Nevertheless, as the guilds began to crumble in Britain, the journeymen, or lower ranks of skilled crafts, began to form their own associations. These early unions were often local and restricted to skilled craftsmen. It was not until the end of the nineteenth century that unskilled labourers began to form general as opposed to craft unions. In England, the Combination Acts made union activity, as well as the formation of other self-help organizations, completely illegal from 1799 to 1824. This led to the development of SECRET SOCIETIES and fostered a strong sense of collective solidarity. Clandestine meetings and oaths of allegiance were thus characteristic of these early years. It was also assumed that to serve as an official would involve frequent periods of imprisonment. Even after combinations were legalized, secrecy was continued because of the violent hostility of employers. In 1834 it was for the administering of an illegal trade union

289

oath that six labourers from the village of Tolpuddle were sentenced to seven years' transportation. OWEN by this time had organized one of the early federations, the Grand National Consolidated Trades Union, which took up the cause of the Tolpuddle Martyrs. After a campaign of mass demonstrations the Martyrs were pardoned. This incident heralded a period of militancy during which industrial action accompanied the political campaigns of Chartism. Trade unions began to develop national organizations led by full-time officials and a paid administration. Conflict between more militant local leadership and a more conservative full-time national leadership has been one common consequence of this structure.

In Britain, these new national union organizations were capable of more sustained campaigning and were partly responsible for the securing of a series of legal reforms in the 1870s that gave legal status for unions and protected the rights of working people. With the official recognition of trade unions in England came a lessening of militancy, with officials largely preferring to present a moderate image in order to further their participation in established political institutions. In other countries, unions have been more revolutionary, adopting anarchist or Marxist principles. Even in Britain, from the 1880s the labour movement began to be dominated by the unifying ideology of socialism. It fostered a strong sense of male working-class identity; of which union activity was an important part. By 1900 there were two million British trade unionists; by 1914, four million. By 1979, 45 per cent of workers were members of unions, the high water mark of trade union membership in the UK.

Though their advance was bitterly contested, trade unions extended their influence into almost every occupation with the development of large general unions. In 1868 the Trades Union Congress (TUC) was founded to coordinate the activities of English and Welsh unions and in 1906 the TUC decided to found the Labour Party to advance the interests of working people in Parliament. (There had been 'labour' MPs before this time who worked in partnership with the Liberal Party). In 1926 the TUC successfully coordinated a general strike of all the major unions in support of the miners. In the post-Second World War period the growth of 'white-collar' unions, particularly in the rapidly expanding public sector, was responsible for much of the increase. By the late 1970s however, unions saw their position weakening throughout the developed world. The post-war economic boom, which favoured the incorporation of unions into national industrial management and relatively consensual collective bargaining with employers, came to an end. Unions saw both their legal rights and their support decline. Many of the functions of collective self-help were taken over by the state, ironically often as a result of union campaigns.

Neoliberal policies across the developed world encouraged a global economic free MARKET. This has increasingly enabled corporations to escape the impact of union action in one country by relocating to the developing world, where sometimes repressive governments violently suppress the development of unions on behalf of their corporate patrons. These processes have been much less marked in some parts of continental Europe than in the US and the UK, but a similar trend has also taken place. As a result, membership has been declining and unions have generally become less radical in their politics. Links between unions and the political parties they helped found have also weakened. As a result unions often find themselves lobbying alongside other competing interest groups, rather than being partners in industrial policy making. Employers are much less willing to enter into collective bargaining agreements, and tougher legal requirements have been set for union recognition in individual workplaces.

Although the US is the global capital of neoliberalism, unions still have a significant presence there. They are strongest amongst public sector employees and concentrate mainly on collective bargaining with employers. Many Northern European countries have single unions for each industry, as well as politically influential national federations. France also has a significant movement, even though it has one of the lowest union densities in Europe, with membership again concentrated in the public sector. However the French public sector is larger than in many other developed countries and trade unionism retains a strongly syndicalist tradition, with unions successfully organizing effective political strikes. The picture is broadly similar in Italy and Spain. In 1930s Spain socialist and anarchist unions used strikes successfully to foment a revolution. In Germany, trade unions have formal rights of codetermination with management in industrial decision making. Australian trade unionism has experienced a similar recent history to that of trade unions in the UK with a spate of recent anti-union legislation weakening their once strong position. South African trade unions, despite their persecution under apartheid, successfully challenged their employers and the state and made a major contribution to the ending of white rule. The Polish trade union *Solidarity* used strike action in the 1980s as an effective political weapon against the Soviet-backed government. In many developing economies, however, trade unions have found it very difficult to organize in the face of the combined hostility of corporate employers and repressive governments.

One response of trade unions to globalization has been to seek to operate at the global level themselves through their representation within the International Labour Organization and through the establishment of international bodies such as the International Confederation of Free Trade Unions. Likewise the European Trades Union Congress seeks to influence the framing of EU policy towards work and labour but does not encourage militancy on the part of its members. The history of trade unions illustrates the ability of common people to create effective large-scale organizations which are capable of bringing about major political changes and significant improvements in the lives of workers. Their great weakness has been in transcending the original conditions that gave rise to them. The hardship and collective nature of working-class life led to a solidarity that sustained unions. The widespread influence of socialism also gave unions a political purpose. Despite this, most union activity has always been aimed at the resolution of individual grievances at a local level. Some would argue that the result has often been success on the part of more powerful workers' groups at the expense of the more vulnerable, leading to a fragmentation of working-class identity. As the general condition of the working classes has improved, support has declined for collective struggle. Many Marxists and anarchists believe that unions have in the end acted as a conservative force, reconciling the working class to capitalism by ameliorating its worst effects whilst not challenging its fundamental structure. These criticisms aside, a world in which trade unions did not exist is unthinkable. The working conditions, pay and the provision of socialized welfare in the West are a legacy of two hundred years of struggle. For those outside the West, who still labour in appalling conditions for the poverty wages paid by corporations, it is difficult to envisage any other form of self-organization which holds out any hope of improving their lives.

TRAVELLERS People who have opted to lead a nomadic life, usually travelling in extended groups, and setting up camps on COMMON land or unused private land. Like SQUATTERS, travellers challenge certain property rights and laws, particularly the use of land for private commercial development rather than the basic human right to shelter. Travellers have a long history and include groups of very different origins. The Roma people (a group more commonly referred to as Gypsies) maybe constitute the largest and best-known traveller group. Originating in North India, they started travelling towards Europe several centuries ago and have been the object of persecution, sometimes state-sponsored (see FASCISM), ever since. There are now between 8 and 10 million Roma people worldwide, mainly in Europe. In order to maintain their independence, they have tended to choose work and occupations that can be done on the move, from craft production and trading, to animal training, music and dance, or fortune telling. The Irish Travellers, or Tinkers, are another nomadic minority group with a long history. Like the Roma people they have a distinctive culture, language and way of life, and travel in extended families. In pre-industrial Ireland, they played an important role in rural COMMUNITIES by doing seasonal agricultural work, BARTERING and selling recycled goods, and bringing news and entertainment. The mechanization of agriculture, together with the development of mass media and production, challenged the lifestyle and economic survival of the Irish travellers, although they have developed new itinerant activities such as market trading and building work.

New Age Travellers are another, more recent nomadic group that emerged in the 1980s out of the free festival circuits of the 1960s and 1970s. New Age Travellers tend to live and travel in extended groups sometimes referred to as tribes. They gained particular notoriety in 1982, when a group of them joined the Woman's Peace Camp on Greenham Common to protest against the deployment of cruise missiles, and stayed there until 1985 when the police evicted them. A group of travellers from this camp developed into the Peace Convoy that roamed the British countryside for over a year, until the mass arrest of 500 travellers trying to reach the Stonehenge summer solstice festival in 1986. Although all travellers live on the margins of society, New Age Travellers have more explicitly developed a counter culture that draws together spiritual, political and cultural elements. One of the most visible aspects of New Age Travellers' counter culture is the CARNIVALESQUE outdoor festivals they organize, for example at Stonehenge in the UK. Like squatters, travellers have had to face persecution, prosecution and eviction threats. The cumulative effects of enclosure, property speculation and development have seriously undermined travellers' culture. For example, in the UK, the Criminal Justice and Public Order Act passed in 1994 effectively outlawed nomadic

293

life by criminalizing 'trespassing', or halting on marginal land that travellers had traditionally used. Various support groups have emerged to defend the rights of travellers and address such issues as eviction, harassment, discrimination, or site provision.

TRUE LEVELLERS, see DIGGERS

TSE-TUNG, MAO, see MAO TSE-TUNG

TUTE BIANCHE, see DISOBBEDIENTI

TWIN OAKS An INTENTIONAL COMMUNITY or COMMUNE in rural Virginia, USA. Inspired by Skinner's WALDEN TWO, it was created in 1967. However, the commune soon abandoned some of the more autocratic principles, whilst retaining other features that included, notably, the labour credit system. In 2005 the commune had 100 members, and claimed to be driven by the values of cooperation, income sharing, equality and ecological awareness. These principles are reflected in the COMMUNITY's economic organization, decision-making process and domestic arrangements. Economically, Twin Oaks is SELF-SUFFICIENT and runs several community-owned businesses (hammock making, soy food production, book indexing) to generate the income needed to purchase what members cannot produce for themselves. The income from the businesses goes to the COLLECTIVE; members do not earn 'wages' or salaries. Each year, the community decides collectively how to allocate the money to its various budgets, such as health and education. The egalitarian principle is also manifested in the allocation of work and distribution of wealth. All members work 42 hours a week, which they divide between the various community businesses, domestic activities (childcare, cooking) and farming activities. In exchange, they receive housing, food, clothing, healthcare and a small personal allowance.

Work is allocated according to a labour credit system: every week members get a labour sheet which they return to the labour manager after recording their own work preferences. The labour manager makes sure all the work shifts are filled for that week, and that each member earns his/her 42 labour credits (see FOURIER, LETS). The only work each member is required to do is one two-hour kitchen cleaning shift each week. All other work is decided by each member according to personal preferences (indoor/outdoor, physical/sedentary, day/evening, etc.). Twin Oaks defines itself as an ECOVILLAGE on the basis of its cooperative and egalitarian organization and its ENVIROMENTAL practices of house and vehicle sharing. The community also tries to use renewable energies, and to practise energy and water conservation. Finally, Twin Oaks is self-reliant for a large proportion of the food it consumes.

TYLER, WAT, see PEASANTS REVOLT

U

UDDEVALLA, see KALMAR

UNDERGROUND ORGANIZATIONS, see SECRET SOCIETIES

UTOPIA

'If I am wrong, and if some other religion or social system would be more acceptable to Thee, I pray Thee in Thy goodness to let me know it.' A Utopian prayer.

1. A fantasy written by Thomas More (1478–1535), published in Latin in 1516 and translated into English in 1551. (For the general meaning of this word, see the second part of this entry, below.) Whether More's work is a satire, a Catholic DYSTOPIA, a learned discussion of themes from PLUTARCH and Plato's REPUBLIC, or a description of a COMMUNIST state is a deeply contested issue. Its two very different parts are encased in various letters of recommendation and clarification. More and his friend Peter Gilles (the town clerk of Antwerp) appear as characters and debate with a fictional traveller. The Latin text contained proper names derived from Greek which almost all undercut their veracity. The river 'Anydrus' means not-water and most famously, the title has two meanings – 'outopia' or no place, and 'eutopia' or good place. Some of these strategies were probably intended to distance the author from the work for political reasons, whilst others were mysteries and puzzles beloved of educated Englishmen of the time. All that being acknowledged, the book was inspirational in both its form and its content (see CITY OF THE SUN; NEW ATLANTIS; OCEANA for early examples). In this entry, *Utopia* will be treated as a radical text.

Leaving aside the various letters of introduction, the first part of the book (which was written second) contains a conversation between the traveller Raphael Hythlodaeus (in Greek, 'Nonsenso'), More and Gilles. During the conversation, which begins with a discussion of the poverty caused by greedy landlords, the enclosure of the COMMONS for sheep farming and the capital punishment of those who were therefore caught stealing, Hythlodaeus complains about the inequalities that result from private property, as well as the impossibility of philosophers giving advice to kings.

He illustrates his arguments with examples from the (real and imaginary) lands he has visited. In the second part of the book, Hythlodaeus describes life on the communistic island of Utopia, established by the lawgiver King Utopus hundreds of years previously, as an illustration of how they have solved all the problems from which England currently suffers. The island was created by dividing a peninsula from the mainland in order to ensure its safety and prevent it from being contaminated with foreign ideas (see PROTECTIONISM).

The island is a FEDERATION of fifty-four CITY STATES, each with a hundred thousand inhabitants. Each is built on the same pattern and divided into four parts, and each has a MARKET. Thirty families elect a Syphogrant ('Sty-Ward'), and over each ten Syphogrants there is a Tranibor ('Bench-Eater'), elected annually. Collectively they form a senate that elects the Prince of the city (for life, unless he abuses his office). Day-to-day decisions are made by the Tranibors and the Prince, but no conclusion can be reached until it has been debated for three days. Each town sends three representatives to the capital Amaurot ('Dreamtown'). The chief magistrate is Ademos ('No People'), but few laws and punishments are needed since the incentives for crime no longer exist. Doors are never locked, there are public honours to encourage good behaviour and informal competition between neighbours as to who has the best garden. If someone did commit a crime, they would generally be enslaved, and made to work alongside the refugees from neighbouring countries who prefer slavery in Utopia to being free outside it. The Utopians are not warlike, and distribute surplus food to neighbouring nations, though they do also establish colonies if their towns become overpopulated. In matters of conflict they tend to prefer the tactics of diplomacy, bribery and propaganda, but hire mercenaries if needed.

All goods are owned COLLECTIVELY, and work is organized by rotation. People are sent to labour in the countryside for two years, but can otherwise choose their occupations (though this might mean they have to move to a family which specializes in their trade). Public stores provide what people need; and cooking and eating is COMMUNAL (though people can cook and eat on their own if they wish). People work for no more than six hours a day because it is not necessary to feed the rich or indolent (though some intellectuals are allowed special leave to pursue their studies), and wasteful overproduction and consumption has ceased. The general demeanour of people is reserved, and forms of ostentatious dress or behaviour are not encouraged. Gold and silver are regarded as only good for chains and piss-

297

pots, and jewels are children's toys, but all are used to buy the services of the foreign mercenaries to defend the island if needed. One of More's innovations, much parodied since, was the idea that men and women should be allowed to see each other naked before marriage. Women were also allowed to become priests, and marriages could be dissolved by mutual consent. Whilst this might sound LIBERAL, once married, women were expected to obey the man, confessing to him on a monthly basis. Recreational sex and adultery were severely punished. Priests are elected but no particular religious beliefs are enforced. Even suicide is permitted. However, any belief must include the possibility of an after-life as a reward for good behaviour (as a means of social control). Other forms of social control include restrictions on travel, continual scrutiny by fellow citizens, the relocation of children if families are too large or too small, and a complete prohibition (punishable by death) on meetings that concern affairs of state but take place outside the elected senate.

Few people nowadays would want to live in More's utopia (though see AMISH). Its slavery, monastic uniformity and rigid patriarchy are alien to us, and reflect a view of human nature that requires the suppression of desire. That being said, its communism and (relative) humanism reflect a man of real principles, a man who felt that kings should listen to philosophers. But even such principles could not be expressed openly when a violent monarch demanded absolute loyalty, and disembowelled alive those who displeased him. The characters of More and Gilles say nothing contentious in *Utopia*, indeed they put the counter-arguments, and More was eventually beheaded for what he would not say (that the king was the head of the church). One of the many ironies in More's text is the reason given for why we don't know exactly where utopia is: Gilles missed what Hythlodaeus said because someone was coughing at the time. Many have since attempted to establish their own utopia in More's image. In the middle sixteenth century, Vasco de Quiroga used *Utopia* to establish a short-lived community near Santa Fe in New Spain. The leader of the first English colonizers to North America, Humphrey Gilbert, carried a copy and attempted to establish settlements using it as a guide (see MASSACHUSETTS BAY COLONY). Etienne Cabet was converted to communism after reading More (see VOYAGE TO ICARIA). MARX's secretary, Karl Kautsky, felt that *Utopia* was the first communist work. Whatever More intended, the book has inspired many radical echoes.

2. A word coined by Thomas More (see above) but now in general use

as a description of a supposedly perfect state of human affairs, or ideal COMMONWEALTH. Most utopias have been written as novelistic fictions that claim some measure of realism, and the literary genre is primarily a Western European and North American one. (There are also substantial traditions in Russia – such as Aleksey TOLSTOY's journey to Mars to establish a communist state in *Aelita*, 1924; in China, such as K'ang Yieu Wei's *United States of the World*, 1935; and in South America.) The assumption in this dictionary has been that utopias are fictional forms of alternative organization, but that they can have the power to inspire forms of practice that can lead to actual alternatives (see, for example, NEW ATLANTIS; VOYAGE TO ICARIA; NEWS FROM NOWHERE). This may be a contentious description for those who prefer to see 'utopian' as an adjective that primarily means 'unworldly' or 'impractical'. Contemporary theories about MANAGEMENT and MARKETS generally claim that the 'one best way' of organizing has now been discovered, and that any attempts to propose serious alternatives are utopian and/or nostalgic. The power of this argument is considerable, but relies on the effacement of the vast variety of all the other ways that human beings have and can imagine different forms of association and organization. In other words, to dismiss utopia is also to dismiss the possibility of any radical change, and hence to accept business as usual.

This is clearly not what utopians have done. Using fiction, practice or both, they have attempted to transcend the social situation that they found themselves in, and sometimes used the 'fictional' form for their own safety, not simply as a literary conceit. This has meant that utopias were routinely to be found elsewhere – on distant islands, beyond far mountain ranges, far in the future, or on some distant planet. As a result, all of the works of fiction to be found in this dictionary bear the imprint of their times – whether this is the stern CITY STATES of the seventeenth century (CITY OF THE SUN; CHRISTIANOPOLIS), the world states of the nineteenth century (LOOKING BACKWARD; WELLS), or the SCIENCE FICTION of the twentieth century (THE DISPOSSESSED; WOMAN ON THE EDGE OF TIME). But this is simply to acknowledge that every age creates its own utopias, and that they reflect the injustices and concerns of the time, as well as the particular interests of their authors in buildings, food or sex (see, for example, THE ISLE OF PINES; SUPPLEMENT TO BOUGAINVILLE'S VOYAGE; SADE).

Key to understanding the different shapes of utopia is some sort of conception of human nature. Are human beings naturally hard-working, creative and communal but corrupted by society (see ARCADIA; GOLDEN

299

AGE; ROMANTICISM), or are they selfish monkeys in need of social systems which prevent them from doing wrong (see OCEANA) or even improve them by 'breeding out' the undesirable traits (see Wells)? One places the emphasis on recovering a pre-social state of nature from the past, the other on the invention of a future (though perhaps one that echoes the glory of a past state such as Greece or Rome). The two poles of COMMUNISM and FASCISM can be imperfectly understood through this dichotomy, but matters are further complicated by whether or not the author believes that some sort of ruling élite is required to keep things in order – from Plato's 'philosopher kings' (see the REPUBLIC), to Skinner's 'Board of Planners' (see WALDEN TWO).

Alphonse de Lamartine called utopias 'premature truths'. If that is accurate, then it is hardly surprising that those who benefit from the status quo have been generally hostile towards them, but their reception on the left has not always been so positive, either. MARX and Engels (as 'scientific' socialists) were highly dismissive of 'utopian' socialists (see FOURIER), on the grounds that they specified no concrete mechanism which would transform the world. Instead, they either set up small-scale alternatives (see OWEN), or retreated into a rose-tinted fantasy that ignored the law-like realities of capitalism. As a result, though SOCIALISM and Marxism are clearly utopian in the sense of attempting to change the world, the word tends to be an insult within such circles. More lately, neo-Marxists such as Herbert Marcuse and Ernst Bloch have attempted to rescue the idea of radical utopianism from scientific Marxism, the latter suggesting that it functions as a 'principle of hope' which allows people to dream that the world could be otherwise. Within ANARCHIST thought, utopianism would be a more respectable concept, though many anarchists would also be highly suspicious of any form of tidy social engineering (NEWS FROM NOWHERE almost always being an honourable exception).

As is evident, utopias can easily turn into, or be seen as, DYSTOPIAS. For example, it is now a commonplace that the BUREAUCRATIC and technocratic utopias of the nineteenth century ended up in the industrialized slaughter of FASCISM, the totalitarian state of which an increasing number fictions warned. As a result, by the second half of the twentieth century, it was being suggested that we lived in a post-utopian age. The grand plans and dreams of the past had only brought closed MONASTIC communities, or grandiose blueprints for modern madness, so a pragmatic, perhaps 'post-modern', politics should avoid such over-ambition. What Anthony Giddens has called 'utopian realism', or the politics of the third way, attempted to seek incremental changes via the public policies of the nation state. Whilst in this dictionary we do not wish to make any particular assumptions about the superiority of any specific alternative organization or utopia, it does seem that undue modesty about alternatives will limit their possibility. In other words, if the dominant politics merely encourages a tinkering with the dominant ideas, then little harm will be done, but great good might be missed entirely. When Isaiah Berlin said that 'the belief in the possibility (or probability) of rational organization ... is the heart of all the utopias', he was right, but the most important question is what 'rational' might mean. Unless my version of rationality is exactly the same as yours, my utopia is likely to look different, too. But then, perhaps utopia can never be pinned down like this anyway. As Louis Marin suggests, maybe it is better thought of as a moving horizon, not a place – 'the unfigurable figure of Infinite Liberty'.

V

VIA CAMPESINA An international movement that coordinates peasant organizations of small and medium-sized producers, agricultural workers, rural women and indigenous communities. It is an AUTONOMOUS and pluralistic movement that is independent of political parties and unites peasants' organizations from Africa, America, Asia and Europe, including, for example, MST. It was created in 1992 to campaign for issues of concern to small farmers such as food sovereignty, agrarian reform, credit and debt, technology, women's participation, and SUSTAINABLE agriculture. In particular, Via Campesina calls for agrarian reforms to democratize the ownership and use of land. This involves not only giving the land to those who work it but also transforming farmers into guardians of the Earth through the promotion of ENVIRONMENTALLY friendly agriculture. Via Campesina has also coined the term 'food sovereignty' to refer to every people's rights to produce their own food, a basic principle to which agricultural trade should be subordinated. In its fight to protect peasants' rights and heritage, it has also opposed seed patenting and genetically modified seeds. Its privileging of LOCAL agriculture, sustainable small-scale farming, food sovereignty and free access to seeds have made Via Campesina a strong opponent of neoliberalism and free trade, and an active participant in the ANTI-CAPITALISM movement (see also SLOW FOOD).

VILLAGES ANARCHISTS like KROPOTKIN looked to existing peasant and worker COMMUNES as having the potential to realize the principles of his ideal society. He believed that the self-governing Russian village or *obshchina* provided a basis for AUTONOMOUS social units managed by direct DEMOCRACY, where work and other social needs would be satisfied in an integrated way. Such villages could be FEDERATED with other communes into a loose REPUBLIC. TOLSTOY and GANDHI also saw the peasant village in a similar way. MARX and Engels, whilst being critical of what they saw as an overly ROMANTICIZED utopianism on the part of anarchists, also identified traditional village-based societies as examples of a primitive form of SOCIALISM. With their COLLECTIVE labour, relatively small differences in wealth and status, and local forms of self-government, villages could be seen as providing historical examples of the feasibility of socialist models of organization. LENIN, though also critical of what he saw as the anarchists' attachment to a decayed tradition, saw the SOVIETS, or workers' and peasants' councils, as the future social building block of COMMUNIST society. It was the pre-existing model of the *mir* or village council that enabled the soviets seemingly to spring into being spontaneously after the 1905 Russian REVOLUTION.

There are many who do not identify themselves as left utopians who also see village life as an ideal. It acts as a powerful symbol of a nostalgic ARCADIAN utopia and the middle classes have been deserting the inner city for decades in favour of the village or GARDEN CITY. There has been a frenzied buying up by the relatively well-to-do of traditional cottages to be 'restored' to their original state. The result is often the construction of a sanitized vision of rural life that would doubtless have been unrecognizable to pre-industrial agricultural workers. The great paradox is that in buying up village property and then commuting to cities for work, the very opposite of the utopian village is created. Many modern villages are no more than monocultural housing estates for the wealthy with no collective life, SELF-SUFFICIENCY or local autonomy. It is an essentially urban lifestyle imposed on the village at enormous ENVIRONMENTAL and social cost, and at the expense of people who are priced out of the housing market. Thus the village provides an ambivalent symbol, one that appeals to both radicals and conservatives for somewhat different reasons. It may be that the principles of local community and self-determination are what is important. These principles may then need to be applied in urban and rural environments as sustainable federations of city 'villages' in the way that SOCIAL ECOLOGISTS have suggested (see BOOKCHIN). ECOVILLAGES provide a contemporary example of the ways in which the model of the village has inspired the development of self-managed sustainable communities in both rural and urban settings.

VOYAGE TO ICARIA Etienne Cabet (1788–1856), like MARX some years later, did the research for his utopia in the reading room of the British Museum whilst a political exile from his native France. Influenced by More's UTOPIA, Harrington's OCEANA and Robert OWEN, his book, originally titled *Voyages et Aventures de Lord William Carisdall en Icarie* (1 83 9), rapidly became a best-selling inspiration for societies of Icarian communists across France.

In 1848, sixty-nine Icarians left to establish a colony at Nauvoo, Illinois. Though this community only lasted until 1856, other Icarian communities survived until the 1890s. Cabet himself died on his second visit to AMERICA, whilst attempting to relocate the Nauvoo community to St Louis. Cabet's utopia is radically COMMUNISTIC, and reflected his own political activism, but was condemned by MARX and Engels as a prime example of ahistorical idealism.

Icaria is symmetrical in design, obsessively clean, and highly ordered in government. New technology and industrial-scale production are employed to generate abundance and ease, which the state then shares equally amongst all citizens. The book consists of an account of how a young English Lord is persuaded of the marvels of Icaria, as well as letters from a young painter who is writing to his brother whom he has left behind in France. The Icarians are isolated from the rest of the world by mountains, river and sea, and travellers have to pay to gain entrance. Their land is divided into one hundred equal provinces, themselves divided into ten COMMUNES which have a town, eight VILLAGES and many farms. The capital, Icara, is a circle bisected by a river and patterned by a grid of straight wide streets down which run 'street cars' every two minutes. In the middle of the river is a circular island, upon which is the Icarians' main public building, at the middle of which is a colossal statue, probably of Icar, the founder. The city is clearly zoned, with sixty residential areas styled on each of the sixty principal nations, and workshops and slaughterhouses kept separate. Everything is collectively owned, and all people receive their allocation of COLLECTIVE products from the public storehouses. The assemblies that take place in the communes, the towns, and in Icara itself are based on DEMOCRATICALLY elected deputies, half of whom are reselected each year. This is also the case for the President, and the fifteen-member executive. All the facts about Icaria, and all the decisions made, are recorded by a department of statistics, and published in a public journal which is distributed to all citizens.

Icarian organization is massively detailed. Committees meet to decide on the best kinds of food, the best ways to distribute food to the places where it is required, and the best ways for women to prepare it at home or for the cooking of collective meals. These are taken at fixed times, and in fixed places such as the magnificent republican restaurants (as fine as the best cafés in Paris), or in silence at work whilst the morning paper is read aloud. A timetable determines when people must get up, when they enjoy themselves, and when they go to bed and observe the common curfew. Similarly, all clothing is designed by experts for ease of manufacture (elastic being commonly used) and tastefulness. Clothes are allocated depending on sex, age, marital status and profession, and also having regard to the requirements of public and private life, and the suitability for the individual (certain colours being more fitting for blondes, and so on). There are no wages, all the different occupations are respected equally, and any unhealthy or immoral trades (innkeeping or dagger making, for example) are simply prohibited.

Cabet's breathless celebration of the beauty of Icarian women, and a marked gender division of labour, are typical enough of his time, but other aspects of this utopia are even more difficult to reconcile for a contemporary reader. All Icarian public work is subject to censorship, and much art was destroyed in the early years of the regime. 'Liberty is not the right do anything indiscriminately; it consists only in doing that which does not harm other citizens, and certain songs can be moral poisons as fatal to society as physical poisons' (see REPUBLIC). As an inspiration to all, Icar is monumentalized in public places and celebrated in songs. Cabet's attempt to organize all aspects of his citizens' lives, and his faith in an all-embracing totalitarianism, make Bellamy's LOOKING BACKWARD seem a rather disordered utopia by comparison. Cabet's understandable enthusiasm for street lighting and public toilets may be creditable, but overall his utopia also points to the limits of a totalizing form of organization as a way of engineering happiness (see BUREAUCRACY, FASCISM).

WALDEN

'I went to the woods because I wished to live deliberately, to front only the essential facts of life, and see if I could not learn what it had to teach, and not, when I came to die, discover that I had not lived.'

The US writer Henry David Thoreau's book *Walden; or, Life in the Woods* (1854) is a massively influential work which could be taken both as a manifesto for simple living and as a condemnation of property owning and competitive society. Thoreau (1817–6 2) was a remarkable fig u re who earned his living variously working as an engineer in his father's pencil factory, lecturing, land surveying and writing. His writing concerned the abolition of slavery; pacifism and civil disobedience; vegetarianism; evolution, ecology and ENVIRONMENTALISM; and the broad sweep of philosophy now usually termed 'American Transcendentalism'. This latter movement was essentially an outgrowth of European ROMANTICISM, initially popularized by Ralph Waldo Emerson, and placing a considerable emphasis on intuition, nature and individualism. From the 1840s onwards many North American INTENTIONAL COMMUNITIES (BROOK FARM, the North American Phalanx, the Clarkson Domain and so on) claimed inspiration from transcendentalism as well as the ideas of FOURIER.

Thoreau's views about modernity were nicely crystallized in his 1843 review of John Adolphus Etzler's 1833 UTOPIA *A Paradise within the Reach of All Men, without Labour, by Powers of Nature and Machinery.* Etzler had proposed completely re-developing the USA using technology: inconvenient mountains would be flattened, people would live in centrally heated palaces with 7,000 inhabitants, and the rivers would be turned into useful canals. Thoreau rejected Etzler's pandering to material comforts, and demolition of nature for human purposes. In summer 1845, he moved to Walden Pond in Concord, MASSACHUSETTS, and lived there until autumn 1847. *Walden* is an account of this time (though condensed into a year with four seasons) in which Thoreau takes various lessons from nature about simplicity, solitude and human development. He builds a hut (with a borrowed axe) and grows vegetables. His view of nature is generally ARCADIAN, and his emphasis is on how people can recover a natural and reasonable way of life that has not been corrupted by false wants.

Thoreau is now often regarded as one of the first theorists of environmentalism as well as an early cultural critic of modernity in AMERICA. Indeed, his views on government ('that government is best which governs not at all') are close to individualist ANARCHISM. He was hostile to voting, organized religion and regular employment. His essay *Resistance to Civil Government* (1849, later titled *Civil Disobedience*) grew from his refusal to pay taxes to a pro-slavery government during the Mexican–American war, and a night he spent in jail in 1846. It influenced TOLSTOY, GANDHI and Martin Luther King (see NON-VIOLENT RESISTANCE). B. F. Skinner's behaviourist utopia was titled WALDEN TWO in homage, though its engineered COLLECTIVISM would have not suited Thoreau at all. On his deathbed, when asked whether he had made his peace with God, he responded that he did not think that he and God had quarrelled.

WALDEN TWO

'*I mean you've got to experiment, and experiment with your own life! Not just sit back – not just sit back in an ivory tower somewhere – as if your own life weren't mixed up in it.*'

A UTOPIA written in 1948 by the US behaviourist psychologist B. F. Skinner (1904–1990). A professor at Harvard for most of his career, Skinner abandoned a career in literature to develop a general theory of positive and negative reinforcement of behaviour in animals and humans. Most importantly, Skinner's radical behaviourism is only concerned with what works to produce the desired effect. Just as we don't need to know what goes on in pigeon's heads in order to make them play table tennis, so we don't need vague ideas about religion, ethics and politics in order to change human behaviour. On publication, the book prompted savage criticism from well-intentioned humanists. Northrop Frye said that 'its Philistine vulgarity makes it a caricature of the pedantry of social science'. More carefully, Lewis Mumford suggested that 'the sugared concept of scientific control, which B. F. Skinner insinuates into his *Walden Two*, is another name for arrested development'.

Skinner's viewpoint is put forward at some length by T. E. Frazier, the founder of 'Walden Two', an experimental community named after Thoreau's WALDEN. As the novel begins, we meet a college professor (a thinly disguised Skinner) who hears about a social experiment in which one of his ex-students has been engaged. He visits with a small party of students and a philosopher colleague, is impressed despite his doubts, and eventually decides to stay. Most of the novel is taken up with interminable explanations and defences of the Walden Two way of life, interspersed with hearty meals and restful sleep, but the overall effect is to depict a remarkably sophisticated and well-arranged society which contains many references to other classic utopias. In addition, by using the device of the combative philosopher, Skinner manages to construct robust defences of his position against the anticipated arguments of his critics – though this did not stop them from making these arguments anyway.

Walden Two is a COMMUNITY in the fullest sense that attempts (through positive reinforcement) to minimize competition and encourage a lifestyle that maximizes supportive social interaction and satisfying labour. Childbearing usually happens early, from about sixteen onwards, when the girl is fit and healthy, and before she begins to participate fully in community life. After children, she is free to organize her romantic and sexual life as she thinks fit, and most adults (of either sex) have their own separate rooms. Children are reared collectively, and intense parental attachments are discouraged. The education system uses experimentally proven techniques of positive reinforcement to discourage negative emotions and encourage self-control. Ethics is reduced to a problem of conditioning, a form of training that domesticates members from birth and ensures that they become happy and compliant members of Walden Two. A system of differential labour credits (see LETS) ensures that all the jobs get done (see LOOKING BACKWARD), but members need work for only four hours a day because the community is arranged to maximize efficiency and reduce pointless labour. For example, the dinner trays are transparent, so that it can easily be seen whether they need cleaning or not, and the babies are kept in a filtered atmosphere so that they don't need to be washed every day.

A general result of this focus on saving energy is that the community is minimally ENVIRONMENTALLY invasive, 'a high standard of living with a low consumption of goods'. It is built around a series of earth buildings, and houses nearly 1,000 people. Four other Waldens are also now growing, the latest (Walden Six) as a process of 'fission' because Walden Two is becoming too large. Governance is conducted by a board of planners (six men and six women, who serve for ten years), and day-to-day decisions are carried out by a series of MANAGERS of various functions – food storage, legal, dairy, behaviour, culture and so on. However, since hero worship of any kind is discouraged, the planners are not widely known, and do what they do from a sense of duty, not for power or recognition. Indeed, 'politics' in general does not happen in Walden Two, merely an endless series of experimentally based changes to fine-tune the collective machinery, 'a government based on a science of human behaviour' (see FOURIER).

In his later book, *Beyond Freedom and Dignity* (1971), Skinner clarifies his hostility to imprecise platitudes by arguing that ideas such as freedom often get in the way of producing a more collectively satisfying society. Since our behaviours are determined, we should engineer the determining factors in a clear manner that achieves our desired goals. Skinner's ideas throw down a clear challenge to anyone interested in social change, and many of his ideas (in the form of cognitive behaviourism) are now routine in a variety of social policy domains (education, probation, clinical psychology and so on). However, others have seen his form of social engineering as producing a DYSTOPIA that disposes of DEMOCRACY and verges on FASCISM. Further, its emphasis on COLLECTIVISM is so overwhelming that there is little room for individuality and difference, as people become elements of a 'superorganism'. Of course these sort of dystopian points have been echoed in many other places. Just as *Walden Two* can be seen as a reinterpretation of Aldous Huxley's earlier *Brave New World*, so can Huxley's later ISLAND be seen as an attempt to put some spirituality into social engineering. Nonetheless, *Walden Two* was written as a radical counter-point to a militaristic state that had just entered the Cold War. Skinner avoids eugenics, state control or REVOLUTION and instead puts forward a pacificist ECOVILLAGE based on sexual equality as a solution. He also wonders whether this might be a form of COMMUNISM, though not like the pro-growth SOVIET UNION. Nearly fifty years after its publication, this utopia has aged well.

An actual INTENTIONAL COMMUNITY inspired by *Walden Two* is 'Los Horcones', founded in 1973 in Sonora in Mexico, which has taken Skinner's ideas, strengthening them with contemporary COMMUNITARIANISM and ENVIRONMENTALISM to produce what they call an 'experimental culture'. TWIN OAKS in Virginia (established 1967) was initially set up on similar principles. It is still in existence, but no longer describes itself as primarily influenced by Skinner's ideas.

WEBER, MAX, see BUREAUCRACY; CULT.

WELLS, HERBERT GEORGE

'No less than a planet will serve the purpose of a modern Utopia'

This English writer (1866–1946) can be described as the last in the classic age of UTOPIAS, and one of the first to write DYSTOPIAS such as *When the Sleeper Wakes* (1899), and SCIENCE FICTION like *The Time Machine* (1895). He is probably best known now for the latter, but his output over his lifetime was massive, covering essays, poetry, social commentary, textbooks and history. His two most significant utopias were *A Modern Utopia* (1905) and *Men Like Gods* (1923), but much of his wider writing is concerned with the destruction and reconstruction of societies (see, for example, *The Shape of Things to Come*, 1933). A further aspect of his early work was an interest in eugenics, and the production of a superior race through breeding out those who cannot cope with social and technical change. Certain formulations of utopia clearly require the elimination of those types who would be an inconvenience in the future, and in the 'New Republic' of his *Anticipations* (1901) Wells uses a quasi-Darwinian logic to suggest that this process may need to be accelerated through state-sanctioned mercy killing.

His later views were more temperate however, and *A Modern Utopia* is a remarkably thoughtful and complex work. It is an academic essay on many of the other utopias that preceded it, a story about two travellers who end up on an Earth which is exactly the same as ours but organized as a utopia, and a musing on the impossibilities and tensions of utopian thought in general. Wells manages to construct a 'reflexive' utopia that reflects his own faith in state SOCIALISM, but without the totalitarianism of Bellamy's LOOKING BACKWARD or what he saw as the rose-tinted optimism of Morris's NEWS FROM NOWHERE. The two travellers, one Wells, the other a lovelorn and rather dim botanist, are transported to a planet millions of miles away. It has the same mountains and is populated by the same people, but has a social system that is rational and humane. While discussing the balance between personal freedoms and state control at length, Wells certainly tips the scales in the direction of the state, and that is a world state, not a mere CITY STATE. Like many radical thinkers, Wells assumed that the world state, like K'ang Yieu Wei's *United States of the World* (1935), was the final solution to problems of international relations. A vast BUREAUCRACY registers and governs the activities of this world state, though many personal freedoms are allowed and encouraged. A common language is spoken by all, the state owns all the land and keeps a gigantic system of records on every individual.

Nonetheless, land is leased to companies, agricultural CO-OPERATIVES and individuals who can then make profits (although not from the production of energy), money is used as a medium of exchange, and the right to travel anywhere is maintained. Broadly, Wells suggests, freedom is allowed in so far as it does not impinge on the freedom of others (as in the case of great wealth, for example). Hence there are no jails or state punishments, and criminals are simply sent to monastic islands for either sex. There, they are free to do what they wish, as long as it does not hurt the other residents.

This 'modern utopia' is a broadly Keynesian state, where demand for labour is stimulated by the state, but private initiative can bring rewards (and a certain proportion of these rewards can be inherited). The laws concerning marriage illustrate this nicely. Certain conditions must be met before marriage is allowed (age, lack of diseases, income and so on), and then each partner is allowed to see the index card that relates to the other. With this full information, the citizens can decide whether they wish to go ahead. Having children is considered a civic duty, and hence women are paid on the birth of a child, and rewarded if the child develops in intelligence or ability above certain thresholds. If no children have been produced, marriages may be allowed to lapse. If any of the initial conditions for the marriage have not been met, the state does not prevent the marriage, but simply ignores it, and no payments are made. These laws, and many others, are formulated and enforced by a 'voluntary nobility' called the 'Samurai', a class of people who are admitted following certain examinations and then have to follow 'the Rule'. This involves prohibitions on certain activities (such as commerce, alcohol and acting), marriage only to another samurai and the performance of certain rather improving activities on a regular basis.

Again set on a distant planet populated by humans, *Men Like Gods* is more science fiction than serious essay, though it might represent the world that could eventually follow from that of *A Modern Utopia*. In what seems like a surprisingly ANARCHIST structure, the state and law have withered away, and decisions are made locally. There is no ruling class (merely some general 'intelligences' who speculate about general matters) and no property, because it is considered a 'nuisance'. These social changes were driven by the realization that competition and struggle were dangerous to the human race, and needed to be replaced by a gradual turn to honest cooperation. Like Swift's Houyhnhnms (see GULLIVER'S TRAVELS), these men like gods speak frankly and truthfully, and (like ROUSSEAU's 'noble savage') are entirely open about the playful satisfaction of their animal instincts. If you do not express yourself with ambition and beauty, there is no punishment, but you are unlikely to find lovers. This remarkably libidinous society (partly prefigured in his *Mankind in the Making* in 1903) is regulated, if that is the right word, by an education system that rewards curiosity, creativity and honesty. Parents play little part in their children's lives until they are about ten, and instead nurses and teachers instil in their pupils the five principles of liberty – privacy, free movement, unlimited knowledge, truth, and free criticism. Yet Wells is not an anarchist, and some sort of state leaks back in. There is no money, but every child is credited with a sum deposited at a bank to last them until they are twenty-five. They are then expected to choose a task that will help them refill their account, and some artists can (in this way) become wealthy.

Wells, like Bellamy, often makes exemptions from his organized states for artists and writers, or more generally for a certain class of people who are (by disposition) called to serve humanity. The over-populated, vulgar and dirty aspects of the present may need to be cleaned away (by Martians, a revolution, eugenics, or a plague) but some sort of social class will still remain or emerge. The paradox of Wells is that (as a writer and thinker) he needed what he called the 'cult called Individualism', and it was this realization that usually prevented him falling into the totalitarianism of organization that can so easily become FASCISM. This attempt to make the future tidy does not assume that human beings are made lazy and corrupt by society (see ROUSSEAU), but that a better sort of human being needs to be cultivated. Wells, in his most prophetic modes, admires the hygienically perfect garden, but the complexity of his thought undoes the vision just as he stridently insists upon its realization. *A Modern Utopia* is one of the few realistic and dynamic utopias, with real people, real problems, and persistent weeds. As he says, for older utopians:

> One beheld a healthy and simple generation enjoying the fruits of the earth in an atmosphere of virtue and happiness, to be followed by other virtuous, happy and entirely similar generations until the Gods grew weary. Change and development were dammed back by invincible dams for ever. But the Modern Utopia must be not static but kinetic, must shape not as a permanent state but as a hopeful stage leading to a long ascent of stages.

WIKIPEDIA One of the most successful examples of internet-based organization, this 'free encyclopedia anyone can edit' has (at the time of writing) over 5 million articles in 200 languages. The English language edition has over 1.5 million articles. It was launched in 2001, based on the expert-written 'Nupedia', and its name derives from the Hawaiian word 'wiki', meaning quick. Its founder, Jimmy Wales, developed the encyclopedia on the basis of two principles – that it should be written from a neutral point of view, and should be free to read and use under the general principles of 'copyleft' or 'creative COMMONS' licences. (That is to say, that authorship is clearly acknowledged, and profits are not made by reproducing the contents.) The capacity for anyone to produce and edit entries has resulted (it is claimed) in a continually developing and improving corpus of entries based on a COMMUNITY of writers, editors and administrators. Whilst ultimate control is maintained by Wales, contentious topics are continually re-edited and discussed on open pages attached to specific entries. No articles are ever declared 'finished', but malicious or offensive editing (as well as advertising) is monitored by a team of volunteer administrators and deleted on a daily basis. Since 2005, following some potentially libellous entries, authors now need to be registered with Wikipedia in order to construct new articles.

Wikipedia has been criticized, often by librarians or the editors of conventional reference works, since there is no robust way of checking the information or the credentials of those who supply it. Its position of 'neutrality' is clearly impossible to maintain to the satisfaction of all its readers, and the quality of its information can be variable. Nevertheless, it has grown massively in influence, and its speed of response and coverage is much greater than that of a normal reference work. It has also spawned a wiktionary, wikiquotes, wikinews, wikibooks and the wikimedia information commons. It is worth considering, as a reader of this paper-based 'Dictionary', just how much wider the coverage could be if it were www- and wiki-based. Wikipedia shows how a DEMOCRATIC or even ANARCHIST approach to information and organization might work (see ILLICH). It is parallelled in technological terms by the OPEN SOURCE SOFTWARE movement, in finance by the 'Ripple Project' (see GRAMEEN BANK), and in news by INDYMEDIA.

WINSTANLEY, GERRARD, see DIGGERS

WOBBLIES (Industrial Workers of the World), see INDUSTRIAL DEMOCRACY

WOMAN ON THE EDGE OF TIME Marge Piercy's 1976 novel has, along with le Guin's THE DISPOSSESSED, been one of the most widely read utopias of recent years. Part SCIENCE FICTION, part contemporary social comment, the time travel plot dramatizes the difference between a sordid DYSTOPIAN present and a UTOPIAN future. Connie Ramos is a Mexican-American who has been diagnosed insane, when she is really just the victim of a racist and patriarchal society that has no other way to deal with its problems. Her story unfolds in the year 2137, in parallel with that of the village of Mattapoisett, which Connie is able to visit and thus temporarily escape her grim present. The village is a small part of a new post-apocalypse world that is still involved in a long war with the old order that has severely damaged the environment. The enemy still have the space platforms, the Moon and the Antarctic, and fight with a cyborg army, but the new world is winning, and beginning to make good the massive environmental problems. (See her later novel *Body of Glass*, for a possible description of the corporate technologized world that precedes this one.)

The key features of Mattapoisett are its fluid gender roles and its ARCADIAN integration with the natural world. The former aspect is most neatly exemplified in the difficulty Connie initially has in deciding who are men and who are women, and in the use of the pronoun 'per' instead of him/his and her/hers. Sexual preferences are fluid and multiple, and there are no family groups, but a self-defined group of friends and sexual partners ('core'). Everyone has their own space, but they eat largely vegetarian food in a communal 'fooder'. Babies are grown in a 'brooder' (which breaks the direct connection between women and reproduction), 'mothered' by three people (some of whom breastfeed, including the men), and educated and cared for in the 'children's house'. When the children feel ready to leave they break from their mothers by spending time in the forest on their own and they can then choose their own names – as many times as they like. They are also forbidden from talking to their mothers for three months, to break unhealthy attachment bonds and allow both mothers and children to become equal members of the COMMUNITY.

In economic terms, Mattapoisett is best described as an ECOVILLAGE (see also ECOTOPIA). It has a population of 600 people, and is organized in order to minimize its impact on the ENVIRONMENT. Most interestingly, there is an attempt to integrate advanced technologies with ecofriendly practices, such as an automated pillow factory that is powered by methane from composting. Flowers and crops grow everywhere, there is rudimentary communication with animals and complementary and shamanistic medicine are practised. Yet at the same time everyone wears a mobile information storage and communication device (a 'kenner'), forms of genetic engineering are routinely practised, and limited 'luxury credits' can be spent on anything that particularly fascinates people.

In institutional terms, the structure is very fluid but organized through a series of key annual and life-stage rituals. After leaving the children's house there is no formal education system, but you choose to study with someone who inspires you, if they choose to accept you. Some people leave their VILLAGES and travel, or try to find a village that specializes in something that interests them. Hierarchy and fixed divisions of labour are actively worked against. Everyone, including children, has to spend time working on the land, in fear of social exclusion or expulsion. Violence is dealt with by marking the individual with a tattoo, but a second violent offence results in a death penalty. Theft is seen as a cry for attention, and the response is the showering of presents. If they wish, people can also join a specific 'workbase' as an equal member to specialize in a particular area of activity. Local governance is carried out through township councils, which encourage short speeches and have a rotating leadership. Matters of wider importance, or that cannot be resolved locally, are passed to the regional 'Grandcil'. The rotating posts on Grandcil come with the dangers of power attached, so they are followed by a spell of six months' service in a more menial job in order to break any attachments (for self and others) between power and the person.

Piercy's utopia is an influential and inspiring FEMINIST UTOPIA. She describes a world in which technology is not rejected, but treated with care for its social and environmental impacts (see AMISH). Her conceptions of sexual politics (particularly with reference to reproduction and family structures) are sophisticated and open up possibilities that radically equalize the relationship between sex, gender and sexuality. This is a book of its time, one highly influenced by the slightly perfumed esoterica of the 1960s (with its rituals, songs and drug use), a certain conception of natural justice, as well as a powerful sense of social change and impatience with the status quo. Its (literal) dream of a new world plays the classic function of utopian literature – to imagine that things could be otherwise.

WORKER OWNERSHIP, see COOPERATIVES; MONDRAGÒN; TOWER COLLIERY; SUMA; WORKER SELF-MANAGEMENT

WORKER SELF-MANAGEMENT Worker self-management (WSM) is the idea that those who produce should control their workplaces. It is based upon the premise that hierarchical forms of MANAGEMENT and organization are unnecessary, undesirable, and can be replaced by DEMOCRATIC forms of decision making. Historically, WSM emerges out of various currents of radical labour organizing including anarcho-SYNDICALISM, council COMMUNISM, and other forms of CO-OPERATIVISM. Forms of WSM often emerge during periods of economic and political crisis and people try to find methods for overcoming the crisis in which they find themselves. Notable historical manifestations of WSM include the emergence of worker COLLECTIVES during the SPANISH Civil War in the 1930s, in MONDRAGÒN, and in plywood cooperatives in the north-west United States. Forms of WSM have included factories, healthcare clinics, transportation services, publishing companies, and so on. While attempts to create WSM are generally not supported by government bodies and TRADE UNIONS, there are exceptions: WSM was the official state policy in Yugoslavia from the late 1940s through to the early 1990s. Other notable examples of state-supported WSM include instances in Bolivia, Peru and Algeria. WSM has been developed and articulated by figures such as Rudolf Rocker, PROUDHON, C. George Benello, Jaroslav Vanek, and many others.

WSM has its critics, ranging from capitalist and MANAGERIAL critiques that argue that it is too slow, inefficient, and undesirable. Critiques from the Left include arguments that WSM does not truly move beyond capitalism but rather constitutes forms of collective production which are most often still subordinated to the discipline of the MARKET. WSM advocates often respond to these arguments by suggesting that WSM provides methods for creating new forms of self-sustaining workplaces and COMMUNITIES that can exist in the present while providing examples and skills for developing post-capitalist forms. Over time forms of WSM and industrial democracy can disintegrate and become transformed into more traditionally organized workplaces (see ONEIDA). Paradoxically enough, such transformations are as often caused by the success of a firm as its difficulties. During the 1970s many capitalist firms and management gurus responded to the massive waves of labour insurgency and unrest that had occured during the 1960s by focusing on ways to increase worker participation, the

QUALITY OF WORKING LIFE, and so forth. These attempts, such as those sometimes described as EMPOWERMENT or INDUSTRIAL DEMOCRACY were often not efforts to create self-determining structures for workers but rather methods for giving greater autonomy within a structure determined by the firm.

Current manifestations of WSM can be seen in the increasing number of self-managed firms in Argentina and through the ideas of Robin Hahnel and Michael Albert who, since the late 1970s, have written a series of books outlining in great detail a process for the creation of a system of participatory economics that builds upon existing traditions of WSM. There have also been recent organizing campaigns that go beyond the usual boundaries of the workplace in their efforts, such as the efforts of the Chainworkers in Italy who focus on organizing precariously employed workers (see AUTONOMIA) and the Downtown Workers' Centre in Vermont, which strives to organize the whole city into one union rather than those based on particular workplaces. These organizing campaigns, which draw heavily from traditions of SYNDICALIST organizing, attempt to address the transformed economic space of post-industrial capitalism. While projects of creating worker self-management continue to occupy a difficult and contradictory position within the social fabric, they remain an important inspiration for those striving to create a more just world. (SS)

WORKPLACE DEMOCRACY see INDUSTRIAL DEMOCRACY; WORKER SELF-MANAGEMENT

WORLD SOCIAL FORUM Every year at the end of January, the world's corporate and government élite, animated by its faith in neo-liberalism and global capitalism, gathers under tight police security in the Swiss resort town of Davos for the World Economic Forum. In January 2001, members of various social movements, non-governmental organizations and other parts of civil society came together in PORTO ALEGRE to create their own alternative meeting: the World Social Forum (WSF). The forum provides an open platform for participants to discuss strategies of resistance to globalization, and to debate alternatives. Since its first meeting, the WSF has organized annual meetings and prompted the development of regional fora such as the European Social Forum, the Pan-Amazon Social Forum and the Asian Social Forum. With its slogan 'Another world is possible', it has become one of the focal points of ANTI-CAPITALISM. From a gathering of 12,000 delegates at the January 2001 meeting, it has developed into the world's largest mobilization of civil society, drawing 155,000 participants from 135 countries to its 2005 meeting.

In opposition to the faith in neoLIBERALISM and capitalism as not only inevitable forces but also forces for the good, the World Social Forum encourages reflection on alternatives that respect human rights, the ENVIRONMENT, DEMOCRACY, social justice and the sovereignty of people. To this end, the World and Regional meetings offer workshops, discussion and cultural events around themes such as 'Environment, Ecology and Livelihoods', 'Aggression against Rural Societies', 'Imperial Strategies and People's Resistance', 'Social Justice, Human Rights and Governance', or 'Life after Capitalism'. Whilst the World and Regional Social Forums come to public attention during their annual meetings, they cannot be reduced to these localized events; the WSF is also a permanent process of seeking and creating alternatives by building connections between movements across the world. Nor can the World Social Forum (or Regional Social Forum) be reduced to an institution. It is a NETWORK for the circulation and exchange of experiences and reflections between movements. The WSF does not aim to 'represent' civil society or any movement within it, but rather to facilitate connections and exchange.

YUNUS, MUHAMMAD, see GRAMEEN BANK

Z

ZAKÂT (or ZAKAAT, or ZAKAH) According to the Qur'an and other Islamic texts, every financially able Muslim adult is meant to pay a proportion of his income to support the poor and needy. So, according to Islamic law (*Shari'a*) once an individual's income has reached a minimum amount (called the *Nisab*, originally a calculation of gold) then a Zakât has to be paid. After deduction of debts and other necessary maintenance and upkeep expenses (see ISLAMIC FINANCE), the individual then pays 1/40th of the money that they have had in their possession for one year. Normally this means Zakât on capital rather than income. Extra may be given (usually in secret) as *Sadaqa* (or *Sadaqah*). Whilst this form of 'charity' or 'alms' is required from every capable Muslim, it is based on the idea that it benefits the needy, those with low incomes, those whose income cannot meet their basic needs of life, Zakât administrators, slaves, those who convert to Islam, people who are in debt, and stranded travellers.

It is based on the idea that giving without desire for earthly reward is both a purification from selfishness and the expression of a desire for fellow-feeling. Zakât also performs redistributive, allocative and educative roles in the economy. It reduces inequality through the transfer of wealth from the rich to the poor. It also promotes allocative justice through the movement of wealth to more productive ventures, since idle funds are penalized. It is different from conventional taxes since it is voluntary, with a stable rate and clearly prescribed beneficiaries. (HM/IU)

ZAPATISTAS The Zapatista TERRORIST, GUERRILLA or freedom fighter movement emerged in opposition to economic liberalism and to promote the rights to self-determination among indigenous people in the Chiapas region of Mexico. The EZLN (Zapatista National Liberation Army) took up arms on 1 January 1994, the day when Mexico joined NAFTA (North American Free Trade Agreement), to protest against the implications of neoliberal policies on Mayan farmers' survival and autonomy. By submitting the price of commodities, in particular corn and coffee, to the 'law of the MARKET', NAFTA was threatening the livelihood of small coffee and corn producers who could not withstand the pressures from global corporations.

In response, Zapatistas have been fighting to reassert indigenous people's right to 'life' – defined not merely in terms of fulfilling basic needs, but also in terms of 'land and freedom', of 'food and dignity, not food and insults'. This emphasis on self-government, self-determination and autonomy is clearly manifested in the Zapatista call for land occupation and collective ownership (see COMMONS). Land access is seen as essential to providing indigenous control over the means of their subsistence. The insistence on self-determination also informs Zapatista anti-authoritarian politics, calling for people to exercise power over themselves and their community, and for bottom-up or GRASSROOTS democratization rather than the seizure of state power. In the words of the main spokesperson for the Zapatistas, Subcomandante Marcos: 'We do not struggle to take power, we struggle for DEMOCRACY, liberty and justice' The COMMUNITY and munici-pality structures that have emerged in the Zapatista-controlled zone of Chiapas are a direct expression of Zapatista belief in people's right to administer their own economic, political and cultural lives.

Zapatismo quickly developed an international dimension as it resonated with the claims of a worldwide spectrum of movements fighting against multiple forms of oppression, based on such divides as gender, race, sexual orientation or class. In addition, its critique of global capitalism and its anti-authoritarianism appealed to the ANTI-CAPITALIST movement. Underlying the Zapatista movement is a critique of global capitalism as excluding the majority of the world's population and fragmenting the disempowered into different minorities subject to various forms of oppression. The movement seeks to reverse the fragmentation of the disempowered and to work for the unity of all oppressed voices in their fight for dignity. Whilst some might condemn them as terrorists, the Zapatistas have inspired many demon-strations of support among civil society at national and international levels.

Further Reading

The many websites relevant to entries in the dictionary are easy enough to find, so here we have listed, along with the references cited in the text, some books that offer pathways into the subject. Although we have tried to select general readings, this is not an exhaustive list but a starter guide to a huge body of alternative practices and ideas. You will also notice that the categories don't really work at all. The distinctions between alternatives, organization and utopianism are simply not stable enough to allow us to order things more neatly. But that was partly the point of this dictionary, so it should hardly surprise you in a further reading section.

ECONOMICS

Albert, M. and R. Hahnel (1991a) *Looking Forward*. Cambridge, MA: South End Press.

Albert, M. and R. Hahnel (1991b) *The Political Economy of Participatory Economics*. Princeton: Princeton University Press.

Benello, C. G. (1993) *From the Ground Up*. Montreal: Black Rose Books.

Birch, J. (1994) *Co-op: The People's Business*. Manchester: Manchester University Press.

Bové, J. (2001) *The World is Not for Sale: Farmers against Junk Food*. London: Verso.

Brinton, M. (2004) *For Workers' Power*. Oakland, CA: AK Press.

DiBona, C., S. Ochman and M. Stone (eds) (2000) *Open Sources: Voices from the Open Source Revolution*. Sebastopol, CA: O'Reilly.

Douthwaite, R. (1996) *Short Circuit: Strengthening Local Economies for Security in an Unstable World*. Devon: Green Books.

Dunkley, G. (2004) *Free Trade: Myth, Reality and Alternatives*. London: Zed Books.

Gold, L. (2004) *The Sharing Economy: Solidarity Networks Transforming Globalization*. Aldershot: Ashgate.

Hines, C. (2000) *Localization*. London: Earthscan.

Madeley, J. (2000) *Hungry for Trade: How the Poor Pay for Free Trade*. London: Zed Books.

Monbiot, G. (2003) *The Age of Consent*. London: Harper Perennial.

Nicholls, A. and C. Opal (2005) *Fair Trade*. Thousand Oaks, CA: Sage.

Ransom, D. (2001). *No Nonsense Guide to Fair Trade*. London: Verso.

Raymond, E. (1999) *The Cathedral and the Bazaar: Musings on Linux and Open Source Software by an Accidental Revolutionary*. Sebastopol, CA: O'Reilly.

Sefang, G. and K. Smith (2002) *The Time of Our Lives: Using Time Banks for Neigh - bourhood Renewal and Community Capacity Building*. London: New Economics Foundation.

Shuman, M. (1998) *Going Local*. New York: Free Press.

Williams, C. C. (2005) *A Commodified World?* London: Zed Books.

Yunus, M. (1998) *Banker to the Poor: The Autobiography of the Founder of the Grameen Bank*. London: Aurum Press.

ENVIRONMENT

Bennholdt-Thomsen, V. and M. Mies (1999) *The Subsistence Perspective*. London: Zed Books.

Bennholdt-Thomsen, V., N. Faraclas and C. von Werlhof (eds) (2001) *There is an Alternative*. London: Zed Books.

Bhalla A. S. (ed.) (1979) *Towards Global Action for Appropriate Technology*. Oxford: Pergamon Press.

Bollier, D. (2002) *Silent Theft: The Private Plunder of our Common Wealth*. New York: Routledge.

Dobson, A. (ed.) (1999) *Fairness and Futurity*. Oxford: Oxford University Press.

Drenson, A. and I. Yuichi (1995) *The Deep Ecology Movement*. Berkeley: North Atlantic Books.

Dresner, S. (2002) *The Principles of Sustainability*. London: Earthscan.

Guha, R. (2000) *The Unquiet Woods: Ecological Change and Peasant Resistance in the Himalaya*. Berkeley, CA: University of California Press.

Hay, P. (2002) *Main Currents in Western Environmental Thought*. Sydney: UNSW Press.

Jackson, H. and K. Svensson (eds.) (2002) *Ecovillage Living*. Totnes: Green Earth Books.

Mollison, B. (1991) *Introduction to Permaculture*. Tasmania: Tagari Publications.

Naess, A. (1989) *Ecology, Community and Lifestyle*. Cambridge: Cambridge University Press.

Norberg-Hodge, H., T. Merrifield and S. Gorelick (2002) *Bringing the Food Economy Home: Local Alternatives to Global Agribusiness*. London: Zed Books.

Pepper, D. (1996) *Modern Environmentalism*. London: Routledge.

Petrini, C. (2004) *Slow Food*. New York: Columbia University Press.

Pretty, J. (1994) *Regenerating Agriculture*. London: Earthscan.

Seymour, J. (2003) *The New Complete Book of Self-Sufficiency*. London: Dorling Kindersley.

Shiva, V. (1997) *Biopiracy: the Plunder of Nature and Knowledge*. Cambridge, MA: South End Press.

Sturgeon, N. (1997) *Ecofeminist Natures*. London: Routledge.

Trainer, T. (1995) *The Conserver Society: Alternatives for Sustainability*. London: Zed Books.

Warren, K. (ed.) (1997) *Ecofeminism*. Bloomington, IN: Indiana University Press.

Whitefield, P. (2000) *Permaculture in a Nutshell*, East Meon, Hampshire: Permanent Publications.

HISTORY

Cohn, N. (1970) *The Pursuit of the Millenium*, London: Paladin.

Cole, J. (1994) *Conflict and Cooperation: Rochdale and the Pioneering Spirit*. London: George Kelsall.

Davis, J. C. (1986), *Fear, Myth and History*. Cambridge: Cambridge University Press.

Dolgoff, S. (1974) *The Anarchist Collectives: Workers' Self-Management in the Spanish Revolution 1936-1939*. Montreal: Black Rose Books.

Epstein, S. (1991). *Wage and Labour Guilds in Medieval Europe*, Chapel Hill, NC: University of North Carolina Press.

Harrison, J. (1969) *Quest for the New Moral World: Robert Owen and the Owenites in Britain and America*. New York: Routledge.

Harrison, J. (1984) *The Common People*. London: Flamingo.

Hill, C. (1971) *Lenin and the Russian Revolution*. Harmondsworth: Penguin.

Hill, C. (1991) *The World Turned Upside Down*. London: Penguin.

Kemp, W. (1991) *The Desire of My Eyes: The Life and Work of John Ruskin*. London: HarperCollins.

Knabb, K. (ed) (1984) *Situationist International Anthology*. Berkeley: Bureau of Public Secrets.

Lambert, M. (1998) *The Cathars*. London: Blackwell.

Marshall, P. (1994). *William Blake*. Freedom Press, London.

Parker, G. (2004) *Sovereign City*. London: Reaktion Books.

Pelling, H. (1992) *A History of British Trade Unionism*. London: Macmillan.

Smith, C., J. Child and M. Rowlinson (1990). *Reshaping Work: The Cadbury Experience*. Cambridge: Cambridge University Press.

Thompson, E. P. (1991) *The Making of the English Working Class*. Harmondsworth: Penguin.

Thompson, P. (1991) *The Work of William Morris*. Oxford: Oxford University Press.

Williams, G. (2000) *The Radical Reformation*. Kirksville: Truman State University Press.

Wilson P. L. (2003) *Pirate Utopias*. Brooklyn, NY: Autonomedia.

INTENTIONAL COMMUNITIES

Bunker, S., C. Coates and J. How (2006) *Diggers and Dreamers: The Guide to Communal Living in Britain*. London: D&D Publications.

Coates, C. (2001) *Utopia Britannica*. London: Diggers and Dreamers.

Communal Societies (an academic journal).

Fellowship for Intentional Communities (2005) *Communities Directory: A Compre - hensive Guide to Intentional Communities and Co-operative Living*. Rutledge, MO: FIC.

Francis, R. (1997) *Transcendental Utopias*. New York: Cornell University Press.

Hayden, D. (1976) *Seven American Utopias*. Cambridge, MA: MIT Press

Hine, R. (1983) *California's Utopian Colonies*. Berkeley: University of California Press.

Sutton, R. (2005) *Modern American Communes: A Dictionary*. Westport, CT: Greenwood.

Trahair, R. (1999) *Utopias and Utopians: An Historical Dictionary*. Westport, CT: Greenwood.

Volker, P. and M. Stengel (2005) *Eurotopia*. London: Edge of Time.

ORGANIZATION

Abers, R. (2000) *Inventing Local Democracy*. Boulder: Lynne Rienner Publishers.

Avrahami, E. (2000) *The Changing Kibbutz: An Examination of Values and Structure*. Ramat Efal, Israel: Yad Tabenkin.

Campling, P. and R. Haigh (1999) *Therapeutic Communities*. London: Jessica Kingsley.

Cheney, G. (1999) *Values at Work: Employee Participation Meets Market Pressures at Mondragòn*. Ithaca: Cornell University Press.

Ekins, P. (1992) *A New World Order: Grassroots Movements to Global Change*. London: Routledge.

Ferree, M. and P. Martin (1995) *Feminist Organizations*. Philadelphia: Temple University Press.

Gribble, D. (1998) *Real Education: Varieties of Freedom.* Bristol: Libertarian Education.

Harley, B., J. Hyman and P. Thompson (eds) (2005) *Democracy and Participation at Work*. Basingstoke: Palgrave.

Kaufman, M. (ed.) (1997) *Community Power and Grassroots Democracy: The Trans-formation of Social Life*. London: Zed Books.

Mellor, M., J. Hannah and J. Stirling (1988) *Worker Co-operatives in Theory and Practice*. Milton Keynes: Open University Press.

Oakeshott, R. (2000) *Jobs and Fairness: The Logic and Experience of Employee Owner-ship*. Norwich: Michael Russell.

Pannekoek, A. (2002) *Worker Councils*. Oakland, CA: AK Press.

Parker, M. (2002) *Against Management*. Oxford: Polity.

POLITICS

Bircham, E. and J. Charlton (eds) (2001) *Anti-Capitalism: A Guide to the Movement*. London: Bookmarks.

Branford, S. and J. Rocha (2002) *Cutting the Wire: The Story of the Landless Move-ment in Brazil*. London: Latin American Bureau.

Callinicos, A. (2003) *An Anti-Capitalist manifesto*. Cambridge: Polity Press.

Cockburn, A., J. St Clair and A. Sekula (2000) *Five Days that Shook the World*. London: Verso.

Corr, A. (1999) *No Trespassing: Squatting, Rent, Strikes and Land Struggles Worldwide*.

Cambridge, MA: South End Press.

Gee, T. (2003) *Militancy Beyond Black Blocs*. Oakland: AK Press.

Harvie, D. *et al.* (eds.) (2005) *Shut Them Down!* Leeds: Dissent.

Jordan, T. (2002) *Activism!* London: Reaktion Books.

Katsiaficas, G. (1998) *The Subversion of Politics*. Atlantic Island, NJ: Humanities Press.

Kingsnorth, P. (2003) *One No, Many Yeses*. London: Free Press.

Starr, A. (2000) *Naming the Enemy*. London: Zed Books.

Starr, A. (2005) *Global Revolt: A Guide to the Movements against Globalization*. London: Zed Books.

Steel, B., M. Paterson and B. Doherty (eds.) (2000) *Direct Action in British Environmentalism*. London: Routledge.

Tormey, S. (2004) *Anti-Capitalism: A Beginner's Guide*. Oxford: Oneworld Publications.

Wright, A. and W. Wolford (2003) *To Inherit the Earth: The Landless Movement and the Struggle for a New Brazil*. Oakland, CA: Food First.

Yuen, E., G. Katsiaficas and D. Burton Rose (eds.) (2001) *The Battle of Seattle*. New York: Soft Skull Press.

THEORY

Bloch, E. (1986/1959) *The Principle of Hope*. Cambridge, MA: MIT Press.

Bookchin, M. (1997) *The Murray Bookchin Reader*. New York: Continuum International Publishing.

Davis, J. (1984) *Utopia and the Ideal Society*. Cambridge: Cambridge University Press.

Etzioni, A. (1993) *The Spirit Of Community: The Reinvention of American Society*. New York: Simon and Schuster.

Goodwin, B. (ed.) (2004) *The Philosophy of Utopia*. London: Routledge.

Hardt, M. and A. Negri (2004) *Multitude: War and Democracy in the Age of Empire*. New York: Penguin Press.

Kelly, P. (2004) *Liberalism*. Cambridge: Polity Press.

Levitas, R. (2004) 'For Utopia: The (Limits of the) Utopian Function in Late Capitalist Society', in B. Goodwin (ed.), *The Philosophy of Utopia*. London: Routledge.

Mannheim, K. (1960) *Ideology and Utopia*. London: RKP Ltd.

Marshall, P. (1993) *Demanding the Impossible: A History of Anarchism*. London: Fontana Books.

May, T. (1994) *The Political Philosophy of Poststructuralist Anarchism*, Philadelphia, PA: Pennsylvania State University Press.

McLellan, D. (ed.) (2000) *Karl Marx*. Oxford: Oxford University Press.

Mulhall, S. and A. Swift (1992) *Liberals and Communitarians*. Oxford: Blackwell.

Newman, M. (2005) *Socialism*. Oxford University Press.

Parker, M. (2002) (ed.) *Utopia and Organization*. Oxford: Blackwell.

Polanyi, K. (2002) *The Great Transformation*. London: Beacon Press.

Putnam, R. (2000) *Bowling Alone*. New York: Simon and Schuster.

Rocker, R. (2004) *Anarcho-Syndicalism*. Oakland, CA: AK Press.

Short, P. (2003) *Mao*. New York: Owl Books.

Ward, C. (2004) *Anarchism: A Very Short Introduction*. Oxford University Press.

Wheen, F. (1999) *Karl Marx*. London: Fourth Estate.

Wright, S. (2002) *Storming Heaven: Class Composition and Struggle in Italian Autonomist Marxism*. London: Pluto Press.

UTOPIAN FICTIONS

Bammer, A. (1991) *Partial Visions: Feminism and Utopianism in the 1970s*. London: Routledge.

Bartkowski, F (1989) *Feminist Utopias*. Lincoln: Nebraska University Press.

Berneri, M. L. (1971) *Journey Through Utopia*. New York: Shocken.

Claeys, G. and L. T. Sargent (eds.) (1999) *The Utopia Reader*. New York: New York University Press.

Fortunati, V. and R. Trusson (eds.) (2000) *Dictionary of Literary Utopias*. Paris: Honoré Champion.

Goodwin, B. and K. Taylor (1982) *The Politics of Utopia*. London: Hutchinson.

Griffiths, J. (1980) *Three Tomorrows*. London: Macmillan.

Jameson, F. (2005) *Archeologies of the Future*. London: Verso.

Kumar, K. (1991) *Utopia and Anti-Utopia in Modern Times*. Oxford: Blackwell.

Lefanu, S. (1988) *In the Chinks of the World Machine: Feminism and Science Fiction*. London: The Women's Press.

Levitas (1990) *The Concept of Utopia*. London: Philip Allan.

Manguel, A. and G. Guadalupi (1999) *The Dictionary of Imaginary Places*. London: Bloomsbury.

Manuel, F. and F. Manuel (1979) *Utopian Thought in the Western World*. Cambridge, MA: Harvard University Press.

Moylan, T. (1986) *Demand the Impossible*. New York: Methuen.

Moylan, T. and R. Baccolini (2003) *Dark Horizons: Science Fiction and the Utopian Imaginary*. London: Routledge.

Sargisson, L. (1996) *Contemporary Feminist Utopianism*. London: Routledge.

Schaer, R., G. Claeys and L. Sargent (eds.) (2000) *Utopia: The Search for the Ideal Society in the Western World*. New York: New York Public Library/Oxford University Press.

Smith, W. *et al.* (eds.) (2001) *Science Fiction and Organization*. London: Routledge.

Utopian Studies (an academic journal).

Weldes, J. (ed.) (2003) *To Seek Out New Worlds*. London: Palgrave.

Index

327